# The United Nations and peacekeeping, 1988–95

Manchester University Press

# The United Nations and peacekeeping, 1988–95

*Chen Kertcher*

Manchester University Press

Copyright © Chen Kertcher 2016

The right of Chen Kertcher to be identified as the author of this work has been asserted by him in accordance with the Copyright, Designs and Patents Act 1988.

Published by Manchester University Press
Altrincham Street, Manchester M1 7JA
www.manchesteruniversitypress.co.uk

British Library Cataloguing-in-Publication Data
A catalogue record for this book is available from the British Library

Library of Congress Cataloging-in-Publication Data applied for

ISBN 978 1 7849 9273 6 hardback

First published 2016

ISBN 978 1 5261 3939 9 paperback

First published 2019

The publisher has no responsibility for the persistence or accuracy of URLs for any external or third-party internet websites referred to in this book, and does not guarantee that any content on such websites is, or will remain, accurate or appropriate.

Typeset by Out of House Publishing

# Contents

| | | |
|---|---|---|
| Acknowledgements | *page* | vi |
| List of abbreviations | | vii |
| Introduction | | 1 |
| 1 A history of UN peacekeeping | | 12 |
| 2 New thinking: UN peacekeeping and the end of the Cold War 1988–91 | | 50 |
| 3 Agenda for peacekeeping 1992–93 | | 85 |
| 4 The failure of peacekeeping as a panacea to civil wars 1993–95 | | 142 |
| Conclusion | | 196 |
| Bibliography | | 208 |
| Index | | 223 |

# Acknowledgements

This work represents several years of sculpting a manuscript out of a huge marble made of thousands of UN pages.

Above all, I owe special gratitude to Prof. Aron Shai, who challenged me to deal with such a large and ambitious project on a global scale.

The tedious and exhausting work mentally, intellectually and sometimes physically would not have been possible without the support, advice and guidance of the following people: Dr. Efrat Elron, Prof. Elie Barnavi, Prof. James Gow, Prof. Arie Kacowitz, Prof. Billie Melman, M. Des. Willy Mizrahi, Dr. Shimon Naveh, Prof. Benni Neuberger, Prof. Iris Rahamimov, Prof. Raanan Rein, Prof. Galia Golan and Prof. Moti Tamarkin. There are many more, but unfortunately space prevents me from naming all of them.

Special thanks are reserved for the archivists at the UN archives in New York and the UN deposit library at the National Library in Jerusalem.

This work was sponsored by the generous funding of the Israeli Council for Higher Education Rotenstreich Fellowship, a research scholarship from the Tami Steinmetz Peace Center at Tel Aviv University and my time as a junior fellow at the S. Daniel Abraham Center for International and Regional Studies at Tel Aviv University.

My parents, Yosi and Ruti, and my brother, Zack, were a fountain of faith in my work.

Last but not least, I owe apologies and gratitude to my dear wife, Hagar, and our three daughters, who had to bear my endless remarks on the UN and peacekeeping, and still encouraged me to continue. This book is dedicated to them.

# Abbreviations

## Organisations and agencies

| | |
|---|---|
| ASEAN | Association South East Asian Nations |
| CIS | Commonwealth of Independent States |
| DPKO | Department of Peacekeeping Operations |
| EC | European Community |
| ECOSOC | Economic and Social Council |
| ECOWAS | Economic Community of West African States |
| EU | European Union |
| ICRC | International Committee of Red Cross |
| MPLA | Movimento Popular de Libertação de Angola |
| MSC | Military Staff Committee |
| NAM | Non-Aligned Movement |
| NATO | North Atlantic Treaty Organization |
| NGO | non-governmental organisation |
| OAU | Organization of African Unity |
| OIC | Organization of Islamic Conference |
| OSCE | Organization for Security and Cooperation in Europe |
| OSPA | Office for Special Political Affairs |
| P5 | Permanent five members of the UN (the United States, the Soviet Union, the United Kingdom, China and France) |
| SCPKO | Special Committee for Peacekeeping Operations |
| SRSG | Special Representative of the Secretary-General |
| SWAPO | South West Africa People's Organization |
| TC | Trusteeship Council |
| UNAVEM | United Nations Angola Verification Mission |
| UNEF | United Nations Emergency Force |
| UNFICYP | United Nations Peacekeeping Force in Cyprus |
| UNHCR | United Nations High Commissioner for Refugees |
| UNIFIL | United Nations Interim Force in Lebanon |
| UNITA | União Nacional para a Independência Total de Angola |
| UNTAG | United Nations Transition Assistance Group |
| USG | Under-Secretary-General |

## Cambodia

| | |
|---|---|
| CPP/SOC | Cambodian People's Party/Phnom Penh government |
| DK | Democratic Kampuchea |
| FUNCINPEC | Front Uni National pour un Cambodge Indépendant, Neutre, Pacifique, et Coopératif |
| ICORC | International Committee on the Reconstruction of Cambodia |
| KPCP | Kampuchean People's Revolutionary Party |
| KPNLF | Khmer People's National Liberation Front |
| PDK | Party of Democratic Kampuchea / Khmer Rouge |
| SNC | Supreme National Council |
| UNAMIC | United Nations Advanced Mission in Cambodia |
| UNTAC | United Nations Transitional Authority in Cambodia |

## Former Yugoslavia

| | |
|---|---|
| FRY | Federal Republic of Yugoslavia (Serbia and Montenegro) |
| ICFY | International Conference on the Former Yugoslavia |
| ICTY | International Criminal Tribunal for the Former Yugoslavia |
| KFOR | Kosovo Force |
| NIOD | Netherlands Institute for War Documentation |
| SFRY | The Socialist Federal Republic of Yugoslavia |
| UNMIK | United Nations Interim Administration Mission in Kosovo |
| UNPA | United Nations Protected Areas |
| UNPROFOR | United Nations Protection Force |
| YNA | Yugoslavia People's Army (Jugoslavenka Narodna Armija) |

## Somalia

| | |
|---|---|
| SNA | Somali National Alliance |
| TNC | Transitional National Council |
| UNITAF | Unified Task Force |
| UNOSOM | United Nations Operation in Somalia |
| USC | United Somali Congress |

# Introduction

Between the late 1980s and the early 1990s, there was a major shift in the position of the United Nations in the world. After the organisation had been shunted aside for most of the Cold War years, it returned to enjoy international centre stage; the large, multifunctional peacekeeping operations were catalysts in this process. The organisation's member states mobilised themselves to promote those initiatives that encouraged both political arrangements and other political, economic and security measures – such as humanitarian aid, resettlement of refugees, demobilisation of armed forces, economic development and advancement of good government – in order to resolve active conflicts using these tools. Simultaneously, intensive discussion was held between the member states and United Nations institutions regarding the potential of these operations.

This global history study examines the concept and practice of United Nations peacekeeping operations from 1988 to 1995. The research is anchored primarily in United Nations documents produced following the diplomatic discussions that took place in the organisation on the subject of peacekeeping in general and in the cases of Cambodia, the former Yugoslavia and Somalia in particular. Studies on peacekeeping operations tend to overlook the importance of the diplomatic discussions that occurred, and are still occurring, at the United Nations. In this study I chose to examine these discussions in order to uncover the routine realignment of members in political groups that worked on different issues of peacekeeping and thus to offer different explanations from the ones that are usually given on the motivation for executing peacekeeping operations, the way they were executed, and their outcomes in different regions and on the work of the United Nations.

There is a wide consensus in the peacekeeping operations literature that there were two types of United Nations peacekeeping operations, based on the time of their execution: 'traditional operations' and 'multidimensional operations'.

Operations of the 'first generation', sometimes termed 'traditional', were executed during the Cold War, from 1947 to 1987. These operations were limited in their objectives and size. Their main aim was to prevent escalation in interstate conflicts through the deployment of peacekeeping forces as a buffer between the belligerent armed forces. During their deployment, the United Nations forces investigated and reported breaches of ceasefire agreements. The aim of this technique was to assist ongoing international mediation efforts in order to resolve the conflict. The principles of success of these operations were to gain the support of international and local actors, to be impartial and under no circumstances to use force. In total, the United Nations deployed thirteen operations during this period. This mode of action focuses on the prevention of wars between states and not on the initiation of actions that could prevent the development of conditions for conflict.

According to most of the peacekeeping research literature, 'second-generation' operations have been executed since 1988 and they continue to this day. These studies highlight the fact that from 1988 to 2014 the Security Council authorised fifty-six new peacekeeping operations, four times the number of operations that were deployed during the Cold War. Furthermore, the number of personnel involved in these operations has risen to more than one hundred thousand troops, policemen and civilians. The cost of the operations rose in parallel, from less than half a billion dollars in the late 1980s to approximately seven billion dollars during 2014.

Another argument is that Cold War era peacekeeping operations differ from later operations not only in their numbers and size, but also in their objectives, which in the latter included interventions on political, security, economic and social levels during an active conflict inside states. Thus sometimes terms such as 'multidimensional' or multifunctional operations are used to define the second generation of peacekeeping operations. They emphasise that these operations are characterised by multiple objectives, such as democratisation, building new national security institutions, providing humanitarian assistance and the advancement of human rights. Their main goal is to end intrastate conflicts through these multiple functions. Others prefer to view these operations as supporting the basic foundations for the maintenance of peace.[1]

Literature which supports the dichotomy between the two periods, from 1947 to 1987 and from 1988 until today, tends to conclude that a fundamental change occurred in the way international politics was practised at the United Nations in the context of peacekeeping operations after the Cold War. According to many studies, the end of the Cold War created two major political alliances in the organisation. The first alliance represents the developing states and is led by China and Russia; it supports the execution of traditional operations. The second and more dominant alliance represents the Western states, led by the United States, the United Kingdom, France and Canada. This alliance pushed for a change in the concept of traditional peacekeeping operations in order to intervene in intrastate conflicts while promoting democratisation, human rights, economic development, etc.

Reviewing the scope of peacekeeping operations from 1988 onwards reveals that it is divided into three periods. The first period, from 1988 to 1995, was the crucial period of transformation. Between 1988 and 1995, the period examined by this work, the Security Council decided on the deployment of twenty-six new operations, half the number of operations that were deployed after the Cold War. Furthermore, the number of peacekeepers rose from a low of 15,390 at the end of 1991 to a high of 80,000 in 1994. The cost of the operations rose in parallel, from approximately half a billion dollars in 1991 to 3.5 billion dollars three years later. Most of these changes are connected to the execution of three large missions in Cambodia, the former Yugoslavia and Somalia.

The United Nations operations in Cambodia, the former Yugoslavia and Somalia were executed in order to achieve multiple objectives, such as supervising demobilisation processes, monitoring ceasefires, delivering aid, monitoring civilian institutions and advancing human rights. During the time of execution they were perceived in the United Nations deliberations as the main test cases for the implementation of new concepts and principles in peacekeeping. In this sense, they represent the best cases for the examination of the will of the international community to intervene in intrastate conflicts in order to end conflicts in this period.

The results of these operations are questioned. Although conventional wisdom holds that the intervention in Cambodia was successful, the intervention in the former Yugoslavia was a partial success and the intervention in Somalia was a failure. In the case of Cambodia, the Security Council decided to terminate the operation in mid-1993, after the United Nations had managed an election that resulted in the formation of a new government by the two biggest political parties. In the case of the former Yugoslavia, it was decided in December 1995 to transfer many of the operation's powers to the North Atlantic Treaty Organization (NATO) after the belligerent parties in Bosnia signed a peace agreement. In the case of Somalia, it was decided to end the operation in March 1995 although the conflict continued.

In 1995 the number and size of peacekeeping operations started to decline until it reach a low of approximately 12,000 soldiers in mid-1999. In June 1999 the tide turned again when the Security Council decided to deploy operations in East Timor, Kosovo and Sierra Leone. The number and size of peacekeeping operations continued to rise after 2001, with most of the new operations deployed in Africa. Moreover, the period after 2001 is also characterised by the subcontracting of large, multidimensional operations to regional organisations such as NATO and the African Union.

The brief review leads to a conclusion that the period of 1988 to 1995 was a transformative period in the history of United Nations peacekeeping and that something undermined the international support for these operations. Researchers such as Alex Bellamy, Paul Griffin, Stewart Williams and Adam Roberts raise several possible reasons for this. These researchers argue that the main cause for the drop in support for multidimensional operations in the mid-1990s is connected to three humiliating failures of the UN: the political crisis that erupted in Somalia after the fighting in Mogadishu between the UN forces and one of the Somali factions, on 3 October 1993; the inaction of the UN in light of the genocide in Rwanda between April and July 1994; and the pullback of UN forces from Srebrenica in July 1995 that allowed Bosnian-Serbian forces to kill thousands of

Muslim youths and men. Additional reasons given by the researchers for scepticism regarding the operations were the unwillingness of UN member states to donate sufficient resources, human as well as material; the fact that most of the soldiers were poorly equipped and sometimes lacked weapons and means of transportation; and inadequate coordination between the various units on the ground. In addition, the budgets for financing operations arrived so late that the organisation was forced to take out bank loans. Another cause is that the UN Secretariat did not have appropriate organisational means to conduct so many large, multidimensional operations simultaneously.[2]

However, when we examine these research arguments in comparison with their explanations regarding the reasons for the change that took place in operations from 1988 to 1995, we reveal several contradictions. For example, it is argued that the end of the Cold War contributed to the resolving of disputes and served as a catalyst for the proper functioning of the Security Council. However, the facts show that numerous existing conflicts continued to develop after the end of the Cold War and new ones were even created. Also, one of the reasons given for the development of peacekeeping operations is that countries ostensibly wanted to contribute to the operations in order to increase their influence in the region or in the UN, and to increase their income. However, this is contradicted by the fact that countries were not willing to invest enough of their resources for the proper execution of the operations. And if we assume that Western countries were eager to promote new democratic norms in the various disputed sites, we have to ask why they were unwilling to invest sufficient resources to accomplish this goal. Finally, the managerial-organisational-logistical problems involved in the execution of the operations had existed in the Cold War period as well; they were not new to the post-Cold War period. The important question is whether the organisation made any changes in order to deal with these problems. This study deals with those issues that have not been sufficiently addressed previously. Because the international political context of the early 1990s was different from that of the first decade of the twenty-first century, the manuscript limits itself to the transformative period that was terminated in 1995.

The changes that occurred to the concept and the execution of peacekeeping operations after the Cold War raise several questions: To what extent do these interventions represent a fundamental change in the international politics at the United Nations regarding the management of conflicts after the Cold War? Were these interventions a result of 'new politics' in the United Nations which Western states supported and advanced against the policies of developing countries?

This research demonstrates, using the records of diplomatic discourse at the United Nations, that although there was an attempt to change the concept and principles of peacekeeping operations and with it to launch an organisational reform, it eventually failed. The international politics at the United Nations could not reconcile the tension between the forces of global reform and those that advanced narrow national interests. The best explanation for this outcome is that international politics at the United Nations – at least as it concerns peacekeeping operations – is conducted according to the principles of each state's realpolitik. States formed their stance on a case-by-case basis, while calculating power relations in order to advance their own national interests. Therefore their position on each topic on the concept of the operation or on organisational reform did not necessarily match the declared position of any particular political alliance. Furthermore, many multidimensional operations were still executed in accordance with the traditional concept. The main objective of these operations was international mediation between belligerent sides in order to form sovereign governments and to deploy a 'peacekeeping force' in accordance with the traditional principles of international and local consent, impartiality and the non-use of force. Traditional objectives were preferred over new objectives such as democratisation, human rights and economic development.

## The theoretical framework and research design

Since the last decade of the twentieth century, hundreds of books and articles have been published on the subject of peacekeeping operations. There is a lively academic community exploring questions concerning peacekeeping. Research in the field discusses diverse issues that cannot be reviewed here in detail. However, peacekeeping scholars can be broadly categorised into six clusters: regional studies, country studies, functions and objectives studies, international law studies, organisational studies and generational-historical studies.

The first and second clusters, which are the largest in the field, are of regional studies. These studies discuss a conflict in a particular region or the decision-making process in a specific state that is involved in the peacekeeping operation. Many of these studies describe UN actions in a specific region in detail, while trying to reach conclusions about how the operations contributed to the solution of a conflict. A different way is to assess the role of one country in an intervention.[3]

The third cluster of studies includes comparative analysis of the operations' objectives and their functions in a particular conflict. These studies tend to focus on one objective and compare the methods for its achievement in several operations. Therefore, there are many studies on international mediation, humanitarian assistance and enforcement action.

A fourth cluster of studies on peacekeeping operations is related to international law. These studies usually try to evaluate whether the operations were applied, developed or deployed in accordance with the norms of international law. This research tends to make comparisons between accepted interpretations of the norms of international law and the practice of the United Nations. For example, cases of massive breaches of human rights are evaluated in light of international law.

The fifth cluster is organisational studies. Researchers in this field try to explain how the concept of peacekeeping was transformed by reviewing the interplay of politics and the organisation.

The last cluster, which I call *historical-generational studies*, includes studies which try to explain the changes in the concept and practice of peacekeeping from their first use in 1947 to the present day. These studies deal with the impact of international politics on the execution of peacekeeping operations in the last seven decades, while trying to characterise the uniqueness of each period in the history of UN operations. The main emphasis is on support or rejection by the international community of the use of such operations.

Overall, the six clusters studying peacekeeping do not give much attention to the historical evolution of peacekeeping operations within the UN in the crucial period that this work analyses. Students of regional studies tend to emphasise the importance of the interests of specific states or specific interventions that they review, without providing the proper context of the discussions that went on in the UN on the operations. The result tends to neglect the wider global historical context of the operation.

Studies that compare specific objectives between different operations tend to emphasise a specific function in the operation beyond the original intentions of the United Nations personnel or the persons who were responsible for the planning and the execution of the operations.[4]

International law studies tend to give greater weight to the development of international law at the expense of the practice, but fail to mention that many of these cases grew out of a political activity within the UN.[5]

While pointing to organisational deficiencies, studies on the work of the UN organisation in relation to peacekeeping fail to explain how the concept of peacekeeping evolved in the organisation during the period analysed in this work. They also choose certain aspects that they think are most important for the discussion and avoid using the UN structural and organisational preferences in its work on peacekeeping.[6]

Finally, historical-generational studies, which strive to review the historical change in the concept and practice of peacekeeping operations, mainly draw their conclusions from secondary sources and neglect to analyse the discussions within the UN.[7] As a result, although our knowledge on the potential use of peacekeeping as a conflict management and resolution measure is improving, neglecting to understand the internal evolution of peacekeeping may lead research in inaccurate directions. The review of analytical frameworks for the study of peacekeeping shows that there is no sufficient explanation of how peacekeeping was transformed from 1988 and why the support of this transformation wavered in 1995. In order to fill the lacuna in our knowledge, Benner, Mergenthaler and Rotmann acknowledge in their study on organisational reform in the early twenty-first century that there is a need to zoom in and out from the organisation process to adopt comparative cases not only between operations but between different issues in management and organisational level. Michael Barnett and others support this argument by claiming that the main problem in peacekeeping lies in the lack of a clear concept and operationalisation in peacekeeping operations.[8]

In this study I challenge the accepted notion in the field of peacekeeping that operations executed by the United Nations until 1987 and those executed from 1988 to 1995 differ significantly in all their aspects. As far as I know, there is no research on the discussions that took place at the United Nations in this period on the concept of peacekeeping and organisational reform, or a comparison between these discussions and the execution of the major operations at the time, in Cambodia, the former Yugoslavia and Somalia. In order to shed light on the processes that took place in the United Nations organisation, this work adopts historical methodology through the analysis of the diplomatic discussions. It covers more than 600 official UN documents that reveal the interrelations between the discussions on the principles of peacekeeping and organisational reform and the practice of executing such operations in the field. As I demonstrate in the study, the examination of these discussions draws a different picture from the one that is usually depicted.

Diplomatic discussions at the United Nations took place in the three central bodies of the United Nations – the Security Council, the General Assembly and the Secretariat.[9] In the Security Council there were discussions on the concept of the operations and their execution in different conflict areas of the world. Scholars of peacekeeping usually point to the important role of the Security Council in the decision-making process.[10] However, even prominent scholars such as Mats Berdal, who has written a lot on the subject, do not compare the work of the Security Council on the concept of peacekeeping with its decisions on different peacekeeping missions.[11] This study analyses the positions of the member states in the Council. A special focus is given to the policies of the privileged Permanent Five (China, France, Russia, the United Kingdom and the United States). The corpus of sources includes different speeches, resolutions, draft resolutions, statements of different speakers, official statements of the presidents of the Security Council and different letters and reports submitted to the Council from 1988 to 1995. The focus will be on the documents produced in connection with the work of the Council on the three largest operations of that period. It also covers all Security Council documents that relate to the principles of peacekeeping. In general, all UN documents that are related to the work of the Council receive the official symbol S/.

Most studies on peacekeeping missions use Security Council documents. The work on peacekeeping in the General Assembly in that period is generally overlooked.[12] During discussions that took place at the General Assembly, many states' representatives expressed their government's views and positions on the concept and practice of the operations. The main body in the General Assembly which was responsible for developing the concept of peacekeeping was the Special Committee for Peacekeeping Operations (SCPKO) founded in 1965 (UN symbol A/AC.121). However, there were other discussions in different forums of the General Assembly such as the Special Political Committee (UN symbol A/SPC/) the Fourth (de-colonisation) Committee (UN symbol A/C.4) and the Fifth Committee. In 1994 it was decided to unite the Special Political Committee and the Fourth Committee. Therefore the discussions of the Fourth Committee from 8 February 1994 received the UN symbol A/C.4/48/SR.23. Although encompassing the official view of dozens of member states on the changes in objectives, principles, management, organisational and logistical aspects of peacekeeping, these discussions have been overlooked by writers who cover this period. The protocols of dozens of these discussions help to trace the formal and unique positions on the concept of the operations and their practice in every case.

The final major player in the politics of the UN on peacekeeping is the Secretariat. It has played an active part in all of the discussions that took place in the Security Council and the General Assembly. As noted recently by writers on the role of the Secretariat, it has the power to influence countries and policies, but it is also influenced by international politics.[13]

In order to simplify the reference of each document, which sometimes includes two or three lines, I have decided to quote in this book only the official symbols used by the UN with the date of its publication. For the complete UN reference list the reader should use http://research.un.org.

Taken together, the scope of United Nations sources reveals the arguments and justifications which diplomats and Secretariat personnel raised on each issue. Meticulous reading of these primary documents allows the researcher to map the different alliances that were formed on each subject and action. It helps to identify what processes gained support and from whom and what processes were cut short and why.

In addition to the corpus of UN primary sources, this study is based on other sources, such as diplomatic correspondence, which includes official governmental exchange of letters, professional reports to the organisation on the concept and practice of different operations, and published official literature such as the United Nations' periodicals and yearbooks. A different corpus of sources is the official documents of states which had specific influence on a particular peacekeeping operation.

### The outline of the book

Chapter 1: A history of UN peacekeeping offers a brief review of United Nations peacekeeping operations from 1947 to 2014. The purpose of this chapter is twofold. First, it puts the current work in its historical context within the wider background of the discussion on the history of peacekeeping and the main UN bodies who influence peacekeeping, the Security Council, the General Assembly and the UN Secretariat. Second, it reviews the main conceptual differences between 'first-generation' and 'second-generation' peacekeeping operations as they are usually represented by studies in the field. This chapter provides the reader with the main terms that are used throughout this work.

Chapter 2: New thinking: UN peacekeeping and the end of the Cold War 1988–91 examines international politics at the United Nations from 1988 to 1991 (when the Union of Soviet Socialist Republics (USSR) dissolved), and challenges the accepted premises concerning the change in the objectives and principles of success in peacekeeping operations at the time. The chapter is divided into three parts: the discussions on the concept of peacekeeping at the United Nations and the objectives that were given to ten new peacekeeping operations from 1988 to 1991; the main focus of the discussion will be on the execution of the transitional-type mission in Cambodia.

Chapter 3: Agenda for peacekeeping 1992–93 examines the diplomatic discussions at the Security Council, the General Assembly and the UN Secretariat on the objectives and principles of success of the operations from January 1992 to mid-1993. During this time period, it was proposed to change the objectives and principles of the operations. At the time, most member states supported the new initiatives to use large, multidimensional peacekeeping operations in order to manage and end civil wars.

During this time, the Security Council decided to execute three large multidimensional operations to maintain global security. In Cambodia it developed a new model for an international transitional administration. In the former Yugoslavia it developed a model for humanitarian intervention. Finally, in Somalia, faced with the challenge of a collapsed state, it developed the model of state-building. Furthermore, the chapter concludes that in most cases, the United Nations continued to work according to the peacekeeping operations' Cold War principles of execution – it emphasised consent, non-use of force and impartiality – and strived to achieve mainly traditional objectives.

Chapter 4: The failure of peacekeeping as a panacea to civil wars 1993–95, offers new explanations for the dwindling support for UN peacekeeping operations from late 1993 to 1995. The discussions on the concept of the ambitious multidimensional operations and their practice created tensions between member states. The chapter reveals that international politics at the United Nations had unique characteristics with regard to each of the conflicts that did not necessarily correlate with the efforts by certain alliances in the organisation to agree on a new concept for peacekeeping operations. By 1995, UN members had failed to reconcile their differences on the concept and practice of multidimensional peacekeeping as a panacea to civil wars. The organisation was in political and financial crisis and mistrust was widespread among the member states. Therefore, most member states declared their resolve to support the traditional objectives and principles of peacekeeping. Moreover, it was recommended that future multidimensional operations would be executed by regional organisations.

The final chapter concludes the main arguments of the book. It summarises the political grouping that was formed in the organisation on each subject from 1988 to 1995. It shows how international politics was interlocked in routine realignment, which formed the basis for the transformation of the role of peacekeeping operations in conflict zones but also failed to reconcile many issues that are still relevant in the twenty-first century.

## Notes

1. For a review of the literature see below and in Chapter 1.
2. An elaboration of the accepted research argument regarding the backtracking from the execution of multidimensional operations can be found in: A. Bellamy, P. Williams and S. Griffin, *Understanding Peacekeeping* (Cambridge: Polity Press, 2nd edn, 2010), pp. 93–111; A. Roberts, 'The Crisis in UN Peacekeeping', in C. A. Crocker, F. O. Hampson and P. Aall (eds), *Managing Global Chaos: Sources of and Responses to International Conflict* (Washinton, DC: United States Institute of Peace Press, 1996), pp. 297–319. For a more nuanced explanation for the transformation of UN peacekeeping during the early 1990s, see: J. T. O'Neill and N. Rees, *United Nations Peacekeeping in the Post-Cold War Era* (Abingdon, Oxon: Routledge, 2005).
3. For an example of studies on national interests of states for participating in peacekeeping operations or for regions in which such operations were executed see: A. Adebajo, *UN Peacekeeping in Africa: From the Suez Crisis to the Sudan Conflict* (Boulder, CO: Lynne Rienner, 2011); S. Autesserre, *The Trouble with the Congo: Local Violence and the Failure of International Peacebuilding* (Cambridge: Cambridge: University Press, 2010); W. J. Durch (ed.), *The Evolution of UN Peacekeeping: Case Studies and Comparative Analysis* (Basingstoke: Macmillan, 1993); W. J. Durch (ed.), *UN Peacekeeping, American Policy and the Uncivil Wars of the 1990s* (London: Macmillan, 1997); J. Mayall (ed.), *The New Interventionism, 1991–1994: United Nations Experience in Cambodia, Former Yugoslavia, and Somalia* (New York: Cambridge University Press, 1996); L. G. Murray, *Clinton, Peacekeeping and Humanitarian Intervention: Rise and Fall of a Policy* (Abingdon, Oxon: Routledge, 2008); O'Neill and Rees, *United Nations Peacekeeping in the Post-Cold War Era*; D. S. Sorenson and P. C. Wood (eds), *The Politics of Peacekeeping in the Post-Cold War Era* (London: Frank Cass, 2005); T. G. Weiss, *The United Nations and Civil Wars* (Boulder, CO: Lynne Rienner, 1995).
4. C. T. Call and V. Wyeth (eds), *Building States to Build Peace* (Boulder, CO: Lynne Rienner, 2008); R. Caplan (ed.), *Exit Strategies and State Building* (Oxford: Oxford University Press, 2012); P. F. Diehl, D. Druckman and J. Wall, 'International Peacekeeping and Conflict Resolution: A Taxonomic Analysis with Implications', *The Journal of Conflict Resolution*, 42:1 (1998), 33–55; M. Finnemore, *The Purpose of Intervention: Changing Beliefs about the Use of Force* (Ithaca, NY: Cornell University Press, 2004); T. Findlay, *The Use of Force in UN Peace Operations* (Oxford: Oxford University Press, 2002); J. M. Welsh (ed.), *Humanitarian Intervention and International Relations* (Oxford: Oxford University Press, 2004); N. J. Wheeler, *Saving Strangers: Humanitarian*

*Intervention in International Society* (Oxford: Oxford University Press, 2000); T. Woodhouse and O. Rambotham (eds), *Peacekeeping and Conflict Resolution* (London: Frank Cass, 2000).
5   N. D. White, *Keeping the Peace: The United Nations and the Maintenance of International Peace and Security* (Manchester: Manchester University Press, 2nd edn, 1997).
6   M. Barnett and M. Finnemore, *Rules for the World: International Organizations in Global Politics* (Ithaca, NY: Cornell University Press, 2004); T. Benner, S. Mergenthaler and P. Rotmann, *The New World of UN Peace Operations* (Oxford: Oxford University Press, 2011).
7   The most comprehensive attempt to review all methodologies while suggesting an historical generational explanation is given in Bellamy *et al.*, *Understanding Peacekeeping*. See also P. Kennedy, *The Parliament of Man: The Past, Present and Future of the United Nations* (New York: Vintage Books, 2006).
8   Autesserre, *The Trouble with the Congo*; M. Barnett, H. Kim, M. O'Donnell and L. Sitea, 'Peacebuilding: What Is in a Name?', *Global Governance* 13:1 (2007), 35–58.
9   For a general discussion of the work of the United Nations, see: Kennedy, *The Parliament of Man*; T. G. Weiss and S. Daws (eds), *The Oxford Handbook on The United Nations* (Oxford: Oxford University Press, 2007).
10  S. D. Bailey and S. Daws, *The Procedure of the UN Security Council* (Oxford: Clarendon Press, 3rd edn, 1998); D. M. Malone, *The UN Security Council: From the Cold War to the 21st Century* (Boulder, CO: Lynne Rienner, 2004); V. Lowe, A. Roberts, J. Welsh and D. Zaum (eds), *The United Nations Security Council and War: The Evolution of Thought and Practice since 1945* (Oxford: Oxford University Press, 2010).
11  M. Berdal, 'The Security Council and Peacekeeping', in Lowe *et al.* (eds), *The United Nations Security Council*, pp. 175–204.
12  The best work on the General Assembly is still M. J. Peterson, *The UN General Assembly* (London, New York: Routledge, 2006). However, this work does not cover the work of the Assembly on peacekeeping.
13  See, for example, the detailed analysis of the role of the Secretariat on police assistance, judicial reform and mission integration in the first decade of the twenty first century in Benner *et al.*, *The New World of UN Peace Operations*.

# 1

# A history of UN peacekeeping

The history of UN peacekeeping is intertwined with the evolution of the concept and practice of these operations. In this research study, the term 'concept', in the context of peacekeeping operations, refers to agreed-upon UN principles regarding the objectives, principles for success, and managerial and organisational aspects of the operations. The term 'practice', on the other hand, refers to the actual implementation of the operations and the political conduct of the states with regard to those conflicts where the decision is made to intervene. 'Practice' also refers to the contribution of the UN member states to the execution of the operations and to the effect of the operation on the conflict.

This research study examines the validity of the accepted research arguments regarding changes in the concept and practice of UN peacekeeping operations from 1988 to 1995. Therefore, this chapter provides the wide historical context and the main issues that are analysed in detail in the other chapters of the book.

The first section of the chapter is devoted to an overview of the United Nations' objectives, work principles and organisational structure, with an emphasis on the work of the United Nations' three central organs: the Security Council, the Secretariat, and the General Assembly. The second section of the chapter is devoted to a historical survey of operations executed by the United Nations until 1987. These operations are usually called 'traditional operations' or 'first-generation operations', and were aimed at preventing the renewal of wars between states. In the third section of the chapter I survey the peacekeeping operations executed by the United Nations from 1988 until our own times. These operations are usually called 'multidimensional' or 'second-generation' operations and they are intended to promote change in the political, security, social and economic conditions that are at the heart of the conflict.

In the fourth section of the chapter I present the accepted research arguments regarding the characteristics of peacekeeping operations, while focusing on the generational differences between the United Nations peacekeeping operations prior to 1987 and those that began in 1988. I focus on some of the issues appearing in the major studies dealing with the research of United Nations peacekeeping operations, especially their incomplete treatment of the role of international politics in the organisation's work with regard to peacekeeping operations. At the end of this section, I specify the main issues that are examined in the research chapters regarding the history of peacekeeping operations from 1988 until 1995.

## The UN and the maintenance of international peace and security

The best way to describe how international politics are conducted in the United Nations regarding peacekeeping operations is to review the objectives, work principles and organisational structure of the UN. These represent the foundation for the organisation's modus operandi and are anchored in the organisation's Charter that was signed on 26 June 1945. The establishment of the UN was the second attempt of the world states to found a global system to ensure stabilisation and collective security, after the first attempt to achieve these goals by the League of Nations failed to prevent the Second World War. The UN system represented an alternative to the system that had arranged the relations between European states from the second half of the seventeenth century: the balance-of-power system.[1]

The United Nations collective security system is intended to deter states from using force against other states, because this will lead to a collective response by the rest of the members of the system. This response on the part of all the member states will endanger all their interests and alliances on the collective principle that is supposed to guarantee their security.[2]

One of the basic principles that were formed to enable the functioning of the system was the prohibition against intervention in the internal affairs of the member states. This was so as not to violate a state's sovereignty, even if the state was in the throes of a civil war.[3] Therefore, the supreme goal of the organisation that is imposed on all the UN member states is to 'maintain international peace and security'. This is considered one of the greatest achievements of the Charter. It formally removes the normative validity behind the well-known expression coined by Prussian military philosopher Carl von Clausewitz (at the beginning of the nineteenth century), that 'war is the continuation of policy by other means'.[4] This step was the climax of a political, religious and legal discussion that continued over hundreds of years regarding the 'just war' theory (*jusadbellum*).[5]

The main responsibility within the UN for maintaining international peace and security lies with the Security Council. Three researchers (Goodrich, Hambro and Simons) note that the Charter emphasises two means for maintaining international peace: resolving disputes by peaceful means and employing a collective security system.[6] Below I describe UN powers with regard to the peaceful settlement of disputes and the organisation's powers of enforcement.

In order to maintain international peace and security, the UN Charter gives the Security Council several powers, described in Chapters 6 and 7 of the Charter;[7] Chapter 6 (Articles 33–38) deals with resolving disputes by peaceful means.[8] Thus, all parties involved in a dispute that is likely to develop into a threat to the maintenance of international peace and security must use these tools to try to resolve the dispute peacefully. The tools at the disposal of the disputing parties are taken from the fields of diplomacy and international law, and focus on resolving the dispute by way of negotiation, enquiry, mediation, compromise, arbitration, legal settlement and more.[9] The work-language of the UN distinguishes between diplomatic activity before the eruption of an armed conflict, called *preventive diplomacy*, and diplomatic activity for restoring peace after an armed conflict has erupted, called *peacemaking*.[10] The premise of resolving disputes and conflicts peacefully is that all the mediators sent by the UN must be totally impartial. Yet there are those who argue that during the mediation process mediators also try to promote their own interests.[11]

Together with the powers for resolving disputes by peaceful means, the UN Charter defines in Chapter 7 (Articles 39–51) the enforcement actions that are available to the Security Council in its efforts to maintain international peace. The chapter also describes two exceptional cases in which force may be used, while violating the principle forbidding the use of force in interstate relations.[12] The first circumstance in which the use of force is permitted is when there is a threat to the peace, breach of the peace or acts of aggression. According to Article 39, the Security Council has the sole authority to declare the existence of such a situation. Before it determines enforcement actions, the Council must verify that the disputing parties have exhausted all the means detailed in Chapter 6 of the Charter. When all the means adopted by the Security Council have failed, it has the right to use force in accordance with Chapter 7, Articles 41 and 42. The use of force is divided into three categories according to the Security Council's level of intervention from imposing sanctions of various types, such as severance of economic relations, to imposing a maritime blockade and no-fly zone etc. Finally, if all these fail, Security Council resolutions may be enforced by the use of military forces against the parties that do not carry out the resolutions.[13] When a resolution to use force is adopted, the organisation's member states are required to provide the requisite military forces to the organisation's command in order to execute the enforcement operation.

The second situation in which the use of force is permitted is defined in Article 51. This article states that nothing mentioned in the Charter can undo the 'natural right of an individual or collective for self-defence, if a UN member should be militarily attacked before the Security Council will adopt the necessary steps to maintain international peace and security'.[14] These two exceptional situations – the right of the Security Council to use force, and the right of a state to defend itself while using force – are not compatible. This situation exists because the UN member states have never succeeded in agreeing on a formulation regarding the use of force, despite or perhaps because of the great importance of the issue.[15]

The two exceptional situations above in which it is permissible to violate the prohibition on the use of force reflect the conflict of interests between those powers that support a collective, universal security system whose main objective is the absence of war between states, and those states that want to maintain their decision-making freedom.

The majority of the articles in Chapter 7 are commensurate with the goal of establishing a system of collective security and present the UN as an entity that designates itself as responsible, *interalia*, for collective military activity. All states are required to assist the organisation in every way possible, by the very fact that they have signed the United Nations Charter, and this assistance includes contributing armed forces to the multinational force; providing assistance of any type to this force; and bestowing transit rights to armed forces on their territory, if and when the forces act to maintain international peace and security. Therefore the Charter calls on the states to sign agreements with the Security Council. Every state that contributes manpower to the international force acting under the directives of the Security Council has the right to be involved in the decision-making process of the Security Council regarding the force's mode of operation.

In addition, the chapter explicitly notes the need for the establishment of an international airforce that can deal immediately with international threats on peace and security. In order to streamline the process, each state is, according to the Charter, required to place military forces on standby for the use of the Security Council when the need arises. An entity called the Military Staff Committee (MSC) was supposed to have been formed in order to advise the Security Council on all its military issues. The MSC was supposed to determine the type of forces to be used, the organisation of the forces' command, and the control and overall strategic regulation of these military forces. This entity, which was supposed to comprise the heads of the armies of each of the permanent member states in the Council, would discuss various military issues in parallel to the discussions in the Security Council. Its goal was to provide for efficient planning of the collective military activity of the powers. In other words, most of the articles in Chapter 7 were, in fact, designed to give the Security Council enforcement measures as part of its responsibility of acting to maintain international peace and security, while revoking the rights of the states to initiate war.

However, the MSC has never succeeded in realising the vision of the Charter and is defunct. At the end of the 1940s, severe disagreements erupted between the powers on the size of the forces they would give the UN. These disagreements grew as political tension between the United States and the Soviet Union intensified.[16] When we review the implementation of Chapter 7 by the Security Council, we see that during the Cold War, the Council members were rarely able to agree on the situations that constituted a threat to the maintenance of international peace and security and that required use of enforcement as detailed in Chapter 7.[17]

In order to strengthen the motivation of the states not to violate international peace, the UN Charter defined additional objectives for the maintenance of international peace and security. The premise was that if the states would act to fulfil these goals, there would be less chance that they would resort to the use of force versus other states. According to Article 1 in the Charter, these objectives are:

1. To develop friendly relations among nations based on respect for the principle of equal rights and self-determination of peoples, and to take other appropriate measures to strengthen universal peace;
2. To achieve international cooperation in solving international problems of an economic, social, cultural, or humanitarian character, and in promoting and encouraging respect for human rights and for fundamental freedoms for all without distinction as to race, sex, language, or religion; and
3. To be a centre for harmonising the actions of nations in the attainment of these common ends.[18]

These secondary goals won consensus during the time the Charter was written, and since then have become entrenched in UN work norms and international rhetoric. They are supported by a series of General Assembly resolutions, such as the Declaration on the Right of Peoples to Peace from 1984 and the Declaration of the International Year of Peace from 1985.[19] Historian Akira Iriye views these objectives as an additional stage in the development of the vision of a global community of nations with a unique 'international culture', with common economic, social, humanitarian, ethical and intellectual values. According to Iriye, these objectives are antithetical to the chauvinist 'nationalistic culture' that characterised the 1920s and 1930s, a culture that may be viewed as one of the major causes of the Second World War. Also, the new international culture helps states work cooperatively while trying to find joint objectives they can promote. Hundreds of international and non-governmental agencies work cooperatively on projects.[20] For this reason, Iriye and other researchers suggest that the globalisation process contributes to the entrenching of these norms in world politics.[21]

So far, the discussion has revolved around the goals of the United Nations, and the means defined in the Charter. In order to understand the organisation's political dynamics that affect the choice of goals and means to realise those goals, we first must recognise its main actors and their relative positions and importance. It is important to emphasise that the main political entity recognised by the UN is the political organisation called the 'state'. Therefore, membership to the organisation is only bestowed on states (see Chapter 2 of the UN Charter). Article 2(1) in the Charter states explicitly that the organisation is based on the principle of sovereign equality between all the member states. A 'state' is usually defined as a political entity with effective administration; a state must have clear borders with regard to neighbouring states to avert territorial disputes; there must be a monopoly on enforcement measures within the state; and a state must be independent (i.e. non-dependence) regarding other states. Therefore, the UN formally recognises only states and the relations that prevail between them, champions state sovereignty and forbids intervention in intrastate internal affairs.[22] At the same time, Weiss, Forsythe and Coate argue that 'most of world politics is comprised of the tension between aspirations to preserve the principles of state sovereignty on the one hand, and the hopes to improve security, human rights, and sustainable human development, on the other.'[23]

The UN has the following six major organs: the General Assembly, the Security Council; the Secretariat; the Economic and Social Council (ECOSOC); the Trusteeship Council (TC which has been inoperative since 1994); and the International Court of Justice. But the heart of the discussion on peacekeeping operations takes place in the Security Council, the General Assembly and Secretariat. This is not meant to suggest that ECOSOC and the International Court of Justice do not do important work, but rather that their work is not in the sphere under discussion here – i.e. the concept and execution of peacekeeping operations.

The main organ in charge of the maintenance of international peace and security is the Security Council.[24] The Security Council was designed to be an effective organ that would rectify the shortcomings in the League of Nations' working methods. The League of Nations' methods, adopted from the tradition of European diplomatic principles of the nineteenth century, were sometimes called the 'European concert [balance of power] system' that included such tenets as passing of resolutions only by unanimous vote. Another principle was that once a resolution was passed to take action in the wake of an aggressive act by one of the states, the member states' contributions to the action were purely voluntary. These principles stymied the League of Nations when incidents took place during the 1930s that flagrantly violated the international peace principle, such as in Manchuria in 1931 and Ethiopia in 1935.[25]

By contrast, the Security Council is much more effective because it includes powerful states that can make decisions quickly and then take immediate action. This approach was promoted by the victorious powers of the Second World War and ensured the creation of an oligarchy in the work of the UN. The superpowers wanted to ensure freedom of action for themselves, thus the Charter gives practically unlimited power to the Security Council to decide whether a given scenario threatens international peace and security. The Council's only constraint is that it is supposed to act in accordance with the objectives and principles formulated in the UN Charter.[26]

At the time the UN was founded, it was decided that the Council would be composed of eleven members, out of which five are permanent: the United States, the Soviet Union, the United Kingdom, China and France (the P5). Council resolutions were passed by a majority of seven votes. At the beginning of the 1960s, the number of UN member states increased significantly, thus the Council was enlarged as well.[27] From 1965 until the present, the Council has contained fifteen members; resolutions are passed by a majority of nine votes. Except for the P5, the other elected non-permanent members in the Council are divided according to geographic representation: five states from Africa and Asia-Pacific, one from Eastern Europe, two from Latin America and the Caribbean Islands, and two from Western Europe and other states.[28]

According to Article 27(3), any issue not procedural in nature requires a majority of votes in the Council that includes all the permanent members. Thus, even if fourteen members vote unanimously for a resolution, it will not pass if one of the P5 votes against it. Thus, in effect, the P5 have veto power. Sidney Bailey, a prominent researcher of the UN's work, argues that this anti-democratic method ensures two things. First, that no Security Council decision can harm the interests of the superpowers; this increases the chances of cooperation among them, and of implementation of resolutions. Second, it ensures the continued existence and partial functioning of the Council even during severe international crises between the Council members, thus ensuring the continued existence of the entire United Nations system.[29]

This method increases the effectiveness of the Council by preventing discussion on disputes in which the P5 have an interest. It also allows the five superpowers to exploit their military and economic power in order to influence other member states in the Council. In addition, the rich, powerful states can naturally finance large delegations to the United Nations. They have the resources to process information quickly and exert pressure in UN 'corridors' more effectively than small delegations can. Finally, veto power is most effective when used to prevent, *apriori*, the raising of certain issues to discussion even though they have ramifications on the maintenance of international peace and security.[30] In 1979, nine states raised a proposal that was discussed in the General Assembly regarding changing the modus operandi of the Council, but this attempt failed. With the conclusion of the Cold War, the question arose whether the Council, and principally its five permanent members, would change their mode of operation.[31]

The second most important organ in the United Nations on the subject of peace and security is the General Assembly. The Assembly is the main organ of the organisation (see Chapter 4 in the Charter). The Assembly meets every year between September and December, though there are usually exceptions. The Assembly is composed of all the organisation's member states, and each state has one vote. But its authority is limited by Articles 11 and 12 in the Charter that forbid the Assembly from passing resolutions and making recommendations regarding subjects connected to the maintenance of international peace and security that are being discussed by the Security Council. Nevertheless, the Assembly has dealt with the whole range of goals of the organisation, ever since it began operating in 1946.

Resolutions on important subjects in the Assembly are passed either according to a regular majority or a two-thirds majority, depending on the subject under discussion. The Assembly can discuss any problem or issue mentioned in the Charter. While it cannot discuss the execution of an operation, it can recommend such an operation. Only the Security Council has the authority to authorise the execution of a specific operation that is connected to peace and security. Thus, as opposed to the League of Nations, in which the Assembly and Council had the same powers, the UN Charter clearly emphasises the division of powers between the main supervisory organ, the General Assembly, and the executive authority, the Security Council.[32]

However, despite the limitations noted above, the Assembly is granted other important powers by the UN Charter. These include supervisory and decision-making responsibility over the organisation's budget and deciding on the admission of new member states (i.e. determining whether they are entitled to become members of the organisation or if they are rejected from the organisation). It also elects the non-permanent members to other UN organs. The Assembly is also entitled to establish various committees to assist it in its work, and it examines the reports submitted to it by the Security Council on the Council's work. Through these duties, the Assembly serves as an international forum for clarifying all the problems that concern the states. Sometimes, when there is a consensus over certain issues, it succeeds in advancing treatment of these issues by multilateral agreements that contribute toward the development of international law and interstate relations.[33]

Thus it is clear that the Security Council must also take into account political procedures in the Assembly. The member states of the organisation are the ones that grant legitimacy to the actions taken by the Security Council, from the very fact of their diplomatic and practical support for the resolutions passed by the Council. Thus, for example, the Assembly fulfilled an important role in promoting the de-colonisation process, and served as a major forum for activities against South Africa's apartheid policy.[34] Similarly, continuous pressure of the Assembly member states was instrumental in the removal of the China seat in the Assembly from the 'Chinese Republic' (Taiwan) and giving it to the communist Chinese government (in 1971) – against the interests and desires of the United States.[35] The Assembly also exerts diplomatic pressure on Israel to withdraw from the territories it conquered in 1967; it promoted the 1975 resolution that equated Zionism with racism; and in 2012 it upgraded the status of the Palestinian Authority to that of a non-member state in the organisation, against the official stance of the Security Council.[36]

Over the years, as the number of member states in the UN increased, it became increasingly difficult to conduct discussions and organise the political alliances in the Assembly. In order to streamline the work of the Assembly in its regular sessions and sub-committees, it was decided over the years to divide the organisation's members into regional groups. This practice became fixed in the 1963 General Assembly resolutions that officially formed five regional groups, in use to the present day. The UN groups are: the African Group; the Asia-Pacific Group; the Eastern European Group; the Latin American and Caribbean Group (GRULAC); the Western European and Others Group (WEOG). Yet, geographical representation is not the only criterion in UN political alliances. For example, the 'Group of 77' – the UN's political organ of the Non-Aligned Movement (NAM) – represents the interests of the developing nations vis-à-vis those of the developed nations. In this case, the criteria are economic. By contrast, the League of Arab States (also called the Arab League) is based on ethnic-religious identity, and is a federation of Arab and Islamic states. These alliances and others exert great influence on the

UN organisation because they can recruit a large number of states to vote a certain way on an issue that is compatible with the group's interests. Within the groups, the strongest states are at an advantage: They can put pressure on the rest of the members to vote for them to represent the group in the United Nations' various organs.[37]

Chapter 8 of the Charter adds another dimension to the role of the organisation while addressing additional actors in the international arena. This chapter emphasises the importance of regional organisations with regard to the maintenance of international peace and security. This does not conform to one of the general work principles of the UN, which views itself as a universal organisation of states that is responsible for interstate peace. Instead, Chapter 8 explicitly states that the UN must give preference to resolving disputes via regional or local organs. Moreover, Article 53 states that the Security Council is privileged with the right to initiate enforcement actions (according to Chapter 7) by using regional organisations. The source of this departure from the founding logic of the organisation is the pressure exerted by the Latin American and Arab countries at the United Nations Conference on International Organization, held in San Francisco in 1945. The representatives of these countries wanted to ensure their sovereignty and to prevent the Security Council from intervening in their affairs. Afterwards, the delegations of the United States, the United Kingdom and the Soviet Union also joined in support for Chapter 7, in an effort to preserve their countries' dominance in their spheres of influence in the world.

However, the Charter emphasises that these organisations' activities must adhere to the following rules: They must be consistent and conform to the goals and principles of the Charter regarding maintaining international peace and security; They may not prevent the right of the Security Council to intervene and decide on the best course of action to ensure peace; Any regional settlement must have the agreement of the Security Council. In practice, the status and functions of the regional organisations have grown politically, economically, culturally and security-wise in the international arena. Yet the support of these regional organisations for the universal principle of collective security, at the expense of their regional interests, remains inconclusive.[38]

The Security Council and the General Assembly, together with the Secretariat, represent the three legs on which the UN is based with regard to its peacekeeping operations. The Secretariat is headed by the Secretary-General (Chapter 15 in the UN Charter). It is difficult to make a clear distinction between the Secretariat and its Secretary-General (though the Secretary-General has certain powers that the Secretariat does not have), and together they comprise one organic unit. The Secretariat is only subordinate to the UN international community, and its composition must be as geographically diverse as possible.

The Secretariat provides administrative support services for the other main UN organs (it writes drafts of resolutions, reports and studies; provides ongoing facts and figures; organises conferences, prepares translations, prepares the budget plan, etc.). It is also responsible for publication of information and public relations. The Secretary-General is responsible for overall administration, and also has a variety of political responsibilities. Articles 98 and 99 of the Charter give the Security Council, the General Assembly, ECOSOC and the TC the right to entrust the Secretary-General with 'other functions' that are not expressly defined in the Charter. Article 99 also gives power to the Secretary-General to initiate any issue that, in his opinion, threatens international peace and security – then bring it to the Security Council for discussion. Occasionally the Secretary-General conducts secret diplomacy in attempts to resolve international disputes. The Secretary-General also has direct influence on the decision-making process of the Security Council; he prepares the yearly reports of the General Assembly, supervises the entire budget, and may express his opinion regarding the gamut of subjects discussed in the meetings of major UN organs such as the Security Council.

Contemporary researchers disagree regarding the amount of influence wielded by the Secretariat on UN workings. The Charter encourages the Secretary-General and Secretariat to be active in the development and design of the organisation's objectives due to the special powers it granted to the Secretary-General, the professionalism of the staff at his disposal, and the efficiency of the Secretariat – as all these are quite centralised in nature. On the other hand, the Secretariat is dependent on the constant political support, on the funds provided by the member states and is constantly being supervised by the UN Security Council and the General Assembly. Indeed, the powers of the Secretariat are given to different interpretations. This contributes to the tension between the Secretary-General and the permanent members of the Security Council, who have not infrequently attempted to limit the Secretary-General's range of activities. In this context, it seems that Stephen Schwebel's question regarding the Secretary-General's role, a question formulated more than sixty years ago – as to whether he is actually a 'secretary' or a 'general' – is still a valid one.[39] Recent studies on the UN Secretariat and peacekeeping in the early years of the twenty-first century arrive at a similar conclusion.[40]

This chapter, dealing with the principles of international politics in the UN with regard to the organisation's goals, leads to several conclusions. It seems that the UN tries to establish a world order composed of relations between states. This order almost does not relate – at least officially – to the influence of other actors (aside from states) on political, security, economic, social, and cultural issues in the global arena. As part of its world order, the organisation attempts to fulfil its primary goal as formulated in the Charter: to maintain international peace and security – the absence of war between states. To reach this objective it maintains secondary goals, such as economic cooperation and advancement of universal norms, that are designed to promote political, economic, social and cultural conditions for peace, within, and between, the states.

One of the justifications for the collective enforcement system is that it protects the weaker states from intervention by stronger states. In effect, however, a number of superpowers (the P5) benefit from the system's existence because it helps them strengthen their relative advantage even more. These countries and others have even violated world peace on more than one occasion, when it suited their interests.[41] Nevertheless, it is commonly accepted that, in most cases, governments prefer to settle disputes among themselves via negotiation or multilateral forums. In order to maintain international peace, the UN Charter encourages the resolving of conflicts through negotiation, and in extreme cases it allows the use of force. The Charter also entrusts two non-state actors with a small role in resolving disputes: regional organisations and Secretariat employees. In addition, it also recognises the importance of additional international organisations in promoting the conditions necessary for maintenance of international peace and security.

The following question arises: Why were peacekeeping operations developed despite the coherent means for the maintenance of international peace and security? The peacekeeping operations model does not appear anywhere in the articles of the Charter. Nevertheless, they were developed only a few years after the founding of the organisation and became a major tool in the maintenance of international peace and security.

### The first generation: UN peacekeeping 1947–87

The majority of studies published since the beginning of the 1990s address all the peacekeeping operations carried out in the forty years between 1947 and 1987 as belonging to one category. These are called 'first-generation operations' or 'traditional operations' (henceforth traditional operations).[42] Nevertheless, some researchers disagree with this approach and they distinguish three sub-periods: the first was 1947–56, the second was from 1956 until the mid-1960s, and the third period was from the end of the 1960s to the end of the 1980s.[43] I adopt this latter approach in my work because it is historical and nuanced, thus conforming with the goal of this work to historicise the study of UN peacekeeping operations.

The main argument that emerges from studies dealing with the generational changes mentioned above is that the United Nations failed in the forty-year period (1947–87) to carry out its main mission of maintaining international peace and security. This was due to the Cold War that existed at the time between the Soviet Union and its allies and the United States and its allies. The Security Council, as the body entrusted with the goal of maintaining international peace and security and preventing wars between countries, was not able to take action in most disputes during the Cold War period because the veto power given to the superpowers in the Council neutralised its abilities. Therefore, diplomats at the UN, with the great assistance of the UN Secretariat workers, invented the concept of peacekeeping operations. The UN manual on peacekeeping says the following about the operations as a 'technique … that is the reversal of the planned use of military force in the Charter. It was developed for situations in which there is no clear determination of the aggressor. Its practitioners have no enemies, they are not taking action in order to win, and they can use weapons only in self-defence. Its effectiveness is dependent on voluntary cooperation.'[44] This technique also allows the UN to operate on low volume after an agreement has been reached to stop the dispute, in order to encourage a reconciliation process leading to a peace agreement between countries or the disputing parties.

### The first period: UN peacekeeping from 1947–56

Peacekeeping operations between 1947 and 1956 attempted to support the new international world order after the Second World War. But it soon became clear to all the involved parties that the vision of peace as it appeared in the UN Charter, a vision of a world composed of countries that do not fight with one another, is not a sustainable ideal in the reality of a Cold War. Four permanent members of the Security Council – the United States, the Soviet Union, the United Kingdom and France – were mired in numerous local disputes around the world (the result of the colonial 'legacy').

In four cases at the end of the 1940s, the Security Council decided to initiate operations under the UN aegis to reduce the involvement of these superpowers in the disputes: in the Balkan states, with the establishment of the United Nations Special Committee on the Balkans (UNSCOB) in 1947–52, and a Balkan Sub-Commission of the Standing Peace Observation Commission (1952–54); in Indonesia, via special UN Committee (1947–50); in the conflict between Israel and the Arab countries, via the United Nations Truce Supervision Organization (UNTSO) which contained military observers and began operating in 1948; and finally, the United Nations Military Observer Group in India and Pakistan (UNMOGIP) has been deployed the length of the border between India and Pakistan ever since 1949, and remains there today.

Rivalry over influence in the Balkan countries was one of the bones of contention during the Cold War. As a result, many of the countries involved in the dispute did not agree to cooperate with the operation initiated by the UN. On the other hand, the other three operations were the result of the de-colonisation process. Due to their geographic distance from Europe, they received the greatest support of the UN among the four such operations. Evidently, however, only the operation in Indonesia greatly contributed to stopping the violent conflict. The contributions of the three other operations – in the Balkans, the Middle East, and between Pakistan and India – are still doubtful.

Although some researchers view the above four operations as belonging to the same category, the UN officially recognises only the last two (in the Middle East and Pakistan–India) as peacekeeping operations, according to official UN publications.[45] In terms of this study, these four operations had great significance in demonstrating the importance of 'military observers' in the maintenance of international peace and security. Even more important was that they contributed to forming the criteria for the execution of future operations, as these types of operations had not been defined in the organisation's Charter at all. In most cases, such operations were 'born' in the Security Council, though in some instances the General Assembly intervened as well. UN Secretary-General Trygve Lie (1946–52) was responsible at the time for managing and organising the operations. He was also responsible for clarifying the objectives of the operations and implementing them as they were defined by the Security Council or General Assembly. Regarding all four instances mentioned above, action was taken only after an agreement was reached among all the parties involved. The UN mission sent to the region of the dispute was usually small, numbering from dozens to a few hundred soldiers at most; these were unarmed and served as observers for implementation of the agreements. Each mission comprised representatives from numerous countries around the world, including the powers, in contrast to the norm that developed later on – which rejected the presence of power representatives in UN operations.

In summary, the main reason for the lack of success of the majority of the early operations is rooted in the fact that the UN could not operate according to the UN Charter principles. In addition, the organisation was constrained by the hostility between the superpowers during the Cold War. Their representatives repeated to the UN Secretariat, time and again, that it was not the organisation's role to attempt to solve disputes, only to contain them.[46]

The UN's role in conflict containment was put to the test on 25 June 1950 when North Korea invaded South Korea. The invasion was a flagrant violation of the UN Charter that forbids aggressive actions of one country toward another. Despite the unmistakable violation of UN principles, it was clear that, due to the system of international alliances, the Soviet Union would not support an operation against its protégé, North Korea. At the same time, the Soviet Union even boycotted the work of the Security Council, since the latter refused to recognise Mao Zedong's regime as China's legitimate government. As a result, the Western member states in the Council were able to pass a series of resolutions according to Chapter 7 of the UN Charter that gave authority to use force (in UN language, 'enforcement power') against North Korea.[47] As a result, the Soviet Union representatives hurried to rejoin the Security Council where they could use their veto power to remove the boycott imposed by the Security Council. Thus they began using their veto power starting from 1 August 1950.[48] In response, the United States took advantage of the dominance of Western countries in the General Assembly to pass resolutions for an enforcement operation against North Korea via an initiative for a new programme called 'Uniting for Peace'. This programme enabled the General Assembly to convene and pass the resolution that:

> if the Security Council, because of lack of unanimity of the permanent members, fails to exercise its primary responsibility for the maintenance of international peace and security in any case where there appears to be a threat to the peace,

breach of the peace, or act of aggression, the General Assembly shall consider the matter immediately with a view to making appropriate recommendations to Members for collective measures, including in the case of a breach of the peace or act of aggression, the use of armed force when necessary to 'maintain and restore international peace and security'.[49]

This kind of resolution was an innovation, as it was not mentioned in the UN Charter. The Soviet Union immediately condemned this resolution as illegal; the only section of the entire resolution that remained legal in their eyes was the part about convening the General Assembly within twenty-four hours. After the United States circumvented the power of the Security Council by use of resolutions taken in the General Assembly, it led a multinational force that finally brought an end to the Korean War in 1953.

The Korean War that was waged from June 1950 to July 1953 proved that, in effect, no use was made of the procedures described in Chapter 7 of the UN Charter against aggressive countries. The international operation led by the United States on behalf of South Korea proved the limitations of the enforcement of the UN Charter's principles regarding disputes between nations. In effect, this relegated the UN to the status of an entity limited to traditional diplomacy tactics of providing forums for meetings between diplomatic delegations, conducting negotiations and forming international committees. The resolution in the General Assembly to execute an operation, such as the activation of Chapter 7 in the Korean War case, stemmed only from the dominance of Western nations in the Security Council and General Assembly. From the 1950s until 1990, the UN never again adopted the same tactics as it did in Korea.[50]

## The second period 1956-67

During the 1956-67 period of the Cold War, the UN executed eight new peacekeeping operations. In 1956 the Sinai Desert operation was executed; the First United Nations Emergency Force (UNEF I) was sent to serve as a buffer between the Israeli and Egyptian armies after the war in the Sinai Peninsula in 1956 (*MivtzaKadesh*). Additional operations were executed in Lebanon in 1958, by the United Nations Observation Group in Lebanon (UNOGIL); in the Congo in 1960-64, by the United Nations Operation in the Congo (ONUC); and in West Irian, also known as Western New Guinea,[51] in 1962-63 (UNTEA/UNSF). The United Nations Yemen Observation Mission (UNYOM) was deployed on the border between North Yemen and South Yemen for a short period in 1964; the United Nations Peacekeeping Force in Cyprus (UNFICYP) has been deployed in Cyprus since 1964; DOMREP was deployed in the Dominican Republic in 1965; the United Nations India- Kuwait Observation Mission (UNIPOM) was deployed on the western border between India and Pakistan in 1965-66. Since this study does not deal with peacekeeping operations during the Cold War, I will only briefly review the four most prominent, complex and ambitious operations conducted in the second period. These operations were the basis for consolidating the guidelines of future peacekeeping operations.

UNEF I was executed at the end of 1956 on the heels of the war against Egypt that was conducted by the United Kingdom, France and Israel (Sinai War, or *MivtzaKadesh* in Hebrew). This war in the Sinai Peninsula created an international crisis; the Security Council could not take action as it was neutralised by the vetoes cast by the United Kingdom and France. Thus it was up to the General Assembly to accept a series of resolutions as part of the Uniting for Peace plan to find a creative solution to the situation. The solution was the creation of the Emergency Force, which was successful beyond all expectations and improved relations in the Security Council between the Soviet Union and the Western states, and between the United States and the United Kingdom–France. The UN emergency force concept was shaped in the early days of November 1956 by the following: then-Secretary-General Dag Hammarskjöld; Canada's Foreign Minister Lester B. Pearson; and high-level officials in the UN Secretariat. They discussed the objectives and principles of success of the operations, and also solutions for the managerial and organisational problems caused by the execution of the operations. Similar to the early operations in which military observers took part, here they emphasised the need to obtain the agreement of the disputing parties for the deployment of the operation's forces and for international support in the form of a mandate given by the General Assembly or Security Council.

The goal of the UNEF I was to help supervise the withdrawal of Israeli forces from Sinai and create a buffer zone between them and the Egyptian forces. Thus it was decided to deploy UN forces over hundreds of square kilometres, within which they would temporarily maintain civil order among the civilian population. Nevertheless, these troops were not allowed to use force, except for self-defence. In addition, they were not allowed to intervene in internal affairs. The countries supplying the forces for the operation were supposed to be countries not involved in the dispute and capable of contributing the soldiers promptly. Hammarskjöld recommended that the P5 powers not take part in operations. It was decided that the soldiers would be lightly armed and wear blue helmets and blue insignias on the sleeves of their uniforms. At its height, the force numbered about 6,000 soldiers. The cost of the entire operation was tens of millions of dollars but the countries that contributed the soldiers agreed to finance the equipment and salaries of their soldiers.[52]

Secretary-General Hammarskjöld decided to establish the Office of Special Political Affairs (OSPA) to assist the Secretariat in managing this complex operation. The OSPA was headed by Ralph Bunche, who had won the Nobel Peace Prize in 1950 for his efforts in bringing about a ceasefire between Israel and the Arab countries in 1949. Bunche served in this role until he retired from the UN in 1970. OSPA was in charge of managing all peacekeeping operations until it was superseded by the Department of Peacekeeping Operations (DPKO) in 1992. Thus in effect, Hammarskjöld increased the influence of the Secretariat over the operations.[53]

We see from the information above that the UNEF I operation initiative, and the actions taken to implement it, defined the execution objectives and principles of these types of operations, as well as the rules for their management and organisation. ONUC, executed between 1960–64, overshadowed the earlier operation in Sinai and became the largest peacekeeping operation ever initiated by the UN, until the Cambodia operation in 1992. The background for ONUC was the civil war that broke out in the Congo after the country gained independence in 1960. The United States and Soviet Union backed different leaders, and the Security Council was not able to agree to discuss the dispute. Therefore, Secretary-General Hammarskjöld exploited the authority invested in him by Article 99 of the UN Charter to convene the General Assembly to discuss the Congo situation. There it was decided to take the unprecedented step of intervening within the country, in contradiction to the Charter's principles. The argument for this was that such intervention was legitimate since the elected head of state, Patrice Lumumba, expressly asked for this help.

The force of the UN operation in the Congo numbered almost 20,000 soldiers at its height. The objectives of the force were to protect Congo's territorial integrity and its political independence, and to avert a civil war. The means at its disposal were the selective use of force within the state; providing assistance to Congo's military forces; and exerting prolonged political pressure on the disputing parties. The ultimate objective was to end the civil war and create one government.

The United States and the Soviet Union each backed different political factions in the Congo dispute. This fact, and the high costs of the operation, provided fertile ground for the lively discussion conducted in the UN regarding the limits of General Assembly powers with regard to peacekeeping operations; the limits of the Secretary-General's authority in conducting the operation vis-à-vis the Security Council; and especially with regard to the method of financing these operations. The UN representatives finally decided that the Congo operation had not been conducted according to the principles of the accepted concept of traditional peacekeeping operations. Thus it was decided to forbid the organisation from executing similar Congo-like operations in the future.[54]

Two additional operations over which a discussion later developed regarding the concept and practice of peacekeeping operations are the West Irian and Cyprus operations. West Irian was under Dutch control, and the UN operation there was a combination of a 'UN Temporary Executive Authority' and a 'UN Security Force', and was executed from October 1962 to April 1963. This operation was relatively smaller than the peacekeeping operations on the Israel–Egypt border, in the Congo, in Cyprus, and years later in South Lebanon. Yet the West Irian operation was important because the UN assumed temporary sovereign authority for a transition period, including responsibility for law and order in the territory, until authority over the territory was transferred to Indonesia, which annexed it into its country. Although one could argue that this, too, involved deviating from UN Charter powers, no doubts arose regarding the legitimacy of this operation in General Assembly discussions, in the Security Council or among the Secretariat staff of then-Secretary-General U. Thant. Ironically, in the same time period there were great disagreements within the organisation about UN conduct in the Congo. The reason for agreement on the West Irian situation as opposed to the Congo situation is probably that there was mutual agreement between the Dutch and Indonesian governments regarding the way they would conduct the transfer of authorities between them. There were no violent clashes on the ground, the mandate for the UN force was short term only, and the two countries agreed to bear the burden of the operation's costs. Thus, this operation left only a minor impression in the UN collective memory.[55]

Another important operation was UNFICYP. This operation was executed in 1964 and has not been terminated to this day. When the force was first deployed, it numbered almost 6,500 soldiers. The force received responsibility for territories within the country, and its mandate included maintaining law and order. The United Kingdom provided a large percentage of the military force and thus exerted greater influence; this was most unusual. However, although the force operated within the country, it maintained the basic principles of peacekeeping operations, including obtaining agreement and support for the operation by the local players as well as the P5 powers. Finally, UNFICYP was neutral and did not use force to achieve its goals.[56]

Decisions about execution of operations in the second time period were disputed among the diplomatic delegations in the organisation mainly because of budgetary constraints. In those years the operations were funded by allocations taken from the organisation's regular budget, which was on the verge of economic collapse due to the great strains placed by the large operations in Sinai (UNEF I) and the Congo (ONUC) on UN purse strings. Also, due to political tension and rivalry, the Soviet Union refused to pay its assessed part of the Congo operation, while the United States, in response, refused to pay its assessed part of the Sinai operation. Evan Luard claims that by 1964, the UN deficit had reached about 112 million dollars, even though the organisation had issued bonds and received contributions from the countries totalling about fifty million dollars.[57] Thus the budgetary problem aroused considerable dissension in the UN regarding the execution of operations. Another problem arose: UNFICYP failed to promote a political process between the Greek and Turkish factions in Cyprus and this, in turn, deepened the UN controversy regarding operations in general.

During 17–19 May 1967, Secretary-General U. Thant received a demand from the Egyptian authorities to evacuate the UN emergency forces from Egyptian territory along the Israeli border. Since some of the countries that had contributed forces argued that they would withdraw their soldiers, and since Israel refused to allow the force to redeploy on its land near the border, U. Thant decided to withdraw the UN force.[58]

The war that broke out between Israel and Jordan, Egypt and Syria on 5 June 1967 was to change the map of the Middle East and raise question marks not only regarding the effectiveness of UN operations in solving disputes, but also regarding its very ability to limit the disputes.

### The third period 1967–87

The peacekeeping operations during the Cold War from 1967–87 were characterised by more sober, realistic expectations. Delegations in the UN, and researchers who specialised in the organisation's work, began to lose faith in the ability of operations to contribute to the solving or containment of conflicts. During this period the UN executed three new operations, all in response to the wars between Israel and its neighbours. The two first operations were international responses, whose roots went back to the Yom Kippur War [in 1973], to prevent expansion of the conflict beyond the region. The first operation, called the Second United Nations Emergency Force (UNEF II), was executed from 1973–79 in southern Sinai, with the goal of providing a buffer zone between the Egyptian and Israeli forces. At its height, the emergency force numbered about 7,000 soldiers from various countries. The second operation, the United Nations Disengagement Observer Force (UNDOF), was established in 1973 and was deployed the length of the Golan Heights slope as a buffer between the Syrian and Israeli forces. This force is still stationed on the territory and operates to this day. The third operation, the United Nations Interim Force in Lebanon (UNIFIL), was deployed in 1978, only four days after Israel invaded South Lebanon in response to terrorist attacks against it from Lebanese territory.[59]

Thus, the third-period operations were carried out in an international atmosphere of political scepticism regarding the ability of these operations to contribute to the resolution or containment of conflicts. Nevertheless, these operations are accorded great importance in the fundamental discussion about the management and organisation of operations. The report of Secretary-General Kurt Waldheim (of 26 October 1973), which proposed the execute of UNEF II between Israel and Egypt, also proposed solutions to many of the managerial and organisational problems that had been discussed throughout the 1960s. Since then, UNEF II, which had been activated as a buffer between the disputing parties and not only as an observer force, became a model for subsequent peacekeeping operations.

Waldheim's report determined that all peacekeeping operations must be conducted under UN command as represented by the Secretary-General; the Secretary-General is under the authority of the Security Council. The second managerial principle was that command on the ground would be given to a commander appointed by the Secretary-General and subordinate to the Security Council agreement. This commander would be directly responsible and subordinate to the Secretary-General. A third managerial principle was that the Secretary-General would be required to report to the Security Council on all developments on the ground regarding the functioning of the force, and anything else that might influence this functioning. Waldheim's report determined that the weapons given to the force would only be those intended for self-defence, and such personnel would be allowed to use force only for self-protection. Regarding the bone of contention – funding of the operations – it was decided to impose a special assessment (assessed contribution) on all UN members, according to Paragraph 2 of Article 17 in the UN Charter. This resolution was later approved by the General Assembly as well. The Soviet Union insisted that this monetary arrangement must be ad hoc and not constitute a precedent, but this work norm has been activated from then until the present, renewed each time. Finally, Waldheim emphasised that all countries around the world from all political blocs must send representatives to the UN forces. The result was that, for the first time in the history of peacekeeping operations, a country from the communist bloc also took part – Poland. Thus, in effect, the General Assembly was stripped of its powers regarding decisions about the initiative for, and ongoing management of, the peacekeeping operations.[60]

The original mandate for the UNIFIL operation that was carried out in March 1978 was to monitor the border between Israel and Lebanon and ensure that Lebanon's sovereignty was not violated.[61] However, after Israel's invasion of Lebanon on 6 June 1982, the UNIFIL force found itself on territory under Israeli control. Afterwards the UNIFIL mandate changed several times, most recently in the summer of 2006, on the heels of the war between Israel and the Hezbollah organisation in southern Lebanon. As part of its mandate, the force was instructed to ensure the security of the civilian population and provide humanitarian aid when required. The force numbered only a few thousand soldiers, and was deployed within Lebanon over a territory of hundreds of kilometres.[62]

Despite the resolutions to execute these three operations on Israeli borders, the Security Council did not initiate new operations in 1978–87. Some researchers view the 1980s as a separate operations-era unto itself and emphasise that, in this period, regional powers or organisations adopted the method developed by the UN, and implemented it to execute peacekeeping operations by themselves. This was because everyone realised that UN activity during the Cold War was almost totally paralysed as a result of the political dissension between the East and West blocs. Thus we are aware of international interventions in Rhodesia, Lebanon and Sri Lanka in the 1980s,[63] but since the UN did not take part in them they are not discussed in this study, nor are they listed in the chronology of UN peacekeeping operations.

Towards the end of the 1960s, the opinion began to take root among statesmen, diplomats, researchers and members of the UN Secretariat that peacekeeping operations were only a passing episode in the chronicles of the United Nations. Brian Urquhart, who worked in the UN from the day of its inception, headed

OSPA, which was responsible for the management of peacekeeping operations, from 1971 until his retirement in January 1986 and summarised the overall atmosphere of the organisation that had heavy financial debts and was torn by political divisions: 'As one who had watched the Security Council from the beginning, I sometimes felt that only an invasion from outer space would be a sufficiently non-controversial disaster to bring the Council back to the great power unanimity that the Charter required in order to make the United Nations effective.'[64]

On the other hand, it should be emphasised that even when there was doubt that the operations could be revived, the concept behind them (which was first consolidated in 1956, with only a few changes in later years) was not cast in doubt. Thus, although in fact each operation was adapted to specific circumstances and the local arena, the managerial-organisational structure was preserved, as were the spheres of authority and modes of execution. The objective of the peacekeeping forces remained the same: to observe the opposing parties and serve as a buffer between the military forces of disputing states. In any event, the Security Council was required, in each specific case, to define the goals of the operations on the basis of an agreement between the disputing parties. The operations were managed and led by the Secretary-General, and each operation was required to receive authorisation for action and support from the countries in which the UN forces acted, and from all the countries involved in the dispute. In addition, the countries permitted to contribute people to the forces were only those countries viewed as impartial (without personal interests) in the specific dispute. Representation was also given to the various geographic regions around the world. The operative forces were not permitted to use force or intervene in the internal affairs of the countries to which they were sent.[65] All these principles were meant to help establish peace (peacemaking) between the disputing states. Despite the limited success of the operations, the delegation representatives renewed the discussions on peacekeeping operations every year, with the support of the Secretariat workers and researchers who specialise in operations. It seems that they have all reached the conclusion that the execution of the operations according to the traditional concept is still the best means we have to deal with international disputes and conflicts.[66]

### The second generation: UN peacekeeping from 1988 to 2014

The end of the Cold War reopened the issue of the role and position of peacekeeping operations in the international arena to new discussion. During the Cold War, the Security Council had great difficulty in responding to intrastate disputes, as explained above. Therefore, one might have anticipated that the end of the Cold War would have created the conditions for minimising the use of traditional operations, while the Council would attempt to solve disputes according to Chapters 6 and 7 of the UN Charter. But this was not the case. Instead, the Council authorised the implementation of dozens of new peacekeeping operations with more objectives than those of the traditional operations. Therefore, these later operations were often called multidimensional operations in the UN. These campaigns were supposed to provide solutions to a variety of facets of the conflict, not only the diplomatic-military aspects.

There is no consensus on the answer to the question as to when the 'second generation' began. For Bellamy, Williams, Griffin, Roberts and Zaum it started in 1988.[67] Berdal, Economides and Mayall point to 1991 as a starting point.[68] Doyle and Sambanis alternatively use the late 1980s and early 1990s as points of departure but they avoid specifying a certain year.[69] In this work I argue that 1988 should be the point of departure for the analysis of the concept and practice of peacekeeping, for several reasons. First, in 1988, after a ten-year break, the Security Council authorised the execution of five new operations in a period of a year and a half. Second, in the same year, the UN's peacekeeping operations received international acclaim and recognition as contributing to world peace when the Nobel Peace Prize was awarded to them. In the same year, the discussion on the concept of peacekeeping was renewed in the General Assembly Committees.

The period after the Cold War, from 1988 to the present day, is characterised by an increasing will of the Security Council to use peacekeeping missions, and one way of differentiating it from the Cold War era is to call it the 'second generation'. This period can be divided into several sub-periods. Thus second-generation operations can be subdivided into the following three time periods: the first period, a period of transformation between 1988 and 1995; the second period, a decline in the support for multidimensional operations, between 1995 and 1999; and the third period, a renewal of support to operations from 1999 until the present.[70]

## The first period 1988–95

The first period, which extended for eight years, was characterised by the attempt to terminate regional conflicts, many of which were considered proxy wars from the Cold War era.[71] In addition, there were attempts to terminate new conflicts that erupted after the conclusion of the Cold War. In contrast to the Cold War era, the Council succeeded in reaching agreement over most of the issues that were discussed between 1988 and 1995. In those eight years, the superpowers used their veto power only sixteen times (out of which eleven occurred in 1988–89), as opposed to almost 290 vetoes cast during the Cold War period. Within eight years, the Council passed 429 resolutions, in contrast to only 606 resolutions passed between 1946 and 1987.[72]

The Security Council resolved to execute a total of twenty-six peacekeeping operations between 1988 and 1995, twice as many as the UN had executed during the first generation of peacekeeping operations over forty years between 1947 and 1987. Some of these latter operations received multidimensional mandates designed to promote political, economic, social and security-related conditions to neutralise the agents that had caused the dispute to begin with. Some of the new objectives of the multidimensional operations were: promotion of a proper civil administration, supervision of elections, disarmament, promotion of human rights, humanitarian aid and economic development. These goals were added to the basic goals of first-generation operations that mainly focused on prevention of the renewal of fighting between two disputing states. Simultaneously, changes were occasionally made in the underlying principles on which the traditional operations were based. Thus, for example, some of the new multidimensional operations even received authorisation to use force.[73]

The period from 1988 to 1995 was a transformative period in which the international community tried to change the traditional concept of peacekeeping to a new one that would allow the execution of large multidimensional operations during conflicts. These new operations were meant to be one of the main pillars of international security in the post-Cold War era.

The operations implemented from 1988 onwards were deployed over much greater territory than those during the Cold War: in five Latin American countries (El Salvador, Guatemala, Honduras, Nicaragua, and Costa Rica), and Angola, Afghanistan, Georgia (FSU), Haiti, Tajikistan, the former Yugoslavia, Liberia, Mozambique, Namibia, Western Sahara, Somalia, Iraq, Cambodia, Chad and Rwanda. In addition to these operations, the Council decided to implement an enforcement operation in Iraq while using military force (according to the UN Charter Chapter 7), after Iraq conquered Kuwait on 2 August 1990 and refused to withdraw. As opposed to the Korea operation at the beginning of the 1950s, there were no differences of opinion among the five permanent Council members regarding authorising the mandate for the enforcement operation in Iraq.

The number of states that contributed to the aforementioned operations grew steadily. Between 1988 and 1994, no less than forty-one new countries participated in peacekeeping operations; these were countries that had never taken part in operations before.[74] Similarly, and as opposed to the norm during the Cold War era, the five permanent Security Council members also participated in these operations, and even contributed large forces. The scope of the forces grew steadily during this period, until the UN commanded about 80,000 soldiers and about 3,000 civilian policemen.

Nevertheless, it is important to emphasise that when the organisation intervened in conflicts during this period, its levels of power and determination often varied from one region to another. Thus, for example, it is customary to emphasise the UN's great contribution at the beginning of the 1990s to bringing an end to the long civil war in Mozambique. However, its scope of intervention there was restricted from the beginning; the number of UN force members there never rose above 7,000 soldiers.[75]

Operations of similar scope were also executed in Haiti, for example, and Rwanda as well; today, researchers are in agreement that the UN did not activate enough force to avert the genocidal mass slaughter [of the Tutsis by the Hutus] that ensued in Rwanda in the summer of 1994.[76] For most of the operations executed by the UN in this period, the same traditional goals were set as had been the norm for operations during the Cold War era. This is another reason that the forces in these operations were limited in size and sometimes numbered only several dozens of soldiers. One extreme example is the UN operation on the Chad–Libya border between May and June 1994. The force numbered only nine soldiers.

The great burden on members of the international community stemmed mainly from the execution of three multidimensional operations in Cambodia, the former Yugoslavia and Somalia. For part of the time, the UN was preoccupied with all three operations simultaneously. The accepted argument in the major research studies on this subject is that these operations were meant to create conditions for the speedy resolution of conflicts and the establishment of peace. This is in contradistinction to the main goal of the operations during the Cold War period: conflict containment and promoting negotiation. The forces that took part in the large operations in this study numbered tens of thousands of soldiers. Their cost to the organisation was billions of dollars a year. Below I will briefly describe the main characteristics of the three operations.

Between October 1991 and September 1993, the UN executed two consecutive operations in Cambodia; the United Nations Advance Mission in Cambodia (UNAMIC), and the United Nations Transitional Authority in Cambodia (UNTAC). Formally, the operations represented an attempt on the part of the international community to assist the Cambodian disputing factions to resolve their conflict, thus bringing an end to the one of the longest, harshest disputes of the twentieth century. The UN was in charge of managing UNTAC in all of Cambodia's territory; UNTAC's mission was to supervise the termination of the conflict in the country and the founding of democracy. The Transitional Authority was headed by a special representative of the Secretary-General, who was charged with working with the four local Cambodian factions. Conceptually, this was an unprecedented operation. The organisation set a wide variety of objectives for itself in the fields of civil administration, elections, human rights, army, police, resettlement of refugees, economic reconstruction and rehabilitation. Despite difficulties in its execution, it is generally agreed that this operation was successful and can serve as a model for other multidimensional operations.

From February 1992 to December 1995, the UN executed the United Nations Protection Force operation (UNPROFOR) in the former Yugoslavia. Various objectives were adopted in the course of the operation in the three regions where UN forces were deployed: Croatia, Bosnia and Macedonia. In Croatia, the force focused on demilitarising four regions of the Serbian minority and restoring security there. In Bosnia, the force focused on securing humanitarian aid throughout the country, and securing Sarajevo and five 'areas' from attacks. The force was also responsible for preventing military flights in the Bosnian airspace (a no-fly zone). Macedonia was the site of a preventive operation, i.e. before the eruption of a conflict (the first time in UN history), to supervise activities that might threaten the country's stability and security, and to report to the Security Council when necessary. All these goals were meant, first and foremost, to contain the dispute to within Yugoslavian territory, to minimise its damage and promote a political arrangement between the antagonistic factions. Researchers are divided regarding the extent of success of the operation.

Between April 1992 and March 1995, the UN executed two consecutive operations in Somalia: United Nations Operation in Somalia I and II (UNOSOM I and UNOSOM II). Simultaneously, between December 1992 and May 1993, the Unified Task Force (UNITAF) operated under American leadership to ensure the delivery of humanitarian aid to famine centres in the south and centre of Somalia. Additional objectives were set for Somalia, such as military-related goals (which at one point even included the arrest of the leaders of one of the strongest factions in South Somalia); reconstruction and development of civil political institutions and of the country's economy. The researchers all agree that this operation failed to achieve its objectives.[77]

## The second period 1995–99

As of late 1995, most UN member states had lost faith in peacekeeping operations as a panacea for civil wars. This conclusion stems from the following facts: the Security Council decided to reduce the use of such operations and especially of the large multidimensional ones; the world's countries cut back on the resources and manpower that they contributed to the UN for these operations; and as a result, the UN operations returned to the more modest dimensions of the Cold War peacekeeping operations. At the same time, there was an increase in support for the execution of multidimensional peacekeeping operations by regional organisations such as NATO and the Economic Community of West African States (ECOWAS) in Western Africa but only according to the traditional principles of peacekeeping. This study will explain what occurred in the UN during 1995 that called for a re-examination of the new concept and practice of peacekeeping in civil wars. The low point was in June 1999, when only 12,084 people were involved in UN peacekeeping operations, including administrative workers, soldiers and civilian police, in a total of fifteen operations. This is in sharp contrast to about 80,000 people in 1994 who served in the operations.[78]

## The third period 1999–2014

During the Cold War, the decrease in the number, scope, and status of peacekeeping operations as a means for treating conflicts extended over a period of about two decades. During the second-generation period, the decline was shorter and took only four years. 1999 signalled the beginning of the third period in the annals of UN peacekeeping operations after the Cold War, and has continued to the present. This period began in the second half of 1999, when the attitude towards the operations changed to the positive and the Security Council decided to initiate four new interventions for maintenance of international peace and security in Kosovo, Sierra Leone, East Timor and the Congo. Thus for a few months, the number of UN peacekeeping operations increased, together with a rise in the numbers of peacekeepers who took part in them. The renewed interest in multidimensional peacekeeping from 1999 onwards is beyond the scope of this work. However, it is important to point out several of its characteristics.

The new support for the execution of peace operations from 1999 onwards encouraged the UN Secretariat to launch an organisational reform. The first outcome of this process was the 'Brahimi Report'. It was submitted by international experts who encouraged the initiation of operations only after specific conditions were met. It also called for a reform in the work of the UN Secretariat. During this period, the United Nations Under-Secretary-General (USG) for Peacekeeping Operations, Jean-Marie Guéhenno (2000–8), and a young generation of officials with experience in field missions began a comprehensive organisational reform to support the change.[79] In the past five years this trend has continued with the publication of several important policy papers by the Secretariat, such as the 'Capstone Doctrine' and the 'New Horizon', which try to establish the main conceptual and organisational lessons in dealing with peace missions.[80]

In 2014, the DPKO in the UN managed sixteen operations.[81] In addition to nine operations executed in Africa, there were five other operations (a legacy from the Cold War period) that Security Council members chose to continue in order to contain conflicts. This was despite the fact that no diplomatic solutions to the disputes were on the horizon at all.

In fact, during the first decade of the twenty-first century, the UN Secretariat was confident that the Security Council was ready to return to the use of peacekeeping operations as the main tool for maintaining international peace and security. The UN USG for Peacekeeping Operations, Jean-Marie Guéhenno, even convened a press conference on 4 October 2006 in which he made a public statement about expanding the use of peacekeeping operations. Guéhenno noted that more than 93,000 soldiers, civilian policemen and civil administration personnel were serving in various UN operations at the time; out of that number, almost 70,000 were soldiers. He anticipated that the total number would reach about 140,000 during 2007, when the operations would be fully deployed. Unlike in 1994, the momentum to support peacekeeping operations continued in the following years.[82]

Since 1999, the mixed trend has continued: Traditional peacekeeping operations have been executed together with second-generation, large multidimensional operations which received authorisation for use force in conflict zones.[83] Researchers who have analysed the operations executed in recent years connect the change since 1999 to the use of the 'peacebuilding' technique. Former UN

Secretary-General Boutros Boutros-Ghali was the one who coined the term 'peacebuilding' in 1992, though other terms are also used for this concept, such as state-building, nation-building, peace support operations and international transition administrations.[84] Researchers claim that these operations are executed after the termination of disputes. The goals of these operations were, and still are democratisation and advancement of human rights; cooperation with and between regional organisations; and the creation of civil institutions. All these steps are also directed towards economic development of the country, via the integration of local economies in global economic institutions. With regard to the more grandiose operations, the Security Council gives the UN sovereign power over the country. This usually involves cooperation on the part of local parties, but it means that the UN administers all the civil authorities in these countries. These goals were implemented most extensively and comprehensively in the Kosovo and East Timor operations. In these two operations, the concept of 'peacebuilding' was used extensively.[85]

The United Nations Interim Administration Mission in Kosovo (UNMIK) has been operating in Kosovo from 1999 to the present. The UN executes this operation in cooperation with the Organization for Security and Cooperation in Europe (OSCE) and the European Union (EU). The objectives of the operation include the following: administration of civil institutions in Kosovo; development of autonomy and self-administration; advancement of human rights; maintenance of law and order; ensuring resettlement of refugees and displaced persons; and economic reconstruction and development. At the beginning, the operation focused on humanitarian aid to the population but this goal was abolished in June 2000, after the conclusion of the humanitarian crisis in Kosovo. NATO's Kosovo Force (KFOR), responsible for the security issues in the region, operates together with the UNMIK operation. At the height of its activity, about 50,000 soldiers took part in the KFOR force, but it has since been reduced, and today it numbers only about 5,000 soldiers. Although the Kosovan government declared independence on 17 February 2008, the multidimensional intervention continues.[86]

In East Timor the UN executed the United Nations Transitional Administration in East Timor (UNTAET) between October 1999 and May 2002. The goals of the operation were: to create an effective civil administration; to develop civil and social services; to prepare the country for self-government; to ensure personal security and law and order throughout the entire country; to coordinate and transfer humanitarian aid with assistance for reconstruction and rehabilitation; and to assist in establishing conditions for sustainable development. At its height, the force numbered more than 10,000 soldiers, policemen and civilians.[87]

In addition to these two operations, the UN is focusing its large, multidimensional operations in several African countries. The United Nations Organization Mission in the Democratic Republic of the Congo (MONUC, MONUCSO) has been operating in the Congo since the end of 1999; in recent years more than 20,000 soldiers are taking part in this mission. The United Nations Mission in

Liberia (UNMIL) has been operating in Liberia since September 2003; approximately 15,000 people are involved in this mission. The United Nations Operation in Côte d'Ivoire (UNOCI) has been operating in the Ivory Coast since April 2004, involving about 10,000 people.

Furthermore, the UN has been executing large-scale operations in the south and west of Sudan since 2004. Multidimensional objectives were set for all these operations, including intervention in the country's political, security, economic and social systems in order to end the conflicts in Sudan and South Sudan. Some of the goals set for the operations are: assistance in the reconstruction of the civil administration, maintenance of law and order, humanitarian aid and economic reconstruction. Since these operations do not have the power to administer local territories like the operations in East Timor and Kosovo since 1999, they are similar to the large, multidimensional peacekeeping operations during the early 1990s, the subject of the present study.

Unlike the operations in the early 1990s, many of these field missions in the twenty-first century are characterised by cooperation between UN missions and regional organisations, such as with NATO in the Balkans, Afghanistan and Iraq; the African Union in Somalia, Sudan and, from 2013, in the Central African Republic; the EU in the Balkans, the Congo and, since 2014, in the Central African Republic.

The impression of a continued rise in international support for the deployment of peacekeeping forces after 1999 in order to deal with intrastate conflicts and primarily civil wars is misleading. Although the United States, Japan and the EU provide approximately 80 per cent of the UN peacekeeping budget, in the early twenty-first century, African and south Asian countries provide more than two-thirds of military and police personnel to UN peacekeeping missions. In the past decade, the bulk of Western countries' forces were deployed in the context of NATO operations in Iraq and Afghanistan in the context of the American-led 'War on Terrorism'.

No large UN peacekeeping mission was deployed in Libya after the air campaign that aided the opposition in toppling the reign of the country's dictator, Muammar Gaddafi, in 2011. The brutal civil war in Syria that began in March 2011 and caused the deaths of approximately 150,000 people saw the deployment of a short-lived small observer operation (UNSMIS) from April to August 2012.

## Characteristics of peacekeeping operations

In the discussion above, we see how the history of peacekeeping operations seems to support the view that distinguishes between the operations executed by the UN before 1987 and those executed from 1988 onwards.

The conflict between the superpowers in the Cold War period led to a situation in which every dispute became a focus for dissension, and each of the superpowers used its veto power in the Security Council to avoid adopting resolutions regarding the disputes. The political paralysis that ensued in the Council as a result of the veto privilege drove the active forces in the organisation to blaze another trail in world politics via the technique of 'peacekeeping', which included operations with military observers and operations with peacekeeping forces. In this study I chose to call these 'traditional operations'.

The main objective of the traditional operations was to lower the intensity of regional conflicts so that they would not escalate to cause a wider conflagration between the Eastern and Western blocs during the Cold War. It was feared that that, in turn, could lead to a world war. In other words, the operations' main goal was to discourage war. Simultaneously with these operations, diplomatic mediation attempts (peacemaking) were also conducted to help bring an end to conflicts, and the UN took part in these as well. To ensure the success of the operations, they were executed only after the disputing parties reached agreement regarding discontinuing an armed conflict. When an agreement was reached, peacekeeping forces or military observers were deployed between the warring forces, usually on the international border, where they functioned with the agreement of the disputing parties. One of the basic requirements of these forces was neutrality; in the language of the organisation's official correspondence, they were required to act impartially. In addition, these forces were forbidden to use force with the exception of self-defence. In accordance with these requirements, an operation based on Chapter 7 of the UN Charter, such as the operation in Korea from 1950 to 1953, is not a peacekeeping operation.[88] Usually, operations were terminated after a political agreement was reached between the disputing parties, which rendered the continued presence of UN forces superfluous. When such an agreement was not reached, such as in the disputes between Israel and its neighbours, between India and Pakistan, and in Cyprus, then the forces remain in place to this day.

It seems that a change took place in international politics after 1988 which led to a change in the concept and practice of peacekeeping operations. This change was related to an accelerated process of globalisation and corresponded to the political hegemony of the United States and Western states in the UN. As part of the change, the position and status of regional organisations were strengthened. Some even operated in partnership with the UN's execution of peacekeeping operations.[89] According to Jakobsen, Kaldor and others, the new political reality allowed the United States and its Western allies to create a consensus in the Security Council regarding conflicts in the world. However, the studies emphasise that most of the world's developing countries, including China and Russia, oppose the use of peacekeeping operations for promoting Western norms as these are expressed in the operations executed by the UN since 1988. The researchers argue that Western hegemony is what facilitated the change of the traditional concept of peacekeeping, and its adaptation to the post-Cold War period.[90]

In addition to the main goal of the traditional operations, goals were added that sometimes seem to supersede the traditional goal. Since the traditional technique of peacekeeping operations was not appropriate for activity within a state and is even explicitly forbidden, goals were added that included the following: supervising democratic elections; building civil institutions; supervising human rights; disarming ex-combatants; providing humanitarian assistance and economic development. The changes in the goals of peacekeeping operations led to the coining of new terms to differentiate these later operations from the ones executed by the UN between 1947 and 1987. Among the prominent terms are 'second-generation peacekeeping operations', 'expanded peacekeeping operations', 'humanitarian assistance operations', 'peace support operations', 'peace enforcement operations', 'peacebuilding operations'. In this study I chose to call them multidimensional operations since by the very definition and nature of their goals, they clearly differ from first-generation operations. These multidimensional operations attempted to provide a sturdy basis for peace by creating the political, economic, social and security-related conditions that would encourage the termination of a conflict. While traditional operations were implemented after some kind of agreement was reached between the disputing parties, multidimensional operations were executed sometimes without clear consent by the local parties. The forces involved were larger than in the traditional operations. They deployed throughout the country in which the conflict erupted. While the success principles of the traditional operations focused on political support on the part of the disputing parties and the world's states in UN activities, the success or failure of the operations after the Cold War was dependent on the scope of contributions from UN member states to the operations (political support, manpower and financing) and the amount of time the world's states were willing to continue to invest in the operations. The mandatory precondition for execution of the traditional operations – agreement of the disputing parties to UN involvement – became less important than achieving other goals, such as forestalling humanitarian calamity (e.g. following the war in Bosnia and the famine in Somalia, rescuing the Albanian population in Kosovo in 1999 or protecting the Syrian people from their ruthless leader in 2011). For this reason, the operations sometimes received enforcement power according to Chapter 7 of the UN Charter that called for the use of force against local armed factions. These UN missions were not limited to use of force for self-defence only.[91]

It is clear that the period of 1988 to 1995 was an important transformative period in the history of peacekeeping and global affairs. During these years there was an effort to transform the concept and practice of peacekeeping in order to confront intrastate conflicts. However, this was short-lived since something happened that caused member states to have reservations about using such operations.

As mentioned in the introduction, the interplay between the discussions on the concept of peacekeeping, its organisational implications and the practice in the field was not confronted in detail in academic writing. This research lacuna prevents the important UN operations researchers from detecting the causes and factors behind many crucial resolutions connected to the execution of the operations and the day-to-day practice of their implementation. In the following chapters of this research study, I attempt to rectify this shortcoming.

From the description above of the peacekeeping operations executed by the UN from 1947 to the present, we can conclude the research questions should revolve around the following issues: the search for an alternative 'operations concept' that is not written in the UN Charter; the role of international politics in the development of this concept and in the execution of the operations. Other questions touch upon the goals of the operations and principles for their execution, the regions in which it was decided to conduct operations, the way the operations were managed, their funding sources and the contribution of the forces that took part in them.

In this context, based on the subjects dealt with in the UN on peacekeeping, I argue that the following issues should be examined: Which countries pushed for a change in the conception? Did they receive support from most of the countries in the organisation? How did they reconcile the traditional principles of peacekeeping and the various goals – democratisation, promotion of a proper civil administration, economic development, promotion of human rights and the right to enforcement? What organisational reform was initiated in order to adapt to the increasing demands? Finally, can we identify any coherence in states' actions towards peacekeeping?

In order to answer these questions, I break down the discussion in the following chapters as follows: Chapter 2 examines the 1988–91 period, Chapter 3 examines 1992 and 1993, Chapter 4 examines the period from the second half of 1993 to 1995. The first section of each chapter examines the discussion held in the UN on the goals and success principles of the operations, and their managerial and organisational aspects. The second section examines the practice of the operation with special emphasis on the operations executed in Cambodia, the former Yugoslavia and Somalia. As was shown in this chapter, these operations were the most ambitious in terms of their mandates and size and therefore seem to be the most appropriate cases to examine the change in UN politics towards peacekeeping operations as a panacea for civil wars. I use these test cases to examine the changes that occurred in each of the interventions: in the goals and principles of success on the one hand, and the actual organisation and course of the operation, on the other.

### Notes

1  I. L. Claude Jr., *Swords into Plowshares: The Problems and Progress of International Organization* (New York: Random House, 2nd edn, 1961), pp. 250–294; Kennedy, *The Parliament of Man*, pp. 3–47; H. Kissinger, *Diplomacy* (New York: Simon & Schuster, 1994), pp. 56–199; V. Lowe, A. Roberts, J. Welch and D. Zaum, 'Introduction', in Lowe *et al.* (eds), *The United Nations Security Council*, pp. 10–17; M. Sheehan, *The Balance of Power: History and Theory* (London: Routledge, 1996), pp. 2–4, 15–23, 152–162; T. G. Weiss, D. P. Forsythe and R. A. Coate, *The*

*United Nations and Changing World Politics* (Boulder, CO: Lynne Rienner, 3rd edn, 2001), pp. 21–27, 38–44.

2  Claude, *Swords into Plowshares*, pp. 250–294; A. C. Lamborn, 'Theoretical and Historical Perspectives on Collective Security: The Intellectual Roots of Contemporary Debates about Collective Conflict Management', in J. Lepgold and T. G. Weiss (eds), *Collective Conflict Management and Changing World Politics* (Albany, NY: SUNY Press, 1998), pp. 31–56; J. Lepgold and T. G. Weiss, 'Collective Conflict Management and Changing World Politics: An Overview', in Lepgold and Weiss (eds), *Collective Conflict Management*, pp. 3–21; P. J. Opitz, 'Collective Security', in H. Volger (ed.), *A Concise Encyclopedia of the United Nations* (Hague: Kluwer Law International, 2002), pp. 25–32.

3  According to the UN Charter, the word combination 'maintenance of international peace and security' refers to a basic concept that provides the rationale for the very foundation of the UN. Therefore, in principle, any action adopted by the Security Council must be justified on the basis of its contribution towards the maintenance of international peace and security.

4  C. von Clausewitz, *On War*, trans. M. Howard and P. Paret (Princeton, NJ: Princeton University Press, 1976), p. 87.

5  S. C. Neff, *War and the Law of Nations: A General History* (Cambridge: Cambridge University Press, 2005).

6  L. M. Goodrich, E. Hambro and A. P. Simons, *Charter of the United Nations Commentary and Documents* (Boston, MA: World Peace Foundation, 1969), pp. 25–36.

7  In the original, Article 24(2) directs the Council to Chapters 6, 7, 8 and 12 of the Charter. However, since Chapter 8 deals with the functions of regional organisations, I chose to discuss it in the context of the General Assembly, in which political coalitions, in the form of these organisations, received broader functions. Chapter 12 discusses the International Trusteeship system that is not relevant to this study.

8  Resolving conflicts via peaceful methods also appears in Article 2(3) in the Charter as one of the norms of the organisation's member states.

9  UN Charter, Articles 33–38. For an overall review of the accepted techniques for resolving conflicts peacefully, see: M. N. Shaw, *International Law* (Cambridge: Cambridge University Press, 2003), pp. 914–950; C. Tomushcat, 'Article 33', in B. Simma, D.-E. Khan, G. Nolte and A. Paulus (eds), *The Charter of the United Nations: A Commentary* (Oxford: Oxford University Press, 3rd edn, 2012), pp. 1069–1085; T. Schweisfurth, 'Articles 34–35', in Simma et al. (eds), *The Charter*, pp. 1086–1118; T. Glegerich, 'Articles 36–38', in Simma et al. (eds), *The Charter*, pp. 1119–1170. Regarding the powers of the Security Council and ramifications of Chapter 6 in the Charter on the peaceful resolution of conflicts, see: United Nations, *A Handbook on the Peaceful Settlement of Disputes Between States* (New York: United Nations Department of Public Information, 1992).

10  Goodrich, Hambro and Simons, *Charter of the UN*, pp. 257–289; Tomushcat, 'Article 33'.

11  S. Touval, *Mediation in the Yugoslav Wars: The Critical Years, 1990–95* (Houndmills, Basingstoke: Palgrave Macmillan, 2002), pp. xi, 1–7.
12  For more information on the principle of the use of force in the Charter, see: Shaw, *International Law*, pp. 1119–1147; Y. Dinstein, *War, Aggression and Self-Defence* (Cambridge: Cambridge University Press, 4th edn, 2005), pp. 85–328.
13  UN Charter, Articles 39–51; N. Krisch, 'Articles 39–42', in Simma *et al.* (eds), *The Charter*, pp. 1272–1356; Goodrich, Hambro and Simons, *Charter of the UN*, pp. 290–353.
14  A. Randelzhofer and G. Nolte, 'Article 51', in Simma *et al.* (eds), *The Charter*, pp. 1397–1428.
15  A. Randelzhofer and O. Dörr, 'Article 2(4)', in Simma *et al.* (eds), *The Charter*, pp. 200–234; Randelzhofer and Nolte, 'Article 51', pp. 1397–1428.
16  E. Grove, 'UN Armed Forces and the Military Staff Committee: A Look Back', *International Security*, 17:4 (1993), 172–182; J. Soffer, 'All for One or All for All: The UN Military Staff Committee and the Contradictions within American Internationalism', *Diplomatic History*, 21:1 (1997), 45–69.
17  For a list of the occasions on which the Security Council adopted resolutions and used the powers that appear in the Charter's Chapter 7, see: T. Schindlmayer, 'Obstructing the Security Council: The Use of the Veto in the Twentieth Century', *Journal of the History of International Law*, 3:2 (2001), 218–223; P. Johansson, 'The Humdrum Use of Ultimate Authority: Defining and Analysing Chapter VII Resolution', *Nordic Journal of International Law*, 78:3 (2009), 309–344.
18  For information about the social and economic goals, see the elaboration in the UN Charter's Chapters 9 and 10, which deal with international cooperation on social and economic issues and in the activities of the Economic and Social Council, ECOSOC.
19  A/RES/39/11, 12 November, 1984; A/RES/40/3, 24 October, 1985; R. Wolfrum, 'Article 1', in Simma *et al.* (eds), *The Charter*, pp. 107–120.
20  Iriye's studies from the end of the 1990s focus on global history and deal with the development of an international culture and community in the twentieth century. The three major works in which he introduces his doctrine are: A. Iriye, *Cultural Internationalism and World Order* (Baltimore, MD: Johns Hopkins University Press, 1997); A. Iriye, *Global Community: The Role of International Organizations in the Making of the Contemporary World* (Berkeley, CA: University of California Press, 2002); A. Iriye (ed.), *Global Interdependence: The World after 1945* (Cambridge, MA: Belknap Press, 2013).
21  Bellamy, Williams and Griffin, *Understanding Peacekeeping*, pp. 14–21, 189–210; Kennedy, *The Parliament of Man*; P. V. Jakobsen, 'The Transformation of United Nations Peace Operations in the 1990s: Adding Globalization to the Conventional "End of the Cold War Explanation"', *Cooperation and Conflict*, 37:3 (2002), 267–282.
22  B. Fassbender, 'Article 2(1)', in Simma *et al.* (eds), *The Charter*, pp. 133–165; M. van Creveld, *The Rise and Decline of the State* (Cambridge: Cambridge University Press, 1999), pp. 1, 416–417; A. Giddens, *The Nation-State and Violence: Volume Two of A Contemporary Critique of Historical Materialism*

(Cambridge: Polity Press, 1985), p. 121; Weiss, Forsythe and Coate, *The UN and Changing World Politics*, pp. 4–12.

23  Weiss, Forsythe and Coate, *The UN and Changing World Politics*, p. 9.

24  See UN Charter, Chapter 5, Article 24.

25  Kennedy, *The Parliament of Man*, ch.1; E. Luard, *A History of the United Nations*, Vol. II: The Age of Decolonization, 1955–1965 (London and Basingstoke: Macmillan Press, 1989), pp. 3–14; S. Schlesinger, *Act of Creation: The Founding of the United Nations: A Story of Superpowers, Secret Agents, Wartime Allies and Enemies, and Their Quest for a Peaceful World* (Boulder, CO: Westview Press, 2003), pp. 19–31.

26  For comprehensive studies on the Security Council see: Bailey and Daws, *The Procedure*; Malone (ed.), *The UN Security Council*; Lowe et al. (eds), *The United Nations Security Council*.

27  A/RES/1991A (XVIII), 17 December, 1963.

28  For elaboration on the subject of regional representation, see below in the discussion on politics in the General Assembly.

29  A. Zimmerman, 'Article 27', in Simma et al. (eds), *The Charter*, pp. 871–938; S. D. Bailey, *Voting in the Security Council* (Bloomington, IN: Indiana University Press, 1969), chs 3–5; Goodrich, Hambro and Simons, *Charter of the UN*, pp. 192–256; Ruth B. Russell, *A History of the United Nations Charter: The Role of the United States 1940–1945* (Washington, DC: The Brookings Institution, 1958), chs 25–26, 28.

30  For specific criticism see: K. Mahbubani, 'The Permanent and Elected Members', in Malone (ed.), *The UN Security Council*, pp. 253–266. C. Nahory, 'The Hidden Veto', *Global Policy Forum*, May 2004; A. Roberts and D. Zaum, *Problems and Opportunities of Selective Security Today* (Oxford: Oxford University Press, 2008), p. 54.

31  A/34/246, 14 November 1979.

32  Goodrich, Hambro and Simons, *Charter of the UN*, pp. 24–28, 106–191; Russell, *A History of the UN Charter*, pp. 750–776.

33  For a general overview of the powers of the Assembly, see articles 9–22 in the Charter, also: Peterson, *The UN General Assembly*, pp. 41–121; White, *Keeping the Peace*, pp. 148–206.

34  United Nations, *United Nations and Apartheid 1948–1994* (New York: United Nations Department of Public Information, 1994).

35  Bailey and Daws, *The Procedure*, pp. 179–187; E. Luard, 'China and the United Nations', *International Affairs*, 47:4 (1971), 729–744.

36  The 'Zionism is racism' resolution was adopted in 1975 and repealed in 1991. A/RES/3379, 10 November, 1975; A/RES/46/86, 16 December, 1991; Y. Manor, *The 1975 'Zionism Is Racism' Resolution: The Rise, Fall, and Resurgence of a Libel* (Jerusalem: The Jerusalem Center for Public Affairs, 2010); A. Beker, *The United Nations and Israel: From Recognition to Reprehension* (Lexington, MA: Lexington Books, 1988), pp. 55–64. The most recent resolution adopted by the General Assembly was: A/RES/67/19, 29 November 2012.

37  I. Winkelmann, 'Groups and Grouping in the United Nations', in Volger (ed.), *A Concise Encyclopedia*, pp. 158–162; I. Winkelmann, 'Regional Groups in the UN', in Volger (ed.), *A Concise Encyclopedia*, pp. 455–458; S. Daws, 'The Origin and Development of UN Electoral Groups', in R. Thakur, *What Is Equitable Geographic Representation in the Twenty-first Century?* (Hong Kong: United Nations University, 1999), pp. 11–29.

38  S. Forman and A. Grene, 'Collaborating with Regional Organizations', in Malone (ed.), *The UN Security Council*, pp. 295–309; Goodrich, Hambro and Simons, *Charter of the UN*, pp. 354–369; C. Walter, 'Articles 52, 54', in Simma *et al.* (eds), *The Charter*, pp. 1445–1477, 1525–1534; G. Ress and C. Walter, 'Article 53', in Simma *et al.* (eds), *The Charter*, pp. 1478–1524; Russell, *A History of the UN Charter*, pp. 688–712; I. J. Rikhye, *The Theory and Practice of Peacekeeping* (New York: St. Martin's Press, 1984), pp. 131–178; B. Reichenstein, 'Regionalization', in Volger (ed.), *A Concise Encyclopedia*, pp. 458–464; Schlesinger, *Act of Creation*, pp. 36, 39–49, 175–192.

39  T. E. Boudreau, *Sheathing the Sword: The U.N. Secretary-General and the Prevention of International Conflict* (New York: Greenwood Press, 1991), pp. 1–101; S. Chesterman, 'Articles 97–99', in Simma *et al.* (eds), *The Charter*, pp. 1991–2021; T. F. Franck, 'The Secretary-General's Role in Conflict Resolution: Past, Present and Pure Conjecture', *European Journal of International Law*, 6:3 (1995), 1–29; L. Gordenker, *The UN Secretary-General and the Maintenance of Peace* (New York: Columbia University Press, 1967); W. Stöckl, 'Article 101', in Simma *et al.* (eds), *The Charter*, pp. 2054–2088; Russell, *A History of the UN Charter*, pp. 854–863; C. Ebner, 'Article 100', in Simma *et al.* (eds), *The Charter*, pp. 2022–2053; S. M. Schwebel, *The Secretary-General of the United Nations: His Political Powers and Practice* (New York: Greenwood Press, 1969, originally published in 1952).

40  Benner, Mergenthaler and Rotmann, *The New World*.

41  H. K. Tillema, *International Armed Conflicts since 1945: A Bibliographic Handbook of Wars and Military Interventions* (Boulder, CO: Westview Press, 1991); N. P. Gleditsch *et al.*, 'Armed Conflict 1946–2001: A New Dataset', *Journal of Peace Research*, 39:5 (2002), 615–637.

42  The main researchers who delineated the dichotomy between the generations are: S. Ratner, *The New UN Peacekeeping: Building Peace in Lands of Conflict after the Cold War* (New York: St. Martin's Press, 1995); J. Mackinlay and J. Chopra, 'Second-Generation Multinational Operations', *Washington Quarterly*, 15:3 (1992), 113–134.

43  M. Goulding, 'The Evolution of United Nations Peacekeeping', *International Affairs*, 69:3 (1993), 451–464; D. Segal, 'Five Phases of United Nations Peacekeeping: An Evolutionary Typology', *Journal of Political and Military Sociology*, 23:1 (1995), 65–79; H. Wiseman, 'United Nations Peacekeeping: An Historical Overview', in H. Wiseman (ed.), *Peacekeeping Appraisals & Proposals* (New York: Pergamon Press, 1983), pp. 19–58. This was later accepted in principle by other scholars although in less detail: Bellamy, Williams and

Griffin, *Understanding Peacekeeping*, pp. 81–92; P. F. Diehl and A. Balas, *Peace Operations* (Cambridge: Polity Press, 2nd edn, 2014), pp. 36–51.

44  UN, *The Blue Helmets: A Review of United Nations Peace-Keeping* (New York: United Nations Department of Public Information, 1985), p. v.

45  UN, *The Blue Helmets: A Review of United Nations Peace-Keeping* (New York: United Nations Department of Public Information, 3rd edn, 1996).

46  R. Higgins, *United Nations Peacekeeping 1946–1967 Documents and Commentary*, Vol. I: The Middle East (London: Oxford University Press, 1969), pp. 5–220; R. Higgins, *United Nations Peacekeeping 1946–1967 Documents and Commentary*, Vol. II: Asia (London: Oxford University Press, 1970), pp. 3–92, 315–420; R. Higgins, *United Nations Peacekeeping Documents and Commentary*, Vol. IV: Europe 1946–1979 (Oxford: Oxford University Press, 1981), 5–80; E. Luard, *A History of the United Nations*, Vol. I: The Years of Western Domination, 1945–1955 (Basingstoke: Macmillan, 1982), pp. 118–208, 275–294; A. Nachmani, *International Intervention in the Greek Civil War: The United Nations Special Committee on the Balkans, 1947–1952* (New York: Praeger, 1990); B. Urquhart, *A Life in Peace and War* (New York: Harper & Row, 1987), pp. 113–115, 118–119; Wiseman, 'United Nations Peacekeeping', pp. 22–31.

47  For the initial resolutions of the Security Council against North Korea, see: S/RES/82, 25 June, 1950; S/RES/83, 27 June, 1950.

48  H. W. Briggs, 'Chinese Representation in the United Nations', *International Organization*, 6:2 (1952), 192–209; Luard, 'China and the United Nations', 729–744.

49  The Uniting for Peace Resolution, A/RES/377 (V), 3 November, 1950. para. A.1. Bailey, *Voting in the Security Council*, pp. 49–54.

50  D. W. Bowett, *United Nations Forces: A Legal Study of United Nations Practice* (London: Stevens & Sons 1964), pp. 29–60; A. Boyd, *Fifteen Men on a Powder Keg: A History of the UN Security Council* (London, 1971), pp. 125–132; Higgins, *UN Peacekeeping*, Vol. II, pp. 153–312; Luard, *A History of the United Nations*, Vol. I, pp. 229–274; B. Urquhart, *Hammarskjold* (New York: Harper Colophon Books, 1994), pp. 7, 175.

51  The names 'West Irian' or 'Western New Guinea' refer to the western section of the New Guinea island. This territory had been a Dutch colony until 1961.

52  A/3302, 6 November, 1956; A/3302/Add., 6 November, 1956; Bowett, *United Nations Forces*, pp. 90–152; Higgins, *UN Peacekeeping*, Vol. I, pp. 221–534; E. Luard, *A History of the United Nations*, Vol. II, pp. 18–57; UN, *Blue Helmets*, 3rd edn, pp. 35–55; Urquhart, *A Life*, pp. 178–182, 205, 228–230.

53  Urquhart, *Hammarskjold*, pp. 75–83.

54  Bowett, *United Nations Forces*, pp. 153–254; R. Higgins, *United Nations Peacekeeping 1946–1967 Documents and Commentary*, Vol. III: Africa (Oxford: Oxford University Press, 1980); Luard, *A History of the United Nations*, Vol. II, pp. 217–316; O'Neill and Rees, *UN Peacekeeping in the Post-Cold War Era*, pp. 46–77; UN, *Blue Helmets*, 3rd edn, pp. 173–199; Urquhart, *Hammarskjold*, pp. 389–520, 545–589; Urquhart, *A Life*, pp. 145–196.

55  Bowett, *United Nations Forces*, pp. 255–264; Higgins, *UN Peacekeeping*, Vol. II, pp. 93–152; Luard, *A History of the United Nations*, Vol. II, pp. 327–347; UN, *Blue Helmets*, 3rd edn, pp. 173–199.
56  Higgins, *UN Peacekeeping*, Vol. IV, pp. 81–411; Luard, *A History of the United Nations*, Vol. II, pp. 407–442; O'Neill and Rees, *United Nations Peaeckeeping*, pp. 78–106; UN, *Blue Helmets*, 3rd edn, pp. 149–170.
57  Luard, *A History of the United Nations*, Vol. II, pp. 443–466; Higgins, *UN Peacekeeping*, Vol. III, pp. 274–303.
58  Higgins, *UN Peacekeeping*, Vol. I, pp. 480–482.
59  Wiseman, 'United Nations Peacekeeping', pp. 19–56; UN, *Blue Helmets*, 3rd edn, pp. 73–80.
60  See: S/11052 and Rev. 1, 27 October, 1973; A/RES/3101, 11 December, 1973; I. J. Rikhye, M. Harbottle and B. Egge, *The Thin Blue Line: International Peacekeeping and Its Future* (New Haven, CT: Yale University Press, 1974), pp. 309–339; Urquhart, *A Life*, pp. 238–243; UN, *Blue Helmets*, 3rd edn, pp. 59–70.
61  S/RES/425, 19 March, 1978; S/RES/426, 19 March, 1978.
62  B. Skogmo, B., *UNIFIL: International Peacekeeping in Lebanon* (Boulder, CO: Lynne Rienner, 1989).
63  Bellamy, Williams and Griffin, *Understanding Peacekeeping*, pp. 88–91; Diehl and Balas, *Peace Operations*, pp. 48–51.
64  Urquhart, *A Life*, pp. 371.
65  UN, *Blue Helmets*, 1985, pp. 3–4.
66  A/RES/40/163, Dec. 16, 1985; A/RES/41/67, 3 December, 1986; A/RES/42/161, 8 December, 1987; Goulding, 'Evolution of UN Peacekeeping', pp. 451–464; Rikhye, Harbottle and Egge, *The Thin Blue Line*; Rikhye, *The Theory and Practice of Peacekeeping*; Urquhart, *A Life*, pp. 178–179.
67  Bellamy, Williams and Griffin, *Understanding Peacekeeping*, p. 93; M. Kaldor, *New and Old Wars: Organized Violence in a Global Era* (Cambridge: Polity Press, 1999); Roberts and Zaum, *Problems and Opportunities*, p. 54.
68  M. Berdal and S. Economides, *United Nations Interventionism 1991–2004* (Cambridge: Cambridge University Press, 2007); Mayall, *The New Interventionism*.
69  M. W. Doyle and N. Sambanis, *Making War and Building Peace: The United Nations since the 1990s* (Princeton, NJ: Princeton University Press, 2006).
70  Bellamy, Williams and Griffin, *Understanding Peacekeeping*, pp. 1–3, 76–93.
71  O. A. Westad, *The Global Cold War: Third World Interventions and the Making of Our Times* (Cambridge: Cambridge University Press, 2005).
72  S/24111-A/47/277, June 17, 1992, para. 14–15; Bailey and Daws, *The Procedure*, p. 50; Schindlmayer, 'Obstructing the Security Council', 226–229.
73  For a general overview of all the changes in the peacekeeping operation concept over the years, regarding their goals and the way they were executed, see: Diehl, Druckman and Wall, 'International Peacekeeping', 33–55; Findlay, *The Use of Force*; Finnemore, *The Purpose of Intervention*; G. H. Fox, 'Democratization', in Malone (ed.), *The UN Security Council*, pp. 69–84; D. M. Malone, 'Conclusion',

in Malone (ed.), *The UN Security Council*, pp. 618–622, 626–630; Ratner, *The New UN Peacekeeping*; A. Roberts, 'The Use of Force', in Malone (ed.), *The UN Security Council*, pp. 133–152; J. Weschler, 'Human Rights', in Malone (ed.), *The UN Security Council*, pp. 55–68; T. G. Weiss, 'The Humanitarian Impulse', in Malone (ed.), *The UN Security Council*, pp. 37–54; Welsh (ed.), *Humanitarian Intervention*; Wheeler, *Saving Strangers*; Woodhouse and Rambotham (eds), *Peacekeeping and Conflict Resolution*.

74 T. Findlay, 'Introduction', in T. Findlay (ed.), *Challenges for the New Peacekeepers* (Oxford: Oxford University Press, 1996), p. 3.

75 A. Ajello and P. Wittmann, 'Mozambique', in Malone (ed.), *The UN Security Council*, pp. 437–450; M. Hall and T. Young, *Confronting Leviathan: Mozambique since Independence* (London: Hurst, 1997); R. Synge, *Mozambique: UN Peacekeeping in Action 1992–1994* (Washington DC: United States. Institute of Peace Press, 1994); UN, *The United Nations and Mozambique:1991–1995* (New York: United Nations Department of Public Information, 1995); UN, *Blue Helmets*, 3rd edn, pp. 319–338; S/RES/797, Dec. 16, 1992.

76 H. Adelman and A. Suhrke, 'Rwanda', in Malone (ed.), *The UN Security Council*, pp. 483–499; R. Dallaire with B. Beardsley, *Shake Hands with the Devil: The Failure of Humanity in Rwanda* (Croyden, Surrey: Arrow Books, 2004); B. D. Jones, 'Rwanda', in Berdal and Economides (eds), *United Nations Interventionism*, pp. 139–167; UN, *Blue Helmets*, 3rd edn, pp. 339–398.; S. von Einsiedel and D. M. Malone, 'Haiti', in Berdal and Economides (eds), *United Nations Interventionism*, pp. 168–191; D. M. Malone, *Decision-Making in the Security Council: The Case of Haiti, 1990–1997* (Oxford: Clarendon Press, 1998); UN, *Blue Helmets*, 3rd edn, pp. 611–636.

77 For elaboration on the operations in Cambodia, the former Yugoslavia and Somalia, see the relevant sub-sections.

78 Simultaneously with the decline in the number of peacekeepers who took part in UN operations, about 40,000 peacekeepers served in various regional organisations (disconnected from the UN) such as NATO, ECOWAS, and OSCE. These operations were connected to specific interests of these organisations in their regions of influence. Bellamy, Williams and Griffin, *Understanding Peacekeeping*, p. 84.

79 Benner, Mergenthaler and Rotmann, *The New World*.

80 UN, *United Nations Peacekeeping Operations Principles and Guidelines* (New York: Department of Peacekeeping Operations, 2008); UN, *A New Partnership Agenda: Charting a New Horizon for UN Peacekeeping* (New York: Department of Peacekeeping Operations 2009).

81 DPKO was created in 1992.

82 UN, 'Top UN peacekeeping official warns of "overstretch" as mission staff numbers surge', *UN News Centre*, 4 October 2006.

83 In this context it is important to note that some of the new operations executed by the UN since 1999 had traditional goals. Most important in this regard is the operation executed on the border between Ethiopia and Eritrea from September 2000 until July 2008. A. Adebajo, 'Ethiopian/Eritrea', in Malone (ed.), *The UN Security Council*, pp. 575–588.

84  For details about the way that this peacebuilding concept struck root, see the discussion on the concept of the operations in Chapter 3 of this study.
85  Call and Wyeth (eds), *Building States to Build Peace*; R. Caplan, *A New Trusteeship? The International Administration of War-Torn Societies* (Oxford: Oxford University Press, 2002); S. Chesterman, *You the People: The UN, Transitional Administration and State-Building* (Oxford: Oxford University Press, 2004); F. Fuyama, *State-Building: Governance and World Order in the 21st Century* (Ithaca, NY: Cornell University Press, 2004); R. Paris, *At War's End: Building Peace After Civil Conflict* (Cambridge: Cambridge University Press, 2004); M. Pugh and N. Cooper (eds), *Whose Peace? Critical Perspectives on the Political Economy of Peacebuilding* (Houndmills, Basingstoke: Palgrave Macmillan, 2011).
86  Chesterman, *You the People*, pp. 79–83, 132–134, 147–149, 165–169; S. Economides, 'Kosovo', in Berdal and Econimides (eds), *United Nations Interventionism*, pp. 217–245; P. Heinbecker, 'Kosovo', in Malone (ed.), *The UN Security Council*, pp. 537–550.
87  The UN did not halt its intervention in East Timor at the conclusion of the operation. Instead, it decided to execute an additional operation (UNMISET) that ended in May 2005, which involved about 5,000 soldiers and civilians. Over time, the forces taking part in the operation were reduced to 600. After a break of more than a year, and in light of the political instabililty and lack of security in East Timor, it was decided to execute another operation, UNMIT, that began in August 2006 and ended on 31 December 2012; about 500 police participated in UNMIT. Also see: Chesterman, *You the People*, pp. 60–64, 135–143, 149–150, 169–174; S. Chesterman, 'East Timor', in Berdal and Economides (eds), *United Nations Interventionism*, pp. 192–216; S. Eldon, 'East Timor', in Malone (ed,), *The UN Security Council*, pp. 551–566; I. Martin, 'International Intervention in East Timor', in Welsh (ed.), *Humanitarian Intervention*, pp. 142–162.
88  For a concise and succinct definition, see, for example: UN, *The Blue Helmets: A Review of United Nations Peace-Keeping* (New York: United Nations Department of Public Information, 2nd edn, 1990), pp. 3–8.
89  The most prominent of these organisations was NATO. As a European security-oriented organisation, NATO was very active in the Balkans, and from the beginning of the twenty-first century it even extended its sphere of action beyond Europe. Bellamy, Williams and Griffin, *Understanding Peacekeeping*; H. A. Frantzen, *NATO and Peace Support Operations, 1991–1999* (London: Frank Cass, 2005), pp. 58–88.
90  Regarding this argument, see especially: Bellamy, Williams and Griffin, *Understanding Peacekeeping*, pp. 23–25, 399–401; Jakobsen, 'The Transformation', pp. 267–282; Kaldor, *New and Old Wars*, pp. 69–111; Weiss, Forsythe and Coate, *The United Nations and Changing World Politics*, pp. 111, 313–315; Paris, *At War's End*, pp. 5–8, 13–37, 235–236.
91  Finnemore, *The Purpose of Intervention*, pp. 52–84; Wheeler, *Saving Strangers*, pp. 139–284; Welsh (ed.). *Humanitarian Intervention*.

# 2

# New thinking: UN peacekeeping and the end of the Cold War 1988–91

It is accepted by researchers and even the UN Secretariat that peacekeeping operations can be divided into two separate time periods: from 1947–88, or the Cold War era, and from 1988 to the present, the post-Cold War era. In 1988–91, the UN carried out ten new peacekeeping operations: in Afghanistan, on the Iran–Iraq border, in Central America, Africa and Cambodia. We can also note the enforcement operation in Iraq after Iraq conquered Kuwait. But although most studies label these as second-generation missions, no research study was ever conducted that focused on the changes that took place at the end of the Cold War and their effect on the execution of operations on the one hand, and on the development of the concept on the other. The absence of such a study casts doubt on the accepted research argument that a new period in international politics began in 1988 in which the Western states developed a new concept for peacekeeping operations and executed them as part of UN operations in order to promote their own interests.

In order to clarify what, indeed, took place in these years in the peacekeeping operations context, it is necessary to examine the most important change that occurred in the time period under discussion, the change that affected the international arena – the end of the Cold War – with an emphasis on the worldview and actions of USSR President Mikhail Gorbachev until 1991. Later in the chapter I review the discourse in the UN on the concept of peacekeeping operations in 1988–91, to ascertain whether agreement was reached regarding a change in the traditional concept of operations. Finally, I investigate possible similarities between the five operations that were carried out in this period and those executed by the UN during the Cold War. In addition, I describe the response of the international community towards Iraq after the conquest of Kuwait in August 1990 – an enforcement operation carried out in accordance with the directives of Chapter 7 in the UN Charter. Finally, I present the chain of events leading to the execution of the most ambitious operation of the UN until that time: the United Nations Transitional Authority in Cambodia (UNTAC).

At the conclusion of the chapter, I argue that while it was clear to everyone at the end of the Cold War that a new world order had been created, it was not clear how the differences between the new and old orders would be expressed, and how peacekeeping operations would contribute to the benefit of the new order. Despite this lack of clarity, there was productive cooperation among all the member states of the Security Council, leading to the decision in 1991 to carry out five new operations: on the Kuwait–Iraq border and in Western Sahara, Angola, El Salvador and Cambodia.[1]

## The strange alliance and the renewal of the debate on peacekeeping

Researchers of peacekeeping operations agree that Gorbachev assumed a significant role in leading the process that led to the end of the Cold War. According to the widely held view, from 1988 onwards the Western states took advantage of the winding-down of the Cold War and the Soviet Union's weakness to promote the new concept of multidimensional peacekeeping operations, a concept that would serve their interests. However, this viewpoint is not substantiated in the primary sources – in other words, protocols of UN discussions in the relevant time period. In fact, it was the Soviet Union, together with mid-sized Western countries (such as Denmark, Canada and Sweden), that were veteran supporters of the operations and called for adoption of 'new thinking' regarding the role of the operations in the new world order, and not powers such as the United States, the United Kingdom and France. Below I discuss the diplomatic dialogue that took place in the UN regarding the concept of the operations from 1988 to 1991.[2]

The main UN organ that had the authority to discuss issues connected to peacekeeping operations was the UN Special Committee on Peacekeeping Operations (henceforth, the SCPKO or Special Committee), also known as the Committee of 33, after the number of countries that are members. This committee was formed in the 1960s and conducted lively discussions on the subject of peacekeeping for about a decade. However, from the early 1970s, a number of factors led to the cessation of discussions on the subject. First, controversies arose on fundamental issues, disagreements that were rooted in the conflict between the superpowers during the Cold War. These differences of opinion lowered the motivation of the parties to continue to discuss and indulge in polemics. Second, after 1973 the General Assembly was excluded from the decision-making process regarding peacekeeping operations and this adversely affected the work of the SCPKO. Finally, the fact that the Security Council did not execute new operations turned the discussions of the SCPKO into hypothetical, empty dialogue. For these reasons, the SCPKO met only rarely and usually dispersed without coming to conclusions that were agreed upon by all the parties. The SCPKO did not meet at all from 1984 to 1987. But the General Assembly continued to renew the SCPKO's mandate every year, in the hope that change would take place in the international system that would facilitate renewal of the committee's work.

This situation started to change when the first hints were dropped by the Soviet Union regarding its willingness to end the Cold War.[3] In 1987–88 discussions took place in the SCPKO in which the delegations recognised the need to discuss the concept of the operations, but the Committee's sphere of influence was still very limited. In 1987, New Zealand sent a report to the UN in which it expressed its willingness to enlarge its contribution to peacekeeping operations.[4] The Nordic countries – Sweden, Denmark, Finland, Norway and Iceland – reported on an updated study they had published regarding the total Nordic forces they held on standby for deployment to operations.[5] In response, the General Assembly realised that discussions on operations should be renewed; thus a resolution was taken, after a long discussion, that the SCPKO would be reconvened in 1988.[6]

However, despite the hopes of a number of UN delegations for renewal of discussions of the SCPKO (mainly from Eastern and Western Europe), this did not lead to new initiatives changing the traditional concept of the operations over the course of 1988. The combination of a positive international atmosphere, the initiatives of the Security Council for new operations, and what seemed like initial successes – all these helped promote renewed hopes among most countries of the world regarding the centrality of the UN and the peacekeeping operation technique in the emerging world order. In that same year, the Nobel Peace Committee decided to bestow the peace prize on peacekeeping operations. At the same time, and despite the theoretical support for execution of operations, the organisation's members refrained from raising new ideas regarding the concept of the operations. In light of the futile discussions, in 1988 the General Assembly called on the UN member states to raise concrete proposals regarding the concept of peacekeeping operations.[7]

From 1989 to the middle of 1991, a discussion was held in the General Assembly regarding the concept of peacekeeping. Only a few dozen delegations took part in this discussion, most of which represented European countries. In general, there were two discussion camps: the reformists, who supported a change in concept, and the traditionalists or pragmatists, who did not want to change the concept in a fundamental way.

The reformist group that advocated a change in the practice of peacekeeping was composed of two main groups of states. The members of the first group were delegations from veteran Western contributor states to UN operations. The main member states in this context were: Australia, Austria, Canada, Ireland, New Zealand and the Nordic countries (Denmark, Finland, Iceland, Norway, Sweden). During the Cold War, the veteran contributor group members were consistent in their support for the traditional concept of peacekeeping and for the execution of peacekeeping operations. The members of the group were also willing to back their political support with human and material resources. In the late 1980s, they called for the renewal of the debate on the role of peacekeeping in global security. They backed their advocacy with printed guidebooks, independent commissions and diplomatic statesmen. One of the most familiar products of their endeavour was the Independent Commission on Disarmament and Security Issues (also known as the Palme Commission). This Commission published its recommendations on global security for the twenty-first century in April 1989.[8]

The second group supporting a change in the use of peacekeeping operations was composed of Eastern European Group members led by the USSR. Under influence of the Soviet 'new thinking' (*novoe myshlenie*) on foreign policy, these states' previously hostile stance towards peacekeeping changed at the conclusion of the Cold War. The Soviets now paid their debts to the UN and supported the Secretary-General's efforts in peacemaking around the globe and the deployment of peacekeeping forces to conflicts in Latin America, South West Africa and Cambodia.[9] They even continued their support for the UN peacekeeping operations when non-USSR Eastern bloc members replaced their communist governments with democratically elected ones.[10]

Together, these two political groups toiled to forge a new understanding of the threats to global security after the Cold War and the potential role of multidimensional peacekeeping operations in dealing with these threats. Both groups envisioned a world that abides by international law, and in which the UN is the main implementer of this law. In this world order, the sustainability of the ecology and economy were considered as important as security issues. In this new vision, it was important to deter aggressors by taking measures to prevent disputes from turning into violent conflicts. To achieve this goal, they encouraged the combination of peacemaking efforts with peacekeeping operations. The new ideal envisaged a network of military observers and fact-finding missions working constantly to de-escalate conflicts. Suggestions were made to use operations for monitoring democratic elections, protecting humanitarian missions and fighting global threats such as international terrorists and naval pirates. Peacekeeping operations were supposed to be supported by peacebuilding, a term which was used to describe a myriad of political, economic and social actions. Finally, in mid-1991, the Soviet Union delegation tried to advance these innovative ideas by integrating them into a formal declaration of the General Assembly on peacekeeping.[11] However, the Soviet Union disintegrated several months later and the Cold War was officially brought to an end.

The main difference between the two groups was in the emphasis on capacity building. The veteran contributor countries put much more emphasis on practical issues. They emphasised that the UN should improve and overhaul its administrative and management functions such as financing and logistics, and shorten the duration of deployment of UN forces.[12]

The clear alliance in ideas between the Western veteran contributors and the Eastern European Group received mixed responses from other UN delegations. Other Western countries – including France, the United Kingdom, the United States and members of the European Community (EC) – were quite indifferent to changes in the role of peacekeeping in the world. The EC's main recommendation was that the Security Council should increase the use of peacekeeping operations. They were especially encouraged by the success of UN operations in Namibia and Nicaragua in the late 1980s. However, until October 1991, they claimed that only traditional principles for the execution of peacekeeping operations were being applied.[13] As for the 'Permanent Three' – France, the United Kingdom and the United States – they had no interest in changing the traditional doctrine of peacekeeping. They supported the increased use of UN operations on an ad hoc basis when such missions would advance their own global interests. France and the United Kingdom worked together with the European Council at least until late 1991; at that time they discerned the change in the world order and initiated a meeting of the Security Council in the presence of heads of states on 31 January 1992.[14] The United States representatives did not offer new insight into the use of peacekeeping and preferred to emphasise the need to cut the costs of these operations in order to minimise US expenditure.[15]

In comparison with the repeated publication of European states' opinions on the matter, most of the other states preferred not to express their views on peacekeeping. The few that did participate in the discourse supported the new operations but disagreed with the new functions. Several states – such as Argentina, Bangladesh, Chile, Japan and Thailand – supported innovations such as the increased use of civilians. Other countries – such as Brazil, Egypt, India, Mexico and Pakistan – while supportive of the new operations, warned that the new ideas proposed by the European states were unclear and might even result in the escalation of conflicts. Finally, China, a permanent member of the Security Council, adopted a similarly hesitant stance towards suggestions regarding the deployment of multidimensional operations before or during conflicts. However, it started participating and supporting the operations: In September 1989, China filed a request to join the work of the SCPKO. In April 1991, it hosted an international symposium on UN peacekeeping operations, and during the Cambodia operation, China contributed an engineering battalion.[16]

This inconsistent stance was understandable when placed in the context of global change. The Non-Aligned Movement (NAM), which represented most of the world's states, declared its satisfaction with the increased involvement of the UN in global security. However, its support was given to traditional operations and it provided no new insights into the potential use of peacekeeping outside its doctrinal conceptualisation.[17]

The final actor involved in the peacekeeping discussions was the UN Secretariat. During the Cold War, the Secretariat was the sole UN organ responsible for the management of peacekeeping operations. As a result, the UN Secretariat had accumulated the most experience on the potential use of peacekeeping.[18] From 1988 to 1991, UN members in the Security Council and General Assembly requested more information on peacekeeping execution from the UN Secretariat.[19] In response, Javier Pérez de Cuéllar, UN Secretary-General from 1982–91, published detailed reports, recommendations and letters on different issues such as military and civilian personnel, material and the technical resources and services that were required by UN operations.[20]

Secretariat personnel were pleased at the new support for peacekeeping operations. They especially appreciated the fact that peacekeeping operations now enjoyed wide international support. From their perspective, the small operations executed at the time were a new and positive model for the future of peacekeeping. Therefore they estimated in October 1990 that

> in recent years, the main demand has been for United Nations field missions consisting of military observers, United Nations civilian police elements, other civilian personnel (whether United Nations staff or personnel provided by Governments) or combinations of all or any of the above. There have been fewer calls for the rapid deployment of multi-battalion infantry forces.[21]

At the same time, the Secretariat faced criticism that its management methods were obsolete. For decades, peacekeeping management was divided between various UN Secretariat departments responsible for different aspects of the operations, such as planning, finances, personnel allocation and political guidance. However, when the Secretariat requested the General Assembly to authorise an increase in the number of its personnel in order to cope with the increasing demands, it received only a minimal increase.[22] Another example of the unwillingness of the international community to support the operations can be seen by its response to the UN Secretariat questionnaire, which tried to assemble a standby group of countries willing to contribute troops. Only forty-five states replied, and even then, some of the answers were only partial.[23]

The continued global momentum by the Security Council during 1991 to execute five new operations in El Salvador, Angola, Cambodia, Kuwait and Western Sahara, and the increased use of peacekeeping operations during 1992, especially for multidimensional operations, overwhelmed the UN Secretariat. The Secretariat was simply unprepared to manage so many operations simultaneously, some of which were also large and multidimensional.[24]

Thus we understand that, from the end of the 1980s, the atmosphere in the UN began to improve regarding cooperation in peacekeeping operations and understanding of the role of the peacekeeping operations in the world order. The new cooperation crossed traditional political alliances and characterised the entire diplomatic arena. Most of the delegations that took part in discussions regarding peacekeeping operations shared a positive view of the new operations executed by the UN in recent years, and expressed hope for the execution of additional ones.

But although basic agreement was reached regarding the need for operations (as we see from the relevant discussions as well as in the resultant resolutions), the multiplicity of ideas and opinions did not lead to a change in the traditional concept of peacekeeping operations but, on the contrary, it aroused dissension and disagreement. The Soviet Union delegation initiated a change in the traditional concept of the operations and tried unsuccessfully to enlist the agreement of most of the organisation's members. Part of the reason for its lack of success was that the Soviet Union was not willing to exhibit flexibility regarding issues connected to the special authorities of the five permanent Council members on decision-making processes. The P5 even torpedoed an initiative of the veteran countries that contributed to the operations; these contributors wanted to establish an advisory committee to the Security Council. The P5's rationale for opposing the initiative was that they felt it could impinge on the Council's authority. They used the same rationale to reject a proposal to set guidelines for Security Council resolutions regarding operations. The P5 raised the following argument: that enlarging the goals of the operations to include 'conflict prevention' missions such as supervision and control over election and referendum processes could lead to intrastate intervention. In fact, they argued, there is no direct connection between what is defined as a peacekeeping operation and supervision over intrastate civic elections. Therefore, the organisation must first receive authorisation from the state in which these tasks are supposed to take place, in each individual case.[25]

The question of time-frame – the dates marking the beginning and end of missions – did not even appear on the agenda. Regarding the issue of centralised management of operations by the UN headquarters in New York, most of the delegations (in the SCPKO) rejected the various alternatives that were raised, including transferring management of the operations to regional organisations or to the authority of a state.[26]

Another debatable subject was the participation of the powers in the operations. In this issue, discussion in the UN garnered results, as all representatives who participated in the discussion, with the exception of Uruguay, encouraged the powers to take part in operations.[27] Similarly, it was decided to integrate citizens into the operations, despite the disagreements on this issue.[28] Another operations-related subject that was discussed during this time period was the organisational structure of the UN Secretariat, and modifying it to fit the new circumstances. Since voices only called for improvement of the Secretariat's functioning but no concrete proposals were raised, no resolutions were taken on the subject. Finally, regarding the financial issue that came up for discussion numerous times, mainly by the countries that actually contributed forces to the operations, a number of ideas for improvement were raised. However, these did not lead to the passing of resolutions but only to a statement that 'the major problem of peace-keeping was that of resources'.[29]

An analysis of discussions in the UN during 1988–91 reveals that the governments and the Secretariat believed that peacekeeping operations could really contribute to peace. Nevertheless, the functions of the operations were not sufficiently clear. While there was a broad consensus that they should be employed more frequently, and that the traditional concept should probably be improved and refined, whenever they tried to set new definitions for the goals of operations, the principles of their success and their managerial and organisational aspects, the discussion always ended with a backtracking to the traditional concept – even in the discussions held in 1991.

In contrast to what one would expect, in light of accepted arguments in the research regarding the reasons for change of concept in peacekeeping operations, the inability to reach agreement regarding change of the traditional concept did not stem from a deep division of opinion between the Western and communist countries, or the developed and developing countries. The real reason was that relatively few countries expressed interest in tailoring a new concept to the operations in light of the emerging new world order. Another factor that emerged as a stumbling block to an agreement on change of concept was the complacency of the Secretariat personnel, who rested on the laurels of international support and therefore did not express any special interest in development of the concept. Instead, they mainly focused on attempting to obtain additional resources so as to execute operations more effectively. The third factor that contributed to the torpedoing of resolutions on the subject of operations in the UN was the inexperience and lack of knowledge on the part of most member states in the organisation, regarding everything connected to execution of peacekeeping operations. Finally, in light of the lack of clarity that surrounded the new emerging world order, all the UN members and the Secretariat preferred to cling to the familiar concept of operations, if only on the declarative level.

## Traditional peacekeeping in new times

Thus we see that, in contrast to the accepted research argument, no conceptual change regarding peacekeeping operations was actually agreed upon during 1988–91. Therefore, it is appropriate to examine whether the ten operations executed by the organisation in these years, including the enforcement operation in Iraq (according to the Charter's Chapter 7), were different in practice from the traditional operations executed by the organisation during the Cold War. If the data shows that the practice did change, this could testify to the fact that the Security Council members – and mainly the P5 – did set multidimensional objectives, in contrast to the professed stance of most of the organisation's members.

The new diplomatic tidings of the Soviet Union at the end of the 1980s transformed the Security Council all at once from an arena of diplomatic struggle to one of diplomatic cooperation with the objective of resolving conflicts around the world. Within four years, the Council adopted 119 resolutions, in contrast to the 60 resolutions it had adopted in the four years that preceded this period. This agreement was the beginning of the oligarchic conduct of the Council members, and mainly of the five permanent members, that escalated in later years. In the short period between 1988 and 1991, the Security Council initiated ten new peacekeeping operations.

Ostensibly, these operations differed in format from the traditional operations. The peacekeeping operations that were executed in these years were connected, one way or another, to the Soviet Union's withdrawal policy from various regions in the world. This withdrawal involved removal of military forces, cessation of economic assistance, and adoption of a policy of cooperation with the United States in the Security Council. Contrary to the accepted notion, these operations were not executed to prevent a renewal of military conflicts such as those between Israel and Syria or in Cyprus, but as part of a political arrangement to resolve conflicts, some of which continued for many years. All the operations were executed within countries, except for the observer operation between Iran and Iraq called the United Nations Iran–Iraq Military Observer Group (UNIIMOG) and the observer operation between Iraq and Kuwait, called the United Nations Iraq–Kuwait Observation Mission (UNIKOM). Similar to the important peacekeeping operation period in the early 1960s, the Israeli–Arab conflict in this later period also assumed a marginal position in international political activity. Given these differences between the operations of the Cold War period and those executed from 1988 onwards, and in light of the willingness of the states to adopt new goals for the operations, we must ask the obvious question: Were the goals defined for these latter operations an expression of the adoption of a new concept for operations? In order to elucidate this issue, I will briefly review the relevant operations while placing special emphasis on the shaping of the goals for the largest operation ever undertaken by the UN until that time: UNTAC.

Ten years after it was decided to execute the UNIFIL operation in southern Lebanon in 1978, the Security Council decided to execute an Afghanistan operation called the United Nations Good Offices Mission in Afghanistan and Pakistan (UNGOMAP). This operation was the direct result of Gorbachev's decision to remove all Soviet Union forces from Afghanistan after an intervention spanning more than eight years, which began on 27 December 1979 when the Soviet army invaded the country. Gorbachev turned Afghanistan into a test case that would serve as an example of the importance of cooperation with the UN and the 'new thinking'. On 14 April 1988 the Geneva Accords were signed by the representatives of the Republic of Afghanistan, the Republic of Pakistan, the United States and the Soviet Union.[30] In the agreement, it was decided that fifty military observers would supervise the withdrawal of the Soviet army on behalf of the UN. The operation had its difficulties and UN representatives received hundreds of complaints from all the parties involved regarding violations of the agreement. Despite this, the Security Council decided not to extend the operation since no regular Soviet military forces remained in Afghanistan. Thus it was decided to terminate the operation in March 1990.[31] Although the operation in Afghanistan was executed within a state, its goals were traditional ones: to observe and supervise the withdrawal of the Soviet army. The UN force was forbidden to intervene in the state's internal affairs. Humanitarian activities were undertaken simultaneously with the operation, but these were not directly linked to the operation itself but were part of the activities of the UN humanitarian agencies in general, and specifically of the United Nations High Commissioner for Refugees (UNHCR).[32]

The second operation executed by the UN at the end of the 1980s was UNIIMOG, the observer operation between Iran and Iraq. Similar to the conflict in Afghanistan, this conflict, which had begun with the invasion of the Iraqi army into Iran in 1980, lasted for many years.[33] After the battles came to a standstill in the summer of 1989, the parties agreed to the Security Council compromise of a traditional observer force of about 400 soldiers of all ranks. In February 1992, the operation was officially terminated.[34]

The third operation that was executed by the UN at the end of the 1980s was the first United Nations Angola Verification Mission (UNAVEM I). This was the first operation out of several that were executed in Angola by the UN until 1999, and as opposed to the later missions, this one was connected to international efforts to protect Namibia's independence. When Namibia was liberated from the colonialist regime of Portugal in 1975, it was only after fifteen years of internal guerrilla warfare. The strongest of the rebel groups was the People's Movement for the Liberation of Angola (Movimento Popular de Libertação de Angola, or MPLA), which founded the Popular Republic of Angola in November 1975. This group received support from the Soviet Union and from Cuba; at its height, Cuba even sent about 50,000 soldiers, who fought on the side of the National Front for the Liberation of Angola against South African military forces. The main group that opposed the MPLA was União Nacional para a Independência Total de Angola, or UNITA (National Union for the Total Independence of Angola), which received assistance from the United States and South Africa.

Gorbachev's policy, aimed at reducing military and economic support of conflicts around the world, cut off support for the Cubans; they, in turn, were unable to continue to support the MPLA. In addition, the thaw in international tension following Gorbachev's new policy facilitated the political agreement signed in 1988 between South Africa, Cuba and Angola. South Africa agreed not to send its army on raids into Angola, while Cuba agreed to remove all its forces from the country. One ramification of the agreement was the initiative for the verification operation for withdrawal of Cuban forces from Angola (Security Council Resolution 626, of 20 December 1988). UNAVEM I numbered seventy military observers and received assistance from international and local personnel. Its objective was to supervise the withdrawal process that took place as planned; the last of the Cuban soldiers left Angola on 25 May 1991. This process brought about the termination of an operation with traditional objectives.

The force remaining on the territory became the foundation for a later, more ambitious operation in Angola – the United Nations Angola Verification Mission II (UNAVEM II) that was executed in July 1991 and designed to supervise the implementation of the Bicesse Accords that were signed by the opposing sides in Angola.[35] The total number of personnel involved in this operation was about a thousand soldiers and civilians of all ranks. Since this operation received additional mandates in the course of 1992, it will be discussed in the following chapter.[36]

Another operation that was executed in the period under discussion was that of the United Nations Observer Group in Central America (ONUCA). The Security Council initiated the operation on 7 November 1989 (Resolution 644). The force's mandate was derived from the Esquipulas II Accord from 1987, which was signed by the heads of five countries in the region – Costa Rica, El Salvador, Guatemala, Honduras and Nicaragua. This agreement came on the heels of years of fighting, starting from the 1970s, between and within these countries. The lines were drawn between regimes that ideologically supported capitalism and those that supported socialism, while receiving assistance in weapons and funding from the United States or the Soviet Union, respectively. But it was only in 1989 – after the changes in the international arena began to be evident – that it was possible to begin to implement the agreement. The role of the peacekeeping forces was to verify that assistance to the irregular forces and insurgency movements had ended, and that the countries which signed the accord would not allow their territory to be used for attacks against other countries.

The ONUCA force numbered 260 unarmed military observers. They were split into small mobile groups that travelled in vehicles, boats and helicopters over the territories they supervised. In December 1989, the presidents of the five Central American countries asked to enlarge the force's mandate to include the following: verification of cessation of hostile acts; supervision of the disarmament process; and dispersion of the irregular forces of both sides in Nicaragua. After UN Secretary-General Pérez de Cuéllar prepared a report proposing such a role for the Secretariat, the Security Council resolved (Resolution 650) to accept de Cuéllar's proposals on 27 March 1990. This mandate was enlarged on 20 April (Resolution 653) in light of the progress in talks between the representatives of the Contras, who won the support of the United States, and the socialist Sandinista National Liberation Front in Nicaragua. This time, it was decided that ONUCA would also supervise the separation of forces in Nicaragua. They would concentrate the Contras into 'security zones' – each zone extended over 500–600 square kilometres – from which the Sandinista government forces would retreat. They would also supervise the dissolution of all the Contras forces. On 29 June 1990, the Secretary-General reported to the Security Council that, except for a small number of persons in one area, all the opposition forces in Nicaragua had completed the demobilisation process by 5 July. The number of fighters from the Contras opposition movement who were demobilised were 19,614 from Nicaragua and 2,759 from Honduras. After completion of the process, the UN force continued its original verification functions until January 1992.

Some researchers argue that this operation does not belong to the group of first-generation operations but instead belongs to the second-generation ones. They accord symbolic importance to this operation because no operation had been executed in Central America for decades, since the Dominican Republic mission in the mid-1960s.[37] In addition, as opposed to traditional peacekeeping operations, the ONUCA forces operated in several countries simultaneously. Ostensibly, the operation attempted to achieve goals that were not characteristic of traditional operations. It was responsible for supervising the demobilisation of tens of thousands of fighters from the ranks of the organisation. Furthermore, at the same time as the operation was underway, additional UN forces were active in another mission. These forces included the United Nations Mission for Verification of Electoral Process in Nicaragua (ONUVEN), and forces for a mission to resettle the demobilised fighters (International Support and Verification Mission; Central America, CIAV) in Central America.[38]

My claim is that ONUCA does not belong to the second-generation category of multidimensional operations. This is due to the fact that the operation was executed only after a comprehensive agreement was attained for the end of the conflict between the conflicted sides, the regional countries and the large powers. While supervision of disarmament was a rather unusual step at the time, it did not include active operations and, instead, focused on the narrow security aspect, thus one would be hard pressed to categorise it as a multidimensional goal. In addition, ONUCA soldiers were not allowed to use force and their soldiers were unarmed; this is similar to all the traditional operations. The main difference between this operation and its predecessors is connected to the supervisory mission of free and fair elections in Nicaragua, and the resettlement mission of demobilised soldiers. But these missions were not an integral part of the peacekeeping operation. Each mission received a separate mandate, similar to many other missions executed by the UN in the course of the Cold War, often without connection to the conflicts.[39]

A certain change became evident in July 1991 when the Security Council decided to execute an operation in El Salvador called the United Nations Observer Mission in El Salvador (ONUSAL). This operation, which continued for four years and ended in April 1995, numbered a maximum of one thousand soldiers, policemen and civilians. It was executed after an agreement had been reached between the opposing sides in the country and mainly monitored the implementation of the agreements and was conducted according to the traditional principles of operations.[40]

In contrast to the operations reviewed above, the most significant contribution to the conceptual and practical discussion of the operations is the largest operation that was executed in Namibia between April 1989 and May 1990, called the United Nations Transition Assistance Group (UNTAG). Six years after its conclusion, it was described by the UN Secretary-General as 'a political operation, in which the missions of each element – civil, police and military – were combined on the ground under supervision of the special representative, with the goal of attempting to attain a structural change in society by means of a democratic process, according to an agreed-upon timetable'.[41] The operation combined all the issues that the UN had dealt with in the past, such as supervision and monitoring of elections, law and order, and borders, via peacekeeping forces. Special Representative of the Secretary-General (SRSG) Martti Ahtisaari was in charge of the process and every step taken needed his authorisation. On one hand, the operation was not viewed by the organisation's Secretariat as an operation charged with supervising standard de-colonisation processes in which the colonising powers withdrew and local government was established, but on the other hand, it was also not a traditional operation. At its height, between 7 and 11 November 1989, the UN force numbered close to 8,000 personnel, out of which 2,000 were civilians (1,000 local workers and another 1,000 members of the international staff that came specially to supervise the elections), 1,500 policemen and about 4,500 soldiers.

The process was relatively calm and without bloodshed except in the first month, when fierce battles were waged between the South African security forces and guerrilla movement fighters who fought for independence, South West Africa People's Organization (SWAPO). About 400 soldiers and civilians were killed in these battles. In the elections held under UN supervision in November 1989, the SWAPO party won. An independence ceremony was held after midnight on 21 March 1990. At the ceremony, Secretary-General de Cuéllar swore in the new President Sam Nojuma in accordance with the new constitution. Thus, Namibia was officially born as a sovereign, independent state in the world.[42]

I disagree with the studies that view the operation conducted in Namibia as an example of a conceptual change in the organisation; these are the studies that view the beginning of the second-generation operations as those that began in 1988. I argue that the operation's goals were a result of the Cold War, and not of its termination process.

Namibia in the modern era had been under German colonial rule until the end of the First World War. The broad territory (824,269 square kilometres), known as 'South West Africa', became mandate territory of South Africa in 1920, and came under the auspices of the League of Nations. After 1946, criticism grew in the UN over the way that South Africa managed the territory in its attempts to annex it. The growing international criticism, and the imposition of the apartheid regime on South West Africa in the 1960s, led to the decision of the UN's General Assembly in 1966 to revoke South Africa's mandate to manage the territory, and transferred it instead to the UN's direct responsibility. This act immediately transformed South Africa from a legal administrator of a territory to an occupying power. The guerrilla warfare of SWAPO, and the violent response of the South African security forces, intensified the international consensus against de facto South African administration of the territory.

In the course of the 1960s and 1970s, several resolutions were formulated – in the General Assembly and the Security Council – for realising the self-determination principle in Namibia. One of these resolutions was the initiative for the peacekeeping operation to Namibia in 1978. However, although there was a basic consensus regarding this operation in the organisation, its execution was delayed due to the inter-bloc tensions of the Cold War. Thus this issue was only resolved at the end of the 1980s, just as many other conflicts in Africa connected to South Africa were resolved at this time. In 1988 the South African government agreed to the political programme originally proposed by the Security Council in 1978 (Resolution

435), towards giving self-determination to a variety of tribes and residents in the country numbering about 1.4 million people.[43] The South African agreement was also the result of talks with Angola and Cuba and the pressure of both the United States and the Soviet Union in 1988.

When we examine the goals of UNTAG, which was only executed in 1989 although it had been resolved in 1978, we see that the operation was based on the traditional concept. The diplomatic process was based on the fact that the goals of the operation won agreement and support of all the global and regional powers as well as the local participants. Therefore, the mission was only executed after final agreement was obtained from the South African government and from SWAPO in December 1988.[44] Similar to other missions that were reviewed above, UNTAG's main objective was to supervise the civil process for election of a legitimate local government that would receive international recognition. The operation's goals did not include managing the country, Therefore, the operation's force was ordered to maintain neutrality and not intervene in internal affairs except those connected to the election process. As part of the force's responsibility for maintenance of law and order and ensuring free and fair elections, it was instructed to supervise the existing civil administration, not to replace it. The UN force did not receive authorisation to use force. For these reasons, the mission also did not receive powers in civil affairs, such as human rights reform or economic development of the country – goals that characterised the multidimensional operations at the beginning of the 1990s. Similarly, traditional principles dictated the management and organisation of the operation. Furthermore, pressure was applied to Secretary-General de Cuéllar to reduce the scope of the forces taking part in the operation.[45]

The operation's goals as determined in the UN resolution for execution of the operation are not compatible with the avowed aspirations of the organisation's Secretariat for a structural change in Namibian society. Instead, the defined goal of the operation was connected to changing the political status of the region from the position of a mandated territory to that of an autonomous country. The means for achieving this objective was to organise a democratic election system – and nothing else. Thus the UN force was not required to change the society by means of goals of democratisation, civil security, promoting human rights and economic development. Since its main goal was to supervise and report on the process of political status change from the perspective of conducting an election campaign, it did not deal at all in internal affairs connected to Namibian society, and certainly not in any attempts to influence those affairs.

Nonetheless, the fact is that the operation was part of the de-colonisation process. The role of UNTAG was unusual in comparison with most traditional operations preceding it in the period under discussion. The political status it was responsible for – i.e. transforming a mandated territory into a sovereign state – was not a traditional goal for peacekeeping operations. However, Marrack Goulding, USG for Peacekeeping Operations in that period, claimed that a similar mission had been executed in the past, for example in West Irian in the 1960s.[46] The two operations had similar mandates, and both are considered to have been successful. One of the differences between them was in scope; while only several dozens of soldiers were involved in West Irian, about 8,000 soldiers and civil personnel were involved in Namibia. Another, more important, difference is connected to the historical-international context of their executions. The operation in West Irian had been very marginal in the international discourse of the time, because the UN was very preoccupied with differences of opinion regarding the future of peacekeeping operations and the political tension that prevailed at the time between the powers regarding the Congo operation at the beginning of the 1960s. Therefore, the Irian case remained a marginal footnote in the documented memory of the UN's work in the field of peacekeeping operations. By contrast, the international political climate at the end of the 1980s was favourable regarding peacekeeping operations, and the Namibia operation was supported by all the powers, as part of the trend towards improving the relations between East and West. Thus, although the operation was originally only intended to serve as an escape hatch for an outdated mandatory regime that had outlived its usefulness and had deviated from its original goals, the mission did influence the discussions on changing the concept of peacekeeping operations. In this way it was similar to the operation in Nicaragua, and it was also inspiration for the operation in Cambodia. Later, the Namibian operation model became the basis for discussions on the new concept of multidimensional peacekeeping operations.

### The Gulf War: enforcement by the Charter

At this point we address the case of the international response to the occupation of Kuwait, in an attempt to position it in the wider context of peacekeeping operations. This war threatened to spoil the positive atmosphere that had prevailed in the international arena at the end of the 1980s, when the powers began to cooperate with one another in aspects connected to the maintenance of international peace and security. The termination of the Iran–Iraq war left Iraq with tremendous debts of about eighty billion dollars. In the course of 1990, the Iraqi government blamed the Gulf emirates for increasing their crude oil production, thus causing a drop in oil prices around the world.[47] Talks were held between Iraqi and Kuwaiti representatives over the rise in oil prices, and when no progress was evident by July 1990, Saddam Hussein decided to conquer Kuwait. On 2 August 1990, the Iraqi army – one of the largest and strongest armies in the world – conquered its neighbouring country Kuwait, in a mere few hours. With this act, Iraqi ruler Saddam Hussein attempted to wipe out his country's enormous debts. On 28 August, Hussein even declared Kuwait to be Iraq's nineteenth district. These proceedings were a flagrant breach of the Charter's principle of sovereignty that forbids aggression between countries. This principle is, as previously mentioned, the very basis of the UN's work; it revokes the rights of states to initiate war, and all the more so forbids the occupation of one country by another.

On the day Kuwait was conquered, the General Assembly convened for an emergency session in which it adopted Resolution 660, calling for the retreat of Iraqi forces and demanding that the two states solve their differences by negotiation.[48] Four days later, the UN imposed sanctions on Iraq. On 25 August, the Security Council attempted to convene the MSC that was, according to the Charter, supposed to plan military coordination between the powers.[49]

Simultaneously, behind the scenes of the Security Council discussions, hectic talks were held in the international arena between the United States, the Soviet Union, the countries of the EC, and the members of the Arab League. United States President George Bush (senior) promoted an aggressive policy and was ready to activate any force needed. His viewpoint, as expressed in his statements and decisions, was that the UN was a means for turning a military action into an international one. In addition, he viewed this as an opportune moment to improve relations with the Soviet Union and China:

> I was prepared to deal with this crisis unilaterally if necessary, I wanted the United Nations involved as part of our first response, starting with a strong condemnation of Iraq's attack on a fellow member. Decisive UN action would be important in rallying international opposition to the invasion and reversing it.[50]

The events at the end of the 1980s and the sense of deterioration caused larger and larger schisms to form in the Soviet Union's policy; policy ranged from supporting the United States' unilateral steps, to a policy adopted in accordance with its new perspective of 'New [political] Thinking' (the formation of a world order in which regional disputes would be resolved in international summit meetings), to one that considered that the United States was using the conquest of Kuwait as an excuse for improving its grip in the Middle East and that Saddam Hussein needed protection from the United States. Since none of these three diplomatic perspectives was dominant, the Soviet Union's policy with regard to the conquest of Kuwait by Iraq resulted in slight changes that it added to the resolutions that had been advanced by the United States in the Security Council.[51]

The EC countries unanimously and decisively denounced the conquest of Kuwait. Most of the member states sent financial aid or symbolic forces to the region. The exceptions were the United Kingdom and France, which both sent larger forces to the Persian Gulf after consolidation of the international coalition.[52] The Arab states were also not united in their response to the conquest of Kuwait; some exploited the opportunity to improve their status in the regional and international arena. Thus, for example, Egypt, which had been a close ally of Iraq in the 1980s, hurried to take advantage of the opportunity and send a large force. It had a dual goal in doing so: to strengthen its position in the Arab world, which had weakened as a result of its peace agreement with Israel, and to receive hoped-for economic assistance from Western countries. Syria also sent forces to shore up its position in the Arab world and to ameliorate its isolation in the international arena as a terror-backing state. Six Gulf states (Kuwait, Saudi Arabia, United Arab Emirates, Bahrain, Qatar and Oman) also rose up against Iraq, while the other Arab states, mainly Yemen and Libya, adopted a more moderate, cautious approach while warning that the operation could set a dangerous precedent of giving carte blanche to the United States to intervene in other cases as well.[53]

Thus a situation arose which was a unique combination of diverse factors: a violent attack on Kuwait that flagrantly violated the principles of collective security, on the one hand, and Saddam Hussein's tenacious refusal to retreat from his position on the other; an American determination to take action, accompanied by Soviet indecisiveness; and wide consensus among the world's states to intervene to change the situation while promising military or economic assistance for the mission. All these factors led to an operation that was unprecedented in UN history in its scope, and which produced Security Council Resolution 678, was passed on 29 November 1990. This resolution authorised the member states to adopt 'all the necessary means' according to Chapter 7 of the Charter, in order to force Iraq to observe Resolution 660 – full withdrawal of its forces from Kuwait and resolution of conflicts by means of negotiation. The final deadline given to Iraq to withdraw its forces was 15 January 1991.[54]

By the month of December, a multinational force of unprecedented size in comparison with all preceding peacekeeping operations had been assembled. The force numbered almost 600,000 soldiers, composed mainly of United States forces.[55] On 16 January, airstrikes commenced against Iraqi targets. On 24 February the ground invasion began; within a few days, the Iraqi military collapsed. Fears of a 'war of all wars', a 'second Vietnam', or even a second Korean war – disappeared. On 28 February, Saddam Hussein commanded his soldiers to retreat and honour the ceasefire. On 2 March, the Security Council formulated an official model for a ceasefire with the acceptance of Resolution 686. On 11 March, Iraq annulled its annexation of Kuwait in an official letter to the UN Secretary-General.[56]

The Gulf War of 1990–91 was an unusual case in terms of the discussion in this study regarding UN peacekeeping operations. Ostensibly, one might think that the war proved the readiness of UN states to take collective action while changing the concept of the operations. However, the Gulf War was not executed as a peacekeeping operation. The war was a unique case in which international politics succeeded in implementing the Charter and activating Chapter 7 in its original meaning, that is, authorisation of an international enforcement operation against an aggressor, and not the execution of a traditional, or multidimensional, peacekeeping operation. The unique combination of factors leading to the Gulf War and its result was documented in the history of the UN as a success in maintaining the principle of collective security. Security Council Resolution 687 congratulated the states on 'welcoming the restoration to Kuwait of its sovereignty, independence and territorial integrity and the return of its legitimate Government'.[57] More than a decade after the international success, a second Gulf War erupted in 2003. The fact that in this second war, Iraq was conquered by a coalition of states led by the United States without receiving a mandate to do so from the UN, only serves to strengthen the argument of this study: that the war coalition in 1990-91 was an anomalous event that differed widely from other peacekeeping operations – it was the exception that proved the rule.

Thus we see how the peacekeeping operations initiated by the UN at the end of the Cold War were generally more successful than many of those executed in the Cold War era. The earlier unsuccessful missions included the United Nations Emergency Force that failed to prevent a war between Egypt and Israel in 1967; the Congo operation in the early 1960s that led to a political crisis in the UN; and the operations in Israel, India and Cyprus that extended for dozens of years and were largely ineffective. By contrast, post-Cold War operations initiated by the UN won world recognition for their peacemaking influence in conflict sites around the world. Most of these later operations described above began and ended within a short time period and were viewed as successful in the UN. But, as this review shows, these operations were, in essence, traditional and not multidimensional in nature. True, they are not identical in all their components and the differences between them may be erroneously viewed as innovations. I, however, argue that the differences between the traditional operations described above should be viewed as resulting from the emphasis on supervision of resolving intrastate conflict after signing a peace agreement instead of on supervising a ceasefire between states. Furthermore, as demonstrated above, except for the operation in Namibia that was planned earlier at the end of the 1970s, all the other operations were of small scope, and were executed according to traditional operation principles and according to the organisation's accepted management and organisational principles.

We do see a significant change in the setting of the goals of the operations and their mode of action, starting from 1991 with the Security Council resolution to initiate five new operations in Angola, on the Iraq–Kuwait border, in El Salvador, in Western Sahara and in Cambodia. Aside from the observer operation on the Kuwait–Iraq border, the UN forces in the new peacekeeping operations were needed to supervise the disarmament and election processes by means of small forces numbering about one thousand soldiers and civilians of all ranks. Nevertheless, the decision to combine all the assignments in one large operation, whose agenda was to promote the end of the conflict by advancing multidimensional goals, was accepted for the first time at the end of 1991 in the context of Cambodia.

## Cambodia: inventing a new model for peacekeeping in the land of genocide

The UN intervention in Cambodia from 1991–93 was the first multidimensional intervention after the Cold War in which the UN attempted – in addition to founding a legitimate government – to also promote political, economic, social and security-related changes. Two Cambodia operations were executed with these goals in mind. The first, called United Nations Advance Mission in Cambodia (UNAMIC), henceforth the 'Advance Mission', began in October 1991 and ended in March 1992. About a thousand military and civil personnel served in this operation. As indicated by its very name, this mission was intended as a prelude to the second operation, called UNTAC; henceforth, the 'Transitional Authority'. At the time of its planning, the mission was considered the largest, most complex peacekeeping operation in the history of the UN. The Transitional Authority operation began in March 1992 and ended in September 1993; the units that had served in the Advance Mission were merged into this one. At its height, between May and June 1993, almost twenty thousand personnel served in the mission, including more than fifteen thousand soldiers, thousands of civil policemen and hundreds of international supervisors who supervised the civil administration institutions in the country as well as the election process. The two operations cost the UN about 1.6 billion dollars.

The Secretariat workers and representatives of the delegations in the UN viewed the Cambodian intervention as a success story. The UN Secretary-General at the time, Boutros Boutros-Ghali, claimed that the intervention instilled in Cambodia a democratic legacy and the will to resolve internal disputes diplomatically and not militarily.[58] Yasushi Akashi from Japan served as SRSG for Cambodia between January 1992 and September 1993. Akashi, who was responsible for achieving the goals of the intervention, also claimed that a fundamental change had transpired in the Cambodian regime: It had changed from an autocracy to a liberal democracy based on pluralism and freedom of choice.[59] Several years later, Force Commander of the Transitional Authority, John Sanderson from Australia, concurred with this view.[60] Similar views were frequently expressed in the organisation's diplomatic discourse that dealt with development of the concept of peacekeeping operations as multidimensional missions, known as 'second-generation operations'.[61] Below I describe how the specific historical context of the conflict in Cambodia, together with the broad historical context relating to attempts to change the goals and principles of peacekeeping operations, shaped a revolutionary operation that preceded the transitional administration operations of Bosnia, Kosovo and East Timor in the second half of the 1990s.

The geographical area known today as Cambodia, inhabited by the Khmer ethnic group (as well as other minority groups), was caught in a civil war from at least the 1960s. The height of the brutal war was between April 1975 and January 1979, during which time the country was ruled by the Communist Party of Kampuchea, more commonly known as the Khmer Rouge. In this time period, almost a quarter of the Cambodian population perished – numbering almost eight million human beings – alongside systematic destruction of physical and cultural infrastructures.[62] After the defeat of the Khmer Rouge genocidal regime in 1979 by Vietnamese armed forces, a civil war developed in Cambodia. Approximately 90 per cent of the country's territories were controlled by the Kampuchean People's Revolutionary Party (KPCP); the KPCP was, in turn, under the supervision of Vietnamese occupation forces. In its attempt to attract foreign investments and hide its autocratic nature, the KPCP changed the country's name to the State of Cambodia (SOC) from 1989 to 1993. In 1991, it reorganised itself as the Cambodian People's Party (the CPP). Most of its members were former Khmer Rouge who had defected from their party. From 1985, Hun Sen served as leader of the KPCP; he was only 34 years old at the time. This puppet government was heavily based on continuous aid from Vietnam and the USSR.[63]

The following groups fought against the KPCP: a loose coalition of royalists (National United Front for an Independent, Neutral, Peaceful, and Cooperative Cambodia, or FUNCINPEC, based on the French name); nationalists (Khmer People's National Liberation Front, or KPNLF); and the radical communists, the Khmer Rouge (DK) factions that operated from the Thai border and received support from Thailand, China and the USA. The fighting forces numbered approximately forty thousand troops, more than half of which were Khmer Rouge soldiers who were responsible for the genocide. Most of the foreign weapons, equipment and supplies (including clothing, food, etc.) also went to the Khmer Rouge.[64]

Under international pressure to resolve their conflict and as a result of the threat of cessation of aid to them, the four factions were pressured to sign a peace agreement known as The Final Act of the Paris Conference on Cambodia (23 October 1991). Central to the peace agreement was the call for the UN to execute a multidimensional peacekeeping operation, entitled UNTAC. The operation, argued the various sides, was to support the peace process through the management and monitoring of democratic elections that would elect a legitimate government for Cambodia. In order to support this state-building objective, the operation was given additional goals, such as: the advancement of democracy and human rights; the demobilisation of 70 per cent of the armed forces of all four factions; assisting the return and resettlement of refugees; and assisting in rehabilitation and reconstruction of the country's economy.[65]

As already mentioned, some researchers attribute the multidimensional goals to changes in the international political landscape in the UN. According to this approach, the conclusion of the Cold War led to a situation in which the United States and its Western allies enjoyed dominance in the UN, thus succeeding in promoting a new concept for peacekeeping operations. However, the discussion above demonstrates that in the 1988–91 period, the UN members had not yet agreed to the need for a new peacekeeping operation concept.

Throughout almost the entire process of peace-agreement negotiations between the rival Cambodian factions in the course of the 1980s, the idea of deploying peacekeeping operations in Cambodia was not brought to discussion. The UN viewed the conflict as a civil war that would end when an agreement was reached between the opposing sides. The UN mediators, headed by Rafiuddin Ahmed from Afghanistan, preferred that elections would constitute part of the agreement and that the elections would determine which of the factions would establish a legitimate government. This was the way the mediators operated, in accordance with the traditional technique of peacemaking. However, in the course of the 1980s, it became clear to the UN mediating teams that the factions would be hard pressed to end the conflict. This was due to the backing they received from the superpowers and the ideological rifts between them.[66]

The merging of a peace process (conducted in accordance with traditional principles of peacemaking) and a multidimensional operation was the result of a combination of factors. These factors include the process of terminating the Cold War, which directly affected the conflict in Cambodia, and the basic dispute between representatives of the conflicted sides that could not find a way to cooperate in the transition period between the end of the civil war and the creation of an elected, legitimate government. Finally, an original and unique initiative arose from an unexpected source – Australian Foreign Minister Gareth Evans. Evans exploited global processes – including local peacemaking successes in Afghanistan, Central America and Namibia – to propose a solution for the dispute between the Cambodian factions: an unprecedented peacekeeping operation in Cambodia. Below, I discuss these circumstances at length.

The effects of the winding-down of the Cold War on bringing an end to the conflict in Cambodia should not be underestimated. As a result of Gorbachev's 'new thinking' policy and the economic crisis in the Soviet Union, the Soviet Union cut off the assistance it had long provided to Vietnam and the Phnom Penh administration.[67] Simultaneously with this policy, or perhaps because of it, criticism peaked in the United States on the continuous support provided by the American administration to the Khmer Rouge since 1979. Throughout the 1980s, pressure increased on the American administration with the dissemination of more and more reports of the culpability of the Khmer Rouge for genocide in their country.[68] During that period, China supported the Khmer Rouge and Sihanouk factions. But towards the end of the 1980s, China also began to support the option of a comprehensive peace arrangement on the site, without defeating the KPCP administration.[69] The United Kingdom and France, Security Council members with no vested interests in any of the rival Cambodian factions, also increased their pressure to end the conflict with a compromise. Thus the Vietnamese government supporting the KPCP remained without assistance from any superpower and strived to improve its economic condition by searching for a way to become integrated in the regional economy. At the same time, the ASEAN member states (Association of Southeast Asian Nations) were working on initiatives to develop the regional economy by becoming integrated in the global market economy. Therefore, they had a clear interest in making peace in Cambodia.[70] Their stance was supported by most of the members of the UN General Assembly, most probably because those countries were members of the non-aligned bloc movement.[71]

Yet although the winding-down of the Cold War played an important role in the willingness of the Cambodian factions to end the conflict between them, in actual fact they failed to accomplish this. By 1989, the conflicted sides had reached overall agreement on most of the clauses of the peace agreement; this was with the support of the UN members and the Secretariat staff. However, the mediators from the UN and from other countries failed to resolve three issues that remained disputable. The first issue was how the Cambodian factions would divide the country's powers during the transition period until the holding of democratic elections and the formulation of a new constitution for the state. The three opposition factions wanted the KPCP, which ruled over 90 per cent of Cambodian territory at the time, to relinquish its control over the state apparatus. The second irreconcilable issue was the question of Khmer Rouge participation in the democratic regime that would arise. The third bone of contention was the very existence of, and nature of, the apparatus that would supervise the entire transition process.[72]

The last issue was the hardest of all to solve, because the Cambodian and international representatives could not reach agreement on the apparatus that would supervise the implementation of the peace agreements. The UN was not the only alternative.[73] Only after numerous discussions was it decided, at the beginning of 1990, that the UN was the proper entity to supervise the entire process. This idea was, surprisingly, advanced by then-Australian Foreign Minister Gareth Evans – and not one of the five permanent members of the Security Council or the Secretariat. Australia was one of the few countries that traditionally supported the UN and the peacekeeping operations. At the beginning of 1988, the Australian government was one of the first countries to send its official opinion to the SCPKO regarding the development of peacekeeping operations. In this document, the government expressed support for the goals and success principles of the traditional peacekeeping operations, while emphasising the need to solve the organisational problems connected to the execution of these operations.[74] Evans, with the backing of the Australian government and Senate, published an 'Australian Peace Proposal' of about 150 pages, dealing with proposals for ending the Cambodian conflict.[75]

The Australian Peace Proposal – a detailed plan that was also called a 'working paper' – was submitted to the representatives of the Cambodian factions and the countries that were interested parties in the conflict. These were instructed to discuss the proposal at a work meeting set to take place in Jakarta, Indonesia, in February 1990. The proposal was divided into six work documents that were drafts of agreements regarding the following: the general structure of the Cambodian government during the transition period; the civil administration during the transition period; the organisation of the elections in the transition period; security arrangements during the transition period; securing the country's sovereignty, independence and neutrality; and, finally, reconstruction of Cambodia after the conclusion of the conflict. In effect, all the work documents led up to the fact that the UN would be the de facto sovereign ruler of the country during Cambodia's transition stage, as it began the stages of return to the international community.

The Australian sources of inspiration were various international agreements and mandates crafted in the past by the Security Council, such as the West Irian and Afghanistan mandates. But mainly they were influenced by the work of the UN operation in Namibia; during that period, elections were held under UN supervision. The Australian proposal called for taking an additional step towards working together with the UNHCR, that of returning the displaced people and refugees to their homes. This was to be done cooperatively with the International Committee of the Red Cross (ICRC), to locate missing persons, and the United Nations Development Programme (UNDP), to coordinate development programmes, together with a special representative of the UN Secretary-General on the territory. Finally, military forces would be available to the Secretary-General to supervise the disarmament of 75 per cent of all fighters of the four Cambodian factions.[76]

The Australian Peace Proposal and the Australian diplomatic efforts in marketing it enlivened the diplomatic discussions about resolving the Cambodian conflict and placed the UN in the very centre of the process. At the time, the foreign ministers of Indonesia and France served jointly as chair of the Paris Conference – an international diplomatic forum entrusted with the peacemaking process – where the foreign ministers discussed the Australian document and transformed it into a cornerstone for future deliberations in resolving conflicts. And in the discussions of the P5 member delegations regarding Cambodia that began in January 1990, it was agreed that the document would serve as a useful foundation for resolving the conflict. In the spirit of the era, in which the UN enjoyed an important role in resolving conflicts around the world, and due to the desire of the involved countries to terminate the conflict in Cambodia – the Australian programme became the only guideline for implementation of the agreements. In the sixth work meeting of the five permanent members that took place on 27–28 August 1990, the member representatives composed a framework document for a compromise agreement among the four Cambodian factions. These, on their part, agreed to the establishment of the Supreme National Council as a legitimate body that would represent Cambodia during the entire transition period. On 20 September 1990 the Security Council passed Resolution 668, in which it adopted the framework-agreement advanced by the P5 members.[77] On 23 October 1991 this draft became the 'Paris Agreements'.

The process of determining the multidimensional objectives of the UN operation in Cambodia, as described above, disproves the commonly held arguments and proves that the mission was an exception proving the rule. As opposed to the description of alliances in the UN regarding various issues discussed in this study, the organisation's members were unanimous regarding the need to end the conflict in Cambodia by means of a multidimensional operation. In the Cambodia context, diverse nations joined together – Western and developing nations, veteran contributors and new contributors – to support the unique, local initiative of the Australian government. It is ironic that while there was no agreement in the UN regarding resolution of conflicts by means of execution of multidimensional operations, such an agreement was based solely on the Australian initiative.

As opposed to operations implemented during the Cold War, multidimensional goals were determined for the Cambodian operation in the diplomatic, economic-humanitarian and security realms. From the diplomatic perspective, the Transitional Authority headed by the SRSG was in charge of promoting good governance, democratisation and human rights. The Transitional Authority was designed to end after democratic elections had been held and the elected government had been formed. The elections were set for the beginning of May 1993 and they were considered the peak of international supervision in the country, a place where democratic elections had last taken place in 1955. In the security-related sphere, the UN forces received the task of supervising the disarmament and demobilisation of 70 per cent of the fighting forces of the rival Cambodian factions that were deployed throughout the country. According to various estimates, these forces numbered about two hundred thousand fighters. In the economic-humanitarian view, the UN's civil authority was required to supervise economic activity in the country, to ensure that it would follow the principles of good governance, to advance the return of about 360,000 refugees to Cambodia, and assist the National Council to invest the contributions received from the international community in projects facilitating the country's development.

The force that was supposed to carry out these objectives numbered about twenty thousand military personnel, policemen and civilians. Despite the ambitious goals of the Paris Agreements, no great changes were made in the execution principles of the operation, which remained traditional in nature. The Transitional Authority operation was carried out after an agreement (the Paris Agreements) was reached between the conflicted sides, including the Khmer Rouge; the agreement supported the deployment of UN forces on the ground. The UN representatives in Cambodia committed themselves to operating impartially and without bias, and they were given extensive authority and powers. Furthermore, the UN forces enjoyed wide international support. As is customary in peacekeeping operations, the UN personnel were committed to the non-use of force with the exception of self-defence.

### Resources for the new peacekeeping operations

Reservations regarding the diplomatic processes that led to the execution of the largest peacekeeping operation at the time were voiced, ironically, by the UN Secretariat – the organ that is in charge of managing such operations. The Secretariat saw that while the international community supported the Secretariat's role in managing numerous new operations, including the large, complex one in Cambodia, it did not give it the resources it needed to succeed.

At that point in time, the Secretariat had not received the additional personnel it needed in order to administer the operation properly. Only a minority of member states responded to the questionnaire sent by the Secretariat regarding allocation of forces, equipment and supplies for peacekeeping operations.[78] East European countries and others that revealed an interest in the operations lacked practical experience; thus the Secretariat was forced to rely on the veteran contributor countries such as the Nordic countries and Canada, countries that trained their soldiers for the operations. Others argued whether it was enough for the training to be done on the national level alone, or whether the UN ought to supervise it.[79] In a response to the shortage of resources for operations, more and more voices argued that the Security Council's permanent members ought to contribute a significant percentage of the forces needed for the peacekeeping operations, under the pretext that they have the greatest influence over decision-making in the Security Council. Since they are the world's most powerful countries, they should carry most of the military burden. This viewpoint contrasted with one of the iron-clad principles of execution of peacekeeping operations during the Cold War, which negated the participation of superpowers in these operations in order to maintain their neutrality.[80]

In the wake of rising demands for additional personnel in peacekeeping operations at the beginning of the 1990s, voices began to be heard supporting the integration of civilian staff in operations, mainly in operations that did not require the involvement of soldiers. Some of the delegation representatives argued that the operations in Namibia and Nicaragua should serve as examples of integrating civilians in operations.[81] The main rationale behind the integration of civilians in operations was not connected to claims that it would improve the effectiveness of the operations, but that it would enable many more member states to take part, and ostensibly would contribute to the neutral status of the operations.[82] Representatives of veteran countries active in peacekeeping operations (the five Scandinavian Nordic countries and Canada, New Zealand and Australia) disagreed over the political trend that was expressed in this issue. They supported the integration of civilian staff with regard to supervision of elections and human rights. However, they warned against excessive use of civilian staff because it could sabotage the effectiveness of the operations; unlike soldiers, civilians cannot cope with complex security situations.[83]

The multitude of operations created logistical problems that, similar to the issues above of the allocation of military and civilian forces, were not divorced from economic and political considerations. The discussions in the General Assembly show that most of the veteran contributor countries strongly and overwhelmingly supported the establishment of a logistic standby arrangements system, while other countries, despite expressing support in principle, raised doubts regarding the scope of the repository and its sources. The end result was that the Secretariat was forced to continue to equip each operation anew in a slow, cumbersome process.[84]

Another prominent obstacle of the operations was the financing issue. In order to encourage countries to allocate forces, it was customary to compensate them with monthly payments for each soldier and for the equipment they sent to the operations. The tariff was set by a designated UN organ. As a result of the tremendous income gaps that exist between the various countries in the world, the monetary compensation offered by the UN to the developed countries did not cover their expenses, as opposed to that offered to the developing countries. Nevertheless, at the end of 1990, the five Nordic countries supplied about 30 per cent of the peacekeeping operation forces.[85] This balance sheet was to change at the beginning of the 1990s, when the scope of the forces in operations grew by a factor of six. The developed countries continued to send forces, but the overall percentage of the developed countries in the operation forces dropped significantly in contrast to the developing countries. It was worthwhile for the developing countries to allocate forces to operations from a financial standpoint and they constantly pressed for higher reimbursement. Other factors made it difficult for developed countries. Most of the world's countries did not possess advanced logistical-organisational skills that could support peacekeeping operation forces in the long range.[86]

In the discussions held in the UN at the end of the Cold War, the members of the SCPKO could not anticipate the end result of the increase in the number and scope of operations. Even though the ongoing expenses of the organisation were not very high in that period, the organisation's budget already had a deficit. In effect, the same countries that traditionally contributed forces to the operations were the ones to absorb a large portion of the economic burden and the organisation owed them tens of millions of dollars. It was clear to everyone that although the developing countries expressed willingness to join the operations, they lacked the financial, logistical and organisational abilities to do so properly. Therefore, most of the countries represented in the SCPKO agreed that the main economic burden should rest on the wide economic shoulders of the five permanent members of the Security Council. Therefore, the SCPKO demanded that they pay all their debts and increase their share of the financial participation in the operations.[87] Furthermore, proposals were raised to re-examine the way the assessments were calculated. Proposals were also heard to request economic assistance from other entities such regional organisations, corporations and non-governmental organisations (NGOs), as these organisations are the prime beneficiaries of the peace that the UN advances.[88] In an attempt to reject this demand, the twelve EC members argued that in recent decades, Western Europe had funded about 38 per cent of the total UN operational budget.[89] At that point in time, the United States and Japan together paid more than 40 per cent of the operating budget.[90]

Veteran UN Secretary-General Pérez de Cuéllar was aware of the gamut of problems faced by the organisation he headed. His worries increased exponentially when the decision was made to launch the Cambodian operation. In his book *Pilgrimage for Peace*, in which he shares his memories of his UN tenure, he testifies to the fact that he was uncomfortable with the new multiple spheres of responsibility on his watch. These new roles – such as managing elections and bearing responsibility for Cambodian internal security – were thrust on the organisation by the Australian initiative. As a long-standing diplomat in the UN, de Cuéllar felt that the main importance of the initiative was rooted in the fact that it strengthened the diplomatic process of peacemaking, because the Cambodian factions took part in the process, as did Vietnam and Thailand. Also, the initiative motivated the five permanent members of the Security Council to commit themselves to supporting the operation. On the other hand, de Cuéllar publicly opposed the objectives defined for the operation. In his memoirs, he claimed that 'for more than four decades, the Permanent Members had been reluctant to give the United Nations any independent authority at all. Now they seemed prepared to have it administer a whole country, a task that was, in my view, inappropriate and beyond its capacity.'[91]

Despite his doubts, and in light of his great experience with the administrative and organisational difficulties connected to the execution of peacekeeping operations, de Cuéllar hurried to establish a task force within the Secretariat. He placed responsibility for planning the Cambodian operation on this task force, and did this even before details of the operation had been decided. Marrack Goulding, in charge of peacekeeping operations in the Secretariat, supported these actions.[92] Regarding monitoring of the civil administration, de Cuéllar realised that the Secretariat could not actively control the ministries of the KPCP administration that ruled over 90 per cent of Cambodia, and he tried to clarify this issue in a series of diplomatic contacts. However, since he was at the end of his term of office as Secretary-General, he preferred to leave the treatment of the problem to his replacement, Boutros Boutros-Ghali.[93]

### The change in the support to UN peacekeeping after the Cold War

The content of the discussions held in the UN's various organs on the subject of peacekeeping operations during the waning years of the Cold War (1988–91) contradicts the following accepted research tenet: that second-generation peacekeeping operations commenced in 1988. The contrary is true: discussions in the organisation regarding peacekeeping operations from 1988 until the middle of 1991 show that during these years not only was no new concept formulated for the operations, but the operations that were executed were not intended to serve as conceptual precedents.

Thus we see that the waning years of the Cold War should be viewed as a transition period that had the potential to develop in different directions. The importance of the transition period to the history of peacekeeping operations is the inspiration it provided to the discussion of the concept of those operations on the one hand, and the Security Council's willingness to execute them (due to their potential contribution to conflict resolution) on the other.

Regarding the new content injected into operation-related discussions, such as advancement of new goals of economic development and environmental protection, it turns out that these new goals were advanced by the contributor countries. These were the veteran countries such as Canada and the five Nordic countries, but also the Soviet Union and its allies. This conclusion totally contradicts the accepted premise that the United States, the United Kingdom and France were the ones to develop the new peacekeeping operation concept.

One of the causes for the significant change in international politics as expressed in UN discussions during 1988–91 was Gorbachev's attempt to end the Cold War and inject the spirit of his 'new thinking' into international affairs. The UN's peacekeeping operations had an important role in resolving conflicts, which was part of the 'new thinking' policy, thus proposals were raised for advancing the concept behind the operations. However, it seems that most of the delegations in the UN viewed Gorbachev's vision with cynicism (or as realpolitik). Thus while his vision did not arouse antagonism, it also did not lead to real changes in the countries' actions.

In addition, all the representatives of the countries that proposed ways to develop the concept continued to advocate the superiority of the traditional objectives and principles of success. They did not advocate advancement of objectives such as promotion of human rights, humanitarian aid, or disarmament of the armed parties. In any case, even those limited concept-changing initiatives that were attempted ultimately failed and did not receive the support of the relevant UN organs.

The Security Council, which had been effectively paralysed throughout most of the Cold War, found the operations to be a means for resolving many of the proxy wars founded in the Cold War inter-bloc period. The lack of real innovation in the concept of operations was also expressed by the deployment of operations in Afghanistan, Iran–Iraq, Iraq–Kuwait, Angola, Namibia, Western Sahara and Central America, and the enforcement operation in Iraq. In light of the accepted research arguments, we would have expected that the United States and its Western allies would have exploited the peacekeeping operation technique to promote their own interests, mainly goals such as promoting human rights and inculcating democratisation. In practice, however, the goals and principles of the operations were traditional. The operations were deployed after agreements were reached by the opposing sides, the regional countries, and the world powers. They banned the use of force and forbade involvement in the countries' internal affairs. The UN forces assumed that the local sides would cooperate with them in implementing the mandate. Before 1991, goals such as peacemaking, humanitarian aid and monitoring of elections were not integrated, with the exception of two instances: Namibia and Cambodia. The main objective of these two operations was to assist in founding peace – in the form of a legitimate government – and, afterwards, to leave the state in which there had been an intervention. Thus, the operations were generally small in size. The enforcement operation against Iraq was an exception and was similar, in certain ways, to the circumstances surrounding the Korean War in 1950. In both cases, enforcement powers were based on the Charter's Chapter 7 (the use of force to ward off an aggressive nation), and the peacekeeping operation technique was not used.

The most important development in those years was the decision to deploy a large, multidimensional operation in Cambodia, which preceded the later Transitional Authority operations of the UN in Bosnia, Eastern Slavonia, Kosovo and East Timor in the second half of the 1990s. Thus, the Cambodian operation was the exception that proved the rule. It was created in the wake of international support for advancing the operations, but was also a result of the inability of the international community to achieve an agreement between the Khmer factions.

The UN Secretariat was surprised by the change in international politics in favour of the operations. Within a few years, the number of operations it administered had doubled and the peacekeeping operation now returned to international centre stage from its former rather low position. The Secretariat suffered from a permanent shortage in personnel on the one hand, and from cumbersome management on the other. In addition, the Secretariat workers shared the perception that future peacekeeping operations would be only small scale. Despite the difficulties encountered by the Secretariat in running numerous operations, the UN did not take significant steps to improve the situation. Most member states did not train soldiers for operations, did not place soldiers on standby, and failed to reach agreement regarding the role of civilians in operations involving civic objectives such as monitoring elections or advancing human rights. Proposals to create logistic reserves were turned down. The financing issue remained a festering sore in the organisation, with the Western countries bearing most of the financial burden and losing additional money when the compensation received for their soldiers did not even cover their expenses. All this proves that the Secretariat was unprepared to deal with the many demands imposed on it with regard to operations from the end of 1991. However, as mentioned in Chapter 1, this lack of preparedness did not prevent the Security Council from passing a resolution to deploy multidimensional operations.

Many changes were evident in 1991: the end of the Cold War, developments in discussions on the concept of operations, the successes of the new operations and the enforcement operation in Iraq. Thus the question arose in the UN deliberations of that year: Would the traditional concept of peacekeeping operations prevail, or would the issue be discussed again more intensely in light of the new world order and the other changes? On 21 December 1991 this question became even more critical when the Soviet Union was dismantled. Brent Scowcroft, US National Security Advisor, understood that a new era had just ended, and a new one was starting:

> It was over. An event I had never imagined I would see in my lifetime had actually taken place. It left me numb, disbelieving ... The world we had encountered in January 1989 had been defined by superpower rivalry. The Cold War struggle

had shaped our assumptions about international and domestic politics, our institutions and processes, our armed forces and military strategy. In a blink of an eye these were gone. We were suddenly in a unique position, without experience, without precedent, and standing alone at the height of power.[94]

The Security Council was assembled in January 1992 with the presence of the heads of states. That session was supposed to create the new world order, to define the functions of the peacekeeping operations within that new order, and provide the means for the success of the operations.

## Notes

1  The Security Council decided to execute the following operations in 1991: UNIKOM on the Kuwait–Iraq border; MINURSO in Western Sahara; UNAVEM II in Angola; ONUSAL in El Salvador and UNAMIC in Cambodia.
2  For a detailed analysis see: C. Kertcher, 'From Cold War to a System of Peacekeeping Operations: The Discussions on Peacekeeping Operations in the UN during the 1980s up to 1992', *Journal of Contemporary History*, 47:3 (2012), 611–637.
3  See, for example, Gorbachev's speech in the General Assembly on 7 December 1988.
4  A/42/637-S/19190, 9 October 1987.
5  This document was an update of an earlier study from 1978, see: A/42/77, 3 December 1987.
6  A/RES/42/161, 8 December 1987; UN, *Yearbook of the United Nations, 1987* (New York: United Nations Department of Public Information 1992), pp. 120–122.
7  A/RES/43/59, 6 December 1988.
8  Kertcher, 'From Cold War', 620–624.
9  R. L. Garthoff, *The Great Transition: American–Soviet Relations and the End of the Cold War* (Washington, DC: Brookings Institution Press, 1994), pp. 197–372; M. Goulding, *Peacemonger* (London: John Murray, 2002), pp. 117–119.
10  Kertcher, 'From Cold War', 624–628.
11  *Ibid.*, pp. 620–629; A/46/254, 18 June 1991, Annex II.
12  A/C.5/45/Sr.40, 5 December 1990, pp. 3–5.
13  At the time there were twelve members in the EC (Belgium, Denmark, Federal Republic of Germany, France, Greece, Ireland, Italy, Luxembourg, Netherlands, Portugal, Spain, United Kingdom); A/C.5/45/Sr.40, 5 December 1990, pp. 3–5.
14  S/PV.3046, 31 January 1992.
15  Kertcher, 'From Cold War', 617–620.
16  A/43/645, 22 September 1988; A/AC.121/36, 21 March 1989; A/SPC/45/Sr.21, 23 November 1990; A/SPC/46/Sr.13, 30 October 1991, pp. 9–10.
17  Kertcher, 'From Cold War', 617–620; A/43/709, 13 October 1988.

18  The publication of *Blue Helmets* and the *Blue Books* Series by the UN Secretariat is an example of this.
19  A/RES/44/49, 8 December 1989.
20  A/45/217, 8 May 1990; A/45/502, 19 September 1990; A/45/572, 5 October 1990; A/45/582, 10 October 1990; A/45/594, 9 October 1990.
21  A/45/493 Add.1, 30 October 1990, pp. 1-2.
22  A/45/493, 18 September 1990; /46/169, 10 May 1991.
23  A/SPC/46/Sr.11, 28 October 1991; A/47/253, 4 June 1992.
24  A/SPC/46/Sr.11, 28 October 1991, pp. 2-3; Goulding, *Peacemonger*, p. 334.
25  A/46/254, 18 June 1991, para. 17-21, 72-77.
26  *Ibid.*
27  Thus, among all the speeches delivered in the Assembly on the topic, the only representative who warned that the proposal deviated from the accepted operative principles of the Cold War era was Uruguay's representative, Pablo Emilio Sader. A/SPC/46/Sr.14, 31 October 1991, p. 4.
28  A/RES/46/48, 9 December 1991.
29  A/SPC/46/Sr.11, 28 October 1991, p. 5.
30  D. Cordovez and S. S. Harrison, *Out of Afghanistan: The Inside Story of the Soviet Withdrawal* (New York: Oxford University Press, 1995); S. E. Mendelson, *Changing Course: Ideas, Politics, and the Soviet Withdrawal from Afghanistan* (Princeton, NJ: Princeton University Press, 1998).
31  UN, *Blue Helmets*, 1996, pp. 661-666; Goulding, *Peacemonger*, pp. 119-120; S/RES/622, 31 October 1988, p. 31.
32  J. P. de Cuéllar, *Pilgrimage for Peace: A Secretary General's Memoir* (New York: St. Martin's Press, 1998), pp. 210-212.
33  A. H Cordesman and A. Wagner, *The Lessons of Modern War: The Iran-Iraq War* (Boulder, CO: Westview Press, 1990).
34  See UN, *Blue Helmets*, 1996, pp. 669-678; Goulding, *Peacemonger*, pp. 122-138.
35  S/RES/696, 30 May 1991.
36  UN, *Blue Helmets*, 1996, pp. 234-238; Goulding, *Peacemonger*, pp. 142-145.
37  Ratner, *The New UN Peacekeeping*, pp. 124-128.
38  B. Antonini, 'El Salvador', in Malone (ed.), *The UN Security Council*, pp. 423-436; Goulding, *Peacemonger*, pp. 215-224; Ratner, *The New UN Peacekeeping*, pp. 123-130; UN, *Blue Helmets*, 1996, pp. 407-444.
39  UN, *Blue Helmets*, 1996, p. 410.
40  *Ibid.*, pp. 423-444.
41  *Ibid.*, p. 203.
42  *Ibid.*, pp. 203-229.
43  de Cuéllar, *Pilgrimage for Peace*, pp. 293-321; V. P. Fortna, 'United Nations Transition Assistance Group', in Durch (ed.), *The Evolution of UN Peacekeeping*, pp. 353-375; Goulding, *Peacemonger*, pp. 139-175; Ratner, *The New UN Peacekeeping*, pp. 118-123; C. Thornberry, 'Namibia', in Malone (ed.), *The UN Security Council*, pp. 407-422.
44  Goulding, *Peacemonger*, p. 143.

45  S/RES/435, 29 September 1978; S/12636, 10 April 1978; S/12869, 9 September 1978; S/RES/632, 16 February 1989; Goulding, *Peacemonger*, pp. 145–148.
46  Goulding, *Peacemonger*, p. 139.
47  A. Ehteshami, 'The Arab States and the Middle East Balance of Power', in J. Gow (ed.), *Iraq, The Gulf Conflict and the World Community* (London: Brassey's, 1993), pp. 63–64; C. Tripp, 'Iraq and the War for Kuwait', in Gow (ed.), *Iraq, The Gulf Conflict*, p. 19.
48  S/RES/660, 2 August 1990.
49  S/RES/665, 25 August 1990. Aside from the representatives from Cuba and Yemen, who chose to abstain, all the other representatives in the Security Council voted in favour of the resolutions regarding Iraq.
50  G. Bush and B. Scowcroft, *A World Transformed* (New York: Alfred A. Knopf, 1998), p. 303.
51  J. A. Baker and T. M. Defrank, *The Politics of Diplomacy: Revolution, War and Peace* (New York: G.P. Putnam's Sons, 1995), pp. 281–295; J. Gow, 'The Soviet Involvement', in Gow (ed.), *Iraq, The Gulf Conflict and the World Community*, pp. 121–137; Y. Klein, 'Soviet Policy during the Gulf Crisis', in G. Barzilai, A. Klieman and G. Shidlo (eds), *The Gulf Crisis and Its Global Aftermath* (London: Routledge, 1993), pp. 192–194.
52  I. Greilsammer, 'European Reaction to the Gulf Challenge', in Barzilai, Klieman and Shidlo (eds), *Gulf Crisis*, pp. 208–227.
53  Ehteshami, 'The Arab States', pp. 58–59.
54  S/RES/678, 29 November 1990; F. Berman, 'The Authorization Model: Resolution 678 and Its Effects', in Malone (ed.), *The UN Security Council*, pp. 153–161.
55  J. Thompson, 'The Military Coalition', in Gow (ed.), *Iraq, the Gulf Conflict*, p. 140.
56  S/RES/686, 3 March 1991.
57  S/RES/687, 3 April 1991.
58  B. Boutros-Ghali, 'Introduction', in UN, *The United Nations and Cambodia, 1991–1995* (New York: United Nations Department of Public Information, 1995), p. 55.
59  Y. Akashi, 'The Challenges Faced by UNTAC', *Japan Review of International Affairs*, 7:3 (1993), 199.
60  J. Sanderson, 'The Cambodian Experience: A Success Story Still?', in R. Thakur and A. Schnabel, *United Nations Peacekeeping Operations: Ad Hoc Missions, Permanent Engagement* (Tokyo & New York: United Nations University Press, 2001), p. 156.
61  Such opinions prevailed in the discussions of the Special Committee and the Fourth Committee of the General Assembly, see, for example: A/C.4/48/SR.22, 4 February 1994; A/C.4/48/SR.23, 8 February 1994; A/C.4/48/SR.24, 31 January 1994; A/C.4/50/SR.19, 13 November 1995; A/C.4/50/SR.21, 29 December 1995; A/C.4/50/SR.23, 11 January 1996. For studies on the operation, see, for example: M. W. Doyle, *UN Peacekeeping in Cambodia: UNTAC's Civil Mandate* (Boulder, CO: Lynne Rienner, 1995); T. Findlay, *Cambodia: The Legacy and Lessons of UNTAC* (Oxford: Oxford University Press, 1995).

62  D. P. Chandler, *A History of Cambodia* (Boulder, CO: Westview Press, 2nd edn, 1992), pp. 137–199; D. P. Chandler, *The Tragedy of Cambodian History: Politics, War, and Revolution since 1945* (New Haven, CT: Yale University Press, 1991); K. J. Clymer, *The United States and Cambodia, 1969–2000: A Troubled Relationship* (London; New York: Routledge, 2004); W. P. Deac, *Road to the Killing Fields: The Cambodian War of 1970–1975* (College Station, TX: Texas A&M University Press 1997); B. Kiernen, *The Pol Pot Regime: Race, Power, and Genocide in Cambodia under the Khmer Rouge, 1975–1979* (New Haven, CT: Yale University Press, 1996); B. Kiernan, 'The Demography of Genocide in Southeast Asia: The Death Tolls in Cambodia, 1975–79, and East Timor, 1975–80', *Critical Asian Studies*, 35:4 (2003), 586–590; M. A. Martin, *Cambodia: A Shattered Society* (Berkeley, CA: University of California Press, 1994); W. Shawcross, *Sideshow: Kissinger, Nixon and the Destruction of Cambodia* (Bungay, Suffolk, UK: Fontana Press, 1980); P. Short, *Pol Pot: Anatomy of a Nightmare* (New York: H. Holt, 2005).

63  Chandler, *A History of Cambodia*, pp. 227–238; Martin, *Cambodia*, pp. 215–240.

64  Chandler, *A History of Cambodia*, pp. 231–235; Clymer, *The United States and Cambodia*, pp. 121–146; Martin, *Cambodia*, pp. 240–254.

65  S/23613, 19 February 1992.

66  de Cuéllar, *Pilgrimage for Peace*, pp. 443–459; Goulding, *Peacemonger*, pp. 248–251.

67  M. C. Williams, 'New Soviet Policy Towards Southeast Asia: Recognition and Change', *Asian Survey*, 31:4 (1991), 364–377.

68  Clymer, *The United States and Cambodia*, pp. 113–156.

69  A. Ramses, 'Sino-Vietnamese Normalization in the Light of the Crisis of the Late 70s', *Pacific Affairs*, 67:3 (1994), 357–383; C. McGregor, 'China, Vietnam, and the Cambodian Conflict: Beijing's End Game Strategy', *Asian Survey*, 30:3 (1990), 266–283; R. S. Ross, 'China and the Cambodian Peace Process', *Asian Survey*, 31:12 (1991), 1170–1185; J. Song, 'The Political Dynamics of the Peacemaking Process in Cambodia', in M. W. Doyle, I. Johnstone and R. C. Orr (eds), *Keeping the Peace: Multidimensional UN Operations in Cambodia and El Salvador* (Cambridge: Cambridge University Press, 1997), pp. 53–59.

70  S. Narine, 'ASEAN and the ARF: The Limits of the "ASEAN Way"', *Asian Survey*, 37:10 (1997), 961–978; S. Narine, 'ASEAN and the Management of Regional Security', *Pacific Affairs*, 71:2 (1998), 195–214; M. C. Smouts, 'The Political Aspects of Peace-Keeping Operations', in B. Stern (ed.), *United Nations Peace-Keeping Operations: A Guide to French Policies* (Tokyo: United Nations University Press, 1998), pp. 7–39.

71  A/RES/34/22, 14 November 1979; A/RES/35/6, 22 October 1980; A/RES/36/5, 21 October 1981; A/RES/37/6, 29 October 1982; A/RES/38/3, 27 October 1983; A/RES/39/5, 30 October 1984; A/RES/40/7, 5 November 1985; A/RES/41/6, 21 October 1986; A/RES/42/3, 14 October 1987; A/RES/43/19, 3 November 1988; A/RES/44/22, 16 November 1989; A/RES/45/3, 13 October 1990; A/RES/46/18, 20 November 1991.

72  de Cuéllar, *Pilgrimage for Peace*, pp. 453–459; Ross, 'China and the Cambodian', p. 1178; Clymer, *The United States and Cambodia*, pp. 155–161; Song, 'The Political Dynamics', pp. 61–69.
73  de Cuéllar, *Pilgrimage for Peace*, pp. 456–457. Also see: S. J. Solarz, 'Cambodia and the International Community', *Foreign Affairs*, 69:2 (1990), 103–108.
74  A/AC.121/36, 21 March 1989.
75  Australia, Department of Foreign Affairs, *Cambodia, An Australian Peace Proposal: Working Papers Prepared for the Informal Meeting on Cambodia, Jakarta, 26-28 February 1990* (Canberra: Department of Foreign Affairs and Trade, Commonwealth of Australia, 1990).
76  Australia, Department of Foreign Affairs, *Cambodia, An Australian Peace Proposal*.
77  S/RES/688, 5 April 1991; Boutros Boutros-Ghali, 'Introduction', pp. 7–9; de Cuéllar, *Pilgrimage for Peace*, pp. 459–463; Song, *The Political Dynamics*, pp. 69–79.
78  A/SPC/46/Sr.11, 28 October 1991; A/47/253, 4 June 1992, pp. 9–11, 17–18.
79  A/45/572, 5 October 1990; A/SPC/45/Sr.19, 21 November 1990; A/SPC/45/Sr.21, 23 November 1990; A/46/254, 18 June 1991, pp. 6–7; /SPC/46/Sr.12, 29 October 1991.
80  See, for example, the arguments presented by the representatives of the Soviet Union, Bulgaria and Papua New Guinea: A/45/626-S/21869, 12 October 1990, pp. 3–4; A/SPC/45/Sr.19, 21 November 1990, pp. 8–9, 17.
81  A/45/502, 19 September 1990; A/SPC/45/Sr.21, 23 November 1990; A/SPC/46/Sr.12, 29 October 1991.
82  This kind of support was provided by the representatives of Austria, India, Togo and Japan: A/C.5/45/Sr.42, 10 December 1990, pp. 5–6; A/C.5/45/Sr.52, 11 December 1990.
83  A/C.5/45/Sr.40, 5 December 1990, pp. 3–5; A/C.5/45/Sr.52, 11 December 1990, pp. 7–9; A/SPC/46/Sr.12, 29 October 1991, para. 20.
84  A/45/217, 8 May 1990; A/45/330, 12 July 1990, para. 15–16; A/45/493 Add.1, 30 October 1990; A/45/801, 28 November 1990; A/C.5/45/Sr.52, 11 December 1990; A/46/254, 18 June 1991.
85  A/SPC/45/Sr.19, 21 November 1990, p. 9.
86  A/45/582, 10 October 1990; A/C.5/45/Sr.52, 11 December 1990, para. 51; A/SPC/46/Sr.12, 29 October 1991, para. 3.
87  A/44/301, 6 June 1989, pp. 3–4, 10–11; A/44/500, 11 September 1989; A/45/582, 10 October 1990; A/SPC/45/Sr.21, 23 November 1990, p. 16.
88  A/46/254, 18 June 1991, para. 61–70.
89  A/SPC/46/Sr.11, 28 October 1991, para. 26–27.
90  For an example of an estimate of the breakdown of funding between the UN member states, see the funding table in United Nations Transitional Authority in Cambodia (UNTAC): ST/ADM/SER.B/398, June 3, 1993.
91  de Cuéllar, *Pilgrimage for Peace*, p. 461.
92  Goulding, *Peacemonger*, pp. 251–254.

93 *Ibid.*, pp. 245–255.
94 Bush and Scowcroft, *A World Transformed*, pp. 563–564. Also see the realpolitik approach of the American secretary of state at the time, James Baker. He was not interested in the intentions of the Soviets but only in how the USA could maximise its achievements. Baker and Defrank, *The Politics of Diplomacy*, pp. 68–70.

# 3

# Agenda for peacekeeping 1992–93

The positive momentum for execution of peacekeeping operations continued between 1992 and 1993. In 1992, the Security Council resolved to execute four new operations in the former Yugoslavia, Mozambique, Somalia and Cambodia. In 1993, the Council decided to intervene in four new sites: in Georgia (FSU), Haiti, Liberia and Rwanda.

Intensive activity took place in the UN despite the lack of clarity regarding the effectiveness of implementation of the traditional operations with regard to intrastate conflicts. That was one of the foremost challenges in the world order after the Cold War. As mentioned earlier, the main objectives of these operations were to observe or serve as a buffer between national armies. The UN forces were not allowed to use force or intervene in the internal affairs of states.[1] But the operations executed in 1992–93 did not fulfil the conditions of the traditional operations. It was especially difficult to get the sides to sign an agreement in these conflicts, because the violence in these countries was not limited to organised armed forces but sometimes spread throughout the entire society. Due to the multiplicity of factors, the UN states could not agree among themselves about which side to support. Furthermore, the parties were supported by additional, non-governmental, sources. Therefore it was difficult to make decisions about the timing of peacekeeping operations, their goals, the optimal composition of the force involved, the areas for deployment, the mode of action and the timing for ending the activity.[2]

The first part of this chapter reviews the discussions that took place in the UN institutions regarding the goals and principles of success of the operations in the course of 1992 until the first half of 1993. Chapter 2 refuted the research claim that the multidimensional concept of peacekeeping operations was adopted by the UN starting from 1988. This multidimensional paradigm represented political, social, economic and security-related changes in resolving conflicts in contrast to the traditional concept that included only limited goals.[3] This chapter addresses the discussions that took place on the objectives and principles of success of the operations in the context of the new world order, with the goal of determining whether they testify that a conceptual change took place in the worldviews of the organisation's member states regarding the operations. The chapter reviews the developments that took place in the stances of the members of the Security Council, the General Assembly and the UN Secretariat. Reading the protocols of the discussions shows us which countries in the organisation supported the change in the traditional goals and principles of success of the operations, and allows us to examine whether they represented a limited group of Western countries – in accordance with the accepted research argument in this field. Furthermore, we can analyse to what extent the adoption of multidimensional goals contributed to detachment from the traditional goals and principles of peacekeeping operations.

The second part of the chapter is dedicated to the practice of the new multidimensional operations. The main discussion is centred on the development of the three interventions of the organisation in this period: Cambodia, the former Yugoslavia and Somalia. The main argument points to a lack of uniformity in the Security Council resolutions and their implementation in various arenas, and thus also to the different outcomes of these operations. Furthermore, I prove that there was built-in tension between the desire to promote new goals and the tendency to operate according to the traditional principles of operations: international and local agreement, lack of use of force and lack of bias in the work of the forces in the field.

### UN peacekeeping as panacea to intrastate conflicts

Researchers Bellamy, Williams and Griffin (whose studies are reviewed in Chapter 1) argue that Western countries headed by the United States were dominant in the peacekeeping operation discussions and were the ones to promote the new goals as opposed to the traditional ones. The US-led Western states viewed humanitarian catastrophes, human rights violations and civil wars as threats to the maintenance of international peace and security. Therefore, operations needed to be multidimensional in nature, in order to advance such objectives as democracy, economic development and human rights. The accepted argument in these studies is that while Western states headed by the United States infused these new concepts into the discussion of operations in the UN, other, non-Western, states expressed opposition to the new concepts as well as to the new goals.

In order to examine which countries led the introduction of the new operational objectives and which ones opposed them in 1992 and 1993, I first refer to the historic January 1992 Security Council session attended by heads of state, and then to the discussion held afterwards dealing with objectives and success principles of the operations in the new world order context.[4] Following the discussion, Boutros-Ghali (who began his position as Secretary-General that same month) published a report he called the 'Agenda for Peace'. In this document, he proposed a comprehensive solution to the main threat to world peace in the guise of intrastate conflicts by means of a combination of techniques. After I discuss Boutros-Ghali's proposal, I address the General Assembly and Security Council's responses to his report until mid-1993. We can say that in general, the Secretary-General's initiative was basically supported by most of the UN delegations. This support served to create the impression among the Secretariat staff, diplomats, researchers and the media that the multidimensional operations deployed during that period represented a new concept that differed from the traditional one.

There was a pressing need to conduct a discussion on the security-related ramifications of the new world order connected to the end of the Cold War and the break-up of the Soviet Union. This was expressed in the new concepts that were raised regarding the peacekeeping operations from 1988 to 1991, the deployment of ten new operations in the same years, and the enforcement operation in Iraq. In an attempt to deal with the challenges of the new world order, the United Kingdom took the initiative to convene a special Security Council meeting (in 1991) attended by heads of state, for the first time in the history of the UN. Aside from the precedent caused by the very nature of the forum, it was unique in that it raised discussion regarding the character of the operations for the first time. Although the Council had resolved to deploy ten operations between 1988 and 1991, it had not discussed the concept behind these operations.[5]

The members of the Security Council expressed their willingness to cope with the threats facing the new world order through the adoption of systematic methods within the UN. This agreement held great symbolic value because, for many years, the Security Council had been rife with dissent and conflict between the political blocs during the Cold War. In anticipation of the meeting, countries and regional organisations sent detailed letters to the Security Council (following the Council's official request to do so), presenting their stances vis-à-vis the new world order and their expectations from the Security Council on this issue.[6]

I focus on two subjects in this context: the view of the countries towards the new world order, and the techniques employed to maintain international peace and security in that new world order.

Most of the speakers in the special Security Council session attended by heads of state emphasised that a historic change had taken place in the wake of the termination of the Cold War and the globalisation process. They felt that the state remained the main player in the world order, while historic developments were directed towards 'new threats'. The speakers enumerated the many threats, including: intrastate poverty, international terror, environmental devastation, human rights violations, lack of democratic regime; ethnic, national and religion-based intrastate conflicts, disintegration of state powers and the constantly rising numbers of refugees. These problems not only pose threats of war between countries but also threaten international peace and security.[7] Although many of these issues were discussed in the course of the Cold War, their importance in the new period lies in their combination with intrastate conflicts and the emphasis on the UN's obligation to deal with these challenges.

During the discourse on the new threats to the world order, many of the speakers discussed the techniques that could be used to deal with threats to the maintenance of international peace and security. The question was asked: Could the techniques defined in Chapters 6 and 7 (of the UN Charter), which were intended to be applied only to interstate threats – techniques such as peacemaking, enforcement and peacekeeping operations – be applied to intrastate threats as well?

The concluding statement of the Security Council session of 1992 characterised the international atmosphere of the era that approved of combining objectives: 'The absence of war and military conflicts amongst States does not in itself ensure international peace and security. The non-military sources of instability in the economic, social, humanitarian and ecological fields have become threats to peace and security.'[8] In order to address the updated view of threats to the world order, the Secretary-General was asked to prepare a comprehensive report by 1 July 1992, recommending how to transform the new techniques – which were called 'preventive diplomacy', 'peacemaking' and 'peacekeeping' – into more effective tools.[9]

On 17 June 1992, UN Secretary-General Boutros-Ghali published a report under the heading, 'An Agenda for Peace'.[10] This document was to become the focus of discussions in the UN on the maintenance of international peace and security in the following two and a half years. The report still represents one of the basic cornerstones in understanding the role played by peacekeeping operations in the world order after the Cold War.[11]

Boutros-Ghali wanted the document to serve the Security Council but also to firmly anchor the new role of the UN Secretary-General as a political leader, a UN leader, and a statesman with great international influence. Part of Boutros-Ghali's view regarding his position was based on the fact that this was the first time that the Security Council had turned to the UN Secretariat with a request to address security-related issues, which had always been under the sole authority of the Council. Thus the new Secretary-General laboured for many months over numerous drafts of his response, in order to produce a document worthy for the occasion.[12]

At the centre of Boutros-Ghali's polished, well-written Agenda for Peace commentary is the argument that the state is the very cornerstone for the maintenance of peace and security in the world. In light of the changes taking place in the world as a result of globalisation, cooperation in the Security Council in the post-Cold War era no longer served as a guarantee for maintenance of international peace and security. Boutros-Ghali viewed the emergence of supra-national organisations such as the EU and ASEAN as encouraging cooperation between countries and moderating ultra-nationalistic movements. By contrast, intrastate entities undermine these goals. Thus he viewed newly emerging nationalistic movements calling for independent sovereignty on the basis of ethnic, religious, social, cultural and linguistic differences as threats to the cohesiveness of the state, and detrimental to the maintenance of peace. He also enumerated many additional threats, such as the increase in debt of developing nations, poverty, diseases, famine, oppression, and the rise in the numbers of refugees, displaced persons and mass migrations of tens of millions of human beings.

Boutros-Ghali felt that maintaining a world order comprising countries at peace with one another, and resolving intrastate hazards that threaten this order, would strengthen what he viewed as the positive elements of globalisation. Therefore he felt that economic development, maintenance of human rights and democratisation at the state as well as international level were crucial goals.[13]

Boutros-Ghali's ideas and worldview reflected those of the Soviet Union and the veteran contributors to, and supporters of, the peacekeeping operations (at the end of the 1980s). These concepts were also clearly evident in the Security Council discussions of January 1992.

As part of his approach of adopting positive goals to cope with the new threats to the world order, Boutros-Ghali enumerated three techniques mentioned above – preventive diplomacy, peacemaking and peacekeeping – and added a fourth: post-conflict peacebuilding, henceforth peacebuilding. He viewed these techniques as a kind of tool-box available to the UN to deal with threats to the maintenance of international peace and security. Ostensibly, the report suggests choosing the appropriate technique based on the point at which the UN became involved in the conflict: before the conflict – preventive diplomacy, during the conflict – peacekeeping as well as peacemaking techniques, and after the conflict – economic aid and civil reforms. But in practice, the techniques that Boutros-Ghali recommended were meant to be integrated simultaneously as the answer to the 'new threats' to maintenance of international peace and security. At the top of the list of techniques that he proposed were the peacekeeping operations that could be executed in order to advance the goals set before, during or after the conflict.[14]

The first technique appearing in the Agenda for Peace is preventive diplomacy – diplomatic activity that mediates between hostile sides via negotiation, even before active conflict erupts between them. Boutros-Ghali proposed adding additional objectives to this technique. First, he proposed the activation of an extensive, active apparatus of fact finding, accompanied by early-warning apparatuses (nuclear, ecological, large population movements, etc.). Another preventive means he proposed was the early deployment of peacekeeping forces in every country in the world characterised by intrastate tension or tension between the country and its neighbours. In addition, he emphasised the importance of humanitarian aid in these tense situations.[15]

The second technique the report addressed was peacemaking. The foundation of this technique is a diplomatic process adopted after the eruption of active, violent conflict. It is intended to bring the conflicted sides to the negotiating table and encourage them to reach a political arrangement. While Chapter 6 of the Charter addresses this technique at length, Boutros-Ghali discussed and significantly enlarged on the peacemaking goals in his report, and did the same to the preventive diplomacy technique. The Secretary-General insisted that, in the new reality, clear preference should be given to the force-technique that imposes a specific arrangement (which he called peace enforcement) over those diplomatic techniques emphasising mediation and non-intervention. This approach is based on the assumption that an imposed political arrangement is preferable to continuation of the conflict. He emphasised the importance of imposing sanctions as a coercive measure on the conflicted sides. Finally, he tied the peacemaking technique to the use of military power to enforce a settlement according to Chapter 7 Article 42 of the UN Charter. Thus, in effect, he tied the principles of Chapter 6 dealing with peaceful resolution of conflict with the principles of Chapter 7 dealing with enforcement. He felt that Article 43 (part of Chapter 7) should be implemented. This article requires states to allocate sufficient military forces to the UN on a permanent basis in order to be able to deal with any fighting force in the world, below the level of a large regular army armed with heavy weapons.[16]

These action proposals detailed in the report borrow the diplomacy principles of the peacekeeping operation technique (in other words, demanding ongoing consent from all the sides) and transfer them to the sphere of enforcement methods, in which force is used to end conflicts.

But it seems that with regard to peacekeeping operations, there was no change. The Secretary-General reiterated some of the principles that are supposed to lead to success, as detailed in the book *The Blue Helmets: A Review of UN Peacekeeping* from 1985. These principles for peacekeeping operations include: a clear, feasible mandate; cooperation between the conflicted parties in deployment of the operation; ongoing support of the Security Council; willingness of the member states to allocate soldiers, policemen and civilians, including experts; effective management of the operation in the New York UN headquarters and on site; and appropriate logistic and financial aid. Regarding the allocation of military forces to the operations, the report noted the following problems: the poor response of the member states to Secretariat requests in 1990; a paucity of logistical units; a glaring dearth of civilian staff to serve as human rights monitors, election officials, refugee experts, humanitarian assistance providers and police experts.[17] Ostensibly, the basic principles underlying peacekeeping operations in the Secretary-General's report of 1992 seem to be identical to those of the 1985 report. However, the difference is that in the new report, the Secretary-General ignores two basic traditional-concept principles that address the political sensitivity of the operations: the existence of an agreement between the conflicted parties before execution of the peacekeeping operation, and the obligation for all the conflicted parties to agree to the operation. In addition, one issue remained open to interpretation: the practice of executing peacekeeping operations based on the traditional concept simultaneously with the practices of preventive diplomacy, peacemaking and peacebuilding, even at the time of active conflict. How do the new proposals contribute to creating peace? When must they be executed? When must they be halted? How many forces are necessary for these new operations?

After meticulously describing his vision regarding the preventive diplomacy technique and peacekeeping operations, Boutros-Ghali then described a new technique he calls 'peacebuilding'. While the preventive diplomacy technique was intended to prevent escalation and disintegration, the peacebuilding technique was intended to strengthen the institutions of the state and encourage the conflicted sides to carry out the peace agreement at the end of the conflict. To these ends, the Secretary-General proposed the activation of a variety of methods such as disarmament, destroying weapons, returning order to a society torn apart by wars, repatriation of refugees, providing training and consultation to security forces, supervising elections, advancing human rights protection efforts, reforming or strengthening government institutions and advancing formal and informal political processes to strengthen the trust and confidence of the population and its leadership in peace. Boutros-Ghali placed special emphasis on the need to promote democratisation of the society, from the perspective that 'societal peace' is no less important than political peace and strategic peace, and that principles of good governance on the national and international levels must also be advanced. Simultaneously, Boutros-Ghali recommended that the UN encourage economic development in the spheres of agriculture, transportation, water, electricity, and regulatory development by means of allowing for free passage between countries. He wrote about the importance of cultural bridging via programmes for cultural and societal development, youth exchange programmes and educational programmes encouraging rapprochement among teenagers from different sectors of the population.[18]

The peacebuilding technique, as first described in the Agenda for Peace, expressed the Secretary-General's worldview. Boutros-Ghali believed that it was crucial to integrate and combine all the various means and entities – intrastate, nation state, international and non-state – that influence the political arrangement within a country. According to Boutros-Ghali, the Charter's Chapter 6 tools of preventive diplomacy and peacemaking given to the international community were not sufficient. He felt that peacekeeping operations should be executed in parallel to these techniques. Furthermore, the operations should include the possibility of use of force (according to Chapter 7 of the Charter), in order to impose a political settlement to end a conflict. Finally, Boutros-Ghali even called for adding goals designed to cause political, economic, social and security-related changes within countries.

When the Security Council requested that UN Secretary-General Boutros-Ghali recommend how to improve the effectiveness of the traditional techniques at their disposal, the member states did not anticipate a report with so many political and strategic ramifications as were in the report that was finally submitted by the Secretary-General. However, we must remember that they themselves, as well as many other delegations in the UN, had already expressed their reservations regarding the traditional concept of the operations in various discussions held on this topic and on other related topics, such as the new world order and the new threats, and the role of the traditional techniques in the world order. These reservations (on the traditional concept) were also expressed in their special emphasis on the contribution of peacekeeping operations to ending conflicts, and in their decision to execute new, multifunctional, operations in Cambodia, the former Yugoslavia and Somalia from the end of 1991 and throughout 1992.

As a result of the discussions in the Council and the Secretary-General's Agenda for Peace, the definition of 'threats to the maintenance of international peace and security' was enlarged to include intrastate conflicts. The solution found in the UN for the growing number of threats was multifunctional peacekeeping operations that combined the following four techniques mentioned in the Agenda for Peace: preventive diplomacy, peacemaking, peacekeeping operations and peacebuilding.

According to this new way of thinking, one might assume that every time a problem developed on the globe, irrespective of its importance or scope, the UN would rush to send a multifunctional operation there to promote goals such as humanitarian assistance, economic development, human rights and 'good governance' as well as ending the conflict. Thus Boutros-Ghali opened a window to disproportionate action while violating the accepted operational principles of the organisation from the days of the Cold War.

The main influence of Boutros-Ghali's Agenda for Peace was in dictating the UN's internal diplomatic discourse. In effect, the strong impact of the report testifies to the importance and power of the Secretariat within the UN. The main failure of the report was that it did not address the effects of international politics and existing conflicts of interest between the various UN organs; and these, as mentioned above, can have a decisive effect on the status of peace.[19]

Thus the definition of 'threats' to maintenance of international peace and security expanded in the time period between January and June of 1992 to include intrastate conflict. In accordance with this new orientation, the goals of peacekeeping operations enlarged from traditional objectives to multidimensional ones. The question is, how did the delegations of the UN member states relate to these changes? Did only the Western states support the Agenda for Peace, as many researchers claim, or was the report an expression of a consensus in the organisation regarding the functions of the operations in the world order after the Cold War? In order to answer these questions, we must first examine the reactions elicited by the Agenda for Peace report in the General Assembly and then compare them with the responses in the Security Council.

Scrutiny of the Assembly's work regarding peacekeeping operations shows us that the Secretary-General's concepts did not arise in a vacuum but were part and parcel of an active diplomatic discussion on the subject within the organisation. Only a few days before publication of the Secretary-General's report, the members of the UN SCPKO agreed that these operations were 'the most appropriate response the international community could offer for peaceful resolution of conflicts which the parties were unable to resolve by themselves'.[20] The goal of operations was, accordingly, to dissipate tension between the conflicted factions, to stabilise conflicts and get the parties to sign a peace agreement. The UN delegations viewed the broadening of the tasks of the missions as an evolutionary developmental stage of the operations. For them 'the concept of peace-keeping was still at an evolving stage and needed persistent attention and careful consideration by all Member States so as to adapt to the phenomenal changes that had taken place in the world in the past few years.'[21]

Publication of the report raised the issue of whether the UN members agreed with the goals and principles of success of the peacekeeping operations – whether traditional or multidimensional. In August 1992, the SCPKO held a special meeting to discuss the report. The various delegations expressed support in principle for the execution of multidimensional operations in intrastate conflicts. Nevertheless, reservations were expressed regarding each of the techniques used in the multidimensional operations such as, for example, reservations regarding the ability to decide when a specific situation mandates a preventive deployment of peacekeeping forces, and whether the deployment must be performed even without the agreement of one of the parties. In the latter case, this would be detrimental to the concept of UN neutrality. Some of the delegations argued that the organisation was not capable of coping with the execution of such demanding techniques as those outlined in the report, and they viewed the Secretary-General's activism with disfavour. Finally, arguments were heard that some of the activities outlined in the report deviated from accepted principles of peacekeeping operations that had been consolidated during the Cold War.

Regarding the execution of multidimensional operations during an actual conflict, most of the delegations emphasised the diplomatic aspects of the peacemaking technique. There were delegations among the veteran, contributor countries who argued that, in order for the organisation to carry out operations effectively, it must have armed forces at its disposal at all times. Most of the delegations were more moderate in their approach, however. While most expressed overall support for the concepts raised in the Agenda for Peace, voices were heard criticising the development of the traditional peacekeeping operation concept as negating the principle of obtaining agreement of the conflicted parties, and of undermining the sovereignty of the state in the name of globalisation. The inclusion of enforcement within peacekeeping operations also raised doubts, mainly due to the concern that enforcement could violate the neutrality principle of the international force, discourage states from allocating forces for fighting purposes, and impinge on the ability of the Secretariat to manage operations of this large magnitude.[22]

Yet despite the doubts and differences of opinion among the member countries, the General Assembly adopted a resolution on 14 December 1992 supporting the development of the goals and principles of success of the operations.[23] After the SCPKO submitted its recommendations, discussions were held in the Special Political Committee, the UN organ that was responsible at the time for all aspects of peacekeeping operations. Most of the delegations supported the expansion of goals and the changing of the success principles of the peacekeeping operations, while integrating techniques of preventive diplomacy, peacemaking and peacebuilding. By relying on this basic approach, the focus of the discussion was on the methods through which the UN could manage and organise the peacekeeping operations when it deployed new, multidimensional operations. Support for these resolutions crossed traditional alliances and included countries from the entire world. We find that the positions of most East European countries were similar to those of West European states. Delegations from countries that are usually categorised as 'developing countries' or 'third-world countries' (that usually oppose the opinions of developed countries), such as Algeria, Bangladesh, Egypt, Malaysia, Senegal and Pakistan, also supported the resolutions.[24] Even the NAM, which disagreed with the policies of Western countries on many issues, released a joint statement supporting the advancement of the operations.[25] By contrast, the representative of Fiji, a veteran contributor state to peacekeeping operations, raised numerous doubts regarding the techniques of preventive diplomacy or peace enforcement, with the argument that they deviate from the traditional concept of the operations. Representatives from other states made similar statements; the most prominent of them, the Cuban representative, even tried to turn the clock back on the new operations technique and emphasised that the Agenda for Peace was only a proposal for discussion and should not be viewed as a work plan.[26] The SCPKO decided to establish an open work group in the General Assembly that would seek agreement of the various delegations on the definitions of terms that were raised in the Agenda for Peace report.[27]

As mentioned earlier, we see (from the discussions of the General Assembly on the goals and principles of success of the operations in 1992 and the beginning of 1993) that support for changing the goals of operations from traditional to multidimensional was given not only by Western states. In fact, most of the General Assembly members supported the adoption of the multidimensional goals. All the members that participated in the discussion raised questions mainly with regard to managerial and organisational problems. But the focus on these issues during the discussion served to hide a more fundamental problem: that the various delegations were not able to come to an agreement regarding the list of new objectives of these multidimensional operations or the principles for their success in the new world order. Most countries had reservations on issues such as: When is a situation defined as a conflict that threatens international peace and security? Who makes this determination? What technique is appropriate for which situation? How should the various objectives that arose in the course of the Agenda for Peace discussion be integrated into the operations?

The third organ that discussed the goals and principles of success of the operations was the Security Council. As already mentioned, it was during the Security Council's session in January 1992 that the need arose to discuss the contribution of operations to the world order after the Cold War. Here, too, the question was asked: To what extent did the Western countries exploit their relative advantage in the Council to promote multidimensional objectives for operations?

The adoption of the Agenda for Peace with its broadened principles and definitions, gave the Council numerous tools with which to deal with a gamut of situations in the world. They were no longer limited to dealing with situations threatening the maintenance of international peace and security according to the UN Charter alone. Due to the limited number of members in the Council and the great influence of the five permanent members (the United States, the United Kingdom, China, France and Russia), it was easier for the Council members to identify the main stances of each of the Council members regarding each issue, and to forge an agreement.[28] Therefore, it is understandable that the Agenda for Peace was accepted more favourably in the Security Council than in the General Assembly.

Two weeks after publication of the report, the Security Council called on the General Assembly to adopt the recommendations of the Secretary-General.[29] Four permanent members of the Council – the United States, the United Kingdom, France and Russia – addressed the following factors in their statement: they called for the execution of large, complex and multidimensional operations in accordance with Boutros-Ghali's definition but without discussing the value and necessity of the new operations for maintenance of international peace and security on the one hand, and for ending intrastate conflicts on the other.[30] By contrast, the Chinese government expressed reservations regarding the Agenda for Peace report – the only one of the five permanent Security Council members to do so. The Chinese representatives in the Security Council and General Assembly emphasised that the traditional concept of the operations must not be ignored because that concept had been developed over an extended period of time, and conclusions had been drawn based on experience. Therefore (according to the Chinese representatives), the execution of operations should be adapted to the principles of the Charter and result from requests on the part of the conflicted parties, so that both sides would cooperate fully throughout the entire operation. Similarly (they argued) the operation must respect the sovereignty of the countries in which it was deployed, and that force should only be used for self-defence.[31] In other words, the Chinese representatives favoured the tried-and-tested traditional operations concept over the newer, multidimensional one.

Nevertheless, China focused on the situation in China and did not intervene in the actions of other members of the Security Council; this had long been the traditional approach of the Chinese government regarding international peace and security.[32]

Thus, for about a year, the Council acted to expand the goals and principles of success of the peacekeeping operations, without any real opposition. At the end of September 1992, the representatives of the five permanent members of the Security Council met with the UN Secretary-General and emerged with a statement regarding certain conflicts that were taking place in the world at the time, supporting the recommendations included in the Agenda for Peace report.[33] On 29 October, the Security Council declared its intention to concentrate its efforts on recruiting the military and civil assistance that the UN member states were supposed to provide, so that the organisation would be able to deploy the operations in accordance with the proposals of the Secretary-General.[34] Two months later, the Council set up a special work group to discuss assistance to countries harmed by sanctions, in accordance with Chapter 7 of the Charter.[35] As part of the positive trend, the Security Council president announced that the Council approved the Agenda for Peace recommendations regarding fact-finding missions and early deployment as an effective tool in conflict limitation. To strengthen their position, they cited examples of early deployment in former territories of the Soviet Union: Moldova, Nagorno-Karabakh, Georgia, Uzbekistan and Tajikistan.[36]

During the first half of 1993, the Security Council issued a series of statements regarding multidimensional peacekeeping operations while renouncing the accepted principles of success of the traditional operations. The Security Council agreed with the approach of the Secretary-General regarding the connection between humanitarian aid, peacemaking, peacekeeping and peacebuilding, and called on him to integrate the work of the new departments he had established in the Secretariat: the Department of Political Affairs (DPA), Department of Humanitarian Affairs (DHA), and the DPKO. In addition, it was agreed in the Council that any political goals it would set for operations would be subject to change at their discretion in light of unfolding events. In 'exceptional cases', it committed itself to consider an operation without receiving agreement of the conflicted sides in advance and even threatened to take action against local factions that would not carry out its decisions. In order to elucidate the point, it was emphasised that it reserved the right to authorise UN personnel to use force in order to carry out its mandate. (This is in contradistinction to the usual principles of traditional peacekeeping operations, in which use of force is forbidden.) Justification for this was based on the conditions that the operation would contribute to the political process of peacemaking, and that it would not continue indefinitely.[37]

From this stage onwards, all Security Council activities were invested in getting international support from states and regional organisations, as well as recruiting the human and material resources needed to fulfil its ambitious objectives. This involved the constant reinforcement of military and police forces, civilian specialists and logistical aid, as well as humanitarian aid. The Council even expressed its disapproval that the transfer of humanitarian aid in the territories of Iraq, Somalia and the former Yugoslavia was disrupted, so that the aid was not distributed equitably. We see from the Council's subsequent statement that providing humanitarian aid was perceived as a stage leading to development of the society and the country, simultaneously with peacemaking and peacekeeping operations, until the final stage of peacebuilding.[38]

The view that humanitarian aid and development are directly connected to the maintenance of international peace and security was promoted in the UN by two entities: the Secretariat members in the briefings they conducted for government representatives, and the representatives of international organisations such as the ICRC.[39] The prevailing assumption in the Security Council was that any type of threat to the new world order justified intervention. 'On the one hand, humanitarian emergencies may constitute threats to international peace and security or aggravate existing threats; on the other hand, disturbances of the peace may give rise to humanitarian crises.'[40]

As said earlier, the Security Council members (which were mainly Western) did not issue statements opposing the developments. The one exception was China, whose representatives in the Assembly and the Council repeated that all intervention resolutions reflected the political interests of the states that voted for those resolutions, and therefore they felt it important to preserve the traditional concept. Yet even China's representatives did not oppose the joint statements calling for increasing the contributions of UN members to operations initiated by the Council, or to the need to address humanitarian, economic and other factors with regard to the maintenance of international peace and security in the last decade of the twentieth century.

The discussions held in the UN from 1992 to the beginning of 1993 on issues connected to the goals and principles of success of the operations, testify to significant changes that took place in the organisation regarding the prevailing view of peacekeeping operations and techniques used to implement them. According to the researchers in the field, two opposing alliances discussed this issue in the UN: the Western states and the developing states.[41] By contrast, I demonstrate that the trend of enlarging the goals of the operations won the support of most of the organisation's countries in the course of 1992, including that of the developing states. Finally, I show how the adoption of the multidimensional goals – intended to influence political, social, economic and security factors – led to detachment from the traditional goals and principles of peacekeeping operations.

In the course of 1992, most of the countries adopted the view that, due to the processes of globalisation affecting the entire world, intrastate conflicts now represented the main threat to international peace and security. The proposal of Secretary-General Boutros-Ghali in June 1992, to deploy multidimensional operations during intrastate conflicts, promised that the operations would not only terminate the conflicts but also remove the factors that led to the conflict. To this end, the operations were supposed to include an assortment of techniques, such as peacemaking and peacekeeping operations with enforcement powers that aimed for economic development. In contrast to the accepted assertions in the research on the operations, the Secretary-General's proposal won support in principle from most of the organisation's countries, and not only from the Western ones. Simultaneously, both Western and developing states began to have qualms regarding the Secretary-General's initiative. These reservations concerned the following: the setting of priorities among all the goals; determining the ideal time for execution of the multidimensional operation; examination of possible contradictions between the success principles of the multidimensional operations and those of the traditional ones. But despite these qualms, overall support reigned in the UN for the attempt to use operations as a means of intrastate conflict resolution. This support existed at least until the summer months of 1993.

## The use of peacekeeping to tame intrastate conflicts

With the change in the international balance of power brought on by the conclusion of the Cold War came a change in the internal balance of power within the Security Council. The East European countries, headed by the Soviet Union (and later by its successor, Russia) began to adopt policy lines that were similar (if not identical) to those of the Western states. The ramifications for the work of the Security Council were immediate. The Council began to meet more often and even adopted numerous resolutions, including the execution of peacekeeping operations and an enforcement operation against Iraq. These acts usually won broad support in the organisation. The international consensus that existed in the UN with regard to the objectives and principles of success of multidimensional operations may explain the great frequency with which peacekeeping operations were executed in intrastate conflicts. From April 1991 to October 1993, the Security Council resolved to execute fifteen operations in ten different sites.[42]

This consensus was negatively exploited by the delegations of the Security Council members and especially the five permanent Council members, who started to meet for private, informal discussions behind closed doors as a matter of course. They argued that the end of the Cold War allowed the Security Council to operate more effectively. This system allowed the Council to evade external pressures from representatives of other UN member states, to arrive at compromises quickly and reach decisions swiftly. The system also cleared the way for internal pressures within the Council. The ones to benefit from this situation were mainly the five permanent members of the Council and especially the United States, the United Kingdom and France, who took advantage of their military and economic superiority and control of international press to influence world opinion. As a result of this, most of the world's representatives had no influence over the resolutions adopted in the Security Council that supposedly embodied the will of the majority, but in fact operated like an oligarchy.[43] This system allowed the Council to adopt 167 resolutions in 1992–93.

Despite the agreement among the Council members, it is important to note that most of the new operations were executed according to the traditional concept, even in cases where additional goals were added. Thus the operations involved only about a thousand soldiers or less. In this period, aside from the three multidimensional operations reviewed in this study, another three operations were executed: in Haiti, Mozambique and Rwanda. In these latter operations, more than a thousand soldiers were involved and they involved traditional objectives together with goals designed to promote democratic elections. While the Mozambique operation is generally viewed as an outstanding success,[44] Rwanda was not; researchers blame the UN for not taking action to avert the genocide of the Tutsi nation by the Hutus.[45] The Haiti operation was also not considered a success.[46] Although most of the operations in this time period operated according to traditional principles with a few additional goals, most of the discussions focused mainly on the multidimensional, complex, large and expensive operations executed at that time, in Cambodia, Somalia and the former Yugoslavia.

Towards the beginning of 1992, most of the discussions in the organisation focused on the UN peacekeeping operations in Cambodia (UNAMIC, UNTAC). These operations were deployed in October 1991 and concluded in September 1993. Since discussions in the organisation at the time focused on the goals and principles of success of these operations, it would be reasonable to assume that these principles would be implemented in the operations taking place at the time. At the height of the UN intervention in Cambodia, the multinational forces numbered more than twenty thousand individuals. This number included the soldiers, civilian policemen and election observers who were deployed throughout most of the country's territory. When the Security Council decided to stop this operation in September 1993, it was viewed by many in the UN as a model of success.

In the course of 1992, the operations in the former Yugoslavia and Somalia began to attract most of the attention in discussions of peacekeeping operations. On 19 April 1993 the new USG for Peacekeeping Kofi Annan argued before the SCPKO that the operations deviated from their traditional boundaries in three instances, numerically as well as in terms of their goals. First, in Somalia and Bosnia, where the operations were given the mandate of providing humanitarian assistance. Second, in Somalia there was another breakthrough when the UN was given a mandate (based on the Charter's Chapter 7) for enforcing the resolution of the Security Council. Finally, a preventive deployment operation was begun in Macedonia (one of the former Yugoslavian states) whose goal was – for the first time in history – to avert a spillover of the conflict from the former Yugoslavian territory towards Macedonia.[47]

In direct proportion to the increasing involvement of the Security Council in numerous countries of the world (starting from 1991), came an associated increase in demands for contributions of manpower, funding and equipment from the world's countries. This increase was especially felt in the course of 1992 when the Security Council decided to execute large, complex and multidimensional operations in Cambodia, the former Yugoslavia and Somalia. Justification for these operations was based on the new concept of multidimensional peacekeeping operations, according to which these operations neutralise 'new threats' to the maintenance of international peace and security, and mainly help end conflicts. The rest of the chapter examines how the goals were defined for these three large, complex operations that, at their time, represented the emergence of a new world order; how these operations were managed and to what extent they received the necessary resources to achieve the goals assigned to them.

## Cambodia: From transitional to legitimisation peacekeeping

The international efforts to mediate between the conflicted sides in Cambodia at the end of the 1980s created the conditions for the execution of an unprecedented peacekeeping operation in Cambodia. The Paris Agreements that were signed in October 1991 by the four Cambodian factions – KPCP, DK, FUNCINPEC and KPNLF – bestowed extensive powers on Yasushi Akashi, SRSG; Akashi directed UNTAC. The operation was supposed to prepare the ground for conducting democratic elections in a country with a harsh history of human rights violations and genocide. Thus, the operation was to ensure that the state's apparatuses and system would be managed properly and cease serving as a tool of the KPCP. Meanwhile, the country's name was changed to the State of Cambodia (SOC) and the KPCP changed its name to the Cambodian People's Party (CPP) during the intervention; the CPP controlled 90 per cent of the country. Therefore, the operation was charged with the goals of promoting human rights and conducting democratic elections. The forces were also charged with the following tasks: supervising the disarmament and demobilisation of 70 per cent of the forces of the rival factions spread out over Cambodia; assisting the civilian police; resettling about 360,000 refugees; and helping the Cambodian factions channel the contributions received from the international community to develop the country in order to encourage political, social and economic stability.

Out of the gamut of UN objectives in Cambodia, the UN Secretariat understood back in February 1992 that 'the election is the focal point of the comprehensive settlement. The manner in which the elections are conducted would be, and must be seen to be, absolutely impartial.'[40] The main question was, to what extent would the Security Council decide to make changes if there were no appropriate conditions for conducting democratic elections, and whether there would be any point continuing the mission at the conclusion of the elections even if other goals of the operation were achieved only in part.[49]

The discussion on the security aspect focused on two problems that were at the heart of the conflict and dissension between the rival Cambodian sides throughout the 1980s, problems that also assumed a central place in the Paris Agreements. One problem was how to ensure that the warring parties, estimated at about two hundred thousand regular fighters and about another quarter of a million militia fighters, would honour the Paris Agreements and disarm, allowing for the demobilisation of 70 per cent of their fighting forces. The second problem was how to create secure conditions in Cambodia for the holding of democratic elections. As long as UN personnel and the international community refused to adopt enforcement methods, the answer to the question depended on the extent of cooperation of the rival parties and mainly of the two strongest factions, the Khmer Rouge and the CPP. This approach – dependence on voluntary cooperation of the warring factions – was based on the traditional principles of peacekeeping operations. In order to ensure a solution to the two security problems, it was decided to launch a multinational force of about sixteen thousand soldiers and about three thousand five hundred civilian policemen. As of the time period under discussion, such a large regular force had been launched under UN authority only once before, in the early 1960s in the Congo, and had almost caused the collapse of the organisation.[50]

The disarmament process dissolved in May 1992 after the Khmer Rouge refused to concentrate their soldiers in bases, under the pretext that the UN was not weakening CPP control of governmental institutions; in effect, the Khmer Rouge faction abandoned the diplomatic process. The other three factions continued the process only symbolically. In November, Boutros-Ghali was forced to concede that the gathering of the soldiers in the bases had failed. At that same time, battles renewed between the Khmer Rouge and CPP forces in the north-west of the country. Even direr were the incidents in which UN soldiers were attacked by Khmer Rouge fighters. Instead of adopting tools for 'peace enforcement' in the spirit of the discussions that were taking place in the UN at that very time, the Security Council and regional countries supported patient diplomatic mediation between the parties – mediation that did not bear fruit. It was evident that the Secretary-General adopted this route because no country supported an enforcement action:

> I am aware of the fact that there have been discussions on whether the Security Council should adopt a different approach and decide on specific measures to get PDK [DK/Khmer Rouge] to honour its commitments. The feasibility of such measures would depend critically on the full cooperation of neighboring countries and other Member States.'[51]

The main aggressive act that the Security Council agreed to was the imposition of economic sanctions on the Khmer Rouge on 30 November 1992.[52] When Major General Michel Loridon (France), deputy commander of UNTAC, publicly supported the adoption of military action against the Khmer Rouge, he was fired from his post in January 1993.[53]

In addition to the task of disarming the Cambodian factions, UN forces were required to supervise and train the civil police (internal security). After the Khmer Rouge abandoned the diplomatic process, and since the other two factions had only a few hundred policemen, the UN force concentrated on forty-seven thousand CPP policemen. Although the UN forces were successful in upgrading the effectiveness of the local police in coping with civilian crimes, they were far less effective in dealing with political and ethnic-based crimes in the Phnom Penh area throughout the entire operation. Most of the politically based assaults were initiated by CPP activists against political representatives of competing parties such as FUNCINPEC and KPNLF. The situation improved only in the course of 1993 when the Security Council authorised certain changes, at the recommendations of the head of the UNTAC mission, SRSG Yasushi Akashi, and Lieutenant General John Sanderson, Commander of UNTAC forces. The Security Council gave authorisation to change the role of UN soldiers in Cambodia, to provide protection for the election teams that circulated throughout the country and to voting centres and election gatherings. Meanwhile, Khmer Rouge fighters perpetrated attacks against the country's Vietnamese minority. Despite protests of the Vietnamese government, the UN was helpless and did not provide protection to this minority. As a result, about twenty thousand Vietnamese fled the country in fear of their lives.

In contrast to its marginal achievements in the security realm, the UN's treatment of the refugee problem in Cambodia is considered one of the biggest successes of the organisation; about 360,000 refugees returned to Cambodia within nine months. The return of refugees usually implies that circumstances have changed for the better, allowing them to take part in the political process from which they had been previously excluded. And this, in turn, implies improvement in peacemaking and stability. In the Cambodian case, the UNHCR assumed that these refugees would settle on agricultural land that they would be given (since most earned their livelihood in agriculture), would take part in the elections and thus become integrated into Cambodian society as rank and file citizens.[54] In April 1993, the UNHCR representatives announced that they had completed the process of repatriating refugees to Cambodia, added them to the list of electors and closed all the refugee camps under their supervision.[55]

Most studies support the official stance of the UN that views the treatment of the Cambodian refugees as a success. But a deeper examination reveals that the organisation succeeded in removing the entire issue from the international agenda. About 88 per cent of the refugees agreed to accept financial compensation, and the organisation did not monitor the absorption of the refugees into Cambodian society after UN personnel left the country.[56] Similarly, the organisation did not protest or object when the Vietnamese fled the country in fear of the Khmer Rouge. This stance dovetailed with the interests of other countries. For example, most of the Cambodian refugees settled in Thailand, since that country shared a border with Cambodia, thus the Thai government pressured the UN to repatriate the refugees in Cambodia. It even threatened to expel them back to Cambodia without waiting for implementation of the agreement.[57] When warfare in Cambodia in the 1990s led to a new wave of refugees, Thai military forces prevented refugees from entering their country, in effect expelling them back to the war zone.[58] Other countries refused to absorb them as well and put pressure on the composers of the Paris Agreements to clearly delineate that the solution to the refugee problem must not come at the expense of other countries.[59]

The issue of economic development was also included in the UN agenda in Cambodia. The envoy of the UNHCR to Cambodia, Sergio Viera de Mello, hit the nail on the head when he said, 'There will be no peace without development, no development without peace.'[60] UN activities included organising international conventions for raising millions of dollars to invest in Cambodia, when the world's states committed to donate a lump sum of 880 million dollars for development efforts during the time of the operation.[61] In addition, the International Committee on the Reconstruction of Cambodia (ICORC) was founded; its role was to advise the Cambodian government about ways to integrate the country into the world market economy. All the international development organs were supposed to work together with the Supreme National Council (SNC), but instead the latter only served to rubber-stamp decisions made by the Cambodians regarding dozens of projects.[62] This process continued until the conclusion of the mandate of the Transitional Authority. Afterwards, the powers for conducting negotiations with the ICORC were transferred to the Cambodian government.

Simultaneously with approving projects, Transitional Authority engineering units from Japan, China, Poland, France and Thailand operated on the territory to improve Cambodia's infrastructure, especially in rural areas. They mended hundreds of bridges and many kilometres of roads, including the airfields of Pochentong near Phnom Penh and Stung Treng in the north of the country.[63]

However, the humanitarian aid and rehabilitation and economic development programmes did not necessarily contribute to Cambodia's political, economic and social stability. In fact, the contrary was true; the intervention caused a sharp rise in prices, especially in the capital city. UN personnel and additional international organisations rented numerous structures in Phnom Penh and, as a result, rental prices rose by about four hundred per cent within sixty days of the signing of the Paris Agreements. The CPP government responded to the price hikes with a massive printing of money, leading to inflation. The price of rice jumped by two hundred and fifty per cent and the price of fish rose fivefold.[64] Together, this caused a severe economic crisis and spurred the development of phenomena such as prostitution among women and children and a rise in the number of AIDS carriers. The number of prostitutes in Cambodia jumped from about six thousand in 1992 to about twenty-five thousand at the height of the operation.[65] UN reports warned that 'there is a tendency on the part of some personnel to treat women as though they were prostitutes.'[66]

Often, the good intentions of UN representatives remained on paper in light of the intensity of local economic interests. The three Cambodian factions not including the Khmer Rouge signed an agreement to cease the illegal trade in trees that was causing accelerated destruction of the Cambodian forests. Despite the agreement, deforestation continued apace. At the conclusion of the intervention, Hun Sen from the CPP and Ranariddh from FUNCINPEC abolished the agreement altogether. The forest destruction resumed within a few years and, according to estimates, only about 5 per cent of the revenue reached the public coffers.

The rest – 95 per cent – was divided among multinational corporations and Cambodian agents who were close associates of the Cambodian factions and dealt in tree smuggling.[67]

The UN intervention also had a direct benefit for the CPP, which ruled about 90 per cent of the country's territory. The three factions competing against the CPP hoped that the worsening of economic conditions would work to their advantage in the elections. Therefore, they refused to take any action that could have improved the economy. Representatives of the Transitional Authority, who were mainly worried about the fate of the elections, were concerned by the heightening social unrest in the wake of the economic crisis. Therefore, they approached external contributors such as the International Monetary Fund and the Asian Development Bank as well as various countries to resolve the crisis.[68] The heads of the Transitional Authority decided to ignore the requests of the opposition factions not to intervene in financial matters, and instead flooded the Cambodian market with rice in order to prevent public stockpiling and thus encourage prices to drop. In order to refute charges that they acted in unilateral support of the CPP, the UN representatives defended themselves by saying that they acted on behalf of all the Cambodians and not according to party interests, in accordance with the resolutions of the Security Council and of the ICORC.[69]

Researchers within the UN who analysed the UN intervention in Cambodia did not point out that the UN economic initiatives did not directly assist the peace process in Cambodia. Development was connected to interests of the local elites, regional and world powers and of multinational corporations before, during and after the intervention; it is difficult to evaluate their ramifications on the economy and the society. From the 1960s onwards, Cambodia was, and remains, a country dependent on foreign aid in order to survive. To this very day, about 70 per cent of the fast-growing population scratches out a living on subsistence agriculture – the growing of rice and grains – and there is a great shortage of land.[70] The Cambodian elite continues to conduct itself corruptly. About 75 per cent of businesses in the country are forced to pay bribes.[71] It seems that UN efforts at economic development contributed mainly to stabilising CPP party rule in the governmental apparatus rather than contributing to the country's peace process.

Due to Cambodia's dubious reputation in humanitarian issues, great importance was assigned to promoting the issue of human rights in diplomatic discussions. Since the UN ostensibly tried to introduce human rights norms as one of the new goals of peacekeeping operations, one might assume that the organisation would try to promote this in Cambodia – but that is not the case. In the Paris Agreements, no direct responsibility was attributed to the two factions responsible for flagrant human rights violations according to international law (the Khmer Rouge and the KPCP that changed its name to the CPP), not in the past or the present. In fact, the Secretariat renounced responsibility for human rights issues from the very beginning. Its approach was 'The Cambodians themselves thus clearly have the obligation to promote and protect human rights and fundamental freedoms in Cambodia. Others have the responsibility to encourage their respect and observance in order to prevent the recurrence of human rights abuses.'[72]

In other words, UN responsibility was limited to 'encouragement' of 'future human-right norms'. In accordance with this viewpoint of the Secretariat, any act taken by the UN could be considered a success, as long as it was done in good faith – even if it was not successful. Thus it is difficult to gauge the extent of the operation's success, since we cannot accurately determine if the changes in Cambodian human rights in this period or later were connected to UN activities or, alternatively, to those of international human rights organisations, local organisations, or even because of changes in other circumstances.[73] The Secretariat chose to adopt an uncommitted stance towards the promotion of human rights and relied on the cooperation of the rival Cambodian sides.[74] This UN 'encouragement' consisted mainly of the following: having Cambodia ratify international human rights treaties; developing educational programmes for local officials (judges, policemen, teachers, etc.); and referring requests for modifying procedures of the country's civilian administration. The UN also operated its own radio station and encouraged a free press.[75] A few weeks before elections, at the beginning of May 1993, Boutros-Ghali was forced to admit that 'the human rights situation in Cambodia continues to give rise to deep concern. The persistence of politically and ethnically motivated attacks is obviously a serious threat to the protection of human rights as well as to the creation and maintenance of a neutral political environment.'[76]

But the failure to advance human rights in Cambodia is dwarfed when contrasted with SRSG Akashi's unwillingness to implement the powers granted him by the Paris Agreements, and especially with regard to CPP's hold on the government apparatus. As previously mentioned, one of the core issues given to disagreement among the Cambodian factions during the discussion regarding the goals of the Transitional Authority operation was the burning issue of CPP control of 90 per cent of Cambodian territory during the interim period. This period extended from the signing of the Paris Agreements in October 1991 until the establishment of the new government after democratic elections. Since traditional Cambodian political life had always been based on the patron–client (*quid pro quo*) system – in researcher Martin's words, bribery and corruption[77] – it was very doubtful that democratic elections could take place when CPP activists ruled all the governmental institutions. Proposals to dismantle the CPP administration were rejected even by Australia, which initiated the UNTAC execution. Australian Foreign Minister Gareth Evans claimed that the UN would be simply unable to recruit, operate and administer such a staff.[78] Therefore, the UN was only entrusted with a supervisory role, to 'ensure a neutral political environment conducive to free and fair general elections'.[79]

UN personnel attempted to monitor the activities of the Phnom Penh administration by various methods. They also attempted to enable accessibility to information by distributing radios, conducting UN publicity campaigns throughout the country, and establishing a journalist association.[80] They encouraged the SNC to legislate various laws for the running of the legal and police systems.[81] According to the periodic reports submitted for the perusal of the SNC members, they seem to have been satisfied by their degree of control of the governmental ministries such as the Public Security and Treasury ministries. They claim to have tried to enlarge their sphere of control to additional domains such as health, and they set hiring standards for work candidates in the various authorities.[82] Akashi was satisfied with the steps that were adopted and argued that they contributed significantly to a calm diplomatic atmosphere, as befits a proper election campaign. To back up his claim of achievement, Akashi presented a letter of complaint brought by Hun Sen, head of the Phnom Penh administration (March 1993), in which Sen claims that 'UNTAC's method of control was so rigorous and intrusive that it resembled the method used by Pol Pot!'[83]

Similar to its lacklustre treatment of human rights, the Secretariat also neglected to prioritise the advancement of 'good governance' or democratic principles when it monitored the civil authorities of the CPP. UN personnel preferred to follow traditional UN principles of relying on the conflicted parties to comply with the agreements they signed, meaning that in this case they relied on the 'agreement' of the CPP. So even though the Secretariat emphasised that it had 'direct control' of the local authorities, in fact it only focused on supervision of official documents produced by several CPP's ministries, similar to the 'encouragement' of human rights as evinced by the UN organ that was charged with promotion of human rights.[84]

Most of the UN representatives who served as supervisors over the civil authorities made their presence known mainly in the head ministries and were practically invisible in the rest of the country. Thus, for example, a UN expert on public information reported the following on 29 March 1993:

> In Seam Reap, as observed elsewhere, CPP and SOC structures are inseparable, and that there seems to have been no attempt whatsoever to at least make them look even formally separate. It appears that, on the contrary, CPP's control over SOC structures has been reinforced to the point of total fusion, SOC's structures being CPP's instrument to implement its policies and achieve its objectives.[85]

Moreover, the reports prove that UN personnel were dissatisfied with the extent of their control. They complained that the CPP administration did things without consulting with them, and that corruption was rampant in the entire governmental apparatus. They claimed that in many cases, they were informed of procedures only after the fact. Regarding relations with Cambodia's neighbouring countries, representatives of the Transitional Authority emphasised that the Vietnam border near Cambodia was monitored to prevent infiltration, and that the prohibition on exporting trees from Cambodia was enforced.[86] Yet, as a matter of fact, the Phnom Penh administration officials signed a flight agreement with the Malaysian government, without the knowledge of the Transitional Authority representatives.

And, as presented above (in the section on economic and social ramifications), the moratorium on the export of trees failed.[87] The UN report of January 1993 stated explicitly that, starting from the beginning of 1992, the administration managed by the CPP used the lack of Khmer Rouge cooperation as an excuse to limit cooperation between its governmental ministries and the supervisory apparatuses of the Transitional Authority.[88] Concurrently, the CPP administration continued to exploit its control of ministries in order to promote the party's interests. Transitional Authority representatives reported that as the election date neared, 'widespread and persistent use [was made] of the SOC state apparatus to conduct political campaign activities of the Cambodian People's Party (CPP) in which state employees – police, armed forces and civil servants – are mobilized for CPP electioneering.'[89] Among the greatest critics of the Phnom Penh administration was Gerard Porcell, who headed UNTAC's Civil Administration Component and expressed his belief that the UN was not doing enough to enforce its authority, not only over the Khmer Rouge but also over the Phnom Penh administration. In February 1993, Porcell resigned in protest over the fact that the UN would not adopt serious measures against the CPP.[90]

The continuous CPP control over governmental institutions throughout Cambodia – both before, during and after the elections – was a decisive factor in the stability of the Cambodian regime, definitely more powerful than the inefficient supervision on the part of UNTAC's Civil Administration Component. At the conclusion of the operation, the political elites remained at the top of the political system with their power intact, while receiving de facto legitimacy from the UN. After the last of the UN representatives left the country, these elites began to consolidate their 'legitimate' powers in the government institutions.[91] Now, after about twenty years since the conclusion of the operation, Hun Sen still heads the ruling CPP party. Throughout the years, systematic violations of human rights have been attributed to him as well as suppression of the FUNCINPEC party in 1997, routing of the Khmer Rouge in 1998, and persecution of other opposition forces.[92]

Thus, we have observed that the first multidimensional operation deployed by the UN at the conclusion of the Cold War achieved mixed results. On January 1993, Marrack Goulding (UN USG in charge of peacekeeping) aptly described the situation when he met with the conflicted parties in Cambodia. Goulding claimed that the factions did not fully cooperate with the Transitional Authority and that the blame should be divided equally between the Khmer Rouge and the CPP.[93] In spite of only partial cooperation and in the face of protests from all four factions, the UN forces continued to prepare for the holding of elections that were boycotted by the DK party. They passed an elections law, registered those eligible to vote, and finally, despite the harsh conditions, conducted the elections from 23–28 May 1993. Of the eligible voters, 89.56 per cent exercised their voting rights. FUNCINPEC earned fifty-eight seats in the formative Assembly, the CPP won fifty-one seats, the BLDP (an offshoot of the KPNLF) won ten seats and a new party,

MOLINAKA (comprising representatives who defected from FUNCINPEC) won only one seat.[94] Since the new constitution composed under the aegis of the UN determined that a new government must garner at least two-thirds of the members of the General Assembly (80 out of 120 members), there was great difficulty in forming a coalition government. In a surprising diplomatic move, two competing contenders for the state's legitimate government established a coalition that became the country's ruling coalition. The two competitors were Prince Sihanouk's son Ranariddh, FUNCINPEC head, and CPP head Hun Sen. This move caught the UN representatives by surprise, and soon after the forming of the coalition, the new rulers demanded that UN forces leave the country.

In light of this demand of Cambodia's new government, Boutros-Ghali argued that other objectives (besides the holding of elections) had not yet been achieved and that the operation should be continued in order to firmly entrench appropriate political and social norms in Cambodia.[95] This, of course, was based on the concepts raised in the Agenda for Peace. But the international community thought otherwise. The Security Council, and countries in the region, called for an end to the operation.[96] In retrospect, Boutros-Ghali remarks that 'The complicated provisions of the Paris Agreement really came down to a single objective: to create a new Cambodian government with international legitimacy.'[97] Back in 1955, the Cambodian elections and the 'nation's desire for independence' were an important means in the process of recognition and acceptance of Cambodia as a member in the world order of nation-states that do not fight one another. Thirty-eight years later, the elections of 1993 were designed to serve as an instrument for ending intrastate conflict among the opposing Cambodian sides and bring about the establishment of a government enjoying internal authority and legitimacy and external international recognition.

The discussion of the issues above – disarmament, training a civil police force, repatriating refugees, economic development, supervision of the civil administration, promoting human rights and conducting of elections – teaches us that the new conceptual principles that won support in the UN in 1992 and 1993 were implemented only superficially in Cambodia. The UN mission in Cambodia was designed, first and foremost, to support elections that would produce a legitimate government; these were the main interests of the UN and its representatives on the ground. The implementation of other goals was of secondary importance. So while the Paris Agreements set multidimensional objectives for the Transitional Authority in Cambodia, the main interest of the international community was the founding of a legitimate government in Cambodia. Despite the fact that the People's Party (CPP) stopped the spread of democratisation in Cambodia (by political persecution of its opponents, among many other abuses), the Security Council members refused to take action against it. Occasionally, expressions of regret would be heard with regard to human rights violations and violence sponsored by the governmental apparatus, simultaneously with cries for the advancement of reconciliation, tolerance, moderation and a neutral diplomatic atmosphere. Not one representative in the Council called for a clear-cut operation to change the situation, in contrast to the more assertive attitude of the Council members toward the Khmer Rouge. In all the discussions in the Security Council, the responsibility for success or failure of the peace process was imposed on the 'Cambodian nation'.[98]

As described above, the UN's traditional mode of behaviour in Cambodia – which cannot be viewed as a systematic attempt to promote norms of peacebuilding or adopt the peace enforcement technique outlined in the Agenda for Peace report – was backed up by all the nations of the Security Council and nations in the region. In the language used by the organisation, a consensus prevailed among all the Council members regarding the UN's objectives and actions in Cambodia. From 1990-93, the Security Council adopted thirteen resolutions regarding Cambodia.[99] In all the speeches delivered in the Council regarding Cambodia, no protests were heard about the way resolutions were adopted by the Council, or the possibility that some states were taking unfair advantage of their power to impose an agenda in Cambodia that was compatible with their interests.[100]

### Former Yugoslavia: mismanaged disintegration

This section analyses the UN intervention in the former Yugoslavia from the end of 1991 until December 1995. During this period, most of the operations deployed by the UN came under the title of the United Nations Protection Force (UNPROFOR). For the purposes of this discussion, I include operations carried out in the former Yugoslavia with an emphasis on Bosnia and Croatia (under the UNPROFOR umbrella), until the end of 1995. The term 'former Yugoslavia' refers to the six countries that had been part of the Socialist Federal Republic of Yugoslavia (SFRY) that existed (at least formally) from 1943 to 1992. In June 1991, the SFRY was dismantled into the states that made up the federation. The first states to secede were Slovenia and Croatia, which declared independence in June 1991. They only received international recognition in January 1992 (the EC members recognised them earlier, on 17 December 1991). Although Macedonia seceded from the SFRY in September 1991, it received international recognition only in April 1993 due to the long-term opposition of the Greek government, which argued that the name of Macedonia, and the flag it adopted, all represented Macedonian irredentist demands in northern Greece. Therefore, in most of the documents that refer to this country, it is recognised as the 'former Yugoslavian Republic of Macedonia'. A referendum was conducted in Bosnia-Herzegovina in March 1992, in which secession was decided. Its independence was recognised by the international community in April 1992. Serbia and Montenegro remained united under the name 'the Federal Republic of Yugoslavia', which they adopted on 27 April 1992 with attempts by Serbian leader Slobodan Milošević to take control of all the resources of the SFRY. But the state was not recognised by the UN until November 2000. In 2003 its name was changed to Serbia-Montenegro, and in 2006 it broke up into two separate, independent states, Serbia and Montenegro. The autonomous region of Kosovo, originally part of Serbia, was put under international administration back in 1999. It declared independence on 17 February 2008 and today is recognised by most countries as an independent state.

The number of people who served in UNPROFOR varied over the years, but at its height at the end of 1995, its forces numbered a total of 57,000 soldiers, about 800 civilian policemen and 2,000 international personnel. The cost of the force has been estimated to be about 4.6 billion dollars. Thus the UN intervention in the former Yugoslavia was, and still is, considered the largest peacekeeping operation ever deployed by the UN.

Immediately at the conclusion of the operation, opinions were divided within the UN regarding its success. The general agreement was that UN action saved thousands of lives, contributed to numerous localised ceasefires and helped stabilise the conflict. There was also a consensus that the preventive deployment operation in Macedonia forestalled the eruption of a conflict there. Nevertheless, in Security Council discussions at the end of 1995, Botswanan delegate Joseph Legwaila and Czech delegate Dušan Rovenský argued that the UN's great investment did not contribute to resolving the conflict and did not prevent serious hostile acts.[101] In addition, no official UN position or Security Council statement was publicised by the UN with regard to the results of the operation such as they had done after the Cambodian operation, when they announced its success.[102]

According to the research literature on the UN intervention in the former Yugoslavia scholars view the intervention (mainly in Bosnia) as a period in which the concept of international law was developed and during which time it was decided to establish the International Criminal Tribunal for the former Yugoslavia (ICTY). Researchers also agree that the international intervention to provide humanitarian assistance to civilian populations, representing the maintenance of minimal human rights standards, assumed great importance in the political diplomatic discussions. These studies feature lively discussions on the importance of NATO's intervention in the region by using air power against the Bosnian Serbs. In other words, the researchers agree that the traditional principles of operations underwent erosion during these years. The various studies used different terms to describe the operation in the former Yugoslavia, from 'second-generation peacekeeping operation', 'humanitarian operation', 'broad peacekeeping operation', or 'enforcement operation'. All these create a deceptive picture regarding the change in the concept of the operations and, even more, in the extent of international political change in the UN. The studies do not answer the question: To what extent did the various players act out of narrow self-interest or out of the higher principle of collective security? Also: Which players adopted the new concept of operations that was under discussion at the time in the UN?[103] Below, we examine how the intervention developed until the first half of 1993.

The intricacy of the intra-Yugoslavian arena was a significant factor in the dissolution process of the state. First, there were numerous players, too many players, in the conflict. The ethnic heterogeneousness of the Yugoslavian population led, over the years, to the rise of political forces that operated in line with their ethnic identities and conspired to change the character of the regime (at the very least). The Serbs constituted about 36 per cent of the country's population (about 8.46 million people), the Croats represented about 20 per cent of the population (about 4.7 million people), and the Muslims about 10 per cent (about 2.35 million people). However, these ethnic groups were scattered unevenly throughout the country. More than 90 per cent of the Slovenic population (numbering 1.96 million residents) was Slovenian. About 4.7 million residents lived in Croatia, where Croatians constituted 78 per cent of the population and the Serbs were a large minority of about 12 per cent of the population (580,000 people) and were concentrated in specific areas. About 4.3 million people lived in Bosnia and 43 per cent of the population were Muslims (about 1.9 million people), the Serbs represented 33 per cent (about 1.37 million people) while the Croats represented about 17 per cent (about 755 thousand people). Serbia and Montenegro contained about 10.4 million residents, of which the Serbs constituted about 62 per cent of the population (about 6.5 million people) and the Albanian minority constituted about 16 per cent (about 1.7 million people), most of whom were concentrated in the Kosovo region. Finally, in Macedonia in which 2 million residents lived, the Macedonians constituted 65 per cent of the population (about 1.3 million people) and the Albanian minority constituted 21 per cent (427,000 people) of it.[104] The Serbianisation of the Yugoslavian political system under the fist of Slobodan Milošević from the end of the 1980s threatened to remould Yugoslavia into a country serving only Serbs at the expense of other ethnic groups in the country.[105] The main counter-responses to Milošević came from the Croatian and Slovenian leadership that tried to found a confederation.[106] In 1989, the dispute escalated between the various players in the field and reached boiling point; numerous, ethnic-based violent events took place in Yugoslavia. Simultaneously, the government tried (without much success) to adopt a more liberal economic policy in order to solve the economic crisis, and to hold democratic elections in the various republics.[107] All these steps did not succeed in reconciling the opposing sides. The federal government weakened and the communist party broke up into national parties in the republics. The Yugoslav People's Army (YNA) did not take an active part in the process except for an attempt to disarm Slovenian and Croatian militias (called 'territorial units').[108]

An additional problem was that the various leaders held conflicting goals and they were not afraid to threaten to use force in order to get what they perceived as their rights.

Thus, diplomats around the world found it difficult to understand how the country's dissolution process would develop, what new states would be formed, what would be their borders and what their principles of self-determination would be. The Slovenian majority in Slovenia demanded independence. In Croatia there was a confrontation between the Croat majority that wanted to exert its right to self-determination in the recognised borders of Croatia and the Serbian minority that wanted (at least) to be annexed to Serbian areas or exert what it felt to be its right to self-determination. Bosnia featured conflicts between several players. Bosnian Serbs, who wanted to remain within the rubric of a united Yugoslavia, operated against Muslims and Croatians. Dissension reigned between the Muslims and Croatians regarding the character of Bosnia as a unitary state or a state that would give special privileges to ethnic groups. Conflict about the character of the state developed between moderate Muslims under Fikret Abdić and nationalist Muslims under Alija Izetbegović. It was not clear whether the Muslim leadership of Bosnia wanted full independence or would be satisfied to receive additional powers in a new Yugoslavia constitution. On Serbian territory were confrontations with the Albanian minority in Kosovo (that represented close to 90 per cent of the district's population). Macedonia featured tense relations between the Macedonians, who constituted about 65 per cent of the population, and the large Albanian minority in the country.[109]

The multiplicity of local Yugoslavian players, with their conflicting goals and activities, contributed to already existing difficulties between the various mediators in the conflict. In the course of 1991, preventive diplomacy and peacemaking efforts were led by the three large EC members: the United Kingdom, Germany and France. However, they were not able to agree on a mutual strategy for ending the conflict. The Germans pressured the other members to recognise the independence of Slovenia and Croatia, while the British and French representatives emphasised that the timing and manner of recognition had an important role.[110] The European mediators did not have the political and material support of additional powers. Due to events connected to the conclusion of the Cold War, the US administration was, at the time, busy supervising the dismantling of the Soviet Union and also involved in the Gulf War.[111] The Soviet Union was in the midst of disintegration. Therefore, although its representatives usually cooperated with the mediators, they could not offer them any kind of aid.[112] China did not express any stance regarding events in Yugoslavia and, in principle, supported the continued existence of a united Yugoslavia. On the other hand, the Chinese representatives noted in the UN that they would honour the wishes of the nation in Yugoslavia. The Secretariat and most UN members shared views similar to those of China.[113] So despite the increasing national tensions and inner contradictions in Yugoslavia, and despite the lack of agreement in the international community on the right path to take to manage the crisis in the country, most EC members and the United States preferred to preserve the integrity of the Yugoslavian state, until the end of 1991.[114]

The credibility crisis within Yugoslavia between the nationalist political elites led Slovenia and Croatia to declare independence on 25 June 1991.[115] It did not take long for war to erupt after that. Due to the reasons listed above, the influence of the European mediators on the local players was negligible when fighting began in Slovenia and Croatia in June 1991. The war in Slovenia finished within ten days, but not as a result of international intervention. Instead, it was because the Serbian leadership preferred to concentrate the Yugoslavian military forces in Croatia to protect the Serb minority.[116] In contrast to the course of events in Slovenia, the fighting in Croatia continued with no tilt in the balance for many long months, causing by January 1993 the deaths of 6,000 people, hundreds of thousands of refugees and internally displaced people and massive destruction. In the course of the war, international mediators led by Lord Carrington (the United Kingdom)[117] tried to convince the warring sides to sign ceasefire agreements. But even when these were signed, they were violated regularly.[118] Frustrated by their inability to stabilise a ceasefire, the EC member states attempted to involve a multinational force from the Western European Union, a multinational European military organisation.[119] However, it quickly became clear to them that they would be unable to do so because of managerial and organisational difficulties. In their time of need, they had no recourse but to turn to the UN, in September; the UN was the organisation with proven experience in the execution of these kinds of operations. Moreover, France wanted to exploit this appeal to the UN in order to increase its influence on the course of the intervention, due to France's special position in the Security Council, thus counterbalancing the strong influence of Germany within the EC. In contrast to the stance of the European representatives, the American administration did not encourage the use of peacekeeping operations. This was in spite of the fact that the United States felt that Serbia and the Yugoslavian army had acted as 'aggressors' regarding Croatia.[120]

The initiative of the EC member states towards the execution of a UN peacekeeping operation received added support of local players at the end of 1991; these countries were also interested in ending the local conflict.[121] But it was the UN Secretariat, frustrated at the time over the profusion of operations and unwillingness of countries to contribute appropriate forces to those operations, which played a central role in delaying the deployment of forces. The UN Secretary-General at the time, Pérez de Cuéllar, opposed granting international recognition to the independence of Slovenia and Croatia, out of concern that such recognition would accelerate the dismantling of Yugoslavia and lead to escalation of the conflict. He also opposed the deployment of UN forces in Slovenia and Croatia so long as the traditional conditions for deployment of forces did not exist on the ground.[122] Instead, de Cuéllar preferred to support the peacemaking activities of the EC members. He changed his opinion only as a result of pressures placed on him by member states of the EC, and in light of the harsh battles in Croatia.[123]

Therefore, in October 1991, de Cuéllar decided to send his personal envoy Cyrus Vance on his behalf, as well as Marrack Goulding, USG for Special Political Affairs, in order to examine the option of deploying a small force of observers.[124] After consulting with the fighting sides, which had not succeeded in tilting the balance of the conflict by military means, Vance and Goulding consolidated a proposal for a programme for Croatia that emphasised a disengagement of forces. This programme defined a number of objectives. First, UN forces were required to supervise the withdrawal of the Yugoslavian army from the country. Another goal was to deploy into protected areas in Croatia, called United Nations Protected Areas (UNPAs), which contained Serbian majorities, and monitor their demilitarisation. Finally, forces were required to ensure that the local administration and police did not discriminate against the non-Serbian population, but instead encouraged the return of refugees and displaced persons. Yet Vance and Goulding emphasised that the programme would operate according to traditional principles; they would not use force and, instead, strived to obtain the agreement of the conflicted sides.[125] Since the peacekeeping operation programme in Croatia emphasised traditional principles of action, the Secretariat refused to recommend the deployment of forces until a stable ceasefire emerged in Croatia.[126] The fighting in Croatia continued until February 1992, at which time a ceasefire agreement was signed with the mediation of UN Secretary-General Special Envoy Cyrus Vance. At the time (January 1992), new Secretary-General Boutros-Ghali was assuming office. That fact, coupled with the pressures inflicted on the Secretariat, resulted in the following feeble letter of recommendation for an operation, which states that:

> [A]fter careful consideration I have come to the conclusion that the danger that a United Nations peace-keeping operation will fail because of lack of cooperation from the parties is less grievous than the danger that delay in its dispatch will lead to a breakdown of the cease-fire and to a new conflagration in Yugoslavia.[127]

Six days later, the Security Council unanimously adopted Resolution 743 that authorised the deployment of a UN force in Croatia, while emphasising 'that the Secretary-General considers that the conditions permitting the early deployment of a United Nations Protection Force are met'.[128] In contrast to the usual sluggishness in deploying forces typical of most UN operations, this time the European countries hurried to allocate forces. Within two months of the adoption of Security Council Resolution 743, the UN force numbered about 8,300 soldiers and civilians out of about 12,000 planned.[129] Despite the broad goals of the operation, the UN maintained its traditional action principles; in other words, the forces were deployed only after receiving international support and local agreement. In addition, they did not have enforcement powers on the local administrators and also lacked the power to use force, except for self-defence.[130] The force grew in the course of the operation and at its height, almost 15,000 soldiers served in it.

The most important mission entrusted to the deployed forces was to monitor the withdrawal of the YNA from Croatia. This mandate was implemented within a few weeks, when the YNA military forces retreated to Bosnia and Serbia. A bigger challenge was the demilitarisation and disarmament of all the militias in the UNPAs. In order to assure this process, the UN forces were committed to ensuring the security of all the residents from armed assaults, and securing public law and order.[131] In the original plan of the Secretariat representatives, the term 'demilitarisation' meant that people would be barred from wearing army uniforms or carrying weapons, and that all weapons would be handed over to the UN forces for custody.¹³² In fact, the UN forces failed in their mission. No reforms were implemented in the local administration of the UNPAs under Serbian control, and the law and order system collapsed. The local authorities encouraged ethnic cleansing of the non-Serbian residents. The civilian police force was Serbian. In fact, the Serbian authorities declared many Serbian militias to be paramilitary special forces of the civilian police and refused to cooperate with the UN demilitarisation initiative. The Serbian militias even terrified the civil police and the legal system, most of which operated according to professional standards (according to UN reports).¹³³ The deterioration of a stable political and security environment also caused a rise in crime, which was not entirely connected to the ethnic-related violence.¹³⁴

The ceasefire announcement in the Croatian conflict imposed a massive task on the UN's humanitarian aid system under the UNHCR: to treat the displaced and refugee populations (Serbs and Croatians) and encourage their repatriation to their homes. Attempts were also made to encourage economic cooperation between the Serbs and Croatians, and to spur economic recovery and development of the country that had suffered great damage during the war.¹³⁵ The relief agencies faced great challenges. According to estimations made at the time, about a quarter of a million Croatians fled the UNPAs. Those who remained faced harassment and arbitrary arrests. Croatians who held public posts were fired. Due to this ongoing pressure, the UN assistance organisations focused on giving assistance to the hundreds of Croatians who wanted to leave these areas out of fear for their personal security. The Serbs in the UNPAs also severed the Croatians' supplies of water and electricity via the Peruća dam, thus exerting heavy pressure on the Croatian government.¹³⁶ Due to the unsafe and insecure circumstances, the UNHCR representatives argued that conditions were not ripe for return of the refugees and they continued to work at extending humanitarian aid and rebuilding demolished infrastructure such as water and electrical systems, railway lines and oil supply to the UNPAs.¹³⁷ The circumstances of the Serbs were also dismal. While the non-Serbs were driven away from the UNPAs, the Serbs in Croatia found refuge in these areas from the Croatians.¹³⁸ According to UN assessments, as of March 1993, about 251,000 Serbs from Croatia had fled to UNPAs and other regions.¹³⁹

Although a variety of UN goals were achieved in the UNPAs of Croatia, these did nothing to change the policy of any of the conflicted parties. The Croatian government under the leadership of Croatian nationalist franjo tudman viewed the presence of UN forces as a transition stage before the territories under his supervision would return to Croatian sovereignty. The Serbian government in Croatia (Krajina that resided in Knin) was formally under supervision of the UN forces, according to Resolution 743. In actual fact, the Croatian Serbs viewed the UN presence as a transition stage towards realisation of their rights for self-determination. This, in turn, meant being annexed to the Serbs in Bosnia, or to Serbia, or, at the very least, autonomy. They relied on promises that they had been given at the beginning of the negotiation process, when the international mediators had made it clear to them that the international community would be willing to recognise a change in borders, subject to acceptance by both sides. They received the support of Federal Republic of Yugoslavia (Serbia and Montenegro), whose representatives argued that any diplomatic process must be part of a comprehensive solution to the gamut of problems connected to the dismantling of Yugoslavia. They argued that the Croatian army ethnically cleansed about 200,000 Serbs from Croatia, that its forces were involved in Bosnia, that they attacked Serbs in protected areas in contravention of the agreements, and that they violated the embargo on the import of weapons.[140] Despite UN efforts, there was no substantial improvement in diplomacy, security, and humanitarian-economic process in the UNPAs until the middle of 1993.

The UN Secretariat personnel were well aware of this situation. In contrast to the international community's broad support for the Croatian operation, the Secretariat raised numerous reservations about it. In the Secretariat's reports to the Security Council, they claimed that neither side in Croatia fulfilled the agreements. They also raised misgivings about the concept of an enforcement mandate that had begun to be raised occasionally as a tool for breaking the diplomatic stalemate. The Secretariat feared that such a mandate could cause escalation. In addition, the reports stated that the contributor countries were not prepared to endanger the lives of their soldiers in such an operation. The Secretary-General's report (of May 1993) based on the operation in Croatia says that:

> [S]ince any new proposals to change the situation ... would require the consent of both parties, and since such consent is clearly not available, the Security Council could decide not to waste the limited resources of the international community by retaining in Croatia a large force whose mandate has proven to be un-implementable. The Council has already learned from the case of the United Nations Interim Force in Lebanon (UNIFIL) that the prolongation of a peace-keeping force whose mandate cannot be implemented becomes an expensive and open-ended commitment, with a considerable risk of casualties.[141]

The UNPROFOR operation in Croatia helped stabilise a violent conflict that caused the deaths of thousands of people and adversely affected the lives of hundreds of thousands. Despite the speedy deployment of the UN forces within Croatian territory, it operated under the constant threat that the entire operation could turn into a tremendous diplomatic, military and financial burden for the international community without contributing to resolution of the conflict. However, at the beginning of 1992, the international community felt that such an operation was the right course of action to adopt, as part of the second-generation changes in operations. In effect, it was also meant to solve the EC's lack of experience and capabilities to execute this type of operation. It was also intended to prevent the conflict from escalating, similar to peacekeeping operations during the Cold War. The question was, to what extent the international community would agree to adopt the new concept for operations in order to advance the resolution of the conflict in Croatia.

The deployment of peacekeeping forces in Croatia quickly became a kind of preamble to the Protection Force operation in Bosnia. Aside from the involvement of the collapsing Yugoslavian government and Yugoslavian army, three ethnic groups were fighting in Bosnia: the Muslims, the Serbs, and the Croats. A referendum was conducted in Bosnia (from 29 February to 1 March 1992) in which the inhabitants were asked to decide whether to secede from Yugoslavia and become independent. The Muslim and Croats voted in favour, while the Serbs (who wanted to remain part of Serbia) boycotted the referendum because they knew they had no chance of attaining a majority vote. On 5 March, the Bosnian parliament declared independence. The preventive diplomacy initiative of the European mediators, known as the Cutilero Plan (which was submitted to the conflicted sides in March 1992), proposed to divide Bosnia into cantons based on the ethnic identity of the residents. But this programme failed because the Muslims and Croats rejected it, with the encouragement of Croatia and the United States, and instead called for independence. Opinions are divided regarding the contribution of the international community to the eruption of the conflict in Bosnia. Some claim that the promise to recognise Bosnian sovereignty before the conclusion of negotiations helped reduce the intensity of the conflict since it ensured that the Yugoslav army would not take part in it. On the other hand, some argue that the recognition encouraged the Muslim community to strive toward independence and reject other programmes for peace.[142] On 27 March, the Bosnian Serbs declared an independent government of their own, and began to take control of the country's territories. They were well armed and well equipped by the Yugoslavian army that had withdrawn from the country in May of that year. Within a few months they had secured their control over about 70 per cent of the country's territories, while still employing ethnic cleansing practices: violent expulsion of populations accompanied by indiscriminate murders, systematic rape and plunder. But afterwards, the Serbs failed in their attempts to enlarge the territory under their control. The Muslims, who were mainly concentrated in urban areas, succeeded in defending themselves from within the cities because they had great manpower. However, they did not have the necessary military equipment and weapons to launch an offensive. At the same time, the Croats tried to secure control in areas in which they constituted the largest minority group.[143]

Ostensibly, the decision to execute a peacekeeping operation inside a country during an active conflict when there was no peace to keep, in contrast to the traditional principles of peacekeeping operations, seemed to befit the new concepts raised in the UN in that era. However, there are other reasons to explain why the UN decided to deploy forces in Bosnia during an active conflict. First, the Western states, headed by the United States, the United Kingdom and France, refused to consider a military intervention to enforce the cessation of the conflict on all the local factions. Numerous other states – mainly Muslim countries – opposed this view that called for enforcement measures according to its accepted meaning in the Charter, in order to stop what they viewed as violation of the national sovereignty of the mainly Bosnian Muslim government. The rejection of the proposal to use force against the Serbs, and its removal from the UN agenda, still did not solve the need for some kind of international response. At that same time, the European countries were concerned that a flood of millions of refugees were likely to flee to their territories from the horrors of war. Ramifications such as these threatened to expand the conflict to all of south-east Europe. Furthermore, Western countries such as the United States, the United Kingdom, France and Germany faced heavy international pressure to deploy peacekeeping forces in Bosnia from the countries neighbouring Yugoslavia (except for Greece), Muslim states and veteran UN contributor states. Many representatives justified this with the argument that the deployment of UN forces in Bosnia befitted the new world order that had been heralded by the Security Council in January 1992.[144] The result was that although the Western countries continued to disagree among themselves regarding the reasons for the conflict, by the summer of 1992 they all agreed that the appropriate response would be the deployment of a peacekeeping operation, something that was not opposed by the leaders of the conflicted sides.[145]

The main player that opposed the deployment of peacekeeping forces in Bosnia was, surprisingly, the UN Secretariat. At the end of his term of office, Pérez de Cuéllar refused to promote such a deployment. As an extension of this approach, Boutros-Ghali opposed the deployment of peacekeeping forces in Bosnia in the first half of 1992 – despite the fact that at the very same time he was developing his Agenda for Peace and acknowledged the severity of the humanitarian crisis in the country. The main rationale for his opposition was that he felt that the deployment of forces in Bosnia would run counter to the traditional principles of success of operations.[146] But after Goulding reported to him on the severe situation in Bosnia, Boutros-Ghali did recommend an intervention involving a large multinational force numbering tens of thousands of soldiers. According to Boutros-Ghali, this force would operate without the agreement of all the sides, in order to enforce order in the country according to the principles of Chapter 7 in the Charter; this was similar to the UN-authorised operation against Iraq.[147]

But since the European countries and the United States did not agree to this solution, Boutros-Ghali suggested a compromise – the same compromise he proposed regarding an intervention in Somalia at the same time. The compromise proposal included the option of deployment of multinational forces to achieve specific goals such as control of the Sarajevo airport, protection of convoys carrying humanitarian aid shipments, safeguarding of open traffic routes throughout the country and deployment of military observers. Such a deployment authorised specific cases in which the use of force would be warranted in the event that UN forces encountered road barriers.[148] But Boutros-Ghali did not recommend such a course of action, due to the fluid nature of the conflict and because the UN did not have the necessary resources at its disposal. Therefore he recommended that a peacekeeping operation should not be executed, but that the UN should continue to support peacemaking activities initiated by the EC.[149]

Three days later, the representatives of Belgium, the United Kingdom and France promoted a resolution in the Security Council calling for execution of the plan proposed by the Secretary-General for international control of Sarajevo's airport and protection of the convoys transporting humanitarian aid. This plan received the support of all the Security Council members, culminating in the adoption of Resolution 752.[150] Boutros-Ghali immediately instructed his people to ensure the evacuation of UN personnel from Sarajevo. Then he responded to what he viewed as an underhanded deal conducted by Security Council members behind his back with a pessimistic report in which he emphasised that the plan was not feasible and could even cause harm.[151] Nevertheless, he began to plan the deployment of UN forces in Sarajevo.[152] This time, the Security Council supported his activities and hurried to authorise the expansion of goals of the UN peacekeeping forces in Bosnia.

The Secretariat decided that the best way to implement the new mandate was to focus on securing Sarajevo airport for the delivery of aid supplies. This was achieved by the deployment of approximately two thousand troops to the airport, but only after obtaining formal consent for the deployment from the Muslim and Serb leadership according to traditional peacekeeping doctrine.[153]

The decision to protect relief operations in Sarajevo but not to protect the citizens in the same city was presented as part of the revolution in the use of peacekeeping; but it had limited influence on the conflict dynamics. Due to fighting between the local belligerents, the humanitarian aid supplies piled up at the airport and could not be distributed to the hinterland or circulated to the civilian population in need.

In order to address the deteriorating situation, on 13 August 1992 the Security Council called for member states to execute a military operation for the protection of relief operations throughout Bosnia; this act was based on Chapter 7 in the UN Charter that authorised the use of force. This resolution was perceived as an implementation of the peace enforcement model that was first mentioned in the Agenda for Peace report (in June). However, the UN states were reluctant to send their armed forces to fight in Bosnia, thus exposing their soldiers to real danger. After several weeks of intense discussions, a compromise was achieved to deploy an additional 7,800 troops in order to protect the UNHCR aid operations throughout Bosnia. By early 1993, approximately ten thousand UN troops were deployed in Bosnia.[154]

The provision of a limited military operation pleased the European states that had advocated it. They offered to deploy their troops speedily under the UN flag and without charging the UN. This was in contrast to the organisation's usual practice of financially compensating the states for their contributions. By early 1993, European countries had contributed almost all of the UN military personnel in Bosnia. This changed only in mid-1993 when developing countries received financial reimbursement from the UN for their troops. By then, the goals of the operation were again under review.[155]

The injection of thousands of UN troops assisted in ameliorating the humanitarian crisis. From November 1992 to January 1993, the UNHCR reported that it was able to deliver a total of some 34,600 tons of supplies to an estimated 800,000 people in Bosnia.[156] By the end of the war, UN aid operations had supplied approximately a million tons of food, clothing and medications to besieged Bosnia populations.[157]

As presented above in the discussion regarding the goals and principles of success of the operation, the international community supported the connection between humanitarian aid activities and the execution of the peacekeeping operation. At the beginning of the conflict, representatives from some of the developing countries (such as China, India and Zimbabwe) raised criticism that was not related to humanitarian aid. These representatives emphasised the difficulty involved in departing from the working principles of the traditional peacekeeping forces when these forces acted according to the powers of Chapter 7 of the UN Charter. They were concerned that these forces would be biased, and would not secure the agreement of all the opposing sides.[158] On the other hand, many other representatives of developing countries argued that the UN was not doing enough to ensure humanitarian aid, and that it must use more force. Most of these latter representatives were from Muslim countries.[159]

The members of the international community did not address the problem that humanitarian aid became a weapon in the hands of the fighting parties. Each faction tried to get the aid convoys to pass through the territory it controlled so that it could seize the supplies for its own distribution and use them against the other factions. Thus the convoys were routinely delayed at road barriers. In many cases the aid would be appropriated, destroyed or, in the case of fresh foodstuffs, spoiled. These acts were carried out by Serbs, Muslims and Croats equally; all of them allowed the supply convoys to pass, so long as they were able to grab their share of the booty. For example, two well-known Muslim commanders in Sarajevo, Mušan 'Caco' Topalović and Ramiz 'Celo' Delalic, were also high-level criminals who traded on the black market. The (Muslim) Bosnian government only succeeded in gaining the upper hand over these commanders and their forces in October 1993.[160] Michael Rose, UN force commander in Bosnia in 1994, claimed that 'the first priority of both sides was to feed their soldiers in the trenches, and we often found that UN supplies had been diverted to the front line.'[161]

The Secretariat was compelled to manage this ambitious operation under traditional principles of consent, impartiality and non-use of force. Although this was in the spirit of the Secretary-General's Agenda for Peace, in practice, the

Secretariat had no desire to supervise such an operation. Navigating through the different interests of member states and local actors, the Secretariat states that 'criticism of UNPROFOR's performance in the Republic has largely been directed at its failure to fulfill tasks that the Force has not been mandated, authorized, equipped, staffed, or financed to fulfill.'[162] This mode of operation frustrated the UN personnel and troops serving on the ground, who chafed under the narrow mandate and were not permitted to take decisive action to change the military dynamics on the ground.[163]

In addition to the two large operations in Croatia and Bosnia, the Security Council decided in December 1992 to authorise the broadening of UNPROFOR to the former Republic of Macedonia.[164] The objective of the deployment of the multinational force in Macedonia, numbering about a thousand soldiers, was to supervise and report on all developments in its border regions that could undermine the country's stability and threaten its territory. Pressure to execute such an operation emerged from the regional countries that feared a spillover of the Bosnia and Croatia conflicts into their territories. In contrast to the previously unfavourable stance of the Secretariat to the interventions in Bosnia and Croatia, the Secretariat had already recommended an intervention in Macedonia during the course of the summer of 1992, simultaneously with the development of the concept of preventive diplomacy deployment that was also introduced in the Agenda for Peace document. It also called for a wide mandate to deal with political and civil tensions between the Macedonian majority and the Muslim minority. Nevertheless, the Security Council gave the force only a limited mandate. It is commonly believed that this operation prevented the spillover of the conflict in the former Yugoslavia to Macedonia.[165]

In addition to the execution of operations in Croatia, Bosnia and Macedonia, UNPROFOR continued to expand its mandate and with it, its forces and commitments. The major evolution took place in UNPROFOR-Bosnia during the spring of 1993. In January 1993, the conflict's international mediators, Cyrus Vance and David Owen, published their comprehensive peace plan that tried to keep a united Bosnia. It proposed the partition of Bosnia into ten political semi-autonomous units called cantons; three cantons were allocated to each ethnic group and the tenth, Sarajevo, was intended to be neutral. The proposal was a result of approximately eighty official and non-official meetings. But in order to implement the plan, tens of thousands of multinational troops would be needed, with extensive authority to use force – conditions that the international community refused to authorise or supply.[166] The belligerent parties in Bosnia, under pressure of a possible political and territorial compromise, renewed their offensive operations in order to improve their leverage at the negotiation table. By early 1993, the majority of the Muslim population in Bosnia was concentrated in several enclaves surrounded by hostile Serb or Croat forces. By March of 1993, it was estimated that in the vicinity of Srebrenica, the town with the largest Muslim concentration in east Bosnia, approximately thirty to forty people died each day from enemy fire, hunger, exposure to cold or from lack of appropriate medical treatment.[167]

At the time, while promoting the development of the peacekeeping concept in their UN discussions, the ICRC and Western governments wanted to declare the Muslim enclaves as 'safe areas' and protect them with military aircraft and deployment of UN troops.[168] These proposals were rejected by UN officials. They feared that these new initiatives would deflect international resources away from implementation of the Vance-Owen peace plan towards unclear new goals.[169]

Fearing that tens of thousands of Muslims would be massacred in the Srebrenica enclave, the Security Council decided on 16 April 1993 under Chapter 7 of the UN Charter to declare the city of Srebrenica and its surroundings a safe area.[170] The safe area was to be demilitarised and protected from armed attacks against the enclave. UN forces were supposed to collect arms, ammunition, mines, explosives and any fighting gear. On 21 April the Special UN envoy in the city declared that it was officially demilitarised. From 22 to 27 April a Security Council fact-finding mission visited Srebrenica. It recommended that the Security Council declare other regions in Bosnia as safe areas. Although the new concept was unclear, the Security Council decided in May to extend the new safe-area concept to five more regions in Bosnia: Bihać (300,000 people), Goražde (60,000 people), Sarajevo (300,000 people), Tuzla (240,000 people) and Žepa (20,000).[171]

UN troops in the safe areas were allowed to respond with force to any armed action against the safe areas, and not only in self-defence. They were authorised to use force in order to deter assaults on the safe areas, to monitor local ceasefires and to control main tactical posts. NATO – who enforced the naval embargo and the no-flight zone over Bosnia from 1992 – contributed air support for the defence of UN troops on the ground.[172]

The 'safe-area' concept was depicted as the epitome of the change in the concept of peacekeeping by adopting robust measures.[173] In fact, it covered the lack of interest by the international community in terminating the civil war through the use of decisive force or in taking care of the full security of civilians in the fighting areas. From the perspective of the UN Secretariat, the new concept was confusing. The Secretariat personnel raised a list of questions that remained unanswered by the Security Council. For example, they asked: How can an impartial operation protect only one faction (the Muslims)? Should the UN forces protect a geographical area, the people in the area or its own personnel? How will the Security Council respond to attacks on safe areas?[174]

In addition to the confusion surrounding the new concept of safe areas, there were practical and logistical problems. The UN Secretariat estimated that in order to provide security to the six announced safe areas, it would require 34,000 troops.[175] These troops had to be heavily armed and well trained due to the dangerous situation. However, under pressure from Security Council members to reduce these numbers, the Secretariat claimed that 'taking into account the realistic volume of troops and material resources expected to be made available to UNPROFOR', it recommended a 'light option' of 7,600 troops. This option took into account that the safe areas depended on the consent and cooperation of the local belligerents. In contradiction to its support for the development of the peacekeeping concept and the safe-area mandates, the Security Council embraced the light option.[176]

An analysis of the discussion that led to the execution of the peacekeeping operation in Bosnia, Macedonia and Croatia in 1992 and 1993 reveals a lot about the continuity and changes in international politics after the Cold War. The use of UN peacekeeping operations in the former Yugoslavia was not the result of a new concept that took root in the organisation. Local and international circumstances were what led to resolutions to deploy UN forces in Croatia, Bosnia and Macedonia. The main players that promoted the execution of the operation were the following: the United States, most of the EC members, the veteran contributor countries, countries from the region that feared a spillover of the conflict, and members of the Organization of the Islamic Conference (OIC). These countries did not succeed in reaching an agreement to launch an enforcement operation that would terminate the conflict, as determined in Chapter 7 of the UN Charter. Thus, for example, the members of the international community failed to supply the resources to implement Vance and Owen's peace proposals. Instead, they were only able to agree on an intervention based on a vague concept of second-generation peacekeeping in order to contain the conflicts in the former Yugoslavia, and they only contributed the bare minimum of resources. By contrast, the Secretariat expressed a more conservative approach regarding the execution of peacekeeping operations in the battlefields of the former Yugoslavia, in contrast to what one might have expected in light of their attempts to develop the concept. Out of all the players that took part in the discussions, it was the Secretariat personnel responsible for managing the operations who were most sensitive to the real motives of the organisation's members. They understood that the support of these nations for the execution of a multidimensional peacekeeping operation as part of the new concept of peacekeeping operations was the result of their inability to consolidate a clear diplomatic stance regarding the termination of the conflict.

**Somalia: from traditional peacekeeping to peacebuilding**

Simultaneously with the interventions in Cambodia and the former Yugoslavia, the UN also intervened in Somalia. The Somalia intervention was conducted in three stages, and three interventions were deployed under the authority of the Security Council. The first, called the United Nations Operation in Somalia I (UNOSOM I), operated from April 1992 until March 1993. The second operation, called the United Nations Operation in Somalia II (UNOSOM II), operated from March 1993 (when the units serving in UNOSOM I merged into UNOSOM II) until March 1995. Another operation called Unified Task Force (UNITAF) was executed from

December 1992 to May 1993; UNITAF operated a multinational force under the label of Operation Restore Hope, under American and not UN command. About thirty thousand soldiers, policemen and civilians served during the height of the operation in the first half of 1993. This operation became the biggest mission ever managed by the UN up to that point.[177]

The Secretariat personnel and UN diplomats frequently consider the UN intervention in Somalia as a failure, for several reasons. They note that the mandates defined by the Security Council were not sufficiently clear; the allocation of forces to the operations was inadequate; the local factions did not cooperate; and much more besides.[178] Boutros-Ghali argued that, despite its failures, the intervention scored many achievements. For example, he said that the intervention spurred a national reconciliation process and saved the lives of hundreds of thousands of Somalis. In Boutros-Ghali's opinion, the main reason for its failures was the lack of cooperation on the part of the local Somali factions.[179] This stance is also backed by Madeleine Albright, then US Ambassador to the UN.[180]

Most of the studies on the subject support the stance of the diplomats. Similar to the studies cited above regarding Cambodia and the former Yugoslavia, most try to draw conclusions that can be implemented in the future.[181] The common denominator of these studies is that they focus on the US intervention stage while ignoring other time periods in the operation. For this reason they emphasise aspects of humanitarian aid and military intervention but do not connect them to issues of nation-building. And nation-building issues constituted a central part of the discussion on operations in Somalia even before the American intervention, as will be clarified in the course of the chapter below. Aside from references to the Agenda for Peace, the diplomats, Secretariat employees and researchers do not explain to what extent the execution of the operations in Somalia were affected by the UN discussions on the new 'operations concept'. Moreover, existing studies do not provide a comprehensive picture regarding the various positions adopted by the members of the international community regarding the multi-purpose operations in Somalia and the actual contribution of these operations. In this section, I discuss the sequence of events unfolding in the intervention until the first half of 1993.

Somalia, a society based on large extended families (clans), had been engulfed in a civil war since 1988. During the early stages of the conflict, from 1988 to 1991, a war raged between a loose coalition of political factions based on a close-knit clan system to depose the country's dictator, Siad Barre, who had ruled the country since 1969, and his allied clans. Therefore, the political objectives of the factions were formulated according to clan strategic interests rather than state-wide national considerations. The clans were headed by the strongest warlords who fought to maintain their positions by increasing their factions' economic resources and territory, in both the cities and the countryside. This, in turn, increased feelings of alienation from, and animosity towards, the Somali government and among themselves. The continuous fighting caused the state's administration and infrastructure to collapse in January 1991, when Barre's supporters fled from the capital city of Mogadishu. They were finally defeated in a series of battles during 1992. No legitimate government was established in its stead. Under the new situation, vital government services – including security, economic and health services – ceased to function. The incessant fighting destroyed approximately 70 per cent of the livestock and the rich agricultural fields in the south of the country were ruined. The effect of this social upheaval on Somali society was the creation of a dire humanitarian crisis. Tens of thousands of people were killed and a wave of hundreds of thousands of refugees and internally displaced persons flooded the region. In the summer of 1992, it was estimated that 10 to 20 per cent of the seven million Somalis were at immediate risk. Thousands perished each day. By the end of 1992, it was estimated that 300,000 Somalis had perished from fighting, hunger and disease. It seemed as if the entire Somali society was being annihilated.[182]

Confronting the crisis in Somalia, UN personnel and Somali faction leaders generated a conceptual linkage between humanitarian relief operations and military deployment, beginning in early 1992. As in the Bosnia instance, the first paradigms connecting UN military peacekeeping to humanitarian relief operations in Somalia emphasised that a UN military contingency should deploy in the capital, Mogadishu, for three reasons. First, it was estimated that with a population of approximately one million people, this was the largest concentration of Somali people in need. Second, Mogadishu had a large harbour and an international airport. Finally, the city was the centre of fighting between two powerful Somali factions of the Hawiye clan who dominated south-central Somalia. Mohamed Farrah Aidid, Hawiye/Habr-Gidir headed one faction while Ali Mahdi, Hawiye/Abgal headed the other. Mahdi, with many other leaders of splinter factions of the Darod – the largest clan in Somalia, from south and north-east parts of the country – demanded a heavily armed UN force or even some form of transitional administration, as was in place in Cambodia at the time. However, Aidid, who led the most powerful faction in south-central Somalia, the USC/SNA (United Somali Congress/Somali National Alliance), objected to all initiatives as he feared that any intervention would weaken his powers.[183]

At the time there was wide support in the UN for deployment of multifunctional peacekeeping operations for the settlement of civil wars. The Secretariat reports tried to find a way to bypass the negotiation impasse between the Somali factions. In disregard to traditional UN peacekeeping doctrine, they established a linkage between humanitarian relief operations and the need for military forces to protect UN workers even in the absence of a stable ceasefire.[184] After unceasing diplomatic efforts, they received Mahdi's and Aidid's support for the deployment of fifty military observers backed by armed UN military units, which were, in principle, supposed to protect and secure aid operations around Mogadishu.[185] The decision to implement the UNOSOM I was adopted by the UN Security Council on 24 April 1992.[186] As in Bosnia, the small observer force had no impact on the conflict or the humanitarian crisis. But unlike in Bosnia, no country volunteered troops for the protection of humanitarian aid operations in Mogadishu.

The failure to address the worsening humanitarian situation in Somalia generated mounting international pressure for a large military humanitarian intervention. Although Africa lacked a powerful regional organisation such as the EC, three organisations did adopt a proactive stance for Somalia's assistance: the Organization of African Unity (OAU), the Arab League, and the OIC. They called for heavy military intervention with official authorisation for the use of force. These ideas received wide support from the international media and various NGOs and international humanitarian organisations; the latter organisations were frustrated that they could not distribute aid to the Somalis due to the continuous fighting and local violence.[187] However, in the case of Somalia, the international alliances differed from those in the former Yugoslavia. With a lack of any strategic interest in Somalia, the five permanent members of the Security Council adopted traditional measures during most of 1992 to cope with the Somali crisis, such as an arms embargo, peacemaking efforts and the delivery of humanitarian aid. Only slowly did they allow the deployment of small contingencies of UN observers and military forces. The Security Council encouraged the Somali factions to sign a peace agreement that would allow the creation of a transitional government.[188] United Kingdom Permanent Representative Sir David Hannay represented this stance by claiming that 'You can't have peacekeeping if you haven't got a peace to keep.'[189]

UN Secretary-General Boutros-Ghali, frustrated by the deteriorating situation in Somalia while Western attention was focused on Bosnia, admits in his memoirs that he decided to advance a proposal for 'a form of "peace enforcement" as mentioned in the Agenda for Peace'.[190] In a report dated 22 July, he advocated a UN 'presence in all regions and to adopt an innovative and comprehensive approach dealing with all aspects of the Somalia situation ...'[191] Boutros-Ghali proposed establishing linkages between political, security and humanitarian issues. Moreover, in order to encourage the establishment of a peacekeeping operation, he claimed that it enjoyed the support of 'all political leaders and elders in Somalia'.[192]

Based on this fallacious information on the situation in Somalia and under international pressure, the Security Council authorised a peacekeeping mission which was designed to deploy a force of approximately four thousand troops throughout Somalia. This modest, lightly equipped force was expected to escort humanitarian relief operations and supervise demobilisation and disarmament of armed militias, despite the fact that it was relatively small and lacked authorisation to use force exception in self-defence.[193]

Boutros-Ghali's diplomatic success was, unfortunately, followed by failed implementation of his plan. Most countries had no strategic interest in Somalia and thus failed to send troops. Governments rightly feared that even with the dubious consent given by local leaders, their troops would be in physical danger. Pakistan was an exception; the country volunteered a battalion of five hundred troops to Mogadishu, but they only arrived on 14 September 1992. By November of that year, UN personnel in Somalia admitted the failure of the mission, claiming that the 'humanitarian supplies have become the basis of an otherwise non-existent Somali economy' and that the Somali clans were fighting over these resources.[194] By the autumn of 1992, the international lack of commitment was obvious. In the former Yugoslavia there were more than twenty thousand UN personnel, the majority of which were military troops. At the exact same time in Somalia, five hundred troops were bogged down in Mogadishu airport struggling to secure their own protection rather than providing protection for humanitarian relief operations.

An abrupt change of United States policy in late 1992 transformed the intervention. During 1992, the USA was the chief provider of humanitarian aid to Somalia, but US senators and congressmen announced their frustration that most aid failed to reach the needy and was instead exploited by the armed militias. By October, a US Congressional committee demanded that the US government force the distribution of aid to Somalis by providing protection to the humanitarian convoys. The mounting national and international pressure galvanised the American government to take action.[195]

In October, the United States proposed leading a robust peace enforcement operation as advocated by the international community during 1992, but under its control and not the UN's.[196] However, the pressure to intervene was not accompanied by a concrete plan. In late November, UN Secretary-General Boutros-Ghali reviewed five different models of military operation in Somalia.[197] This generated disagreement between US representatives and UN Secretariat personnel over the objectives of the new intervention. US officials insisted that their own military operation, entitled Operation Restore Hope, would be independent from the UN command and control, and that its main objective was only to secure humanitarian aid to the people in need in south-central Somalia. UN officials, on the other hand, wanted the US forces to deploy throughout the country, disarm all Somali militias, and rebuild Somalia according to ideas presented in the Agenda for Peace and other reports. In the words of the Secretary-General, 'The crisis results from the fact that Somalia has become a country without a government or other political authorities with whom the basis for humanitarian activities can be negotiated.'[198]

UN Security Council Resolution 794 of 3 December 1992 tried to resolve the argument between the narrower and broader military humanitarian options. Therefore, it 'determined also to restore peace, stability and law and order with a view to facilitating the process of a political settlement under the auspices of the United Nations, aimed at national reconciliation in Somalia'. At the same time, it authorised the forces 'to use all necessary means to establish as soon as possible a secure environment for humanitarian relief operations in Somalia'.[199]

In practice, the American government decided that a UNITAF in Somalia would follow the narrow interpretation of the Security Council's resolution. As of December 1992, it was three times the size of the forces in Bosnia, with approximately thirty thousand troops, of which two-thirds were from the United States and the rest from other countries. These troops were heavily armed. Although UNOSOM civilian and military operations continued, UNITAF forces operated outside the UN command-and-control structure. UNITAF limited its operations to 40 per cent of Somalia's territory, in the centre of the hunger-stricken area of south-central Somalia. It also enjoyed a mandate to use force when necessary. Although it did not receive a mandate to protect civilians and never established safe areas as in Bosnia, UNITAF forces, and especially the Americans, used lethal fire against any militia that dared to interfere with their aid-protection operations. This practice achieved effective results and the horrific scenes of hundreds of starved and sick people dying daily had dropped dramatically by the early months of 1993.

In order to curtail UN Secretariat criticism of its narrow interpretation of the Security Council mandate, US representatives, together with UN officials, encouraged the signing of a comprehensive peace agreement amongst all Somalia clan-based political parties. The Addis Ababa peace agreement was signed by the representatives of fifteen Somali factions in two stages on 8 January 1993 and on 27 March 1993. The agreements called for the establishment of a Transitional National Council (TNC), which resembled the Cambodian SNC. The TNC was to symbolise Somali sovereignty and for two years to supervise the establishment of new democratic state institutions, while officially inviting the UN to supervise its work.

The Addis Ababa Agreement failed to create a transitional institution. There were several reasons for this. First, the clans had been only slightly affected by UNITAF's operations and thus continued to fight among themselves for political and economic resources. Moreover, with the understanding that the multinational intervention provided lucrative sources of income and that participation in the national political process would increase international political support, many factions began to split; by late 1994, UN officials put the number of factions at twenty-eight.[200]

Second, the intervention failed to establish permanent civilian institutions and a standing national civilian police service that could confront the armed militias. The reconstruction of local government administration was not coordinated among the various multinational players. The international intervention achieved mixed results in advancing sporadic initiatives to collect 'weapons for cash' and making agreements with warlords to hand over their heavy weapons into storehouses.[201]

On 26 March 1993 the Security Council passed Resolution 814, which authorised a new peacekeeping operation named UNOSOM II. This seems to show that the Security Council conceded that the limited UNITAF, emphasising the delivery of humanitarian aid, should be replaced in favour of a comprehensive state-building operation, as advocated in the Agenda for Peace. This resolution changed the operation's goals towards the wider option advocated by the UN

Secretariat. For the first time in its history, the Secretariat received broad authority to command a multidimensional peacekeeping mission of approximately twenty-eight thousand troops with the authority to use force. The operation was also expected to rebuild Somalia's civilian institutions.

Detailed analysis of the international community's incentive for the change points to growing concern about the widening gap between member state declarations in the UN of what was desirable and the actual readiness of member states to support their statements with actions. In other words, the states were unwilling to contribute the personnel (and other materials and resources) needed to carry out operations based on the new expanded concepts – such as peace enforcement and peacebuilding – that they themselves formulated. The US and many European governments wanted to pull their troops out of Somalia for several reasons. The major humanitarian objective – ending the famine – had been achieved. Pressure by both local and international media to take action was waning. They feared that prolonging their troops' presence would also increase their casualties and the demands to invest more in the intervention. Therefore, they preferred to transfer wide-scale powers to the UN Secretariat while creating a false notion of commitment by the international community to state-building goals. Warnings from the Secretariat that it did not have the necessary managerial or logistical capabilities for such an operation were ignored.[202]

During most of 1992, the Security Council was reluctant to implement the new models of peacekeeping in Somalia. Contrary to its recommendations in Bosnia, the Secretariat recommended robust actions in Somalia. However, even when it received the desired mandate, such as in Security Council Resolution 767, the Secretariat lacked the means to implement it. Only in late 1992 was more support raised, when the United States government wanted to launch a humanitarian operation. In public it was presented as the implementation of the new concept of peacekeeping. In practice, it focused on humanitarian aid and ignored many other issues raised by the Secretariat, such as disarmament of the local forces and the creation of new civil institutions. On paper, the Security Council resolution in March 1993 to execute UNOSOM II aspired to implement the most advanced interpretation of the new models for peacekeeping operations. This resolution integrated almost every new suggestion that was raised during the 1992 UN deliberations on the subject, including peace enforcement, peacebuilding, etc. However, this mandate was accepted mainly due to political pressure by Western countries that wanted an excuse to withdraw from the country rather than to invest in it. UN Secretariat personnel were aware of the ruse. They warned that there was a need for a continuous presence in Somalia and large financial and material commitments in order to implement the most ambitious mandate of the time. This warning was put to the test on 5 June 1993 when Aidid's powerful USC/SNA militia attacked UN forces in several locations (see Chapter 4).

## Support for the changes in peacekeeping

An analysis of the discussions that took place in the UN in the course of 1992 and at least until the first half of 1993 reveals a dramatic change in the importance accorded by the international community to peacekeeping operations in the world order after the Cold War. In light of the successes of the operations deployed in the waning years of the Cold War, peacekeeping operations were viewed as a tool with which to deal with, and resolve, intrastate (and not only interstate) conflicts. A variety of proposals were raised regarding the assigning of multidimensional goals to operations, to change the political, social, economic, and security-related environment of the states in which the conflicts were waged. The new proposals integrated new concepts such as peace enforcement, peacebuilding, preventive deployment, and integration of all the activities before, during, and after the conflict. A few isolated UN representatives raised warning bells and posed unanswered questions, including: When does a conflict require the execution of a multidimensional operation? Who makes such a determination? What is the distinction between the various multidimensional operations? To what extent do the multidimensional interventions also affect the principles of execution of the operations? What resources are required for success? Thus these essential, substantive questions were brushed aside in favour of diplomatic support that crossed traditional political alliances. A wide variety of developed and developing countries, from Western and Eastern Europe, supported the new initiatives. One of the main players in these reforms was ambitious Secretary-General Boutros-Ghali. Thus, it was believed that the post-Cold War international community was creating a new method for taming threats in the new, formative world order.

I examined the support for the concept change of peacekeeping operations in light of the international community's response to three conflicts: Cambodia, the former Yugoslavia and Somalia; these three conflicts generated the three largest operations. In Cambodia, the decision to execute the operation did not stem from an accepted conceptual change in the organisation but from an unusual initiative designed to encourage the conflicted parties to sign a peace agreement. The operation was conducted according to traditional principles and did not cause an essential change, as embodied in the concepts that were raised in the organisation in this period. The UN settled for the founding of a legitimate government, at the expense of dealing with the challenges of disarmament of militias, training a civilian police force to operate according to universal standards, entrenching human rights norms and more. This operation was unique in that it enjoyed a clear consensus of the international community.

In the former Yugoslavia, the UN was dragged into a conflict after the EC failed in its mediation attempts. After the international community failed to reach agreement on clear guidelines for resolving the conflict, it was decided to execute a traditional peacekeeping operation in Croatia with a number of new goals. Later on, the Security Council was dragged into a peacekeeping operation in Bosnia to secure humanitarian aid. However, they were required to implement the new goal according to the traditional principles of attaining the agreement of the local sides, impartiality (no bias) and no use of force. A change occurred at the beginning of 1993 when it was decided, for the first time, to create 'safe areas', based on Chapter 7. However, this concept was not sufficiently clarified. The question was: To what extent would the international community succeed in resolving differences of opinion among its members, decide on clear goals, and provide the necessary means so that the operations deployed in Croatia, Bosnia and Macedonia would help resolve conflicts?

Among the conflicts examined in this chapter, Somalia represented the greatest challenge to the new concept of peacekeeping operations. The challenge of a collapsed state was unfamiliar and represented a clear threat to the stability of the region. Despite the fact that there were many conceptual similarities between the discussions conducted in the organisation at that time on operations and the situation in Somalia, the international community refused to authorise, and provide the means for, the execution of an operation of the necessary size in Somalia throughout most of 1992. Only the intervention of the United States in November 1992 caused a change. But even the American humanitarian operation was limited and geared to pacify pressures at home, rather than to implement the new concept of peacekeeping operations. Only the decision to execute UNOSOM II in March 1993 falls into the category of implementing the new concept. As such, it even enjoyed international support. The main challenge was whether the international community would provide the needed funding, personnel and equipment in order to transform the amorphous concept discussed in Agenda for Peace from theory into practice.

## Notes

1   UN, *Blue Helmets*, 1989, pp. 3–4.
2   For the special characteristics of intrastate conflicts after the Cold War, see especially: Kaldor, *New and Old Wars*, pp. 2–12, 69–152.
3   See Chapter 1.
4   In some of the speeches, representatives claimed that they represented the opinions of many other nations. For example, King Hassan II of Morocco claimed to represent the African countries, the Arab League and Islamic countries.
5   S/21323, 30 May, 1990.
6   S/23457, 22 January 1992; S/23486-A/47/77, 28 January 1992; S/23505-A/47/80, 30 January 1992; S/23509, 3 February 1992; S/23512-A/47/82, 5 February 1992; S/23576-A/47/89, 12 February 1992; S/24025-A/47/232, 28 May 1992; S/24238-A/47/312, 6 July 1992.
7   S/PV.3046, 31 January, 1992.
8   S/23500, 31 January 1992, p. 3.
9   S/23500, 31 January 1992.

10   S/24111-A/47/277, 17 June 1992.
11   One of the proofs for this is that during the writing of these lines in 2015, the document appeared as a cornerstone for discussion of peacekeeping operations in UN documents.
12   B. Boutros-Ghali, *Unvanquished: A US-UN Saga* (New York: Random House 1999), pp. 26-27.
13   S/24111-A/47/277, 17 June 1992, para. 8-19, 75-86.
14   S/24111-A/47/277, 17 June 1992, para. 15, 20-22.
15   S/24111-A/47/277, 17 June 1992, para. 23-33.
16   S/24111-A/47/277, 17 June 1992, para. 43.
17   S/24111-A/47/277, 17 June 1992, para. 46-54.
18   S/24111-A/47/277, 17 June 1992, para. 55-59.
19   For an extensive description of the conflicts of interests among the various players, see Chapter 1.
20   A/47/253, 4 June 1992, pp. 3, para. 11.
21   A/47/253, 4 June 1992, para. 12.
22   A/47/386, 31 August, 1992.
23   A/RES/47/71, 14 December, 1992.
24   A/SPC/47/SR.15, 11 November 1992, pp. 6-7; A/SPC/47/SR.16, 12 November 1992, pp. 5-6, 9-11; A/SPC/47/SR.17, 13 November 1992, pp. 21-22; A/SPC/47/SR.18, 16 November 1992, pp. 5-6; A/C.4/48/SR.23, 8 February 1994, pp. 4, 10-12; A/C.4/48/SR.24, 31 January 1994, pp. 5-6, 13-14; A/C.4/48/SR.26, 2 February 1994, pp. 7-8.
25   A/47/675-S/24816, 18 November 1992, pp. 28-33.
26   A/SPC/47/SR.14, 10 November 1992; A/SPC/47/SR.15, 11 November 1992; A/SPC/47/SR.16, 12 November 1992; A/SPC/47/SR.17, 13 November 1992; A/SPC/47/SR.18, 16 November 1992.
27   A/RES/47/120, 18 December 1992.
28   For information about the modus operandi of the Council, see the first section of Chapter 1.
29   S/24210, 30 June 1992.
30   A/AC.121/39/Rev.1/Add.2, 24 April 1992, pp. 2-6; A/SPC/47/SR.14, 10 November 1992, pp. 5-6; A/SPC/47/SR.16, 12 November 1992, pp. 13-16; A/SPC/47/SR.17, 13 November 1992, pp. 6-7.
31   A/SPC/46/Sr.13, 30 October 1991, p. 9; A/SPC/47/SR.17, 13 November 1992, pp. 3-4.
32   This separatist stance of the Chinese was expressed in several speeches delivered by its representatives at several occasions in the Security Council and the General Assembly. See especially the speech of the Chinese Prime Minister at a session of the Security Council on January 31, 1992: S/PV.3046, 31 January 1992, pp. 91-94.
33   S/24587, 25 September 1992.
34   S/24728, 29 October 1992.
35   S/25036, 30 December 1992.

36  S/24872, 30 November 1992.
37  S/25344, 26 February 1993; S/25859, 28 May 1993; S/25944-A/47/965, 15 June 1993.
38  *Ibid.*
39  A/47/253, 4 June 1992, p. 8, para. 32; pp. 18-20, para. 88-103; A/49/136, 2 May 1994, p. 3.
40  A/47/965-S/25944, 15 June 1993, p. 5, para. 23.
41  Bellamy, Williams and Griffin, *Understanding Peacekeeping*, pp. 23-25, 399-401; P. V. Jakobsen, *Nordic Approaches to Peace Operations: A New Model in the Making?* (London & New York: Routledge, 2006), pp. 267-282; Kaldor, *New and Old Wars*, pp. 69-111.
42  According to the chronological order in which they were executed (except if they were executed in the same region as the operations): the Western Sahara (MINURSO), on the Iraq-Kuwait border (UNIKOM), in Angola (UNAVEM II), in El Salvador (ONUSAL), in Cambodia (UNAMIC, UNTAC), in the former Yugoslavia (UNPROFOR), in Somalia (UNOSOM I, UNOSOM II), in Rwanda (UNOMUR, UNAMIR), in Georgia (UNOMIG), in Haiti (UNMIH), in Liberia (UNOMIL).
43  For more on this issue, see especially the admission of French Foreign Minister Alain Juppé of November 1994, regarding the modus operandi of the Security Council even after the conclusion of the Cold War. A/49/667-S/1994/1279, 11 November 1994, pp. 2-4.
44  Ajello and Wittmann, 'Mozambique', pp. 437-450; Hall and Young, *Confronting Leviathan*; Synge, *Mozambique*; UN, *The United Nations and Mozambique*.
45  S/1999/1257, 16 December 1999; Adelman and Suhrke, 'Rwanda'; Dallaire and Beardsley, *Shake Hands with the Devil*; Jones, 'Rwanda'; UN, *Blue Helmets*, 1996, pp. 339-398.
46  Von Einsiedel and Malone, 'Haiti'; Malone, *Decision-Making in the Security Council*; UN, *Blue Helmets*, 1996, pp. 611-636.
47  A/48/173, 25 May 1993, pp. 3-4, para. 12-19.
48  S/23613, 19 February 1992, para. 49.
49  Akashi, 'The Challenges Faced by UNTAC', pp. 195-196.
50  See Chapter 1 for information.
51  S/24800, 15 November 1992, para. 24.
52  S/PV.3099, 21 July 1992; S/RES/783, 13 October 1992; S/PV.3143, 30 November 1992; S/RES/792, 30 November 1992; Goulding, *Peacemonger*, pp. 259-260.
53  Doyle, *UN Peacekeeping in Cambodia*, pp. 67-70; Findlay, *Cambodia: The Legacy*, pp. 36-40.
54  S/23613, 19 February 1992, Section F, para. 135-136; S/25154, 25 January 1993, para. 79-85; S/25719, 3 May 1993, para. 89-94; United Nations, *The United Nations and Cambodia, 1991-1995* (New York: United Nations Department of Public Information, 1995), pp. 14, 32-33; S. Whitworth, *Men, Militarism, and UN Peacekeeping: A Gendered Analysis* (Boulder, CO: Lynne Rienner, 2004), p. 61.

55  S/23613, 19 February 1992, section F; S/23870, 1 May 1992, para. 37–39; S/24578, 21 September 1992, para. 47–51; S/25154, 21 January 1993, para. 6, 79; S/25719, 3 May 1993, para. 88, 93.
56  S/25719, 3 May 1993, para. 88, 94; Whitworth, *Men, Militarism and UN*, pp. 61–62; B. Williams, 'Returning Home: The Repatriation of Cambodian Refugees', in Doyle, Johnstone and Orr (eds), *Keeping the Peace*, pp. 167, 173–173.
57  UNHCR *Tripartite Memorandum of Understanding*, 21.11.1991; de Cuéllar, *Pilgrimage for Peace*, pp. 468–469.
58  H. E. Smith, G. S. Nieminen and M. Kyi Win, *Historical Dictionary of Thailand* (Lanham, MD: Scarecrow Press, 2nd edn, 2005), pp. 215–216; Williams, 'Returning Home', p. 168.
59  A/46/608-S/23177, 30 October 1991; S/23613, 19 February 1992, para. 135–136; UNHCR, *Tripartite Memorandum*.
60  S/23613, 19 February 1992, para. 150–156; E. Uphoff Kato, 'Quick Impacts, Slow Rehabilitation in Cambodia', in Doyle, Johnstone and Orr (eds), *Keeping the Peace*, p. 186.
61  S/25289, Feb. 13, 1993, para. 30–32; S/25719, 3 May 1993, para. 95.
62  S/23870, 1 May 1992, para. 40–43; A/47/285-S/24183, 25 June 1992; S/24286, 14 July 1992, para. 15; S/24578, 21 September 1992, para. 52–56; S/25154, 25 January 1993, para. 6, 86–87; Uphoff Kato, 'Quick Impacts', pp. 193–194.
63  S/25719, 3 May 1993, para. 50–51.
64  Uphoff Kato, 'Quick Impacts', pp. 201–202; W. Shawcross, *Deliver Us From Evil: Peacekeepers, Warlords and a World of Endless Conflict* (New York: Simon & Schuster, 2000), pp. 73–74, 80.
65  Whitworth, *Men, Militarism and UN*, pp. 64–74.
66  *Ibid.*, p. 70.
67  S/24578, 21 September 1992, para. 57–58; S/RES/792, 30 November 1992, para. 13; S/25154, 25 January 1993, para. 88–90; S/25289, 13 February 1993, para. 20–25; S/25719, 3 May 1993, para. 98–103; P. Le Billon, 'The Political Ecology of Transition in Cambodia 1989–1999: War, Peace and Forest Exploitation', *Development and Change*, 31:4 (2000), 785–805; P. Le Billon, 'Logging in Muddy Waters: The Politics of Forest Exploitation in Cambodia', *Critical Asian Studies*, 34:4 (2002), 565, 574–577; S. Peou, 'Cambodia in 1998: From Despair to Hope?', *Asian Survey*, 39:1 (January 1999), 23.
68  S/25154, 25 January 1993, para. 65–69.
69  S/24578, 21 September 1992, para. 52–53; S/25719, 3 May 1993, para. 70–74; Whitworth, *Men, Militarism and UN*, pp. 62–63.
70  I. V. Langran, 'Cambodia in 2000: New Hopes Are Challenged', *Asian Survey*, 41:1 (January 2001), 157; S. Peou, 'Cambodia in 1997: Back to Square One?', *Asian Survey*, 38:1 (January 1998), 72; Peou, 'Cambodia in 1998', 24; K. Un and J. Ledgerwood, 'Cambodia in 2001: Toward Democratic Consolidation?', *Asian Survey*, 42:1 (January, 2002), 104.
71  M. Beresford, 'Cambodia in 2004: An Artificial Democratization Process', *Asian Survey*, 45:1 (January 2005), 138–139; O. Weggel, 'Cambodia in 2005: Year of Reassurance', *Asian Survey*, 46:1 (January 2006), 158.

72  S/23613, 19 February 1992, para. 9.
73  J. L. Ledgewood and K. Un, 'Global Concepts and Local Meaning: Human Rights and Buddhism in Cambodia', *Journal of Human Rights*, 2:4 (2003), 531–549.
74  Reports of the Human Rights Committee: E/CN.4/2003/114, 18 December 2002; E/CN.4/2005/116, 20 December 2004; E/CN.4/RES/2005/77, 20 April 2005; E/CN.4/2006/110, 24 January 2006; E/CN.4/2006/110/Add.1, 8 March 2006.
75  S/24286, 14 July 1992, para. 15; S/24578, 21 September 1992, para.6, 8–11; S/25154, 25 January 1993, para. 6, 16–23; S/23870, 1 May 1992, para. 11–14; S/25719, 3 May 1993, para. 16–19; Akashi, 'The Challenges Faced by UNTAC', 195.
76  S/25719, 3 May 1993, para. 14.
77  Martin, *Cambodia: A Shattered Society*, pp. 21–23, 274–275, 291–293.
78  Australia, Department of Foreign Affairs, *Cambodia: An Australian Peace Proposal*, pp. 11–20.
79  S/23613, 19 February 1992, para. 92.
80  S/23613, 19 February 1992, para. 159–163; S/23870, 1 May 1992, para. 44–45; S/24578, 21 September 1992, para. 59–64; S/24800, 15 November 1992, para. 10; S/25154, 15 January 1993, para. 70–71, 91–93; S/25719, 3 May 1993, para. 104–107.
81  S/24578, 21 September 1992, para. 28, 34.
82  S/24578, 21 September 1992, para. 30–40; S/25154, 25 January 1993, para. 76.
83  Akashi, 'The Challenges Faced by UNTAC', 192, 195.
84  S/23613, 19 February 1992, para. 93–111; S/24578, 21 September 1992, para. 27; Goulding, *Peacemonger*, pp. 245–255.
85  Quoted in M. W. Doyle, 'Authority and Elections in Cambodia', in Doyle, Johnstone and Orr (eds), *Keeping the Peace*, p. 153. The 'State of Cambodia' was one of the names given to the Phnom Penh government.
86  Regarding the country-wide moratorium on the export of logs from Cambodia, see also the section that discusses the economic aspects of the intervention.
87  S/25154, 25 January 1993, para. 57–59, 65, 72–73; S/25719, 3 May 1993, para. 61–63; Findlay, *Cambodia: The Legacy*, pp. 59–63.
88  S/25154, 25 January 1993, para. 56.
89  S/25719, 3 May 1993, p. 14.
90  Findlay, *Cambodia: The Legacy*, pp. 62–63.
91  D. Chandler, 'Three Visions of Politics in Cambodia', in Doyle, Johnstone and Orr (eds), *Keeping the Peace*, pp. 25–52.
92  R. B. Albritton, 'Cambodia in 2003: On the Road to Democratic Consolidation', *Asian Survey*, 44:1 (2004), 103–105; Beresford, 'Cambodia in 2004', 134–137; G. De Launey, 'Cambodia Sentences Sam Rainsy', *BBCNEWS*, Phnom Penh, 22 December 2005; P. P. Lizee, 'Cambodia in 1995: From Hope to Despair', *Asian Survey*, 36:1 (1996), 83–88; P. P. Lizee, 'Cambodia in 1996: Of Tigers, Crocodiles and Doves', *Asian Survey*, 37:1 (1997), 66–69; S. Peou, 'Cambodia in 1997', 69–72; S. Peou, 'Cambodia in 1998', 20–22; Un and Ledgerwood, 'Cambodia in 2001', 101–103; Weggel, 'Cambodia in 2005', 155–161.
93  Goulding, *Peacemonger*, p. 264.

94 S/25289, 13 February 1993, para. 33-39; S/25719, 3 May 1993, para. 22.
95 Boutros-Ghali, *Unvanquished*, pp. 211-213.
96 S/RES/810, 8 March 1993; S/RES/840, 15 June 1993; S/RES/860, 27 August 1993; Akashi, 'The Challenges Faced by UNTAC', pp. 195-196; UN, *United Nations and Cambodia*, doc. 90, 91, 93, 95, 96.
97 Boutros Ghali, *Unvanquished*, p. 36.
98 See, for example, Article 15 of Resolution 826 from 20 May 1993.
99 The thirteen resolutions were: S/RES/668, 20 September 1990; S/RES/717, 16 October 1991; S/RES/728, 8 January 1992; S/RES/745, 28 February 1992; S/RES/766, 21 July 1992; S/RES/783, 13 October 1992; S/RES/792, 30 November 1992; S/RES/810, 8 March 1993; S/RES/826, 20 May 1993; S/RES/835, 2 June 1993; S/RES/840, 15 June 1993; S/RES/860, 27 August 1993; S/RES/880, 4 November 1993.
100 S/PV. 3057, 28 February 1992; S/PV.3099, 21 July 1992; S/PV.3143, 30 November 1992; S/PV.3181, 8 March 1993; S/PV.3213, 20 May 1993; S/PV.3227, 2 June 1993; S/PV.3237, 15 June 1993; S/PV.3270, 27 August 1993; S/PV.3287, 5 October 1993; S/PV.3303, 4 November 1993.
101 S/1995/1031, 13 December 1995; S/PV.3607, 13 December 1995; Boutros-Ghali, *Unvanquished*, pp. 246-248.
102 A/54/549, 15 November 1999, p. 105. Even the report of the UN investigation of the massacre of about 8,000 male Muslims of age 14 and above in Srebrenica in July 1995 avoided stating clearly whether the operation was a success or failure. It did state that the UN intervention saved many lives.
103 Two studies that adopt this approach are: J. Gow, *Triumph of the Lack of Will: International Diplomacy and the Yugoslav War* (London: Hurst & Company, 1997); Touval, *Mediation in the Yugoslav Wars*.
104 S. L. Burg and and P. S. Shoup, *The War in Bosnia-Herzegovina: Ethnic Conflict and International Intervention* (Armonk NY: M.E. Sharp, 1999), pp. 46-56; J. R. Lampe, *Yugoslavia as History: Twice There Was a Country* (Cambridge: Cambridge University Press, 2000), pp. 334-341, 368; UN, *Blue Helmets*, 1996, p. 487.
105 C. Bennett, *Yugoslavia's Bloody Collapse: Causes, Course and Consequences* (London: Hurst & Company, 1998), pp. 83-101; L. J. Cohen, *Serpent in the Bosom: The Rise and Fall of Slobodam Milošević* (Boulder, CO: Westview Press, 2002), pp. 87-163; S. P. Ramet, *The Three Yugoslavias: State-Building and Legitimation, 1918-2005* (Washington, DC: Woodrow Wilson Center Press, 2006), pp. 341-362; W. Zimmerman, *Origins of a Catastrophe: Yugoslavia and Its Destroyers* (New York: Times Books 1997), pp. 17-27.
106 Bennett, *Yugoslavia's Bloody Collapse*, pp. 101-107, 123-131; Ramet, *The Three Yugoslavias*, pp. 364-367, 371-372; Zimmerman, *Origins of a Catastrophe*, pp. 52-56, 61-62, 65-78, 90.
107 Bennett, *Yugoslavia's Bloody Collapse*, pp. 67-82; Lampe, *Yugoslavia as History*, pp. 321-322, 327-345; Ramet, *The Three Yugoslavias*, pp. 234-240, 263-340, 354-359.
108 Bennett, *Yugoslavia's Bloody Collapse*, pp. 106-111, 116-143; Ramet, *The Three Yugoslavias*, pp. 369-379; Zimmerman, *Origins of a Catastrophe*, pp. 28-140.

109 Burg and Shoup, *The War in Bosnia-Herzegovina*, pp. 46–127; Touval, *Mediation in the Yugoslav Wars*, pp. 15–38; Zimmermann, *Origins of a Catastrophe*.
110 Gow, *Triumph of the Lack of Will*, pp. 61–65, 156–183; Touval, *Mediation in the Yugoslav Wars*, pp. 39–133.
111 Baker and DeFrank, *The Politics of Diplomacy*, pp. 478–83, 634–51; M. Glitman, 'US Policy in Bosnia: Rethinking a Flawed Approach', *Survival*, 38:4 (1996–1997), 66–83; Gow, *Triumph of the Lack of Will*, pp. 202–222; D. Halberstam, *War in a Time of Peace: Bush, Clinton, and the Generals* (New York: Touchstone, 2002), pp. 30–127; Zimmermann, *Origins of a Catastrophe*.
112 Gow, *Triumph of the Lack of Will*, pp. 186–201.
113 S/PV.3009, 25 September; Touval, *Mediation in the Yugoslav Wars*, pp. 44–45, 71–77.
114 Touval, *Mediation in the Yugoslav Wars*, pp. 22–38; Zimmerman, *Origins of a Catastrophe*, pp. 63–65, 138.
115 Touval, *Mediation in the Yugoslav Wars*, pp. 78–82; Zimmerman, *Origins of a Catastrophe*, pp. 141–177.
116 Touval, *Mediation in the Yugoslav Wars*, pp. 49–60.
117 Lord Carrington served as official mediator of the EC from September 1991 until August 1992, when he ultimately resigned in frustration over his failure to coordinate a uniform policy to resolve the conflict.
118 A total of fourteen ceasefire agreements had been signed by February 1992.
119 As of 1991, the following nine states were members of the West European Union: Italy, Belgium, the United Kingdom, Germany, Luxembourg, Netherlands, Spain, Portugal, and France. The organisation ceased to exist in 2011. See: www.weu.int.
120 S/RES/713, 25 September 1991; S/PV.3009, 25 September 1991. Touval, *Origins of a Catastrophe*, pp. 45–46, 87–97.
121 S/23240, 26 November 1991; S/RES/743, 21 February 1992.
122 de Cuéllar, *Pilgrimage for Peace*, pp. 482–490.
123 S/RES/721, 27 November 1991.
124 S/23169, 25 October 1991.
125 S/23169, 25 October 1991; S/23239, 24 November 1991; S/23280/Annex III, 11 December 1991; S/23592, 15 February 1992; S/23777, 2 April 1992; S/23844, 24 April 1992.
126 S/23363, 5 January 1992, para. 5–7; S/23513, 4 February 1992.
127 S/23592, 15 February 1992, p. 7.
128 S/RES/743, 21 February 1992; S/PV/3055, 21 February 1992.
129 S/23777, 2 April 1992.
130 S/RES/743, 21 February 1992; S/25264/Annex I, 10 February 1993; S/UN, *Blue Helmets*, 1996, p. 514.
131 S/23280/Annex III, 11 December 1991; S/23513, 4 February 1992; S/23592, 15 February 1992; S/23777, 2 April 1992; S/23844, 24 April 1992; S/RES/762, 30 June 1992; S/RES/769, 7 August 1992; S/RES/779, 6 October 1992.
132 S/23280/Annex III, 11 December 1991; Gow, *Triumph of the Lack of Will*, p. 103.

133 S/24353, 27 July 27, 1992; S/24600, Sep. 28, 1992; S/25264, 10 February 1993, para. 12–17.
134 S/24600, 28 September 1992.
135 S/23280, 11 December 1991; S/23592, 15 February 1992; A/C.2/47/2 22 October 1992; S/26017, June 30, 1993; S/PV.3356, March 31, 1994.
136 S/24600, 28 September 1992, para. 19–22; S/25264, 10 February 1993, para. 13; S/25777, 15 May 1993, para. 9; S/24353, 27 July 1992, para. 23–24; S/25777, 15 May 1993, para. 10.
137 S/RES/871, 4 October 1993; S/26828, 1 December 1993, para. 6–7.
138 S/24353, 27 July 1992.
139 S/25777, 15 May 1993, para. 10.
140 S/23169, 25 October 1991; S/25193, 29 January 1993; S/25218, 1 February 1993; S/25237, 3 February 1993; S/PV.3174, 19 February 1993, pp. 6–13S/25777, 15 May 1993; S/25777, 15 May 1993, para. 18.
141 S/25777, 15 May 1993, p. 6.
142 Gow, *Triumph of the Lack of Will*, pp. 77–89; Touval, *Mediation in the Yugoslav Wars*, pp. 107–112; Zimmerman, *Origins of a Catastrophe*, pp. 188–190.
143 S/24007, 27 May 1992. For a general account of the conflict, see: Zimmerman, *Origins of a Catastrophe*, pp. 172–201; Burg and Shoup, *The War in Bosnia-Herzegovina*; C. R. Shrader, *The Muslim-Croat Civil War in Central Bosnia: A Military History, 1992-1994* (College Station, TX: Texas A&M University Press, 2003).
144 S/23363, Jan. 5, 1992, para. 17, 30; S/23805, 10 April 1992; S/23812, 12 April 1992; S/23830, 22 April 1992; S/23833, 23 April 1992; S/23838, 24 April 1992; S/23840, 24 April 1992; S/23845, 26 April 1992; S/23854, 29 April 1992; S/23874, 4 May 1992; S/23900, 12 May 1992; S/23905,12 May 1992; S/23997, 26 May 1992.
145 S/23363, 5 January 1992; S/23900, 12 May 1992; S/24007, 27 May 1992; A/46/929-S/24011, 27 May 1992; S/24024, 27 May 1992; S/24081, 10 June 1992; S/24096, 15 June 1992; S/24099, 15 June 1992; A/47/225-S/23998, 26 May 1992; Baker and DeFrank, *The Politics of Diplomacy*, pp. 644–651; The Netherlands Institute for War Documentation (NIOD), *Srebrenica: A 'Safe' Area: Reconstruction, Background, Consequences and Analyses of the Fall of a Safe Area* (Amsterdam: Netherlands Institute for War Documentation, NIOD, 2002), Part I, Ch. 6.
146 In April 1992, Boutros-Ghali approved the limited deployment of only forty-one military observers to Sarajevo and Mostar. Yet even they were evacuated from Bosnia when the security situation worsened.
147 S/23860, 30 April 1992; S/23900, 12 May 1992, p. 9, para. 27.
148 S/23900, 12 May 1992, para. 28–30. For the sake of comparison, see below on the development of the intervention in Somalia in the course of 1992.
149 S/23900, 12 May 1992, para. 30.
150 S/RES/752, 15 May 1992.
151 S/24000, 26 May 1992.
152 S/24075, 6 June 1992.
153 S/RES/757, 30 May 1992; S/ 24075, 6 June 1992; S/RES/758, 8 June 1992; S/RES/761, 29 June 1992; S/24201, 29 June 1992; S/25264, 10 February 1993.

154 S/RES/770, 13 August 1992; S/24540, 10 September 1992; S/RES/776, 14 September 1992.
155 UN, S/25264/Corr1, 12 February 1993.
156 S/25264, 10 February 1993.
157 For a description of the many difficulties encountered in the execution of the humanitarian aid mandate, see: P. Corwin, *Dubious Mandate: A Memoir of the UN in Bosnia, Summer 1995* (Durham, NC: Duke University Press, 1999), pp. 11–13, 103, 152–154, 161–162; T. Seybolt, *Humanitarian Military Intervention: The Conditions for Success and Failure* (Oxford: Oxford University Press, 2008), pp. 63–68. For a personal angle and description of the Sarajevo siege, see: Z. Filipović, *Zlata's Diary: A Child's Life in Sarajevo* (New York: Viking, 1994).
158 S/PV.3106, 13 August 1992.
159 See, for example, the arguments of the representatives of Pakistan and Venezuela in the Council regarding these issues. The two representatives emphasised that the Serbs were the aggressor parties, and the Muslims the victims. S/PV.3228, June 4, 1993.
160 S/24100, 15 June 1992, p. 5; S/25264, 10 February 1993, pp. 6–7; S/1994/333, 24 March 1994, para. 2–5; S/1994/674/Add.2, 12 December 1994, pp. 10, 17–18; S/1995/222, 22 March 1995, pp. 5–12; M. Rose, *Fighting for Peace: Bosnia 1994* (London: Harvill Press, 1998), p. 188.
161 Corwin, *Dubious Mandate*, pp. 196–198; Rose, *Fighting for Peace*, p. 190.
162 S/25264, 10 February 1993, para. 19.
163 S/25264, 10 February 1993; S/25700, 30 April 1993; S/1994/94, 28 January 1994; Corwin, *Dubious Mandate*, pp. 31–38; Findlay, *The Use of Force*, pp. 219–255; Rose, *Fighting for Peace*, pp. 75–76.
164 S/RES/795, 11 December 1992.
165 S/23996, 23 May 1992; S/24851, 25 November 1992; S/24852, 25 November 1992; S/24923, 9 December 1992; S/1994/300, 16 March 1994.
166 Burg and Shoup, *The War in Bosnia-Herzegovina*, pp. 214–262; Gow, *Triumph of the Lack of Will*, pp. 232–253; Touval, *Mediation in the Yugoslav Wars*, pp. 120–123.
167 S/25700, 30 April 1993; S/26415, 8 September 1993.
168 D. Owen, *Balkan Odyssey* (New York: Harcourt Brace, 1995), pp. 66–67, 134–136.
169 S/25939, 14 June 1993; Shawcross, *Deliver Us from Evil*, p. 99.
170 S/RES/819, 16 April 1993; S/25700, 30 April 1993; NIOD, *Srebrenica*, Vol. II, Ch. 2.
171 S/25700, Annex II, 30 April 1993; S/RES/824, 6 May 1993; S/RES/836, 4 June 1993; S/1994/555, 9 May 1994; Owen, *Balkan Odyssey*, pp. 177–182.
172 S/RES/713, 25 September 1991; S/RES/757, 30 May 1992; S/RES/781, 9 October 1992; S/RES/787, 16 November 1992; S/RES/816, 31 March 1993; S/RES/824, 6 May 1993; S/RES/836, 4 June 1993; S/26335, 18 August 1993; S/1994/555, 9 May 1994; Gow, *Triumph of the Lack of Will*, pp. 129–141.
173 See the report of the Security Council Mission to Srebrenica, which reinterpreted the concept of 'preventive diplomacy'. The concept was first introduced in Boutros Ghali's *An Agenda for Peace* to denote the deployment of troops before a conflict, mainly as observers; now, the new model interpreted it as providing protection for civilians. In: UN, S/25700, 30 April 1993.

174 S/25700, 30 April 1993; S/25700/Annex II, 30 April 1993; S/1994/555, 9 May 1994.
175 S/25939 and addendum 1, 14 June 1993.
176 S/25939, 14 June 1993; S/1994/555, 9 May 1994.
177 United Nations, *The United Nations and Somalia 1992–1996* (New York: United Nations Department of Public Information, 1996).
178 The official UN study on the operations in Somalia is found in the Comprehensive Report on Lessons Learned from the United Nation Operation in Somalia that was published at the end of 1995. United Nations, *The Comprehensive Report on Lessons Learned from United Nation Operation in Somalia (UNOSOM) April 1992-March 1995*, in www.un.org/Depts/dpko/LESSONS/Somalia.pdf.
179 UN, *Blue Helmets*, 1996, pp. 315–316.
180 M. Albright and B. Woodward, *Madam Secretary* (New York: Miramax Books, 2003), pp. 145–146.
181 C. Adibe, *Managing Arms in Peace Process: Somalia* (New York and Geneva: United Nations, 1995); K. Allard, *Somalia Operations: Lessons Learned* (USA: CCRP, 1995); W. Clarke and J. Herbst (eds). *Learning from Somalia, The Lessons of Armed Humanitarian Intervention* (Boulder, CO: Westview Press, 1997); W. J. Durch, 'Introduction to Anarchy: Intervention in Somalia', in Durch (ed.), *UN Peacekeeping*, pp. 352–353; R. B. Oakley and J. I. Hirsch, *Somalia and Operation Restore Hope: Reflections on Peacemaking and Peacekeeping* (Washington, DC: United States Institute of Peace, 1995); I. Lewis and J. Mayall, 'Somalia', in Berdal and Economides (eds), *United Nations Interventionism*, pp. 108–139; M. Sahnoun, *Somalia: The Missed Opportunities* (Washington, DC: United States Institute of Peace, 1994); UN, *The United Nations and Somalia*; UN, *Blue Helmets*, 1996, pp. 285–318.
182 L. Cassanelli, *Victims and Vulnerable Groups in Southern Somalia* (Ottawa, Canada, May 1995); D. Compagnon, 'Somali Armed Movements: The Interplay of Political Entrepreneurship and Clan-Based Factions', in C. Clapham (ed.), *African Guerrillas* (Oxford: Oxford University Press 1998), pp. 75–79.
183 S/23693, 11 March 1992; S/23829, 21 April 1992; Boutros-Ghali, *Unvanquished*, p. 55.
184 S/23693, 11 March 1992.
185 S/23829, 21 April 1992.
186 S/RES/751, 24 April 1992.
187 C. Kertcher, *The Search for Peace – or for a State: UN Intervention in Somalia, 1992–1995* (Jerusalem: The Harry S. Truman Research Institute for the Advancement of Peace, 2003), pp. 8–11.
188 S/RES/733, 23 January 1992; S/RES/746, 17 March 1992; S/PV.3060, 17 March 1992; S/RES/751, 24 April 1992; S/RES/767, 24 July 1992.
189 S/PV.3060, 17 March 1992, pp. 56–57.
190 Boutros-Ghali, *Unvanquished*, p. 55.
191 S/24343, 22 July 1992.
192 S/23829, 21 April 1992; S/24343, 22 July 1992; S/RES/767, 27 July 1992; S/24480, 24 August 1992 and Annex; S/24480/Add.1, 28 August 1992; S/RES/775, 28 August

1992; S/24531, 8 September 1992; S/24532, 8 September 1992; Boutros-Ghali, *Unvanquished*, p. 55.
193  S/RES/767, 27 July 1992; S/24531, 28 October 1992; S/24532, 8 September 1992; J. Drysdale, 'Foreign Military Intervention in Somalia: The Root Cause of the Shift from UN Peacekeeping to Peacemaking and Its Consequence', in Clarke and Herbst (eds), *Learning from Somalia*, p. 125.
194  S/2489, 27 November 1992.
195  According to the memoirs of former US Foreign Secretary Colin Powell, the only voice in the American government against the US military intervention came from National Security Advisor Brent Scowcroft, who warned that after the ending of the humanitarian crisis the USA would find it difficult to withdraw from Somalia. Boutros-Ghali, *Unvanquished*, p. 56; W. D. Freeman, R. B. Lambert and J. D. Mims, 'Operation Restore Hope: US Centcom Perspective', *Military Review*, 73:9 (1993), 61–72; J. T. Howe, 'Relations Between the United States and the UN in Somalia', in Clarke and Herbst (eds), *Learning from Somalia*, pp. 175–76; H. Johnston and T. Dagne, 'Congress and the Somalia Crisis', in Clarke and Herbst (eds), *Learning from Somalia*, pp. 192–194; A. S. Natsios, 'Humanitarian Relief Intervention in Somalia: The Economics of Chaos', in Clarke and Herbst (eds.), *Learning from Somalia*, pp. 77–82; C. L. Powell and J. E. Persico, *My American Journey* (New York: Ballantine Books, 1996), pp. 550–551; J. L. Woods, 'US Government Decision-Making Process During Humanitarian Operations in Somalia', in Clarke and Herbst (eds), *Learning from Somalia*, pp. 151–156.
196  Boutros-Ghali, *Unvanquished*, pp. 58–59; Woods, 'U.S. Government', p. 158.
197  S/24868, 30 November, 1992.
198  UN, *The United Nations and Somalia*, document 34.
199  S/RES/794, 3 December 1992.
200  C. Kertcher, 'Same Agenda, Different Results: The UN Interventions in Cambodia and Somalia after the Cold War', in U. Rabi (ed.), *International Intervention in Local Conflicts: Crisis Management and Conflict Resolution Since the Cold War* (London: I.B. Tauris, 2010), pp. 28–29.
201  S/24992, 19 December 1992; S/25168, 26 January 1993; S/25354, 3 March 1993; F. M. Lorenz, 'Confronting Thievery in Somalia', *Military Review*, 74:8 (1994), 46–55; F. M. Lorenz, 'Law and Anarchy in Somalia', *Parameters*, 23:4 (1993), 27–41; Oakley and Hirsch, *Somalia and Operation Restore Hope*, pp. 87–91; M. R. Ganzglass, 'The Restoration of the Somali Justice System', in Clarke and Herbst (eds), *Learning from Somalia*, pp. 22–27; G. Prunier, 'The Experience of European Armies in Operation Restore Hope', in Clarke and Herbst (eds), *Learning from Somalia*, pp. 135–141; R. G. Patman, 'Disarming Somalia: The Contrasting Fortunes of United States and Australian Peacekeepers During United Nations Intervention, 1992–1993', *African Affairs*, 96:385 (1997), pp. 519–526.
202  Boutros-Ghali, *Unvanquished*, pp. 92–93; Howe, 'Relations Between the United States and the UN in Somalia', pp. 178–186; H. Smith, 'Intelligence and UN Peacekeeping', *Survival*, 36:3 (1994), 174–192; Woods, 'US Government Decision-Making', p. 161.

# 4

# The failure of peacekeeping as a panacea to civil wars 1993–95

Ostensibly, it would seem that, during the first half of 1993, the UN had succeeded in dealing effectively with all the 'new threats' to international peace and security in the form of intrastate conflicts, by the implementation of multidimensional peacekeeping operations when needed. The operations were viewed as the ideal means for terminating conflicts and establishing peace. However, the truth was that the UN resolutions to execute the operations in their new format were unanimous only in outward appearance. As already discussed, despite the overall support for development of the operational objectives, there were many differences of opinion among the various UN delegations regarding numerous issues that appeared in the Agenda for Peace.

In 1993, the UN's main peacekeeping operations were in Cambodia, the former Yugoslavia and Somalia; these were supposed to become models of success of the new multidimensional operations. However, as explained in Chapter 1, it is generally agreed that, despite the success of the Cambodian operation, three events caused an erosion in the status of the multidimensional operations and international support for them: the fighting in Mogadishu (in Somalia) on 3–4 October 1993; what has been termed the genocide in Rwanda, from April to July 1994; and the withdrawal of UN forces from Srebrenica in July 1995, which created the conditions for Bosnian Serb militias to murder thousands of Muslim men and youths.

In the course of 1995, the viewpoint that large multidimensional peacekeeping operations could resolve conflicts was in crisis. The Security Council did not rush to execute new operations. In July 1995, the number of personnel participating in peacekeeping operations was 67,269 soldiers, civilian policemen and other staff members. By July 1996, the number of personnel had dropped to 25,296. Meanwhile, debts to the organisation reached more than three billion dollars.[1] Thus, by 1995, diplomats as well as Secretariat personnel began to withdraw their support for multidimensional peacekeeping operations.

The section below examines the change in the support given to large multidimensional operations. The chapter demonstrates that the conceptual crisis was not necessarily due to failure of the operations but to disagreements within the United Nations on their management and organisation. At the same time, through qualitative analysis of the interventions in Somalia and the former Yugoslavia from the second half of 1993 to 1995, we will see that when the powers lacked strategic interests in specific operations, the peacekeeping operations suffered as a result – ranging from total abandonment (in Somalia), to dubious alliances that led to deadlock and, later, to tipping the military balance in Bosnia. This explains why the Security Council only infrequently authorised the execution of new operations after that point, and when it did authorise them it preferred to base them on the traditional principles from the Cold War era.

## The victory of old politics over new models

International support for changing the concept of peacekeeping operations represented clear evidence of a new world order after the Cold War. Despite the problems in implementing the amorphous concepts, it seemed – until the first half of 1993 – that the international community, engaged in lively discussion of the new concept, could overcome its differences of opinion and formulate a conceptual model that would be acceptable to all the members. This chapter describes how, from the second half of 1993, the Secretariat, Security Council and General Assembly began to withdraw the support they had earlier given to the concept change of the operations. They withdrew from their earlier commitments, and the controversy surrounding the new peacekeeping concept increased. Each UN organ tended to blame its lack of success on other organs, in an attempt to maintain or increase its political power in the organisation.

### *The international rift over the concept of peacekeeping*

Although there was widespread agreement among UN representatives regarding the need to set new objectives and principles of success for the operations, this consensus did not extend to all the details discussed. In an attempt to clarify the objectives and principles of success of the peacekeeping operations, the General Assembly requested all the world's governments to express their opinions on the operations, including submitting concrete proposals to improve them.[2] In May 1993, the Security Council also joined this request.[3] However, the response to both requests was scant. The following countries were the only ones to submit their opinions: the members of the EU, Australia, the five Nordic countries, Federal Republic of Yugoslavia, New Zealand, Namibia, Canada and Russia.[4] The poor response shows that although the peacekeeping operation as an issue was often discussed in the General Assembly, it was not an issue of great importance to most of the world's countries. When we closely examine the composition of the countries that did rise to the challenge, we see that in most cases, the ones that pushed to improve and refine the peacekeeping operations technique were the same countries that had pushed for a change in concept at the end of the 1980s. It is important to note that Denmark, a veteran contributor to peacekeeping operations and

UN member that was active in the Nordic group of states, was president of the EC in 1987 when the country requested that the work of the Special Committee be resumed. Denmark also was serving as the president of the EU when it made proposals to improve the operations in April 1993. Unfortunately, no study has yet been carried out to examine the internal politics of these bodies regarding the peacekeeping operations after the end of the Cold War Era.

Due to the great experience accumulated by the Western veteran contributor countries in sending forces to UN operations, numerous states turned to them with requests for assistance and clarification regarding the traditional concept of operations, sometimes in order to create forces in their own country that could take part in the peacekeeping operations.[5] At the beginning of the 1990s, Canada led a campaign for promoting a clear logistic doctrine for peacekeeping operations.[6] New Zealand forcefully promoted aspects connected to protecting the personnel taking part in the operations.[7] As mentioned earlier, the five Nordic countries were the most consistent players in discussions of peacekeeping operations, and their involvement was most systematic. Thus, these countries accepted the changes in the goals and principles of success of the peacekeeping operations, almost without reservation.[8]

Starting from 1992, this handful of countries received increasing support from European countries (in contrast to what happened in the late 1980s). The support was mainly from the twelve member states of the EC that were promoting the formation of the European Union at the time.[9] These countries also supported the expansion of the goals and success principles of the operations. Most of the East European states also supported this change, similar to the policies of West European countries, at least with regard to peacekeeping operations. When EU representatives presented the official stance of the EU regarding peacekeeping operations, they also represented the Bulgarian and Romanian governments, which added their names to the EU's announcement, even though they were not official members.[10]

During 1992–94, most of the West and East European representatives gave unqualified support for the advancement of the new goals and principles of success regarding the execution of multidimensional operations. According to these principles, operations could be executed before, during and after a conflict. The new goals were meant to promote human rights and the principles of 'good governance'. Many of the spokesmen even believed that humanitarian aid facilitates peacemaking during conflicts. On the other hand, other speakers argued that operations should feature local support and the non-use of force with the exception of self-defence.[11]

In general, the developing countries supported the execution of multidimensional operations until 1995, but most of the member countries began to quickly backtrack from the new concept in the course of 1993. They felt that the change had been too fast, and that the concept itself was too fuzzy and unclear.[12] The NAM group was the most prominent in its opposition. Until the beginning of

1994, the development of the multidimensional concept won formal support. But in that same year, after the execution of numerous peacekeeping operations, a special discussion was held about the operations in the Eleventh Ministerial Conference of the Non-Aligned Countries that was held in Cairo, Egypt, from 31 May to 3 June 1994. In contrast to the declaration of support for multidimensional operations in 1992, now the members of the movement expressed sceptical viewpoints. While it was agreed that peacekeeping operations are an important technique in the maintenance of international peace and security, it was emphasised that operations should not replace political settlements between the sides involved in a conflict.

In this context, it was noted that all techniques must be exhausted before deciding to use enforcement methods according to Chapter 7 of the UN Charter. This is in accordance with the traditional distinction between the diplomatic methods outlined in the Charter's Chapter 6 and the enforcement methods outlined in its Chapter 7. In order to dispel all doubts, the movement members consolidated ten principles relating to peacekeeping operations that are very similar to the traditional principles of the Cold War days.[13] Similar resolutions were adopted a year later at the Summit Conference of Heads of State or Government of the NAM in Cartagena, Colombia, and since then, they have been regularly ratified at the movement's conferences.[14] This approach received additional backing in the speeches of representatives of scores of UN nations, and at forums of the Special Committee and of the Fourth Committee.[15]

The dispute that prevailed between the members of the international community regarding the concept of the operations also existed within the UN Secretariat between two schools of thought on how to administer the operations. The first, more conservative, viewpoint was presented by Marrack Goulding, who was in charge of managing the peacekeeping operations from the end of the 1980s until the beginning of 1993. He expressed his opposition to the widespread support in the Secretariat for the changes in the operations as expressed by Secretary-General Boutros-Ghali at the time. In March 1993, Goulding was transferred from his peacekeeping operations job to serve as USG for Political Affairs (USG-PA) until 1997. In this capacity, Goulding served as mediator in conflicts that the UN intervened in as part of the peacemaking technique.

At the beginning of his new role in the first half of 1993, Goulding expressed reservations regarding the new goals and the change in the principles of the operations and supported a return to the concept of traditional operations. He argued before the Special Committee that more attention should be paid to the political conditions that facilitate the success of peacekeeping operations. Some of the conditions for success were (according to Goulding) connected to a clearer formulation of the mandate: obtaining the agreement of all conflicted sides to deployment of the peacekeeping operation forces and ongoing cooperation between all the UN member nations and the conflicted sides. Goulding felt that these indispensable conditions must be met prior to execution of all operations.[16]

Representatives of the second school of thought in the Secretariat insisted that the main difficulty in the successful execution of operations was not political-conceptual but managerial-organisational in nature. In 1993, the demand to execute large, complex and multidimensional operations within countries during conflicts, especially in Somalia and the former Yugoslavia, intensified the organisational pressures imposed on the UN Secretariat. On 14 March, Secretary-General Boutros-Ghali circulated a report called *Improving the Capacity of the United Nations for Peace-Keeping*. In his report, Boutros-Ghali emphasised the official stance of the Secretariat, according to which the recipe for success of the gamut of UN operations was support by the member states with regard to organisational aspects such as funding, manpower allocation, equipment and logistics.[17]

At the beginning of May 1994, Kofi Annan (who served as USG for Peacekeeping Operations from March 1993 to December 1996) spoke to the members of the Special Committee on this issue. Annan argued that the primary reason for the organisation's inability to run the operations effectively was the fact that several large countries had avoided paying their debts to the UN. Annan railed against the tendency of countries to abandon the operations before they were finished, due to public pressure, and warned of the destructive ramifications of this conduct on the collective security principle on which the entire organisation was based. He felt it inadvisable to discuss the enlarged goals and principles that had developed unchecked over the previous two years, but recommended instead a focus on the real solution: to increase the resources available to the UN. In addition, Annan believed that operations should be granted flexible mandates that would allow them to cope more successfully with difficulties and dangers on the ground, even including lack of local support and authorisation to use force.[18] Boutros-Ghali was more cautious and, in abrogation of his arguments in the Agenda for Peace, he argued that a distinction must be made between peacekeeping operations and peace enforcement operations. Similarly, he did not mention a connection between enforcement operations and preventive diplomacy and peacemaking.[19]

The more nuanced view of the Secretary-General towards the execution of peacekeeping operations to resolve conflicts around the world was connected to the increased caution exercised by the Security Council in its resolutions regarding peacekeeping operations. Even on 30 September 1993 – a few days before the violent incident in Mogadishu, Somalia[20] – the five permanent members of the Security Council signed a joint declaration expressing a retraction of their earlier declarations. They said the following:

> Given the gap between current demands on the United Nations and its capabilities pending the reforms mentioned above, the Ministers affirmed that new commitments should be weighed very carefully, and made only after fundamental questions of mandate, objectives, adequacy of force, availability of resources, risk to personnel and length of mandate have been examined and satisfactorily resolved.[21]

Seven months later, on 3 May 1994, the more cautious peacekeeping operation approach prevailed when Security Council President Ibrahim Gambari from Nigeria made an announcement on behalf of all the Council members; this declaration was a rejoinder to the Secretary-General's report of 14 March. The declaration consisted of six questions composed by the Security Council members, questions that the Security Council must address before adopting resolutions regarding the execution of an operation. The questions were: Is the continuance of the present condition likely to be a threat (or become a threat) to international peace and security in the future? Are there existing regional arrangements in place which are capable of helping to resolve the situation? Is there a valid ceasefire in place, and are the parties committed to a peace process with the goal of achieving a political arrangement? Does a political goal exist, and can it be expressed in a mandate? Can a precise mandate be determined for a UN operation? Can the safety and security of the operation's personnel be reasonably secured; that is, can reasonable guarantees be provided by the major conflicted sides regarding the safety and security of the UN staff?[22]

### The pressure for reform of the Security Council

In order to understand why the Security Council representatives (and especially the five permanent members) became so cautious, we must understand the global diplomatic context of UN activities and not limit ourselves to a description of the theoretical disagreements regarding the new concept of the operations. Although in 1992 most of the member states were in favour of advancement of the multidimensional goals for peacekeeping operations, they were not at all supportive of the clandestine, arbitrary conduct of the Security Council. In the course of 1992, a demand was raised for managerial reform under the heading of 'World Democratization'. At the end of that year, this demand became one of the 'hot' issues in the General Assembly discussions. On 11 December 1992 the Secretary-General was asked to examine the stances of the interested countries regarding the question of the size of the Security Council and its composition.[23] Within half a year, seventy-nine delegations sent their governments' opinions in response to the Secretary-General's appeal. Some countries even added new ideas regarding the powers of the Council in the new world order.[24]

It was agreed that by the fiftieth year celebration of the founding of the UN, the Security Council would be enlarged, its composition would be changed and its work would be more transparent and efficient. Finally, proposals were raised to insert revisions into the UN Charter.[25] But in actuality, no practical resolutions were accepted. The five permanent members managed to retain their unique privileges in the Council from the Cold War days. Therefore, the subject was supposed to be discussed in the organisation in the future, with expectations for a change in the balance of international powers (in the Security Council) that would resolve the issue.[26]

The Security Council faced increasing pressure on the part of the contributor nations to update them regarding any changes in the operations and include them in the Council's discussions.[27] This was due to a growing demand for manpower, financing and equipment to supply the large, multidimensional peacekeeping operations. Malaysia's representative criticised the Council for not involving those countries that allocated soldiers in the discussions.[28] In the spring of 1994, the Canadian government invited other contributor countries (that allocated soldiers) to a discussion on the variety of problems presented above. In the following months, delegations from developed and developing nations alike took action to compel the Security Council to consult with them regarding any change in the operations, with the threat of withdrawing their political and material support. The Argentinian delegate presented the conflict faced by a member nation in the Security Council on the background of events that transpired that very year, in which a Rwandan representative and member of the Security Council acted on all fronts to prevent a discussion on the country's internal conflict that led to the genocide in the spring of 1994.[29]

International pressure finally left its mark, and from the end of 1994 the Security Council members agreed to receive compromise proposals. According to the new arrangement, meetings would be held between the Security Council members, the countries contributing soldiers, and the Secretariat staff before any kind of resolution would be adopted regarding the operations.[30] The decision of the General Assembly in December represented the culmination of all the achievements that had reduced the absolute power held by the Security Council from the beginning of the 1990s.[31]

Despite the reforms adopted in the mid-1990s regarding the functioning of the Security Council, most of the states claimed that these were temporary successes in the long-range political struggle to change the balance of powers in the UN. This stance was consistently supported by the Secretariat.[32] Most of the delegations felt that the steps taken had not gone far enough, and that the Security Council must do more to achieve the credibility that would encourage more countries to send forces to the operations.[33] Since then, the Council's resolutions – which are supposed to represent international consensus in dealing with conflicts on behalf of the maintenance of international peace and security – are permanently under suspicion of mainly promoting the interests of the permanent members of the Security Council.[34]

The main reason for the formation of alliances in the organisation was not to increase the Council's efficiency and adapt it to the changes in goals and success principles of the operations. Instead, first and foremost, alliances were formed to increase the influence of states on the decision-making process. Each alliance formulated its own criteria for making the Council's work more efficient. Thus, the five permanent members championed 'efficiency'; according to their approach, this required diplomatic discussion in a small forum in order to make decisions quickly. But, in fact, this practice served to maintain their privileges in the organisation. By contrast, most of the countries demanded a consensus before adopting resolutions, to ensure that the principles of collective security and neutrality were maintained in the organisation, thus encouraging countries to allocate forces to operations. In practice, this reform was meant to weaken the Council's powers so that it would not be able to ignore the political interests of the member states regarding the conflicts under discussion. In the summation of the discussion, it was agreed that despite (or perhaps because of) the Council's composition and modus operandi, the Security Council did not define clear mandates and well-defined goals for operations.[35]

*Revision of the new concept*

The theoretical discussions that took place in the organisation, and the ongoing pressure for reform in the Security Council's decision-making process, did not solve the problems faced in deployment of the operations. Three years after Boutros-Ghali had begun to serve as Secretary-General, he decided to re-examine the goals and success principles of the operations. This was due to the following factors: the meagre achievements of the operations; the unwillingness of many countries to allocate forces to the operations; and the expressions of no-confidence (on the part of the member states) regarding the capacity of the Secretariat to achieve satisfactory results.

In January 1995, Boutros-Ghali publicised his viewpoint in a document entitled *Supplement to an Agenda for Peace*. Despite his claims to the contrary – Boutros-Ghali stated that this document did not express a change in the viewpoint and positions he had expressed in the Agenda for Peace – the spirit of the new supplement ran counter to that of the Agenda for Peace of two and a half years earlier. Despite his reservations, Boutros-Ghali still felt that the UN was the most important and suitable body to deal with international crises. In contrast to his arguments in the Agenda for Peace, in the Supplement he integrated preventive diplomacy with peacemaking, while returning the emphasis to diplomacy. Also, Boutros-Ghali dropped any mention of the use of force during these diplomatic endeavours. He also continued to support the peacebuilding technique with the built-in reservation that it is difficult to discern when peacebuilding prevents the eruption of conflict and when it assists in stabilising a diplomatic arrangement.

With regard to peacekeeping operations, Boutros-Ghali again emphasised the existence of three basic principles on which UN involvement has been based since the days of the Cold War: (1) agreement of the conflicted sides; (2) impartiality in the activities of the peacekeeping force; (3) a no-force policy, with the exception of self-defence. He also emphasised the differentiations that were accepted in March 1994: that a clear distinction must be made between enforcement operations and peacekeeping operations. Boutros-Ghali argued that 'peace-keeping and the use of force (other than in self-defence) should be seen as alternative techniques and not as adjacent points on a continuum, permitting easy transition from one to the other.'[36] The enforcement issue was pushed to the end of the document, perhaps with the goal of creating a clear distinction between enforcement and the peacekeeping operations themselves. In the Supplement, Boutros-Ghali flatly opposed the idea of the UN being responsible for the execution of enforcement operations. He presented NATO as an example of a regional organisation with an approach different from that of the Secretariat for resolving disputes, the reason being that the two organisations have different mandates. Boutros-Ghali argued that NATO, as a regional organisation with authority to use enforcement powers, was able to use this authority to promote its biased policies and interests. Thus, even though NATO professes international legitimacy, it does not receive or deserve it (according to Boutros-Ghali).

It emerges, then, that the position espoused by the Supplement is actually contradictory to that of the Secretariat's earlier avowed position during 1992 and 1993, probably as a result of the experience of the UN Secretariat with respect to Bosnia and Somalia. These operations – which were supposed to represent a new, multidimensional model that improved the traditional concept – received harsh criticism during their deployment. In the course of their deployments, the mandates assigned them were changed numerous times and their goals were unclear, as was the entire political process that the peacekeeping operation was supposed to leverage. In the very last pages of the report, the Secretary-General called for coordination between all the entities concerned with the promotion of peace in the world (states, regional organisations, supra-governmental organisations, private foundations, international agencies etc.). However, he still attributed most of the influence to states. Governments were therefore the key entities to be taken into consideration in all activities discussed in the position-paper (i.e. the Supplement). Governments are what facilitate, and fund, the activities. They directly allocate the required personnel and equipment. They also determine the policy of the UN's special agencies and its international organisations. States' willingness to provide ongoing support and intervention to the conflicted parties was vital for the Secretary-General's success in realising the mandates he was given.[37] The placement of the states at the forefront of the discussion and recognition of their supreme importance in the maintenance of international peace and security, even after the Cold War, constitute Boutros-Ghali's tacit confession that his vision of a new world order, characterised by globalisation and supra-state relations, had failed. The new world order, though affected by the conclusion of the Cold War and globalisation, had not changed substantially.

Publication of the *Supplement to an Agenda for Peace* led to a lively public discussion among the Security Council members and representatives of dozens of delegations from other countries, which re-examined the changes made to the concept of peacekeeping operations. There was sweeping agreement regarding a number of issues. First, the organisation's members agreed that an operation cannot succeed without local support. This concept also included the responsibility of the local players for the safety and security of the international community's representatives in their country. Despite the differences among the perspectives and stances of the state representatives in the UN regarding the new concept of the operations, it was evident that a consensus prevailed that intrastate conflicts, and the globalisation process, can threaten the maintenance of international peace and security. Nevertheless, everyone agreed that, despite the changes in the world order, the individual state remained the key player that contributed to or threatened the maintenance of international peace and security. In a discussion on the other issues, the delegate representatives hesitated to reject outright the changes made to operations, but were also unable to formulate points of agreement regarding them.

There was no clear alliance among the five permanent members. The representatives of the United States, the United Kingdom, France and Russia emphasised the importance of preventive diplomacy, peacemaking, peacebuilding, and cooperation with regional organisations. All these techniques help avert conflict and ultimately contribute to lowering the peacekeeping costs of the international community. The countries whose representatives most emphasised the need to combine a variety of techniques while receiving assistance from regional organisations were the United Kingdom and France. These two countries continued to advocate a combination of techniques before, during and after a conflict:

> To contribute to a lasting restoration of peace through measures for coordinated consolidation in the economic, social, institutional, electoral, humanitarian and human rights fields. This method has already been proven on many occasions, particularly in Namibia and Cambodia. It deserves to be continued, as is intended in El Salvador and Mozambique.[38]

The exception in this instance was the Chinese government, which continued to consistently follow the policy that it had adopted at the end of the 1980s; at that time, the discussion on improving the peacekeeping operation technique to solve new threats to the maintenance of international peace and security had only just started. In an open meeting of the Security Council that took place on 18 January 1995, the Chinese representative raised doubts regarding the 'natural' combination of the different techniques:

> In recent years United Nations activities in maintaining international peace and security tend to be increasingly mixed up with those in the economic, social, development, humanitarian assistance and other areas. However, the absence of clear guidelines has resulted in confusion of concept and differences in interpretation of these activities. It is therefore necessary to define, on the basis of extensive discussions and under the guidance of the Charter, the concept and scope of these activities and their mutual relationship, so as to provide them with a solid legal base.[39]

The Chinese statesmen in the UN consistently supported the traditional goals and success principles of the Cold War era. Thus they emphasised the need for the agreement of the conflicted sides, the honouring of the Charter's principles, especially with regard to the prohibition on violating a country's sovereignty, and the non-use of force by peacekeeping troops.[40]

However, this should not be misunderstood to mean that the Security Council featured a coalition of four permanent members of the Council (the United States, the United Kingdom, France and Russia) versus the other permanent member (China), with regard to the discussion of the goals and principles of success of the peacekeeping operations. For example, the delegations of the United Kingdom and France in the UN favoured, in principle, the development of a regular rapid reaction force that would be placed at the disposal of the UN.[41] Such a force would be on standby, ready to be sent rapidly to any arena in which the Security Council could agree that a clear and immediate 'threat' existed to the maintenance of international peace and security. On the other hand, the United States opposed the formation of such standby forces by the UN.[42] The Russian government argued that the issue should be discussed, but it had entirely different motives for doing so. Throughout the end of the 1980s and beyond, the representatives of Russia consistently pushed for the following mechanism: that all military resources entrusted to the UN would become the organisation's regular standing army, subject to the authority of the MSC that had been terminated in the late 1940s due to the Cold War.[43] The Chinese representatives did not express an opinion on the issue in the relevant forums but they most probably opposed it, as their traditional approach would dictate.

All the representatives of the five permanent Security Council members agreed that 'certain situations' would dictate that the Security Council should use its enforcement powers according to the Charter's Chapter 7. However, they could not come to an agreement on the mapping of such situations. Such an agreement would be critical in answering questions such as: When can this power be used, and who executes it? This discourse revealed the vested interests of the powers on a variety of issues. One example was the zigzagging of the Russian government regarding the use of force. In 1994, Russia demanded support for its operations and threatened that if this support was not forthcoming, it would veto the enforcement mandate that the United States had asked to operate in Haiti in 1994. The Russian representatives were also angry that the French did not support Russia in the Council, even though they supported France's Operation Turquoise in Rwanda after the genocide, an operation that included authorisation for the use of force.[44]

Similar arguments prevailed among the developing nations. We see that governments of countries such as Egypt, Thailand and many others, members of the NAM, backtracked from full support of the execution of multidimensional peacekeeping operations from 1992.[45] In contrast, there were other member states of the NAM that did not accept the decisions of the movement as binding on them or as the only basis for forming an opinion on peacekeeping operations. They continued to allocate forces to operations that ostensibly did not conform to the principles defined at the end of the Cairo convention in 1994. Some of the African countries were in favour of deepening involvement of the UN and did not renounce the use of force should it prove necessary.[46] Developing nations such as Ukraine and Mali supported the development of a rapid reaction force. These approaches opposed the spirit of the resolutions of the NAM.[47]

At the beginning of 1995, the delegations of the Western countries also retracted their sweeping support for the concepts introduced in the Agenda for Peace, and now expressed unequivocal disapproval for executing multidimensional operations with the goal of settling active conflicts. They stipulated that such operations had to be executed in the presence of an agreement, or at least willingness for an agreement, of the conflicted sides. Similarly, reservations were expressed in the Assembly at the execution of peacekeeping operations that included enforcement powers according to Chapter 7 of the Charter. The importance of this about-face in the positions of these nations is rooted in the fact that, as opposed to the multidimensional concept promoted in 1992, the execution of peacekeeping operations in 1995 was accomplished only after the conflict ended. These operations were mainly directed at peacebuilding or diplomatic missions or conflict-preventive economic development, with the agreement of the conflicted parties. Many of the speakers called on the UN to cooperate with regional organisations in order to ensure the political and material support needed for the success of the operations.[48]

The lack of agreement among the various UN delegations was also expressed in the organisation's organs that dealt with the peacekeeping operations. In 1996, a work group established by the Assembly to discuss the relevance of the Agenda for Peace published an interim report. The report was mainly a summary of the differences of opinion among the various delegations. Even though it was only an interim report, the work group was never assembled again.[49] The Special Committee (SCPKO), the only UN organ permitted to discuss the principles of the operations, attracted much criticism in 1994 due to its outdated composition.[50] A year later, many of the delegation representatives at the Special Committee emphasised that the Committee should be opened to all the member states of the UN. After all, more than eighty countries allocated soldiers to operations at that time. The representatives of these delegations felt that no resolutions should be adopted regarding operations until the contributor nations were permitted to take part in the associated discussions. On 6 December 1995, after thirty years of a permanent composition, the dam was finally broken. Finally, the Assembly asked to increase the number of committee members in order to provide broader representation to the organisation's member states.[51] A year later, the Special Committee was finally enlarged according to a special system.[52] In 1997, the number of Special Committee members almost tripled and rose from thirty-three to ninety-five.[53]

In summary, between the second half of 1993 and 1995, the organisation went through a process of disillusionment regarding the ambitious ideas raised in the course of 1992. This process was not the direct result of the harsh violent events in Somalia, Rwanda and the former Yugoslavia – a view held by many researchers.

From 1992 onwards, the Secretariat and Security Council attempted to convince the UN states that the main reasons for lack of success of the multidimensional peacekeeping operations were related to insufficient resources for the proper management and organisation of the large operations. They received wide support from Western countries. This emphasis allowed the five permanent members to receive resources while retaining their prerogatives in the Security Council to decide selectively on peacekeeping operations. As this chapter shows, the mounting political pressure to reform the Security Council helps to (partly) explain the Council decisions to decrease the numbers of multidimensional operations.

But the problems with the execution of operations were not only connected to the supply of resources or the pressure imposed by the organisation's members for the need to reform the management of the operations. Instead, the problem was that all the organisation's organs failed to define and agree on the goals and principles of the multidimensional operations. The distinctions between traditional peacekeeping operations, enforcement operations and peacebuilding operations were not at all clear.

Also, discussions on the new concept did not elucidate when new operations should be executed and how these were supposed to actually affect the conflicts. The organisation's members did not succeed in reaching an agreement on the extent to which intrastate conflicts could be resolved through the following new concepts: the integration of the diverse objectives of humanitarian aid; the training of civilian policemen; disarmament; the holding of democratic elections; and the promoting of human rights.

In 1995, most of the states agreed that peacekeeping operations were a temporary means that could only be executed after achievement of a political agreement. Also, it was agreed that these operations must follow the traditional principles of impartiality and non-bias, agreement of the local factions, and non-use of force. Thus, the concept of the large multidimensional operation – whose goal is to end a conflict while simultaneously promoting political, security, economic and social change – was removed from the UN agenda.

Nevertheless, despite everything mentioned above, the General Assembly and Security Council members, as well as the Secretariat, continued to support the multidimensional operations in principle. In fact, the five permanent members continued to address the organisational aspects in their work, and constantly called for an increase in the resources for the operations. Similarly, the Security Council could count on the fact that in almost any conflict, there would be those countries with vested interests that would be willing to recruit allies for interventions. Thus multidimensional operations remained a flexible means in UN hands for future use, when local and international conditions permitted.

## Mind the gap between theory and practice in UN peacekeeping operations

The UN was able to successfully organise the regular provision of forces to peacekeeping operations during the Cold War (by relying on a relatively limited number of countries), so long as the goals and physical sizes of these operations were limited in scope. Most of the regular contributor countries were, as mentioned before, medium or small Western nations such as the five Nordic countries as well as Canada, Australia, New Zealand and Ireland. These countries played an important role in changing the concept of 'new threats' to international peace and security, as well as how the multidimensional operations were supposed to deal with these new threats. In the previous chapter dealing with the changes in operations from 1992 till the first half of 1993, we saw how the international community succeeded in providing only part of the requirements for the many operations executed at that time, and especially for the large multidimensional operations in Cambodia, the former Yugoslavia and Somalia. We also saw that the UN Secretariat personnel and the Security Council members emphasised that the main difficulty in execution of the operations was the intransigence of the international community in allocating sufficient soldiers, civilian policemen and civilian experts, as well as logistical support and financing for these operations. The need for these resources only increased in the beginning of 1993. By 1994, the number of peacekeeping forces had reached about eighty thousand people, almost seven times the number in 1988. In truth, while the Security Council enlarged the goals of the operations, most of the countries were not prepared for the provision of massive numbers of soldiers to various fronts around the world.[54]

In response to the shortage of resources for the operations, and in light of the growing criticism of the decision-making patterns of the Security Council, more and more voices were heard proposing that the five permanent members of the Security Council should be the countries to contribute the lion's share of forces to the peacekeeping operations. The argument was as follows: since the P5 are the most influential countries when it comes to decision-making in the Council and since they are the strongest nations in the world, they must also bear a large part of the UN military burden. This viewpoint was antithetical to one of the principles of peacekeeping operation deployments during the Cold War era that rejected the participation of the powers in these operations, in order to maintain the neutrality of the missions.[55]

Another response to the growing demands for additional manpower in peacekeeping operations at the beginning of the 1990s were the voices calling for integration of civilian staff in the operations, mainly in activities that do not require the involvement of soldiers.[56] The main rationale for the use of civilians in operations was to open the door to additional member states to take part in operations, thus ostensibly contributing to their neutrality.[57] Various representatives had already warned against a massive use of civilians back in 1990, claiming that this could sabotage the effectiveness of the operations, since civilians, unlike soldiers, cannot cope with complex, sensitive security-related scenarios.[58] In fact, the need for civilian personnel in the large multidimensional operations (in Cambodia, the former Yugoslavia and Somalia) forced the Secretariat to create special standby arrangements.[59]

In light of the accumulated experience of previous operations involving intervention in intrastate affairs, it was clear to everyone involved that the civilian police had to be reinforced with more manpower and needed to be better trained. Thus a special department, called the Civilian Police Unit, was set up within the peacekeeping operations unit; this unit significantly shored up the role of the civilian police in the operations, via coordination with the contributor states. Yet it was still difficult to recruit these forces, for several reasons. First, the policemen were committed to their regular work in their own countries, first and foremost. Second, in some cases the governments did not have the authority to send policemen beyond the borders of their own country. Third, the nature of the work required language skills that, in most cases, did not exist. Finally, many policemen lacked basic technical skills such as driving all-terrain vehicles in the operational arenas of the operations.[60]

Thus it turned out that the discussion in the UN regarding integration of civilians in the operations did not contribute to the effectiveness of the execution of multidimensional operations – in fact, it even inflamed the dissent within the organisation. True, the civilian option was a good solution for highly organised, economically robust countries such as Germany and Japan, whose constitutions prevented them from contributing soldiers to military operations outside their borders but permitted them to send civilians. On the other hand, most governments were hard pressed to commit personnel to the civilian staff. In the end, bureaucratic factors and intrastate politics and problems prevailed over good intentions to allocate manpower to the operations.

Another associated issue that arose for discussion in the UN at the time was the logistical problem of provisions of equipment, foodstuffs, vehicles, generators and the like. Here, too – as with the manpower allocation problem – the issue was fraught with political and economic considerations. Below I examine which representatives tried to advance solutions to the logistical problems that multiplied as the operations grew and which representatives placed stumbling blocks instead.

The logistical problems proliferated greatly in the operations executed in Cambodia, the former Yugoslavia and Somalia beginning in 1992.[61] In light of these increasing demands, the representatives of the Canadian delegation proposed the creation of a logistical doctrine for the organisation of the operations.[62] Despite the fact that this plan was backed by the organisation's Secretariat and by the Nordic countries, many other delegations felt that the establishment of such a standby arrangements system was not efficient. Also, the countries were divided as to whether the UN ought to create standby arrangements (regarding provisions) with member states or to maintain ongoing contact with commercial suppliers.⁶³ Finally, in the course of 1995, it was decided to establish a permanent logistical base for peacekeeping operations in the Italian port of Brindisi.⁶⁴

When examining the UN discourse regarding the contribution of military forces to operations, it is important to remember that member states agreed (in 1992 and the beginning of 1993) to the evolution and the execution of multidimensional peacekeeping operations. This means that international politics in the UN continued on its same path. Although there was a rise in the number of countries sending forces, the truth was that these countries committed themselves to sending only very small numbers of soldiers, and even this depended on the arena to which the soldiers were sent. Nevertheless, it is important to note that there were some countries, such as India and Pakistan, that contributed thousands of soldiers equally to all the operations. By contrast, most of the other countries that allocated forces usually did so when a specific operation suited their regional or international interests. Also, most countries did not train their soldiers to serve in these types of operations. Even the demand on the part of UN members to the P5 to supply most of the forces of the operations was not rooted in a desire the upgrade the effectiveness of the operations but only to lower the chances that they, too, would face similar demands to contribute. Thus the member states contributed towards the creation of a gap between empty rhetoric and action. This gap was one of the main causes of the backtracking from the ambitious goals and success principles of multidimensional operations. Member states offered two alternatives in dealing with this gap. The first alternative addressed the creation of a standby multinational force that could rapidly and effectively respond to the demands of new operations. The second alternative was to appeal to regional organisations.

The unwillingness of member states to allocate forces and logistical assistance to operations finally caused several small and mid-sized Western nations to raise a proposal (in 1995 and 1996) to establish an international rapid reaction force (as part of a peacekeeping force), even in the form of a multinational brigade. This proposal aroused the concern of representatives of several states, who felt that such an organised military force would undermine the sovereignty of the state in which it operated and that it would cost too much. These representatives argued that the success of operations was not dependent on the strength of its military component, but on the pre-existence of a political settlement. Some delegations even argued that the formation of a rapid reaction force would be another step towards the transformation of the UN into a military organisation.⁶⁵

*Multinational force and regional organisations*

In light of the pointless and futile discussions in the UN, seven countries finally decided to form a multinational Standby High Readiness Brigade for United Nations Operations (SHIRBRIG). These seven countries were: Austria, Denmark,

Netherlands, Norway, Poland, Canada and Sweden. This initiative was the only concrete action taken by the member states to provide a trained military force to the organisation, a force that could be rapidly deployed to any arena in the world. This scheme was the fruit of cooperation between veteran contributor states to the operations. However, in later years, only a very small number of additional countries joined the project, and in June 2009, it was decided to end the brigade's activity.[66]

Another proposal raised in the organisation to deal with the shortage of resources was to request help from regional organisations. In effect, this was implementation of UN Charter's Chapter 8, calling for cooperation between the UN and regional organisations to establish international peace and security. Since the regional organisations had become dominant players in the international arena and united large numbers of countries, it seemed possible that they could offer significant help to the operations.[67]

In response to a request from the Security Council,[68] the Secretariat turned to dozens of organisations in 1993–94 but received responses from only a minority of them.[69] Some of the organisations argued that they could not cooperate in any way with the UN in accordance with the Charter's Chapter 8.[70] Others offered cooperation solely in the spheres of diplomacy and economics.[71] Few regional organisations complied with most of the UN requests, and even cooperated with the UN in practice, mainly with regard to security issues. All the organisations in this group, with the exception of the OAU, were European.[72] But attempts to create permanent and binding cooperation between the UN and these regional organisations failed; instead, the organisations responded that each request would be examined on a case-by-case basis.[73]

The regional organisations were careful to maintain their autonomy and not to allow themselves to be affected by UN-dictated policy.[74] Thus the documents demonstrate that the Commonwealth of Independent States (CIS, a regional organisation whose participating countries were former Soviet republics) abandoned Gorbachev's path and policy of supporting UN work. Instead, the CIS espoused a division of labour between itself and the UN. From an exchange of letters between the UN and Russia (together with the other countries constituting the CIS), we see that the CIS wanted to retain its political-security aspects of operations while 'allowing' the UN to be in charge of humanitarian and economic aid.[75] Even the governments of European countries which had greeted UN peacekeeping operations enthusiastically starting from 1992 and had even supported cooperation between the UN and regional institutions started to have reservations regarding these cooperative ventures. From the mid-1990s they tightened their military cooperation with regional institutions such as NATO and EU institutions. They clearly preferred collective security activities with regional organisations to collective security with the UN.[76]

Thus, by the beginning of the 1990s, most of the UN members (except for the veteran contributors) evinced little willingness to cooperate with the Secretariat in training military forces and civilian manpower and placing these on standby. Most member states even obstructed efforts to solve the logistical problems of the operations. At the same time, there was no significant responsiveness on the part of most of the regional organisations to cement their relationship with the UN in the pursuit of conflict resolution. This conduct of most of the states – not only the developing states – explains many of the difficulties involved in execution of large, complex multidimensional operations.

In earlier chapters we learned that the Secretariat did not encounter major problems in recruiting manpower for most of the operations from 1988 until the first half of 1993. The change in orientation took place in the course of 1993 as a result of the great increase in the demands and costs of the operations. In June 1993 – before the debacles mentioned in studies as an explanation for the international withdrawal of support to peacekeeping – the Secretariat noted a steep decline in the willingness of countries to contribute to the operations. Simultaneously, the Secretariat also encountered difficulties in recruiting the necessary resources – logistical units, a civil police force, military observers and even regular infantry troops.[77] In one of the Secretariat reports in which the Secretary-General presented data about the operations he managed, he listed thirteen operations in which about sixty thousand soldiers and civilians took part. He argued that the more ambitious goals attributed to the operation in Somalia, and the willingness to execute additional peacekeeping operations simultaneously, necessitated forces of about a hundred thousand soldiers and civilians, a number that the UN forces reached, in fact, only in 2008.[78]

On 5 August 1993 Secretary-General Boutros-Ghali sent a letter to the Security Council president in which he described a meeting he had conducted with the representatives of fifteen developing nations. During the course of the meeting the representatives argued that they 'are aware of the increasing responsibilities of the United Nations in the area of peace-keeping activities, which has necessitated increased contribution of resources by member states in terms of personnel and equipment to the peace-keeping operations'. Nevertheless, they expressed their concern that their countries and other developing nations might not receive their monetary compensation in time. In this case it 'could make difficult the participation of many member states in United Nations peace-keeping operations, in particular that of the developing countries'. The Secretary-General expressed worry over the future of the operations unless a solution could be found to the organisation's financial crisis.[79] But the economic circumstances of the organisation did not improve. In March 1994, the UN executed seventeen peacekeeping operations and additional political missions.[80] In May 1994, the Security Council asked the Secretary-General to prepare a report on the personnel and equipment standby arrangements at its disposal for the reinforcement and replacement of existing units. A month later the Secretary-General reported that only twenty-one countries had committed themselves to allocating manpower, thus creating a standing force encompassing thirty thousand soldiers. This pessimistic report joins his report from March 1994 in which he comments that there is little willingness among the countries to make additional contributions. Many of the operations were characterised by a severe shortage in communication equipment, medical equipment, engineering equipment and vehicles. Also, many of the forces supplied by developing nations arrived without appropriate equipment, thus the UN was required to supplement what was missing. Despite these problems, the Secretary-General was optimistic regarding the future and anticipated that twenty-seven additional states would agree to join the standby arrangement force, thus increasing the total number of forces on standby to seventy thousand soldiers.[81] The Security Council limited itself to calling on the member states to continue to provide more military forces and equipment to the operations; this was in line with its conduct in past operations and in other settings.[82] It should be noted that the promises given by many governments in declaring their willingness to contribute to the UN standby arrangements system were only tentative promises. The governments retained their full right to decide whether to send these forces and when. So, for example, when the UN adopted the resolution to take action in Rwanda, nineteen countries put forces on standby for peacekeeping operations but, at the moment of truth, all of them refused to send their forces to missions.[83]

## The UN financial crisis

The ongoing inefficient management and organisation of the operations after the Cold War was also expressed in one of the salient and important obstacles of the operations: their financing.[84] The operations' expenses rose at a dizzying rate, as we see from the discussions conducted by the Special Committee in June 1993. 'Despite the fact that the pattern of payment improved in 1992, it was noted with a sense of alarm that the amount of outstanding assessed contributions was even higher than in previous years because of a sharp rise in overall peace-keeping expenditures.'[85]

Yet even some of the countries that supported the execution of multidimensional operations did not pay their debts to the organisation. By December 1993, the debts to the UN totalled one and a half billion dollars, out of which more than a billion were connected to the financing of the peacekeeping operations. One hundred and eighty days after the resolution regarding assessment collection, the organisation had received only 68 per cent of the funds that the countries were supposed to contribute.[86] Some of the contributor nations, mainly those owed large sums by the UN, threatened to withdraw their forces unless they received the payment due to them. In order to resolve the crisis, even temporarily, the Secretariat used all the funds at its disposal to cover part of the debts for existing operations, thus leaving new operations without any budgetary coverage at all.[87]

In a desperate attempt to solve the developing financial crisis, Boutros-Ghali, together with the Ford Foundation, initiated an independent advisory group.

But their report also failed to make any change in the financing of the organisation's activities.[88] As a result, by the middle of 1994 the organisation found itself on the verge of financial collapse. By 30 June 1994, the unpaid debts to the UN (for financing of the operations) reached more than 2.1 billion dollars. In light of this situation, on 7 July the Secretary-General sent an urgent letter to the Security Council in which he argued that the financing issue had developed into an unprecedented crisis. The large operations in Somalia and Mozambique remained without financing, and the resources that had been allocated to other operations in the former Yugoslavia, southern Lebanon, El Salvador and the Kuwait–Iraq border were almost all used up.[89]

The diplomatic delegations in the UN agreed that the organisation's financial crisis could cripple its ability to execute peacekeeping operations.[90] Nevertheless, many delegations argued that the UN should increase the compensation they paid to the countries for each soldier they sent to the operations. Some even added that, should the UN fail to pay, this would adversely affect the willingness of most countries to take part in future operations. This, in turn, would sabotage the principles of universalism and universal representation in the operations, a fact that could render the neutrality of the operations in doubt. We must remember that for the developing countries, UN payment constituted a significant supplement to their economies. Thus, in the time period under discussion, a country could expect more than a thousand dollars compensation a month for a regular soldier; this constituted the average yearly income of an individual in India and Bangladesh, and half of that income in Pakistan – three large contributor countries that allocated tens of thousands of soldiers to the operations.[91] At the same time, representatives of the developed nations argued that it was not possible, from an economic point of view, that they should be the primary backers of the operations' costs yet not receive adequate compensation (in the developed nations, the countries paid their soldiers more than the compensation they received from the UN).[92]

The dispute prevailing among the delegations from the developed and developing nations regarding financing of the peacekeeping operations did not only stem from economic interests but was also connected to the very heart of the discourse on the subject of 'development' in the world and the 'new threats' to the maintenance of international peace and security. The representatives of the developing nations started, back in 1992, to pressure the organisation to raise the issue of development to the focus of discussions. These pressures are what led to the publication of a report called *Agenda for Development* by Secretary-General Boutros-Ghali, as well as a series of resolutions of the General Assembly.[93] According to Secretary-General Boutros-Ghali, the 'Agenda for Development would thus complement an Agenda for Peace, by addressing the deeper foundations of global peace and security in the economic, social and environmental spheres'.[94] At the end of 1994, representatives from developing countries added the following interpretation to the peacekeeping operations resolution: that the allocation of resources for financing operations must not negatively affect the allocation of resources for development.⁹⁵ The pretext for this codicil was as follows: the focus of the international political system on the execution of multidimensional peacekeeping operations as a means for resolving intrastate conflicts had led to the diverting of resources from worldwide assistance and development to the benefit of the multidimensional operations. Since the Western countries were the main contributors to assistance and development, as well as the main backers of the operations, now they were asked to directly increase the sums they invested in aid and development.⁹⁶

The analysis above proves that the decision to enlarge the goals and size of the operations was not accompanied by a substantive change in the policy of the UN members. Thus a large and growing gap was created between theory and practice. In this discourse, the veteran contributor states were exceptional in their attempts to provide an accepted, efficient foundation for the allocation of forces (similar to their stance during the Cold War). Otherwise, most of the countries – the five permanent members of the Security Council, and Western and developing countries – organised themselves in various alliances that tried to promote narrow interests, thus sabotaging the initiatives of the veteran contributor countries. Finally, in light of the growth of demands resulting from the execution of numerous operations – mainly multidimensional ones – even many of the contributor countries stopped allocating forces to the operations, criticised the functioning of the Security Council, did not support the Secretariat sufficiently, and did not allocate the manpower and logistical support necessary for speedy, reasonable success of the operations. Only the termination of the large UN operations in the course of 1995 helped the organisation to recover and escape bankruptcy.

Despite the criticisms described above, the UN executed two large, unprecedented operations in Somalia and the former Yugoslavia, from 1993 to 1995. Below we examine how these operations developed and to what extent they reflected progress in the UN discourse regarding the evolution of the concept of peacekeeping operations.

### Somalia: from peacebuilding to collapsed operation

Somalia is described in the research literature as a 'collapsed' or 'failed' state as a result of the civil war that raged there and destroyed the state infrastructure and institutions. As already discussed, the harsh humanitarian crisis was one of the side effects of this collapse. But the collapse of state institutions also had security ramifications because numerous local forces rushed to fill the vacuum that was created; these local forces or factions were based on the Somali clan system. Marauding, well-armed gangs called *moryaan* roamed throughout the country; sometimes they operated alone, sometimes they joined up with the fighting forces of the factions. According to various appraisals, about half a million light arms circulated in Somalia at the time, and the various factions held many heavy weapons as well.[97] Despite their promises and signatures on agreements such as the Addis Ababa Agreement (March 1993), the Somali faction leaders did not succeed in stabilising the security situation. In fact, they were generally the cause of the problem, not part of its solution.

Ostensibly, the Security Council adopted Resolution 814 on 26 March 1993 in order to deal with the great challenges in Somalia. The UN Secretariat administered an operation in Somalia two months before the Transitional Authority in Cambodia supervised the holding of elections in the country, and simultaneously with the execution of UNPROFOR in the countries of the former Yugoslavia. The operation in Somalia was even more ambitious than the UN operations in Cambodia and the former Yugoslavia, because the UN forces in Somalia were expected to rebuild civilian institutions and they received authority to use force when necessary to maintain their mandate. As of March 1993, it appeared that the operation enjoyed the collective support of the international community as well as of the Somali factions. Despite the authorisation to use force, the Secretariat announced that it would be operating impartially in order to promote a consensus among the local factions and bring an end to the conflict. The SRSG was given the difficult mission of implementing the most advanced ideas proposed up to that period in the organisation's discourse, combining peace enforcement with peacebuilding in a country that lacked all state institutions. Thus the international community faced the following test: Would they be willing politically to support an operation over time and allocate manpower and provide logistical support and financing for the operations?[98]

The Secretariat personnel took steps to unify Somali society and restore it to the status of a civil state. This is corroborated by the Secretariat's statement in March 1993 that 'ultimately, all the efforts being undertaken by the United Nations in Somalia are directed towards one central goal: to assist the people of Somalia to create and maintain order and new institutions for their own governance.'[99] As we will see, the multiplicity of missions of UNOSOM II quickly led to piercing the UN's veil of using peacekeeping as a panacea for civil wars.

The organisation worked on five important levels to carry out the goals of the operation. On the first level, the Secretariat personnel encouraged the representatives of the various factions to sign peace agreements and honour them. On the second level, the UN representatives in Somalia tried, over two years, to re-establish civil institutions. On the third level, they tried to create local law and order apparatuses. On the fourth level, they tried to stimulate Somali economic development. All these activities were connected to the fifth goal, demobilisation of the armed militias.

The UN's main goal – even when the factions tried to depose dictator Siad Barre – was to form a Somali government that would be perceived as legitimate by all the Somali factions as well as international recognition. In Chapter 3, we saw that UN representatives understood that humanitarian aid had become an important economic resource in the Somali civil war. However, they did not understand the ramifications of the dismantling of Somali civil society and its return to a traditional clan structure. While the clan system provided security and economic opportunities for individuals in Somali daily life at the beginning of the 1990s, these clans were also given to fierce internecine conflict, unprecedented in scope. After years of war, the clans became extremely distrustful of one another. The survivability of the clans was put to the test in the ongoing conflict. The factions refused to lay down their weapons out of concern that if the fighting were to be renewed they would lose all influence in future negotiations over dividing up power and resources in the country. Thus, the faction leaders jockeyed for international recognition that could give them positions in reconciliation conventions and institutions established under the aegis of the UN, and thus allow them to receive humanitarian aid. The more senior their status, the more the clan representatives would have the opportunity to place their people in positions with high salaries.[100]

This situation led to a zero-sum situation: The achievement of a specific faction or clan came at the expense of the other clans. General Aidid, who led the strongest faction in south-central Somalia, was concerned about his status and justifiably suspicious of any external intervention that could detract from his power. For this exact reason, most of the other factions supported and even encouraged General Aidid's main competitor in Mogadishu, Ali Mahdi, who was in favour of international intervention.

Since the Secretary-General's representatives were not sufficiently attuned to the nuances of the relations between the Somali clans, they adopted an aggressive policy that was opposed by most of the clans. As part of this policy, the UN representatives (with the support of members of the international community) refused to recognise the independence of Somaliland, which had been declared in the country's north-west. Instead they recognised the local leaders who cooperated with them, even though these enjoyed only partial support of the clans.[101] But since the major part of the intervention was concentrated in the country's centre and south, the Secretariat representatives clashed mainly with General Aidid. The UN policy of intervention in a country's internal affairs was compatible with the entire atmosphere in the UN at the time when the organisation called for the execution of a multidimensional operation at the end of 1992. As an echo of the 'the spirit of the times' that prevailed in the organisation, the Secretariat reports on General Aidid viewed him a warmonger who was preventing peace. On his part, General Aidid advanced the notion with other militia leaders that 'the United Nations has decided to abandon its policy of cooperation and is planning to "invade" the country.'[102]

The tension between the UN representatives, who argued that they operated impartially and with the agreement of the local factions, and General Aidid and his representatives temporarily dissipated when the Unified Task Force operated in the south-centre of Somalia until May 1993. The Addis Ababa Agreement was also signed in this period; these agreements were the legal basis (together with Security Council Resolution 814) for the execution of the multidimensional operation in Somalia.[103] Most of the American military forces left and the operative powers were definitively transferred to the UN on 4 May 1993, and that was when the tense relations between the UN representatives and General Aidid began to escalate.

The peacemaking process in Somalia was supposed to have been accompanied by the creation of civil institutions. As opposed to Cambodia, where the Security Council focused on supervision, in Somalia the Security Council resolved that the Secretariat should rebuild the country's institutions in cooperation with the population and the local factions. In order to accomplish this, the Secretariat had to decide how best to establish institutions so that they would not be subject to the country's factional politics. Yet despite the numerous goals, the Secretariat had only a few hundreds of international civilians at their disposal.[104]

Sporadic attempts had been made to establish local civilian councils and local police forces even before the Addis Ababa Agreement was signed, but these councils and forces only really began to coalesce after the signing of the agreements.[105] According to the Addis Ababa Agreement, the UN and the Somali factions were charged with the establishment of a Transitional National Council (TNC) as well as regional and district councils. The TNC did not succeed in operating, and the apparatuses created for the establishment of regional and district councils were not sufficiently clear.[106] The faction leaders preferred to appoint their own people to the councils according to traditional, local formulas, but the UN representatives refused to allow this.[107]

Although the UN failed in its peacemaking process, its financial assistance and security measures helped found more than half of the regional and district councils until the end of 1993. But after a few months of activity, it emerged that the councils were not receiving full local support. The civil, democratic and Western model undermined the foundations of the local, traditional institutions that had consolidated after the collapse of the state's formal institutions and the growing gap between the clans. The councils were not able to achieve the goals that were set in the Addis Ababa Agreement, such as full responsibility for security, a health system, an educational system and reconstruction of infrastructure.[108] A year later, the institutions founded by the UN remained unstable. A study was conducted from July to September 1994 in two regions where the UN had been most successful, Bay and Bakool. The study testifies to the fact that even these institutions were on the verge of breakdown.[109] When the UN left Somalia, the institutions it had established collapsed.[110]

The attempt to reconstruct civil institutions in Somalia was supposed to have been supported by activities to rehabilitate law, justice and penal institutions and restore law and order. This goal was defined in Resolution 814 of March 1993, according to which the Secretariat was given the task of assisting the Somalis in establishing a national police force.[111] The Secretariat claimed that in order to carry out the rehabilitation, the UN would need to establish a force numbering ten thousand policemen, who would be deployed throughout the state until the end of 1994. Before the Somali state had collapsed, a total of eighteen thousand policemen had operated there, that is eight thousand more than the Secretariat had deemed to be necessary to rehabilitate the police force.[112] At the beginning of 1994, 6,737 Somalis served as policemen, 311 as judicial personnel and more than 700 as jail wardens, in total. Furthermore, the UN planned to operate the *Daraawishta* force (a Somali term for a rapid reaction police force) in March 1994.[113]

Unfortunately, the civil police force shared the bitter fate of the local authorities, and began to fall apart in the last months of the UN presence in Somalia. There were several reasons for this. First, due to the absence of organised government institutions such as local or transitional authorities, civil police could not serve as a unifying national force for the entire Somali population. They did not receive the support of the population, which splintered into more and more clans. Another reason for the failure of the civil police was connected to its armament. The administrators of the UN operation opposed arming the police with heavy weapons, with the rationale that civil police are only responsible for public order. The UN administrators argued that should the security situation necessitate the use of heavy weapons, they (the UN) would send soldiers to shore up the police. However, the local police forces, armed with only light weapons, were no real match for the armed militias of the clans. Meanwhile, the UN forces barricaded themselves in their camps. In fact, the local police operated only by virtue of the goodwill of the armed Somalis and with backup of the UN forces. When the UN left, most of the policemen linked up with the clans they had originally belonged to.

A third cause of the failure of the local police was the inadequate and delayed training of the Somali policemen by the international community comprising the UN. The money that was needed for training was mobilised too slowly, due either to inaction on the part of Kofi Annan, USG for Peacekeeping Operations, or to under-funding by the organisation's members. Thus, for example, the USA – the main contributor to these programmes – only began to contribute funds after the resolution was taken to withdraw from Somalia in October 1993.[114] From the second half of 1994, very few Somalis tried to enlist in the police force (even though the UN lowered its acceptance criteria). Only few UN member states still believed there were hopes for this force; most of the states were in favour of withdrawing the UN forces and halting political, financial and security backup for the new civil institutions that were supposed to emerge.[115]

Simultaneously with efforts to form functioning civil institutions, an international convention was convened in March 1993 with the goal of implementing the transition from the humanitarian aid stage to the economic development stage, similar to the ideas proposed in the organisation in the course of 1992.[116] In the absence of a functioning transitional government in Somalia – in contrast to the situation that prevailed in Cambodia and the countries of Former

Yugoslavia – there was no agent in the field to monitor the planned programmes and actions. In the following months, humanitarian aid organisations operated in a broad variety of spheres, in addition to delivering foodstuffs throughout the country. These aid organisations included: the UNHCR, the World Food Programme, the United Nations Children's Fund and the World Health Organization. They ran supply programmes of basic consumer goods, they opened schools, prepared school curriculums, developed medical programmes, fixed roads, reconstructed ruined water systems, dug new water wells, vaccinated people and provided veterinary services together with attempts to stimulate export.[117] Reports from the Secretariat of that period reflect their optimism regarding the chances for changing the social and economic situation of Somalia from top to bottom.[118] In October 1993 the Secretary-General reported to the UN members that 'Somalia has potential for sustainable development, which in the long run can raise all the Somalis above the poverty line.'[119] Unfortunately, this optimism was unfounded and did not match the situation on the ground.

The assistance and development efforts created the illusion of a functioning economy, when in reality these operations actually led to social and political instability. The explanation for this is that the massive injections of aid to urban centres such as Mogadishu and Baidoa transformed them into immigration centres for hundreds of thousands of displaced persons searching for food and work. Also, productive work was replaced by thousands of jobs that were created by the assistance organisations and that paid much higher salaries than the local salaries for productive work. The leaders of the Somali factions observed these developments and understood that the aid centres had become Somalia's chief economic resource. Thus factions began to fight for control of the aid centres; they offered them 'protection' or robbed the provisions from the centres.[120] Also, the assistance organisations encouraged the hundreds of thousands of refugees and displaced persons to return to the communities from whence they came; however, these communities had been taken over by other clans, and the return of the original owners threatened to re-ignite the fighting. Mohamed Sheikh Osman (Hawiye), who had served as finance minister in Barre's government, said 'There are about half a million Somalis living outside Somalia. When they will return, there will be another civil war.'[121]

Although the international community had expressed support for the humanitarian activities and reconstruction and development operations, most of the UN representatives backtracked from their support for the intervention in 1994. In this way, they surreptitiously broke off the connection established in 1992 between a 'peacebuilding' and 'peacekeeping' operation.[122] Supra-governmental and international organisations did try to exert pressure on the UN to increase their investment in Somalia, but they ignored the negative influences of the intervention on Somali society. The Secretariat personnel were among the main forces calling for an expansion of the intervention, with the argument that the peacebuilding process was succeeding. By contrast, most of the organisation's members, developing and developed countries alike, expressed scepticism regarding the allocation of so many resources from worldwide aid to Somalia alone, when there were so many additional regions in need of these resources. They could not see a direct relationship between the aid and development activities of the various aid agencies and the main objective – establishing a government in Somalia. When the UN aid organisations asked for contributions from the world's countries in 1995, the response was poor. As of September 1995, it was estimated in the UN that the total amount of aid to Somalia was about 20 million dollars from the beginning of the year. By contrast, various estimates in the UN placed the sum total of investments for assistance and development in Somalia between 1992 and 1994 at hundreds of millions of dollars.[123]

Along with the creation of civil institutions and initiatives for economic development, UN forces were needed to supervise the Herculean mission of disarmament of the local factions.[124] For about a year, the Secretariat had far fewer forces at their disposal than they needed for this large mission. In contrast to the situation in Cambodia and the former Yugoslavia, the countries in the Somali region did not contribute any forces at all. The Latin American countries also did not contribute soldiers to this operation. The United States agreed to send a logistical force of about 2,700 soldiers. Italy sent a force of about 2,500 soldiers, which deployed in north Mogadishu, but they did not try to enforce the disarmament. France sent just over a thousand soldiers, who deployed in the relatively quiet regions in the country. Most of the veteran Western contributor countries sent small forces. By contrast, the developing countries supplied the main forces. In the course of 1993 until the end of the operation, India and Pakistan together allocated about 10,000 soldiers, about half of the entire UN forces. The following countries contributed forces: Bangladesh, Malaysia and Nepal from Asia, and Egypt, Zimbabwe, Nigeria and Botswana from Africa. The Secretariat staff members decided to implement the concept of 'peace enforcement' that they had devised during 1992 and early 1993; they had reached an understanding with the contributing countries that they were willing for their soldiers to fight against local Somali militias, if that became necessary.[125]

The exaggerated expectations regarding the abilities of the multinational force were based on misunderstanding of the developments in Somalia in the UNITAF period. The truth was that much of the achievements of the multinational force in that period can be attributed to the fact that, in December 1992, the faction leaders preferred not to confront the UN forces directly. They decided to adopt a 'wait-and-see' approach first, to see how the UN forces would operate. The scepticism of the clan leaders, and mainly of Aidid, strengthened as a result of the contradictory messages they received: while UN diplomats emphasised the multidimensional goals of the operation, American diplomats emphasised the humanitarian aid goal. Another reason was that the fierce battles that had waged in the spring of 1992 between Barre's adherents, who were mainly from the Darod, and the Hawiye clans – were behind them. From the end of 1992, Somalia's central and southern territories were ruled by the SNA – the leadership of General Aidid and his allies. Also, General Aidid, Ali Mahdi and the other warlords were willing to place their heavy weapons in storage sites during the UNITAF period because they were able to take them back whenever they wanted, and also because they smuggled most of their heavy weapons over the border. In addition, despite the arms embargo on the country, the warlords exploited the time-out in the fighting to equip themselves with more weapons. They mainly equipped themselves with the weapons of the large Ethiopian army that fell apart at the end of the long civil war in Ethiopia.[126] Furthermore, most of the Somali factions did not store their light weapons with the multinational force.

Programmes such as 'weapons for food' or 'weapons for money', intended to encourage the Somali population to hand over their light arms, were soon abandoned because, in many cases, the local population used the funds received to acquire more arms that flowed into the country from abroad. Thus, after three months of activity, the multinational force succeeded in confiscating only 2,250 light and heavy firearms, out of hundreds of thousands circulating in the country at the time. Finally, the *moryaan* (marauding gang) phenomenon was not halted and continued to threaten the personal security both of the Somalis and of the humanitarian aid personnel.[127]

The security situation began to deteriorate from March 1993, when the fighting between the various factions was renewed in Mogadishu and Kismayu. However, UNITAF preferred not to use force to stop the fighting.[128] This trend was reinforced when the American government, which ran the largest and most professional military force in Somalia, also shirked its responsibility and refused to disarm the factions.

Despite the unwillingness of the United States and many other countries to use force in order to change the security situation in Somalia from its foundations, the UN Secretariat agreed to conduct a second UN operation in Somalia from May 1993. The Secretary-General committed himself to implementing the vague concept of peace enforcement that he had developed at that time in the organisation, even though he did not receive the material resources needed for his goals. According to Security Council Resolution 814, a smaller force and more limited resources (compared to UNITAF) were allocated to the operation to be deployed throughout the country. At the time, the UN had only about eighteen thousand soldiers at its disposal.[129] The quality of the forces was low: their equipment was inferior and the soldiers lacked basic fighting skills. This was especially true after the American army evacuated most of its fighting forces from Somalia. But most critical of all was the fact that the UN was running many other missions simultaneously.[130]

Under the circumstances prevailing in Somalia at the time, and considering the limited resources available to the UN, the disarmament plan was doomed to fail. This result was similar to the situation in Cambodia in the corresponding time period. But in contrast to Cambodia – where UN representatives tried to operate according to the traditional principles of operations – the UN representatives in Somalia decided to implement peace enforcement. This meant that the UN forces would have to directly confront General Aidid's faction.

In their actions, the UN representatives ignored the fact that General Aidid could not waive his relative advantages vis-à-vis the other factions; in other words, he could not disarm when the other factions did not. Much blood had been spilled to achieve the advantages that had turned his faction into the most powerful force in south-central Somalia. Since the UN forces deployed mainly in Mogadishu, these interfered with General Aidid's attempts to secure his influence in the area. Similarly, the pressures inflicted on him to store his heavy weapons in weapon storage sites and hand over his light weapons threatened to weaken him with regard to other clans. Therefore, he chose war over continuation of the peace process.[131]

After most of the American military forces left the country and authority for the operation was definitively transferred to the UN on 4 May 1993, relations between the UN representatives and General Aidid deteriorated. This, in turn, led to discontinuation of the work of the Somali work groups that had been established by the Addis Ababa agreements. The relations between the UN and General Aidid's faction reached a nadir after the violent incident that erupted on 5 June 1993. When Pakistani inspectors came to check a weapons storage site and USC/SNA radio station, against the express request of one of the high-placed members of the USC/SNA, a battle erupted. In the violent incident, twenty-five Pakistanis and fifty Somalis were killed, and hundreds were wounded.

In the wake of this incident, the Security Council decided to conduct an enforcement operation against General Aidid and the leaders of his faction. A 'virtual war'[132] was conducted (from June–October 1993) between UN forces and General Aidid's forces. After the Security Council decided (on 6 June) to bring General Aidid and the USC/SNA leadership to trial, UN and special US military forces conducted raids to either arrest or kill them. These actions, which continued for about four months, violated all the traditional operating principles of UN forces: they used force, they were biased, and they intervened in internal affairs. Thus, in fact, the UN forces conducted themselves as a sovereign entity, competing against General Aidid's faction for control of the country. Instead of peacemaking, they tried to impose peace by force. The war against General Aidid's faction halted the peacemaking process until the end of 1993 because General Aidid and the warlords of the USC/SNA were the leaders of the strongest faction in the south-central area of Somalia, and even received the support of the leaders of other factions. In addition, the other leaders did not want to be viewed by the public as collaborators with a foreign entity fighting Somalis.[133]

As mentioned in earlier sections, by the middle of 1993, countries began to have reservations regarding the sweeping support they had earlier given to development of the goals and success principles of the operations. In addition, criticism increased against the way things were conducted in the Security Council. The events in Somalia throughout the four months of fighting against General Aidid's faction shed light on the fundamental change in support for operations of this type. In June 1993, there was almost wall-to-wall support for the use of forces to defend the UN presence in Somalia. But as the fighting continued and was directed specifically at General Aidid, breaches began to appear in the international front.

A close look at the positions of the five permanent members of the Security Council show us that representatives of the United States, the United Kingdom, France and Russia supported the enforcement actions and viewed them as legitimate methods in the context of the unstable and insecure situation in Somalia. They found backing for their positions in quotes from the Secretary-General's biased reports. The only one who expressed reservations about this viewpoint was China's representative in the Council, Li Zhaoxing. While he was in favour of the enforcement actions in Somalia, this was only so long as it expressed the wishes of the OAU and the Arab League.[134]

The nations of the region and of the African continent did not share a uniform viewpoint. The OAU countries supported the operation, although some of them raised doubts regarding the logic of using force in Mogadishu.[135] They wanted the operation to succeed in order to halt the flow of refugees and instability in the region. Yet they were not sure that enforcement action against a warlord was the right path to take. As time went on, the fighting in Mogadishu caused more and more losses among UN forces as well as among the local populace, and the representatives of these countries in the UN began to argue that the operation had veered off from its original goal of peacemaking. They argued that the Secretariat had tried to enforce peace instead of encouraging cooperation with and between the factions, in order to end the conflict.[136]

One unusual approach was exhibited by representative Roble Olhaye from Djibouti (Somalia's neighbouring country in Africa). Throughout the intervention, Olhaye repeatedly cited the importance of disarmament of the factions, even if the multidimensional force would be required to use force to accomplish this.[137]

In contrast to the case of Cambodia and especially that of the former Yugoslavia, most of the developing countries did not express their positions regarding the events unfolding in Somalia. The few countries that did address the events there held different positions. Brazil's representatives in the Council wondered how the gamut of activities in the security and economic spheres could possibly contribute towards peacemaking.[138] By contrast, in that very same time period, Pakistan's representatives supported enforcement operations against General Aidid (they allocated a large number of forces to the operation and suffered many losses). Thus, in effect, Pakistan called for violation of the traditional principles of the operations.[139]

Since most of the veteran Western contributor nations did not take part in the operation, it is hard to know what their position was. The documents show that New Zealand's representative supported the multidimensional operation as well as the enforcement operation. Yet Italy, which allocated forces to the north Mogadishu area and was on good terms with the various Somali factions, had reservations about the enforcement activities that were adopted.[140]

Thus the Secretariat was almost alone in its readiness for peace enforcement steps against General Aidid's faction. This insistence on peace enforcement operations, when few countries (except for the United States) allocated forces and contributed the necessary resources, led to deterioration in the security situation in Somalia. In the course of the four months of fighting, hundreds of Somalis and dozens of UN soldiers were killed. Many Somalis viewed General Aidid as a nationalist who was trying to protect their country from the dictates of a foreign occupier. All activities to disarm the factions and store the weapons were completely halted. The focus on fighting in Mogadishu shifted attention from the other battlefields of the multinational force in the centre and south of the country, where the factions continued to arm and secure themselves. Finally, the fighting caused the fifteen factions that had signed the Addis Ababa Agreement to split into even smaller factions. These represented a wide variety of clans that all competed for the relief resources and for control over the new civilian authorities that the UN was trying to found.[141]

The aggressive conduct of the Secretariat proved that, when tested, the UN countries refused to allocate the resources necessary for successful multidimensional operations. Most of the countries had qualms over the prolonged fighting and some of their representatives criticised the fact that the operation had deviated from its main goals. They called on the Secretariat to return to conducting the operation according to traditional principles.

Between 3 and 4 October, a battle was waged in Mogadishu between the Special Forces of the United States and the local forces faithful to General Aidid. In this battle, dozens of soldiers from the multinational forces were killed and wounded (most from the United States), along with hundreds of Somalis. In response, the American government decided to withdraw all its forces from Somalia by March 1994. (The USA had allocated special forces and had contributed logistical support to the operation.) On the heels of the US announcement, most of the Western nations announced that they, too, would withdraw their forces by this date, and additional countries joined them. This step caused another crisis between the American administration and the UN Secretariat; the latter was afraid that the American decision would lead to a premature termination of the operation before it achieved its goals.[142]

The early 1994 withdrawal of the forces which had been sent by Western countries and headed by the United States led the Security Council to adopt Resolution 897 in February 1994. This resolution stated that the second UN operation in Somalia would return to operate in accordance with the traditional principles of the operations. Thus, in effect, Resolution 897 voided the security goals specified in Resolution 814, less than a year earlier.[143] The Secretariat then emphasised that peacemaking and humanitarian aid provisions to the Somali population were two separate forms of involvement in Somalia – two separate, unrelated activities that did not necessarily support one other. This was contrary to the Secretariat's position at the beginning of the conflict and to the discussions held in the organisation on the changes to the concept of peacekeeping operations.

The UN forces maintained their presence in the centre and south of the country until the end of the operation, but were mostly involved in securing the civil institutions that the UN had helped to establish and in providing humanitarian aid. Although Pakistan increased the size of the military force it allocated by another two thousand soldiers, the total number of soldiers in the second UN operation in Somalia was only nineteen thousand soldiers. In the course of 1994, when the organisation increased its forces in Bosnia and Croatia, the forces at UN disposal shrank considerably. As a result, the UN operated in Somalia in a format similar to that of the end of 1992: using force only in self-defence and with the agreement of the local factions. The UN forces largely operated in the main cities, and afterwards only in the Mogadishu area. Despite the presence of thousands of soldiers, they stopped intervening in security affairs and focused on defending themselves. In some cases, they secured certain sites or protected convoys of humanitarian aid. On one hand, the UN force had strong firepower and logistic-communication capacities in comparison to the fighting forces of the Somali factions. On the other hand, the UN forces were less willing to use their power. For example, when Somali forces attacked the Indian UN force in September, causing the deaths of nine soldiers from India, the only response was censure on the part of the Security Council[144]

The change in UN policy in Somalia with regard to use of force also led to a return to the peacemaking principle in cooperation with all the Somali clans. Due to the political pressure, the Secretariat representatives in Somalia changed their modus operandi. From the beginning of 1994, there was a change of personnel among the Secretariat representatives to create renewed momentum in the negotiations between the Somali factions; now, General Aidid's authority was recognised. The Secretary-General's representative from March 1993 until February 1994, Admiral Jonathan Howe from the United States, was replaced by Lansana Kouyaté from Guinea. Kouyaté tried to encourage the warlords of various clans to sign local peace agreements in the centre-south Somali environs. Simultaneously, he also tried to promote peace initiatives between all the clans. Kouyaté operated according to the traditional principles of the operations: he assumed an unbiased and neutral position, did not intervene in the internal affairs of territories associated with the factions, and did not use force.[145] The Nairobi Declaration of March 1994 was a direct result of Kouyaté's efforts. It was signed by the factions recognised by the UN and brought hope for redressing the damages of 1993.

The factions announced their commitment to establishing a functional transitional government, and proposed to assign a different function to the local and regional councils that the UN had established in Somalia. But, unfortunately, it was not possible to turn the clock back. The peacemaking attempt came after about a year of stagnation in the diplomatic process between the factions, and the UN had lost its credibility and importance as a peacemaker among the Somali factions.[146]

The warfare in Somalia over territory and economic resources continued. The Somali factions continued to splinter off into smaller and smaller factions, until there were twenty-eight separate factions by the end of 1994 – not including the Somaliland government.[147]

The UN also proved its impotence regarding the financing of the expensive operations, and it failed this mission. Not one UN member state was willing to contribute money to finance the second operation in Somalia, beyond the regular assessments imposed on the member states.[148] And that's not all: many of the countries did not even pay the assessments on time, and many did not pay the entire amount. As of 30 June 1994, the amount of assessments that were not paid to the UN for the operations in Somalia alone, was estimated at 610,652,972 dollars. These arrears contributed significantly to the organisation's financial crisis, which in turn encouraged a more limited use of multidimensional peacekeeping operations.[149]

Most of the members of the international community pressured the Secretariat to terminate the operation in Somalia for two main reasons: first, because the peacemaking process had failed, and second, because demands for international assistance and interventions increased in other places in the world. At the top of the list of those countries pushing for an end to the operation, no matter what the results, was the American delegation. Only a minority of delegations opposed the rapid withdrawal of the forces. On the other hand, veteran contributor states like Australia, New Zealand and Pakistan told Boutros-Ghali that they felt that Somalia should not be abandoned and that the intervention should be continued until peace was established in the country. In October 1994, a special delegation was dispatched to Somalia on behalf of the Security Council in order to assess the chances for continuation of the operation and its success. In its final report, the delegation reached the conclusion that the UN had outlived its usefulness in Somalia. One of the reasons was that even the leaders of the Somali clans saw no point in continuing the operation.[150]

The discussion of the intervention in Somalia from March 1993 proves that it is not true that the decrease in support for the peacekeeping operations was caused by the confrontation with General Aidid in October 1993 (this is the accepted argument in the literature, as presented in Chapter 1). The confrontation with General Aidid did not cause a real change in the international approach but only served to prove more clearly that discussions in the UN on the new concept were mainly theoretical and had never received a consensus among the member states. This is the only way we can explain why most of the organisation's members declared in 1994 that the operation in Somalia should be conducted only according to the traditional principles of the operations, while placing the responsibility for success of the operation on cooperation with the Somali factions.[151]

If we compare all the operations executed by the UN as of the mid-1990s, we see that the 1993 UN intervention in Somalia implemented many of the multidimensional operation concepts, while abandoning the accepted, traditional principles of peacekeeping operations.

Local and international support for this operation did not stem from the adoption of the new concept. The local factions wanted to weaken General Aidid and re-integrate Somaliland into Somalia. Most of the countries of the world had no interest at all in the conflict in Somalia. The United States government only wanted to leave Somalia without being accused of abandoning it. Under those circumstances, the UN Secretariat (headed by the Secretary-General) succeeded in dragging other countries into the conflict, while rationalising this behaviour by citing the new concepts raised in the organisation regarding the potential of the multidimensional operation. For a few months in the course of 1993, it did seem as if the 'Agenda for Peace' vision of Secretary-General Boutros-Ghali would actually be realised.

As opposed to what happened in Cambodia and the former Yugoslavia, the Secretariat representatives lost their discretion and clear-sighted thinking in everything related to Somalia. They pushed the Security Council to adopt multidimensional goals while they quarrelled with the local players. It seems as if the Secretariat personnel 'forgot' that their power stems, first and foremost, from the willingness of the member states to give this power to them. They did not try to act cautiously, as they did in Cambodia, for example. The Secretariat representatives were biased and partial, and intervened in the internal affairs of the local factions. They ignored the declaration of independence of the Somaliland representatives, and they recognised the regimes of local leaders who supported the UN over those leaders who ruled by virtue of local power or position. Thus they labelled the members of General Aidid's USC/SNA faction as recalcitrants who did not cooperate with the UN representatives.

The violation of traditional principles reached its height when the Secretariat crossed the 'Mogadishu Line',[152] in the course of the confrontation that took place in Mogadishu between UN forces and USC/SNA forces (June–October 1993). The campaign in Mogadishu was an important test of the new concept that called for integrating a wide variety of goals such as peacemaking, peace enforcement and peacebuilding during a conflict. Voices denouncing these steps started to be heard in the UN as early as the middle of 1993, and not only after the fierce fighting in Mogadishu between 3 and 4 October 1993.[153] The UN failed in this test, when it became clear that most states refused to give the Secretariat the means and resources needed to enforce a theoretical concept whose ramifications were not yet sufficiently clear. In the course of 1994 until the official termination of the operation in March 1995, the operation returned to a pattern of more limited goals according to traditional principles.

It is important to note that at every stage of the conflict, no clear, uniform alliances ever formed of Western versus developing states in the UN. If such an alliance did occasionally appear, it formed in the context of a local issue or interest. The developing countries contributed the lion's share of the forces for the second

UN operation in Somalia. The Western states, on the other hand, contributed very little in the way of financing and logistical support to the Somalia operation, mainly because these countries were at the time investing heavily in the Balkan operations connected to the former Yugoslavia. This lack of assistance showed the true face of the pretentious rhetoric of 1992. At the same time, peacekeeping operations developed in Croatia and Bosnia that would overshadow all prior operations in size.

### Former Yugoslavia: from protection of civilians to protection of interests

As of the first half of 1993, it appeared that the international community was willing to expand its involvement in the former Yugoslavia and especially in Bosnia. From 1993 to 1995, the Security Council accepted 236 resolutions; out of these, 64 dealt with issues connected to the countries of the former Yugoslavia. For the first time in UN history, a preventive deployment was implemented in Macedonia. Peacekeeping forces deployed the entire length of the country's border with the Federal Republic of Yugoslavia. Relative stability was achieved in Croatia when peacekeeping forces were deployed in protected areas. But the most important developments took place in Bosnia. The Security Council authorised a multinational force to secure humanitarian aid under UN Charter's Chapter 7; six regions throughout the country were declared protected areas, and it was decided to found an international criminal tribunal. It appeared that as an extension of the new principles for execution of the operations, a new consensus was developing that during a civil war, residents of countries not involved in the conflict would receive the protection of the international community.

A few months prior to the renewal of the battles that led to the termination of the war in Bosnia and Croatia in May 1995, the UN forces operating as part of UNPROFOR numbered 39,402 soldiers, military observers and police. This number was about two-thirds of the sum total of all the forces that were deployed in all the UN peacekeeping operations of that time period.[154] A month later, a decision was taken to authorise the deployment of another 12,500 soldiers in Bosnia. Ostensibly, the great military power of the UN force strengthens the claim regarding the change in concept of the operations. However, despite the large numerical size of the force, the operation's goals were limited (throughout most of the operation) and it mainly operated in accordance with the traditional principles of peacekeeping operations – the non-use of force, receiving international legitimacy, and obtaining the agreement of the warring parties. Finally, the operation is remembered mainly because of its failure in preventing the local genocide carried out by Serbs on Muslims in Srebrenica. Since the UN adopted different modes of operation in the successor countries of the former Yugoslavia, I will focus in my discussion below on the following issues, the two main interventions in the protected areas in Croatia and the development of the operation in Bosnia, while paying special attention to the securing of humanitarian aid and protection of the safe areas.[155]

### Croatia

In March 1993, UN forces were deployed in Croatia in what was then the third-largest operation of that period, after the operations in Cambodia and Somalia. But these forces did not contribute to resolving the conflict. In light of lack of progress in the diplomatic realm, the continuation of the humanitarian crisis and the failure of the UN forces to fulfil their responsibility in the security realm, Croatian President Tudman said that he was in favour of an enforcement operation in the protected areas, similar to the operations executed by the UN during the conquest of Kuwait and in Somalia.[156] Since there was no progress, the Croatian government initiated three military operations against the Serbs in 1993. The first operation of the Croatian army was in January 1993, when it tried to return the Peruća Hydroelectric dam to its control. The second operation was held near the town of Maslenica in January–February 1993. The third operation was near the town of Gospić in September 1993. The goal of the last two operations was to prevent the Serb forces from effectively cutting Croatia in half and to facilitate transportation movement along the length of the Adriatic Sea. In the course of the battles, Croatian forces harmed the Serbian civilian population. These operations were limited in scope and designed to return control to the country over sites with strategic and economic importance. Following the operations, ethnic cleansing was carried out by both sides.[157]

Although the UN failed in its attempts to influence the security situation in Croatia, the international community continued to support the operation while condemning both warring sides.[158] However, in the course of 1993, the international community agreed that the conflict of the Serbs in Croatia must be resolved in such a way that the Serbian minority would be re-integrated into the Croatian state with minority rights. Thus, for example, 142 out of 184 members of the UN voted in favour of a resolution calling for the termination of the conflict in Croatia, while accusing the Federal Republic of Yugoslavia of attempting to annex these territories in violation of international law of respecting the sovereign borders of every state.[159] To implement this, the Secretariat adopted a stage-by-stage programme: the first stage was the creation of a ceasefire agreement; afterwards, steps towards economic normalisation; and, finally, merging the Serbian regions into Croatia.[160]

Although the number of refugees on both sides (Serbs and Croats) was roughly equivalent, the main responsibility for the situation was cast on the Croatian Serbs. Thus severe economic sanctions were imposed on them in April 1993. For example, they were forbidden to engage in all commercial activity with the exception of the transfer of humanitarian aid – foodstuffs and medications – to their territory.[161] The great efforts made by the international community to supply humanitarian and economic aid yielded only limited results. Only at the end of 1994 did the talks for cooperation between Serbs–Croats and the Croat government begin to bear fruit. Agreements involving economic cooperation were reached, such as opening the main road from Zagreb to Belgrade, or renewing the pipeline transport of crude oil and petroleum from the Adriatic Sea to the centre of Europe. However, the agreements were only partially implemented and the UN agencies reported that from the beginning of their activities in 1992 only a few thousand Croats had returned to be repatriated in their homes in the protected areas.[162]

As the direct continuation of the change in the international community's position regarding resolution of the conflict in Croatia, most of the UN nations placed the blame for the situation on the Serbs, since they did not cooperate with the UN. The representatives from Russia were of the minority opinion when they argued – with a great deal of truth – that the Croatian government forces were the first to violate the ceasefires. We see from the discussions in the UN at the time that, even in the later stages of the operation, Chapter 7 of the Charter was never invoked to allow the UN forces to enforce their authority over the conflicted sides. The Security Council adopted resolutions to allow UN personnel to use force in order to protect and defend themselves, whether by using their own arms or by receiving air support from NATO. The only dissenting voices were heard from the representatives of China and Brazil, who argued that this permission to use force was likely to escalate the situation on the ground.[163] The UN Secretariat was aware of the inability of the international community to terminate the operation or to give it greater powers. Thus, due to international pressure, the Secretariat was forced to recommend the continued presence of UN forces in Croatia, which operated mainly according to the traditional principles, in the hope that a diplomatic agreement, and not military action, would terminate the conflict.[164]

The absence of a diplomatic solution – and in light of the international backing given to the Croatian government – led to a realisation of the Secretariat's prediction: that without international resolve, war would be renewed. After the Croatian army received American training and support,[165] the Croats attacked the protected areas – the southern, northern and western regions – and conquered them in May and August of 1995. In the wake of the battles, about a quarter of a million Serbs fled to the Federation of Yugoslavia or to territories under Serb rule in Bosnia. Since the UN forces were operating according to the traditional principles, they did nothing to prevent the Croatian army's takeover of these territories. In light of the new circumstances, the majority of the UN forces were evacuated from most of the Croatian territory; the force still remaining on the ground was mainly concentrated in the eastern region. A new operation was executed as part of the new concept of peacebuilding after a peace agreement was signed between the Croatian Serbs and the Croatian government, stipulating that all their (Serb) territories would be merged into Croatia.[166] Following these operations, the Serbs agreed to sign the Erdut Agreement that merged the eastern region in the protected areas (including the districts of Eastern Slavonia, Baranja and Western Sirmium) back to Croatia. Only after the Erdut Agreement was signed on 12 November 1995 did the international community focus on economic development programmes for Croatia. This sequence of events testifies to the negligible influence of UN activities – the military intervention, the humanitarian aid and attempts at economic cooperation – on the willingness of the warring factions to end the conflict between them. The UN forces operated according to traditional principles, and did not attempt to carry out peace enforcement measures against the Serbs who violated the agreements or against the Croats who attacked the protected areas.

*Bosnia*

Against the recommendations of the Secretariat, the Security Council decided to enlarge the sphere of operations of UNPROFOR in Bosnia in the summer of 1992. This placed the UN forces at the very epicentre of an active conflict. Ostensibly, this modus operandi conformed to the conceptual discussion in the organisation regarding the need to combine peacemaking and peacekeeping forces. However, these forces operated in tandem with the diplomatic negotiating teams when no overall agreement had been reached to define the forces' role and contribution to peacemaking. On one level, UN representatives brokered hundreds of initiatives for local ceasefires in order to limit the intensity of the conflict, to create conditions for continued activity of the peacekeeping forces and various assistance organisations, and to encourage support for a comprehensive agreement to resolve the conflict in Bosnia.[167] On a second level, the International Conference on Former Yugoslavia (ICFY – the international mediating body in the conflict) focused its efforts on achieving a comprehensive peace between the opposing factions in Bosnia and Croatia according to traditional principles such as impartiality and honouring sovereignty.[168]

In the previous chapter, we saw how the international community invested many resources in supplying humanitarian aid to the Bosnian population. In October 1993, there were about 4.3 million individuals in need of humanitarian aid in the countries making up the former Yugoslavia, out of which about 2.74 million were in Bosnia-Herzegovina. Two years later, in September 1995, the scope of humanitarian aid remained constant and aimed to assist about 3.5 million needy individuals.[169]

In contrast to the way it worked in Cambodia and Somalia, the Security Council decided not to supervise or manage the work of the governments of the former Yugoslavian states, which in many cases were responsible for gross human rights violations. This was despite the scathing reports received by the UN Special

Rapporteurs regarding severe violations of human rights, and the Commission of Experts that examined grave breaches of the Geneva conventions and other violations of international humanitarian law in the countries of the former Yugoslavia, and sweeping approval for the founding of an international criminal tribunal to judge war crimes in the countries of the former Yugoslavia.[170] The explanation given for this inaction was that such interference in the former Yugoslavian states was considered taboo in the UN, constituting an infringement on state sovereignty.

The UN forces which operated in the very midst of the conflict in Bosnia had two main security-related goals that, when combined, were supposed to minimise the suffering of civilians in the course of the conflict. The first objective remained, in effect, the only objective until the first half of 1993. The UN forces were charged with securing the airlift to Sarajevo and Tuzla, and the convoys of humanitarian aid throughout the country.[171] In the course of 1993, another goal was delineated: the development of the concept of safe areas – defined geographic spaces in which military operations were banned. The UN forces were charged with responsibility for the safety of the civilian population that was mainly Muslim.[172]

Despite the diplomatic support for the safe areas, they were really just fig leaves to hide the unwillingness of the international community to end the conflict by using force or to provide full protection to the civilians in the conflict-ridden areas. An example is the barbed comment of Czech representative Karel Kovanda in a discussion held in the Security Council on 31 March 1994 regarding the need for imposing the concept of safe areas on additional cities in Bosnia. Kovanda ridiculed other representatives who argued that only several hundreds or thousands of soldiers were needed each time. Kovanda cited the case of Srebrenica, in which at least 1,500 UN soldiers had been required but, in actual fact, only 300 soldiers were present in March 1994. Although the number of forces in Bosnia grew and reached about 22,000 soldiers by the beginning of 1995, only limited numbers were allocated to the safe areas outside Sarajevo.[173] Thus, in July 1995 only about 450 Dutch soldiers were deployed in Srebrenica, and of these, only about a half were combat soldiers.[174] During the course of the conflict, proposals were raised to apply the concept to other regions in Bosnia but the Security Council refused to increase the numbers of safe areas after UNPROFOR failed to deploy its forces according to the conservative estimates.[175] And despite the fact that the resolutions regarding the safe areas authorised UN personnel to use force in accordance with the Charter's Chapter 7, the UN forces were dependent on obtaining the agreement and support of all local sides to the conflict.[176]

Debate continued to rage throughout the years in the UN regarding methods to improve security during an active conflict. Most of the proposals raised in the discussions focused on two solutions. One was removal of the embargo imposed on the Socialist Federal Republic of Yugoslavia (SFRY) in September 1991, in order to allow the Bosnian Muslims to arm themselves.[177] Another suggestion was to attack Serbian positions and facilities from the air. However, when it was resolved to use air raids in February 1994 and May 1995, the Serbs responded by taking hundreds of UN soldiers as prisoners. This act led to a change in the organisation's priorities, leading to UN efforts to ensure the welfare of its soldiers on the ground instead of the welfare of the local population.[178] Below I describe one of the instances in which a fierce discussion erupted even before the United States advanced the principle of using one-sided force, starting from the summer of 1995.

On 5 February 1994 a 120 mm mortar shell exploded in the heart of the bustling Markale market in Sarajevo, killing almost seventy people and wounding about another two hundred. In response, numerous governments demanded that the Security Council conduct a special discussion on the issue. The resultant discussion on 14 and 15 February ended without the adoption of a resolution, but it advanced United States involvement in the conflict and the launching of NATO planes to conduct air strikes.[179] A total of fifty-eight spokespersons took part in the discussion and numerous countries sent official letters to the organisation with their opinions and positions, thus revealing the alliances existing in the UN and the different stances taken within the international community towards the conflict in Bosnia. The chief supporters of enforcement actions against the Serbs were diplomats from the United States, Muslim countries and many representatives of developing countries; these represented most of the speakers. They considered the Serbs to be the aggressors, and were in favour of bombing Serb military forces and removing the embargo on Bosnia so that the Bosnian government would be able to legally acquire weapons abroad.

But this view was opposed by EU diplomats who represented the largest contributor states to UN forces in Bosnia. They argued that the use of force was only possible if it would contribute to the resolution of the conflict. They especially emphasised their opposition to air strikes on the Bosnian Serbs, unless such strikes were authorised by both NATO and the UN Secretariat. Finally, they opposed the removal of the embargo on Bosnia, claiming that this would cause an armament race, escalation of the violence, and inevitably force the UN to withdraw entirely, instead of allowing its forces to help restore peace in the area. The UN Secretariat also supported this stance and summarised that adopting any of the more militant options would 'be a fundamental shift from the logic of peace-keeping to the logic of war and would require the withdrawal of UNPROFOR from Bosnia and Herzegovina'.[180] A third point of view was expressed by representatives from countries such as Greece, China and Russia. The representatives of these countries were in favour of the continued embargo and were opposed to any use of force. In their view, the responsibility for the conflict rested on all the conflicted sides in Bosnia.[181]

Thus the way the peacekeeping operation in Bosnia was handled led to the failure of the UN forces to protect the safe areas and disarm the local population (until the military balance was tilted during the final months of the conflict in Bosnia). While most of the organisation's members proclaimed their opposition to the Serbs' actions, the alliance system in the Security Council and the dynamics on the ground paralysed all options for ending the operation or adopting enforcement actions.[182] In the spring of 1995, fighting escalated in Croatia and Bosnia; the continuation of the operation as it was came into question. The escalation of the Bosnian conflict in May 1995 was connected to several events. In May 1995, NATO bombed the Bosnian Serbs in response to Serbian shelling of Sarajevo, and the Serbs did not withdraw their heavy weapons. In reaction to the NATO bombing, the Serbs captured about 370 UN soldiers as prisoners. This proved that the UN forces were, in many cases, unable to defend themselves, let alone defend the local civilian population.

The big change occurred when the American government took control of the diplomatic process and the military modus operandi. This was because the American government came under increasing public pressure in the United States to intervene in the conflict. In addition, the American government was worried that the European governments would decide to withdraw their forces from Bosnia, forcing the United States to assist them in securing the retreat by sending thousands of soldiers. Therefore the US government acted alone to tilt the military balance in the conflict. In this epilogue to the intervention, the UN and peacekeeping forces played second fiddle to American action. The United States violated the embargo imposed on the countries of the former Yugoslavia by supplying weapons and training to the Croats and Bosnian Muslims and encouraging them to cooperate in military operations. Finally, in July 1995, the Americans succeeded in garnering the support of the UN member states for consolidating a model of NATO air strikes against the Bosnian Serbs, only after it was agreed to deploy a rapid reaction force in Bosnia. Simultaneously, the USA promised Slobodan Milošević that it would lighten the economic sanctions imposed on the FRY, in exchange for pressure on the Bosnian Serbs to sign an agreement.[183]

The results of all these actions were not long in coming. In May and August 1995, the Croatian government forces succeeded in conquering most of the Croatian-Serb territories. Meanwhile, a weakened Milošević – whose state had suffered severely under the economic sanctions imposed on the FRY – decided not send military forces to protect these Serbs. In July, the Bosnian Serbs conquered the safe areas of Srebrenica and Žepa and massacred about 8,000 male Muslims. Local and international response was quick. At the end of August, NATO conducted air strikes against Bosnian Serb military infrastructure after a Serbian shell killed scores of people in Sarajevo on 28 August. They did this only after Lieutenant General Rupert Smith (UK), UNPROFOR commander in Bosnia, concentrated all his troops and also deployed a rapid reaction force strong enough to cope with a possible attack by the Serbs. From this point on, UN ground forces cooperated with NATO's air force in joint operations against the Serbs. About two years after the UN's 'peace enforcement' operation in Somalia against the Somali USC/SNA faction of General Aidid, this model was again implemented in the former Yugoslavia. But in contrast to the Somali incident, the Yugoslavian operation was held under joint command of NATO and the UN, and thus had access to considerable resources. At the beginning of September, the Croat and Bosnian-Muslim forces began a joint military raid on West Bosnia. They inflicted defeats on the Bosnian Serb military forces, and at the beginning of October they reached the outskirts of the largest Serbian city in Bosnia, Banja-Luka.[184]

Facing defeat, the Bosnian Serbs were forced to sign the peace agreement submitted to them by mediator Richard Holbrooke, appointed by the United States. Holbrooke employed the experience and knowledge accumulated during the war years to take over the failed mediating process of ICFY (in the name of the American government), and led the conflicted sides to agree to partition the Bosnian territories into two units: 51 per cent to the Bosnian-Croatian Federation, and 49 per cent to the Serbs. The new constitution divided the Bosnian state into two entities: a Srpska Republic (Serbs) and a Bosnian-Croatian Federation, each entity enjoying sovereign rights of states, such as diplomatic relations with neighbouring countries. Finally, the agreement called for large-scale deployment of NATO forces – sixty thousand soldiers in Bosnia – to enforce the ceasefire, supervise the return of heavy weapons, and promote human rights and the return of displaced persons and refugees.[185]

Thus, the largest peacekeeping operation ever held after the resolution of a conflict was not managed by the UN Secretariat (despite the Agenda for Peace vision) but by a regional Western organisation combining US interests with those of EU members. After the signing of the peace agreement, the international community continued to intervene in the former Yugoslavia countries. From the middle of the 1990s to this day, these countries have served as a laboratory for the development of the peacekeeping operation concept. Unfortunately, these developments lie outside the purview of this study. It is important to emphasise that, in all these operations, the role of the UN weakened to the benefit of international or regional coalitions that operated in a variety of political, security, economic and social spheres.

In summary, despite the differences of opinion within the international community regarding the correct way to intervene in the former Yugoslavian conflict, the members of the community were able to unite around the dismantling of the former Yugoslavia according to internal borders that separated the federation's members, and in accordance with international law. The proposal to dismantle the entire Yugoslavia entity in accordance with ethnic identities and the principle of national self-determination was rejected. The key confrontations in the UN were not waged between delegations demanding a large multidimensional operation versus others who demanded a traditional operation. Instead, the disagreement was between those who wanted a multidimensional operation with a focus on limited goals and adherence to the traditional principles, and those who wanted an enforcement operation to subdue the Serbs in the conflict, similar to the international military operation conducted against Iraq after the occupation of Kuwait.

UNPROFOR in the former Yugoslavia was a hybrid of two approaches: a large traditional operation and an enforcement operation according to the Charter's Chapter 7. Therefore, it did serve to stabilise the conflict, but did not promote goals that could have leveraged the sides to resolve the conflict.

Attempts to reform the political systems in the countries of the former Yugoslavia at the beginning of the 1990s had only marginal influence. Economic development activities had no effect on resolving the conflict. Finally, while the military deployment may have succeeded somewhat in moderating the warring sides, it did not prevent them from activating large army operations whenever they felt like it, and it certainly failed to prevent large massacres from taking place. The presence of multinational forces in Bosnia and Croatia, along with large quantities of humanitarian aid, became instruments in the hands of the local factions and international players. This interim condition ended only in 1995 when the United States manifestly entered the picture and used force to tilt the military balance in the conflict in Croatia and Bosnia; this had no connection to the concept behind peacekeeping operations, whether traditional or multidimensional. Only afterwards did the state-building process begin in Croatia and Bosnia. This process was widely supported by the European countries and the United States, and the UN was only a minor partner.[186] This process continues to this very day.

## Notes

1   A/51/1, 20 August 1996, pp. 27–28, 93–94.
2   A/RES/47/71, 14 December 1992.
3   S/25859, 28 May 1993.
4   A/AC.121/40, 1 April 1993; /48/403/Add.1-S/26450/Add.1, 2 November 1993; A/48/403/Add.2-S/26450/Add.2, 1 December 1993.
5   A/AC.121/37/Add.1, 23 April 1990, pp. 11–13; A/SPC/47/SR.14, 10 November 1992, pp. 12–13; A/C.4/49/SR.24, 16 November 1994, pp. 3–5; A/C.4/50/SR.22, 19 December 1995, p. 6.
6   A/AC.121/39/Rev.1, 14 April 1992, pp. 6–12; A/SPC/47/SR.15, 11 November 1992, p. 9.
7   S/25667, 16 April 1993.
8   A/AC.121/39, 2 April 1992, pp. 4–8; A/SPC/47/SR.14, 10 November 1992, pp. 6–8; A/AC.121/40, 1 April 1993, pp. 3–6; S/25996/Add.2, 30 July 1993; A/C.4/48/SR.22, 4 February 1994, pp. 3–4; A/AC.121/41, 16 March 1994, pp. 2–6; A/C.4/49/SR.21, 14 November 1994, pp. 12–14; A/C.4/50/SR.20, 14 November 1995, pp. 7–8.
9   In this context it is important to emphasise that Ireland and Denmark, two countries that promoted the multidimensional concept, were also members of the EC. For information about their politics, see: K. Ishizuka, *Ireland and International Peacekeeping Operations 1960-2000* (London: Routledge, 2004); Jakobsen, *Nordic Approaches*.

10  A/C.4/50/SR.19, 13 November, 1995, pp. 3–5.
11  A/C.4/48/SR.24, 31 January 1994; A/C.4/49/SR.21, 14 November 1994, pp. 10–11; A/C.4/49/SR.24, 16 November 1994, pp. 3–5; A/50/137-S/1995/295, 13 April 1995; A/C.4/50/SR.20, 14 November 1995, pp. 14–16; A/C.4/50/SR.22, 19 December 1995, pp. 12–13; A /C.4/48/SR.22, 4 February 1994, pp. 12–13; A/C.4/48/SR.26, 2 February 1994, pp. 6–7; A/AC.121/41, 16 March 1994, pp. 6–8; S/PV.3492 (Res. 1), 18 January 1995, pp. 15–18; A/C.4/50/SR.19, 13 November 1995, pp. 3–5; A/C.4/50/SR.20, 14 November, 1995, pp. 11–12.
12  A/C.4/48/SR.22, 4 February 1994, pp. 6–9, 16–17; A/C.4/48/SR.23, 8 February 1994, pp. 4–7; A/C.4/48/SR.24, 31 January 1994, pp. 13–20.
13  A/49/287-S/1994/894, 29 July 1994, pp. 17–19.
14  A/57/759-S/2003/332, 18 March 2003; Non-Aligned Movement, NAM, 2008/Doc.1/Rev.2, July 2008; Non-Aligned Movement, AM 2012/Doc.1/Rev.2, 31 August, 2012.
15  See the variety of opinions expressed by many countries in the discussions of the Special Committee and the Fourth Committee: A/C.4/49/SR.21, 14 November 1994; A/C.4/49/SR.22, 15 November 1994; A/C.4/49/SR.23, 16 November 1994; A/C.4/49/SR.24, 16 November 1994; A/C.4/49/SR.25, 17 November 1994; A/C.4/49/SR.26, 18 November 1994; A/50/230, 22 June 1995; A/C.4/50/SR.19, 13 November 1995; A/C.4/50/SR.20, 14 November 1995; A/C.4/50/SR.21, 29 December 1995; A/C.4/50/SR.22, 19 December 1995; A/C.4/50/SR.23, 11 January 1996.
16  A/48/173, 25 May 1993, p. 2.
17  A/48/403-S/26450, 14 March 1994, para. 11–13.
18  A/49/136, 2 May 1994, p. 2.
19  A/48/403-S/26450, 14 March 1994, para. 11–13.
20  On the battle in Mogadishu that took place on 3 October 1993, see the discussion on Somalia.
21  S/26517, 30 September 1993.
22  S/PRST/1994/22, 3 May 1994.
23  A/RES/47/62, 11 December 1992.
24  A/48/264, 20 July 1993, pp. 18–19, 40–42, 82–83, 90–92; A/RES/48/26, 3 December 1993.
25  A/48/47, 2 September 1994; A/49/47, 15 September 1995; A/RES/50/6, 9 November 1995.
26  On the ongoing discussions regarding the council's size, composition and powers in contemporary times as well, see: B. Fassbender, 'Pressure for Security Council Reform', in Malone (ed.), *The UN Security Council*, pp. 341–355; Mahbubani, 'The Permanent and Elected Council Members', pp. 253–266.
27  A/47/253, 4 June 1992, pp. 6, 16–17; A/48/173, 25 May 1993, p. 7; S/26015, 30 June 1993; S/PV.3294, 19 October 1993; A/RES/48/42, 10 December 1993; S/1994/120, 4 February 1994; A/49/136, 2 May 1994, p. 7. And see the criticism expressed by the Malaysian representative about the conduct of the Council regarding the operation in Somalia throughout 1993: S/1994/120, 4 February 1994.

28  S/1994/120, 4 February 1994.
29  S/1994/1063, 18 September 1994; S/1994/1136, 6 October 1994; S/1994/1193, 21 October 1994; S/1994/1201, 22 October 1994; S/1994/1219, 27 October 1994; S/1994/1221, 28 October 1994; S/1994/1231, 31 October 1994; S/1994/1237, 2 November 1994; S/1994/1238, 2 November 1994; S/PV.3449, 4 November 1994, pp. 15–18.
30  S/PRST/1994/62, 4 November 1994; S/PV.3449, 4 November 1994; A/49/667-S/1994/1279, 11 November 1994; S/1994/1313, 18 November 1994; S/1994/1349, 26 November 1994; S/1994/1350, 26 November 1994; A/49/759-S/1994/1384, 6 December 1994; S/PRST/1994/81, 16 December 1994; S/PV.3483, 16 December 1994; Albright and Woodward, *Madam Secretary*, pp. 136–137.
31  A/RES/49/37, 9 December 1994, para. 8–13; S/PRST/1996/13, 28 March 1996.
32  A/50/230, 22 June 1995, pp. 3, 7.
33  A/51/130, 7 May 1996, pp. 3, 9.
34  Fassbender, 'Pressure for Security Council Reform', pp. 341–355; N. Krisch, 'The Security Council and the Great Powers', in Lowe *et al.* (eds), *The United Nations Security Council*, pp. 133–153.
35  A/50/230, 22 June 1995, pp. 4, 9–10; A/51/130, 7 May 1996, pp. 2–3, 8; B. Boutros-Ghali, 'Introduction', in UN, *Blue Helmets*, 1996, pp. 3–4.
36  A/50/60-S/1995/1, 25 January 1995, p. 9.
37  A/50/60-S/1995/1, 25 January 1995, p. 19.
38  S/PV.3492(Res. 1), 18 January 1995, p. 16.
39  S/PV.3492, 18 January 1995, p. 14.
40  S/PV.3492, 18 January 1995, pp. 12–15; A/C.4/50/SR.20, 14 November 1995, pp. 5–6.
41  S/PV.3492 (Res. 1), 18 January 1995, pp. 16–17.
42  S/PV.3492, 18 January 1995, p. 24.
43  S/PV.3492, 18 January 1995, p. 18; A/C.4/50/SR.21, 29 December 1995, pp. 3–4.
44  A/49/114-S/1994/357, 30 March 1994; A/C.4/49/SR.24, 16 November 1994, pp. 9–10; A/C.4/49/SR.25, 17 November 1994, pp. 2–4; S/PV.3492, 18 January 1995, pp. 2–7, 22–24; S/PV.3492 (Res. 1), 18 January 1995, pp. 15–18. Albright and Woodward, *Madam Secretary*, pp. 146–147, 157–158; Boutros-Ghali, *Unvanquished*, pp. 123–125; von Einsiedel and Malone, 'Haiti', pp. 172–173.
45  For more information about the change in policy of the Egyptian and Thai governments, see: A/AC.121/37/Add.3, 9 May 1990, pp. 2–4; A/SPC/45/Sr.19, 21 November 1990, pp. 5–6; A/SPC/46/Sr.13, 30 October 1991, p. 14; A/SPC/47/SR.14,10 November 1992, pp. 8–9; A/SPC/47/SR.17, 13 November 1992, pp. 21–22; A/48/403/Add.1-S/26450/Add.1, 2 November 1993, p. 19; A/C.4/48/SR.24, 31 January 1994, pp. 13–14; A/C.4/48/SR.22, 4 February 1994, pp. 9–10; A/C.4/49/SR.25, 17 November 1994, pp. 17–19; A/C.4/49/SR.26, 18 November 1994, pp. 4–5; A/C.4/50/SR.21, 29 December 1995, pp. 2–3; A/C.4/50/SR.23, 11 January 1996, pp. 6–7.
46  In the following discussions, we see how the following countries continued to express support for the operations and their development,

while committing themselves to continue to allocate forces to the operations: Argentina, Bangladesh, Zimbabwe, Mali, Malaysia and Kenya. A /C.4/48/ SR.23, 8 February 1994, pp. 10–12; A/C.4/48/SR.26, 2 February 1994, pp. 7–8; A/C.4/49/SR.21, 14 November 1994, pp. 5–7; A/C.4/49/SR.23, 16 November 1994, pp. 8–9; S/PV.3492/RES.1, 18 January 1995, pp. 12–15; A/C.4/50/SR.20, 14 November 1995, pp. 4–5, 9–10; A/C.4/50/SR.21, 29 December 1995, pp. 12, 15–16; A/C.4/50/SR.23, 11 January 1996, pp. 5–6.

47  A/C.4/49/SR.23, 16 November 1994, pp. 5–7; A/C.4/50/SR.21, 29 December 1995, pp. 15–16.

48  Lack of space prevents me from exemplifying the gamut of positions held by UN delegations regarding the goals and success principles of the peacekeeping operations from 1993 to 1995. Below I reference only a few prominent speeches. Regarding East European countries, see: A/C.4/48/SR.24, 31 January 1994; A/C.4/49/SR.21, 14 November 1994, pp. 10–11; A/C.4/49/SR.24, 16 November 1994, pp. 3–5; A/50/137-S/1995/295, 13 April 1995; A/C.4/50/SR.20, 14 November 1995, pp. 14–16; A/C.4/50/SR.22, 19 December 1995, pp. 12–13. Regarding Western countries, see: A/C.4/48/SR.22, 4 February 1994, pp. 12–13; A/C.4/48/SR.26, 2 February 1994, pp. 6–7; A/AC.121/41, 16 March 1994, pp. 6–8; S/PV.3492 (Res. 1), 18 January 1995, pp. 15–18; A/C.4/50/SR.19, 13 November 1995, pp. 3–5; A/C.4/50/SR.20, 14 November 1995, pp. 11–12.

49  See the last report of the Open Working Group regarding the Peace Agenda: *Conference Room Papers: Sub-group on Coordination 1996*, in A/WGAP/96/1; *Sub-group on the Question of United Nations Imposed Sanctions 1996*, in A/WGAP/96/2.

50  A/49/136, 2 May 1994, p. 9, para. 42.

51  A/50/230, 22 June 1995, p. 8, para. 34, p. 17, para. 93; A/RES/50/30,6 December 1995, para. 6.

52  A/RES/51/136, 13 December 1996.

53  A/52/209, 28 June 1997, annex.

54  A/48/403-S/26450, 14 March 1994, para. 23–24.

55  A/47/253, 4 June 1992, pp. 4, 6, 16; A/RES/47/71, 14 December 1992; A/48/173, 25 May 1993, p. 7, para. 32–33; A/RES/48/42, 10 December 1993; A/48/403-S/26450, 14 March 1994; A/49/136, 2 May 1994, p. 9; A/RES/49/37, 9 December 1994; /50/230, 22 June 1995, pp. 7–8, pp. 13–14; A/51/130, 7 May 1996, pp. 5–6, 11–12.

56  A/45/502, 19 September 1990; A/SPC/45/Sr.21, 23 November 1990, pp. 2–3; A/SPC/46/Sr.12, 29 October 1991.

57  A/C.5/45/Sr.42,10 December 1990, pp. 5–6; A/C.5/45/Sr.52, 11 December 1990.

58  A/C.5/45/Sr.40, 5 December 1990, pp. 3–5; A/C.5/45/Sr.52, 11 December 1990, pp. 7–9; A/SPC/46/Sr.12, 29 October. 1991; A/49/136, 2 May 1994, p. 8.

59  A/46/254, 18 June 1991, pp. 4–5, para. 24–31; A/48/173, 25 May 1993, p. 5; A/RES/48/42, 10 December 1993; A/49/136, 2 May 1994, p. 8; A/RES/49/37, 9 December 1994.

60  S/26450-A/48/403, 14 March 1994, para. 19; A/51/130, 7 May 1996, pp. 5–6, para. 21–23, p. 12, para. 62–65.

61 Goulding, *Peacemonger*, pp. 145–148.
62 A/47/253, 4 June 1992, p. 16, para. 75; A/RES/48/42, 10 December 1993, para. 35.
63 A/47/253, 4 June 1992, pp. 10–11; A/48/173, 25 May 1993, p. 6; A/49/136, 2 May 1994, p. 8; A/RES/49/37, 9 December 1994; A/50/230, 22 June 1995, pp. 6, 15–16.
64 A/51/130, 7 May 1996, pp. 5, 11.
65 A/49/886-S/1995/276, 10 April 1995; A/50/230, 22 June 1995, p. 6, para. 22–23; A/51/130, 7 May 1996, p. 4, para. 15.
66 J. Koops, *UN SHIRBRIG and EU Battlegroups* (Oxford: Oxford Council on Good Governance, 2007).
67 This is not the place to discuss the gamut of activities of regional organisations in world politics. For a short introduction, see the first chapter of this study.
68 S/25184, 29 January 1993.
69 S/25996, 15 June 1993.
70 S/25996, 15 June 1993, pp. 3–4; S/25996/Add.4, 14 October 1993.
71 S/25996, 15 June 1993, pp. 5–6, 9–15; S/25996/Add.1, 14 July 1993, p. 2; S/25996/Add.2, 30 July 1993; A/48/403/Add.1-S/26450/Add.1, 2 November 1993, pp. 36–39; S/25996/Add.6, 4 May 1994.
72 S/25996, 15 June 1993, pp. 7–9; S/25996, 15 June 1993, pp. 16–20; S/25996/Add.1, 14 July 1993, pp. 2–4; S/25996/Add.3, 1 September 1993.
73 S/1994/61, 20 January 1994; A/RES/49/37, 9 December 1994.
74 A/47/253, 4 June 1992, p. 8, para. 31, pp. 20–22, para. 104–110; A/RES/47/71, 14 December 1992, para. 52–53; A/48/173, 25 May 1993, p. 9, para. 45–46; A/RES/48/42, 10 December 1993, para. 62–65; A/49/136, 2 May 1994, p. 4, para. 16, p. 9, para. 41; A/RES/49/37, 9 December 1994, para. 56–58; A/RES/49/57, Annex, 9 December 1994; A/50/230, 22 June 1995, pp. 5–6, para. 19–21, p. 8, para. 30, p. 17, para. 90–91; A/51/130, 7 May 1996, pp. 4, 10, para. 51, pp. 14–15, para. 78–82.
75 A/49/114-S/1994/357, 30 March 1994.
76 P. Duignan, *NATO: Its Past, Present, and Future* (Stanford, CA: Hoover Institution Press, 2000), pp. 43–84; K. Ifantis, *NATO and the New Security Paradigm: Power, Strategy, Order and the Transatlantic Link* (London: Frank Cass, 2003), pp. 41–71; Frantzen, *NATO*, pp. 58–88. The EU and NATO countries began to develop multinational forces (from the end of the 1990s) that could participate in peacekeeping and peace-supporting operations. It seems that the initial inspiration for this was the success of NATO operations in stabilising the political and security-related tensions in Bosnia and later on in Kosovo.
77 A/47/965-S/25994, 15 June 1993, para. 27; S/25777, 15 May 1993, para. 26.
78 A/47/965-S/25994, 15 June 1993, para. 26.
79 S/26273, 9 August 1993. The representatives were from the following countries: Uruguay, Indonesia, Argentina, Bangladesh, India, Zimbabwe, Jordan, Malaysia, Egypt, Fiji, the Philippines, Pakistan, Chile, Kenya and Thailand.
80 A/48/403-S/26450, 14 March 1994, para. 68.
81 A/48/403-S/26450, 14 March 1994, para. 11–13, 17; S/PRST/1994/22, 3 May 1994; S/1994/777, 30 June 1994.

82  S/PRST/1994/36, 27 July 1994.
83  A/50/60-S/1995/1, 25 January 1995, para. 43. For an additional description of the unwillingness of states to contribute forces throughout the intervention in Rwanda, see: Dallaire with Beardsley, *Shake Hands*.
84  See Chapter 1, for a discussion about establishing UNEF II. S/11052 and Rev. 1, 27 October 1973; A/ Res/3101, 11 December 1973; Rikhye, Harbottle and Egge, *The Thin Blue Line*, pp. 309–339; Urquhart, *A Life*, pp. 238–243.
85  A/48/173, 25 May 1993, pp. 5–6; A/RES/48/42, 10 December 1993.
86  A/48/403-S/26450, 14 March 1994, pp. 12–14.
87  A/47/965-S/259444, 15 June 1993, para. 32–33; A/48/403-S/26450, 14 March 1994, para. 46–59.
88  A/48/460, 11 October 1993.
89  S/1994/845, 19 July 1994; S/1994/846, 19 July 1994.
90  A/49/136, 2 May 1994, pp. 7–8, para. 31–33; A/RES/49/37, 9 December 1994, para. 20–277.
91  A/C.4/48/SR.23, 8 February 1994, p. 15; A/C.4/48/SR.24, 31 January 1994, pp. 5–6; A/C.4/48/SR.26, 2 February 1994, pp. 7–9; A/C.4/49/SR.25, 17 November 1994, pp. 13–14; A/C.4/50/SR.20, 14 November 1995, pp. 9–10; A/C.4/50/SR.21, 29 December 1995, pp. 10–14. The average yearly income calculations are taken from the following yearbook: International Institute for Strategic Studies – IISS, *The Military Balance 1991-1998* (London: Brassey's, 1991–1998).
92  A/50/230, 22 June 1995, p. 6–8, para. 25, 33; p. 16, para. 88–89; A/51/130, 7 May 1996, p. 4; A/57/774, 3 April 2003.
93  B. Boutros-Ghali, *An Agenda for Development* (New York: United Nations Department of Public Information, 1995).
94  Boutros-Ghali, *An Agenda for Development*, p. 12.
95  A/RES/49/37, 9 December 1994, para. 21; A/51/130, 7 May 1996, p. 3.
96  Almost all representatives of developing states that supported the declaration of the Non-Aligned Movement from 1994, emphasised this issue. See mainly the discussions of the Fourth Committee of the General Assembly, 1994–1995.
97  Lorenz, 'Weapons Confiscation Policy', 414–415; P. Tripodi, *The Colonial Legacy in Somalia, Rome and Mogadishu: From Colonial Administration to Operation Restore Hope* (Basingstoke: Macmillan, 1999), p. 138.
98  For example, see the following books: Allard, *Somalia Operations*; Clarke and Herbst (eds), *Learning from Somalia*.
99  S/25354, 3 March 1993, para. 41.
100  Cassanelli, *Victims and Vulnerable Groups*; Compagnon, 'Somali Armed Movements', pp. 75–79.
101  S/1994/614, 24 May 1994, para. 2–12; S/1994/614/Annex I, 24 May 1994; S/1994/839, 18 July 1994, para.2; 54–59; S/1994/898, 30 July 1994; S/1994/977, 17 August 1994, para. 7–16, 17; S/1994/1245, 3 November 1994; A. Guleid and J. L. Davies, 'Is It Peace for Somalia?', *New African*, 319 (1994), 7–9; Sheikh A. Hassan, 'Build a New Somalia', *New African*, 320 (1994), 19; K. Menkhaus, 'International Peacebuilding and the Dynamics of Local and National Reconciliation in Somalia', in Clarke and Herbst (eds), *Learning from Somalia*, pp. 47–48.
102  S/24859, 27 November 1992.

103 Oakley and Hirsch, *Somalia and Operation Restore Hope*, pp. 49–99.
104 A/50/741, 9 November 1995, Annex II. At the end of 1994, it numbered only about 700 people.
105 Ganzglass, 'The Restoration of the Somali Justice System', pp. 27–28; Patman, 'Disarming Somalia', 519–526; Prunier, 'The Experience of European Armies', pp. 135–147.
106 S/25168/Annex I-IV, 26 January 1993; S/26317, 17 August 1993, para. 23–34; UN, *UN and Somalia*, Doc. 53; I. M. Lewis, 'Clan Conflict and Ethnicity in Somalia: Humanitarian Intervention in a Stateless Society', in D. Turton (ed.), *War and Ethnicity Global Connections and Local Violence* (Rochester, NY: University of Rochester Press, 1997), pp. 179–201; T. Lyons and A. I. Samatar, *Somalia: State Collapse, Multilateral Intervention, and Strategies for Political Reconstruction* (Washington, DC: Brookings Institution, 1995), pp. 50–52; Oakley and Hirsch, *Somalia and Operation Restore Hope*, pp. 98–99.
107 Thus, for example, the faction leaders came to an agreement on 30 March; these were called, 'Agreements Reached Between the Political Leaders at the Consultations Held in Addis Ababa, 30 March 1993. S/1994/653, 1 June 1994, para. 55–63. Nevertheless, the UN representatives ignored this development. See: S/1994/653, 1 June 1994, para. 55–63.
108 S/26738, 12 November 1993; S/1994/12, 6 January 1994.
109 B. Helander, M. H. Mhtar and I. M. Lewis, *Building Peace from Below? A Critical Review of the District Councils in the Bay and Bakool Regions of Southern Somalia*, online at http://Arlaadinet.com, April 1995, accessed 18 April 2015.
110 S/26317, 17 August 1993; S/1994/614, 24 May 1994; S/1994/839, 18 July 1994; Helander, Mhtar and Lewis, *Building Peace from Below?*
111 See, for example: S/24343, 22 July 1992, para. 61–64.
112 S/26317, 17 August 1993, para. 21–22; S/26317/Annex I, 17 August 1993; S/26317/Annex II, 17 August 1993; Ganzglass, 'The Restoration', pp. 29–30.
113 S/1994/12, 6 January 1994; S/1994/614, 24 May 1994; S/1994/839, 17 July 1994.
114 S/26738, 12 November 1993; A/48/850, 19 January 1994; A/48/850/Add.1, 15 July 1994; S/1994/839, 18 July 1994; Ganzglass, 'The Restoration', pp. 33–35.
115 S/26738, 12 November 1993; A/48/850, 19 January 1994; S/1994/614, 24 May 1994; A/48/850/Add.1, 15 July 1994; S/1994/839, 18 July 1994; S/1994/839, 18 July 1994; S/1994/1068, 17 September 1994; S/1994/1166, 14 October 1994; S/1995/231, 28 March 1995; Ganzglass, 'The Restoration', pp. 33–35.
116 S/25168, 26 January 1993, para. 51; S/26317, 17 August 1993, para. 43–51. For the sake of comparison, it should be noted that promises of 800 million dollars were pledged for Cambodia.
117 S/25354, 3 March 1993, para. 25–31; S/26022, 1 July 1993, para. 33–38; S/26317, 17 August 1993, para. 43–51.
118 S/1994/614, 24 May 1994; S/1994/839, 18 July 1994; A/49/456, 30 September 1994.
119 A/48/504, 29 October 1993, para. 43.
120 A/48/504, Oct. 29, 1993; T. Liasi, 'Last Days of Saigon?', *New African* (1995), 35; M. Maren, *The Road to Hell: The Ravaging Effect of Foreign Aid and International Charity* (New York: Free Press, 1997), pp. 203–238; Natsios, 'Humanitarian Relief',

pp. 83–91; Seybolt, *Humanitarian Military Intervention*, pp. 52–61; A. de Waal, *Famine Crimes: Politics & Disaster Relief Industry in Africa* (London: African Right & International African Institute in association with J. Currey, Oxford & Indiana University Press, Bloomington, IN, 1997), pp. 174–175; Wheeler, *Saving Strangers*.

121  Maren, *The Road to Hell*, p. 177.
122  A/RES/48/201, 17 March 1994.
123  A/49/456, 30 September 1994; A/50/447, 19 September 1995.
124  It is important to note that despite the large presence of multinational forces from that time until the end of the intervention in March 1995, sporadic attacks continued on the convoys bearing humanitarian aid.
125  S/24976, 17 December 1992; W. Clarke, 'Testing the World's Resolve in Somalia', *Parameters*, 23:4 (1993–1994), 48–49; Kertcher, *The Search for Peace*.
126  RES/733, 23 January 1992; S/23693, 11 March 1992; S/23829, 21 April 1992; S/24343, 22 July 1992; S/1994/12, 6 January 1994; S/1994/1245, 3 November 1994, para. 9–10; S/1996/17, 15 January 1996; Lewis, 'Clan Conflict', pp. 185, 194–195.
127  S/25168, 26 January, para. 43–45; S/25354, 3 March 1993, para. 21; Lorenz, 'Weapons Confiscation Policy', pp. 414–415, 424; Natsios, 'Humanitarian Relief', pp. 84–85; Tripodi, *Colonial Legacy*, p. 138.
128  Drysdale, 'Foreign Military Intervention in Somalia', pp. 130–131; Lyons and Samatar, *Somalia*, p. 50; Oakley and Hirsch, *Somalia and Operation Restore Hope*, pp. 76–77; Tripodi, *Colonial Legacy*, p. 147.
129  The force reached its designated number of 28,000 soldiers only in September 1993.
130  S/25354, 3 March 1993, para. 79–87; S/25354/Add.1, 11 March 1993; S/25354/Add.2, 11 March 1993; S/25354/Add.3, 22 March 1993; S/26317, 17 August 1993, para. 3.
131  S/26022, 1 July 1993; S/1994/653, 1 June 1994.
132  The phrase 'virtual war' is taken from a commission of inquiry report on attacks on the second UN operation in Somalia. This operation was established after Resolution 885 was accepted by the Security Council in November 1993. See report 1994, June 1, S/1994/653.
133  S/RES/837, 6 June 1993; S/25354, 3 March 1993, para. 59–69; Boutros-Ghali, *Unvanquished*, p. 95. Since the essence of the UN policy change was connected to peace enforcement and use of force, this subject is discussed in depth in the following section that deals with UN activities in security-related issues.
134  S/PV.3280, 22 September 1993, p. 11.
135  UN, *UN and Somalia*, Doc. 59.
136  S/PV.3280, 22 September 1993, pp. 6–10; S/26627, 25 October 1993; S/26766, 18 November 1993; S/PV.3317, 18 November 1993, pp. 3–7; UN, *UN and Somalia*, Doc. 59.
137  S/PV.3188, 26 March 1993, pp. 7–10; S/PV.3229, 6 June 1993, pp. 11–12; S/PV.3280, 22 September 1993, pp. 6–10; S/PV.3283, 29 September 1993, pp. 7–9; S/PV.3317, 18 November 1993, pp. 8–12; A/C.4/50/SR.22, 19 December 1995, pp. 17–18.
138  S/PV.3280, 22 September 1993, pp. 23–25; S/PV.3315, 16 November 1993, pp. 6–9; S/PV.3317, 18 November 1993, pp. 13–16.

139  S/PV.3229, 6 June 1993, pp. 6–7, 11–12; S/PV.3280, 22 September 1993, pp. 6–14; S/PV.3315, 16 November 1993, p. 6; S/PV.3317, 18 November 1993, pp. 8–12, 25–27. The change in Pakistan's position was recorded only from February 1994, after most of the Western armies had already left Somalia.
140  UN, *UN and Somalia*, Doc. 59; Albright and Woodward, *Madam Secretary*, p. 146; Boutros-Ghali, *Unvanquished*, pp. 96–97; Tripodi, *Colonial Legacy*, p. 151.
141  Kertcher, *The Search for Peace*, pp. 21–28.
142  UN Press Release, SG/SM/5126, 7 October 1993; UN Press Release, SG/T/1818-SOM/44, 14 October 1993; S/26738, 12 November 1993, para. 77–78; Boutros-Ghali, *Unvanquished*, pp. 104–105; Howe, 'Relations Between the United States and the UN in Somalia', pp. 183–184; Johnston and Dagne, 'Congress and the Somalia Crisis', pp. 197–202.
143  S/RES/897, 4 February 1994.
144  S/1994/614, 24 May 1994, para. 22–26; S/1994/839, 18 July 1994, para. 31–33; S/PRST/1994/46, 25 August 1994; Kertcher, *The Search for Peace*, pp. 29–33.
145  S/1994/614, 24 May 1994; S/1994/839, 18 July 1994; S/1994/977, 17 August 1994; S/1994/1068, 17 September 1994.
146  S/1994/614, 24 May 1994; S/1994/614/Annex I, 24 May 1994; S/1994/839, 18 July 1994, para. 48; S/1994/1068, 17 September 1994; Guleid and Davies, 'Is It Peace for Somalia?', pp. 7–9; Hassan, 'Build a New Somalia', p. 19; Menkhaus, 'International Peacebuilding', pp. 50–52; Helander, Mhtar and Lewis, *Building Peace from Below?*
147  S/1994/1245, 3 November 1994.
148  A/50/741, 9 November 1995, para. 7.
149  A/50/741, 9 November 1995, Annex VIII, pp. 44–45.
150  S/PV. 3432, 30 September 1994; S/RES/946, 30 September 1994; S/1994/1166, 14 October 1994; S/RES/953, 31 October 1994; S/1994/1245, 3 November 1994; S/PV.3447, 4 November 1994; S/RES/954, 4 November 1994.
151  S/PV.3334, 4 February 1994.
152  Rose, *Fighting for Peace*, pp. 126, 184, 201–203, 241–242.
153  See the organisation's discussions on the concept of the operations from 1993–95.
154  A/50/60-S/1995/1, 25 January 1995; A/S/1995/222, 22 March 1995. About 1,100 soldiers served in Macedonia, almost 16,000 soldiers served in Croatia, and about 22,000 soldiers served in Bosnia.
155  I do not address the operation in Macedonia in this section because the peacekeeping force there had only observer status.
156  S/25447, 26 March 1993; S/25601, 15 April 1993; S/25766, 12 May 1993; S/26491, 24 September 1993; A/50/64-S/1995/28, 12 January 1995; A/50/118-S/1995/221, 27 March 1995; A/50/119-S/1995/223, 27 March 1995.
157  S/25264, 10 February 1992; S/25828, 12 January 1993; S/RES/802, 25 January 1993; S/25555, 8 April 1993; S/26436, 14 September 1993; S/1994/367, annex, 30 March 1994; S/1994/1067, 17 September 1994.
158  S/RES/815, 30 March 1993; S/RES/869, 30 September 1993; S/RES/870, 1 October 1993; S/RES/871, 4 October 1993.

159 A/49/630, 1 November 1994; A/RES/49/43, 9 December 1994.
160 S/1994/38, 14 January 1994; A/C.4/49/SR.9, 21 October 1994; A/RES/49/43, 9 December 1994; A/50/64-S/1995/28, 12 January 1995; S/1995/222, 22 March 1995.
161 S/RES/820, 17 April 1993.
162 S/1994/300, 16 March 1994; S/1994/1067, 17 September 1994; /C.4/49/SR.9, 21 October 1994; S/1994/1375, Annex, 2 December 1994; S/1995/38, 14 January 1995; S/1995/222, 22 March 1995.
163 S/RES/802, 25 January 1993; S/25154, 25 January 1993; S/25156, 25 January 1993; S/PV.3163, 25 January 1993; S/PV.3174, 19 February 1993; S/PV.3189, 30 March 1993; S/PV. 3286, 4 October 1993; S/PV.3434, 30 September 1994; S/RES/958, 19 November 1994; S/PV.3512, 31 March 1995.
164 S/25264, 10 February 1992, para. 24–30, 35–39; S/25777, 15 May 1993, para. 2, 13–17, S/25993, 25 June 1993; 20–27; S/26470, 20 September 1993; S/26468, 30 September 1993; S/1994/300, 16 March 1994, para. 4–15; S/1994/1067, 9 September 1994, para. 3–11, 35–40; S/1995/320, 18 April 1995.
165 Boutros-Ghali, *Unvanquished*, p. 240.
166 S/1995/670, 8 August 1995; S/PV.3563, 10 August 1995; S/PV.3564, 10 August 1995; A/50/727-S/1995/933, 7 November 1995; S/RES/1023, 22 November 1995; S/RES/1025, 25 November 1995; S/1995/1028, 13 December 1995; S/RES/1037, 16 January 1996; S/1996/66, 26 January 1996; S/RES/1043, 31 January 1996.
167 Corwin, *Dubious Mandate*; Touval, *Mediation in the Yugoslav Wars*, p. 128.
168 Touval, *Mediation in the Yugoslav Wars*.
169 A/AC.96/808, 12 August 1993; UN, *Yearbook of the United Nations, 1994* (New York: United Nations Department of Public Information, 1995), pp. 512–513; UN, *Yearbook of the United Nations, 1995* (New York: United Nations Department of Public Information, 1997), pp. 519–520.
170 S/RES/780, 6 October 1992; S/RES/827, 25 May 1993; S/RES/827, 25 May 1993; S/1994/674, 27 May 1994; A/50/441-S/1995/801, annex, 18 September 1995; S/1995/933, 7 November 1995.
171 S/25264, 10 February 1993, para. 23.
172 See the previous chapter for an exhaustive discussion of these goals.
173 S/PV.3356, 31 March 1994, pp. 5–6. For more information regarding the difficulties involved in recruiting those 7,600 soldiers, see: J. Traub, *The Best Intentions: Kofi Annan and the UN in the Era of American World Power* (New York: Farrar, Straus and Giroux, 2006), pp. 46–48.
174 A/54/549, 15 November 1999, pp. 53–55.
175 One of the stormiest debates ever held in the Council took place in March 1994 with regard to the city of Maglaj, and ended with the resolution not to include it in the safe areas. S/PV.3344, 4 March 1994; S/RES/900, 4 March 1994; S/1994/291, 11 March 1994; S/PV.3349, 14 March 1994; S/PRST/1994/11, 14 March 1994; S/PV.3356, 31 March 1994; S/RES/908, 31 March 1994.

176 S/RES/844, 18 June 1993; S/1994/94, 29 January 1994.
177 On 25 September 1991, the Security Council accepted a resolution that called on all the countries to impose an absolute embargo on supplying weapons and military equipment to Yugoslavia. A committee was established to monitor the decision. From 1992, NATO member states agreed to assist in the enforcement of a maritime blockade and no-fly zone over Bosnia. From June 1993 onwards, NATO also agreed to the safe areas, first to protect UN troops, and from 1994 onwards, to deter Bosnian-Serb aggression as well. The embargo was lifted only in June 1996; S/RES/713, 25 September 1991; S/RES/724, 15 December 1991; S/1996/433, 13 June 1996; S/1996/442, 17 June 1996; S/RES/757, 30 May 1992; S/RES/781, 9 October 1992; S/RES/787, 16 November 1992; S/RES/816, 31 March 1993; S/26335, 8 August 1993; Gow, *Triumph of the Lack of Will*, pp. 129–141.
178 S/25264, 10 February 1993, para. 19; S/26335, 20 August 1993; S/26470, 20 September 1993, para. 3–4; S/RES/868, 29 September 1993; S/1994/50, 18 January 1994; S/1994/131, 7 February 1994; S/1994/182, 16 February 1994; S/1994/466, 19 April 1994; S/1994/498, 22 April 1994; S/1994/1067, 17 September 1994; S/1995/444, 30 May 1995.
179 Burg and Shoup, *The War in Bosnia-Herzegovina*, pp. 145–152, 166–167; NIOD, *Srebrenica*, Part II, Ch. 1; Owen, *Balkan Odyssey*, pp. 136–142, 246–247, 255–268, 323; Rose, *Fighting for Peace*, pp. 42–68, 85–86.
180 S/1994/1067, 9 September 1994, para. 43; S/1994/1067, 9 September 1994; S/1994/1389, 1 December 1994.
181 S/1994/123, 4 February 1994; S/1994/124, 5 February 1994; S/1994/126, 7 February 1994; S/1994/127, 6 February 1994; S/1994/129, 7 February 1994; S/1994/131, 6 February 1994; S/1994/134, 8 February 1994; S/1994/135, 8 February 1994; S/1994/136, 8 February 1994; S/1994/137, 7 February 1994; S/1994/138, 7 February 1994; S/1994/139, 8 February 1994; S/1994/142, 10 February 1994; S/1994/143, 9 February 1994; S/1994/144, 9 February 1994; S/1994/145, 7 February 1994; S/1994/146, 9 February 1994; S/1994/148, 5 February 1994; S/1994/152, 10 February 1994; S/1994/153, 10 February 1994; S/1994/158, 10 February 1994; S/1994/159, 11 February 1994; S/1994/166, 11 February 1994; S/PV.3336, 14 February 1994; S/PV.3336/Res.1, 14 February 1994; S/PV.3336/Res.2, 15 February1995; S/PV.3336/Res.3, 15 February 1994.
182 S/1994/300, 16 March 1994; S/1994/555, 9 May 1994; S/1994/1389, 1 December 1994; S/1995/470, 9 June 1995; S/RES/998, 16 June 1995; S/1995/707, 18 August 1995; S/PRST/1995/40, 19 August 1995; NIOD, *Srebrenica*, Part III, Ch. 1; Rose, *Fighting for Peace*, p. 99. When the security situation escalated, three countries – Netherlands, France and the United Kingdom – decided, in June 1995, to establish a rapid response force of 12,500 soldiers that could fight against local forces if necessary. But this force was not an influential factor in the fighting of summer–fall 1995.
183 The flow of weapons to Croatia and Bosnia arrived from the United States, Brunei, Iran, Malaysia, Saudi Arabia, the Sudan, Pakistan and Turkey. Burg and Shoup, *The War in Bosnia-Herzegovina*, pp. 307–309, 330–331, 337–339; R. C. Holbrooke, *To End a War* (New York: The Modern Library, 1999), pp. 73, 87–88; Ramet, *The Three Yugoslavias*, pp. 448–449, 452–453, 465–466.

184 Boutros-Ghali, *Unvanquished*, pp. 233–246; Bourg and Shoup, *The War in Bosnia-Herzegovina*, pp. 322–360; Ramet, *The Three Yugoslavias*, pp. 453–466; R. Smith, *The Utility of Force* (London: Penguin, 2006), pp. 346–369.

185 A/50/790-S/1995/999/Annex 4 'The Constitution of Bosnia-Herzegovina', 30 November 1995; C. Bildt, 'Holbrooke's History', *Survival*, 40:3 (1998), 187–191; Burg and Shoup, *The War in Bosnia-Herzegovina*, pp. 317–387; Gow, *Triumph of the Lack of Will*, pp. 276–297; Holbrooke, *To End a War*, pp. 79–324; Ramet, *The Three Yugoslavias*, pp. 471–494; Touval, *Mediation in the Yugoslav Wars*, pp. 141–165.

186 R. F. Baumann, G. W. Gawrych and W. E. Kretchnik, *Armed Peacekeepers in Bosnia* (Fort Leavenworth, KS: Combat Studies Institute Press, 2004), pp. 70–229.

# Conclusion

I chose to devote much space in this research study to the various discussions conducted in the UN, in order to elucidate to readers the labyrinthine depths of international politics with regard to the operations in a unique period in global history. This comparative approach shows the interrelations between discussions on the concept and principles of the operations, the organisational reform and the practice in Cambodia, the former Yugoslavia and Somalia between 1988 and 1995.

One of the conclusions of this book is that, since the Cold War, international politics on UN peacekeeping has been in permanent tension between two political trends. The first political trend supports most variants of peacekeeping operations under certain conditions in order to prevent, contain and terminate intrastate conflicts. On the other hand, member states continue to guide their policies in discussions on the goals, principles, organisational reform and the practice of the operations according to their national interests. This tension explains why UN member states supported the changes in peacekeeping operations while at the same time they failed to reconcile their differences. From the late 1980s, the member states expanded the spectrum of operations between the authorities of Chapter 6 and Chapter 7 in the UN Charter. However, they could not agree on an alternative to the traditional concept and principles that were agreed during the Cold War. Thus, despite the fact that new goals regarding traditional operations were raised in various UN organs between 1988 and 1991, no consensus has ever been reached among the organisation's member states regarding an alternative model. Therefore, when new peacekeeping operations began to be executed in the course of 1992, they were not based on a consensus to change the traditional principles. It is true that, in 1992, UN Secretary-General Boutros-Ghali did propose to enlarge the goals of the operations in a detailed document he called *Agenda for Peace*. In this report, Boutros-Ghali contested some of the accepted principles of the traditional operations, and, for about a year and a half, this initiative received the backing of most UN members. Some writers and diplomats even argue that the operations in Cambodia, the former Yugoslavia and Somalia were executed in the 'spirit' of the new concepts. However, this support was withdrawn by the Security Council, the Secretariat and the General Assembly from the middle of 1993 to 1995; the UN organs backtracked from their support for large multidimensional

Conclusion 197

peacekeeping during active conflict. By 1995, the concept of the collective multidimensional operation – whose goal is to end a conflict while simultaneously promoting political, security, economic and social change – was removed from the UN agenda.

The importance of the discussion was that it outlined the main concepts, terms and conditions for such operations and drew the contours of the second generation. An attempt was made by the UN to implement the lessons learned in the early 1990s in the 1999 operations deployed in Kosovo and East Timor. Together with the Brahimi Report published on 17 August 2000, these two operations signalled what seemed to be a new period in the history of operations which is beyond the scope of this book.[1]

The research concerning the three operations in Cambodia, the former Yugoslavia and Somalia shows us that the traditional concept was the pillar of UN activity in the 1990s. The organisation's principal goals were to reach a political arrangement based on restoring sovereignty to the elected authorities of the relevant states, and the absence of war between countries. This two-sided goal is, in effect, the supreme goal at the top of the priority list of the first-generation operations. The new goals ascribed to the second-generation operations – such as humanitarian aid, advancement of human rights and promotion of good governance – were, and remain, secondary in importance to the central goal of the operation. Thus we can see how, in Cambodia and the former Yugoslavia, the organisation's members made great efforts to restrict the goals of the operations to the bare minimum.

In the three most ambitious operations that were reviewed, the UN strived to achieve legitimacy in the course of each of its interventions. It also tried to maintain neutrality in its operations within the countries in order not to act inequitably towards any of the conflicted sides and to avoid the use of force as much as possible. An unmistakable example of this is the UN intervention in Cambodia. In this study, I have shown how preference was given to traditional goals over new ones (in Cambodia), thus making it much easier for the UN to achieve its primary goal: establishment of a sovereign government in the state. In the Cambodian intervention, the emphasis was on administration of democratic elections and the establishment of a government. Other, new, goals – such as humanitarian aid and promotion of human rights – were considered less important. The realisation of the new government helped the international community to re-absorb Cambodia into its ranks as a state with a fully fledged, legitimate government. The exceptions that prove the rule and strengthen my argument are Somalia in 1993 and Bosnia for a limited but critical period in 1995.

Another conclusion of the study is that the delineation of new goals for UN operations often unintentionally counteracted the actions bound up with achieving the traditional goals: limiting the conflict and creating conditions enabling the establishment of a political arrangement between the warring sides. Thus, for example, a new goal such as humanitarian aid, which became a key UN activity in

Bosnia and Somalia, not infrequently clashed with efforts to reach a speedy political arrangement in these conflicts. This is because the resources sent for assistance often became major economic resources in the conflict battlefield, thus encouraging some of the warring sides to continue to fight, even forcing the UN to use force on the ground (for example, to protect foodstuffs). The very use of force undermined the legitimacy given to the organisation to operate on the ground and cast a shadow on its mediation efforts.

In order to understand the importance of the unique historical happenings in the UN in the first years after the conclusion of the Cold War, I carefully examined the diplomatic discourse within the organisation on the issues of the concept and practice of large, multidimensional operations. It turns out that, in contrast to the arguments of many researchers of UN operations, who emphasise the existence of two political blocs (West against the rest), I maintain that international politics and political jockeying in the UN continued in its traditional format without substantive change. True, opinions in the UN were unanimous in believing that the end of the Cold War and the globalisation process signalled new circumstances and conditions that threatened, but also contributed to, the maintenance of international peace and security. Nevertheless, this recognition did not lead to willingness of the organisation's member states to waive advancement of their individual interests, even when these were at the expense of the UN's higher goals of resolving conflicts. This hypothesis contradicts those studies that claim that, after 1988, a clear dichotomy existed in the UN between the policies of Westphalian countries, which promoted the traditional concept of peacekeeping operations, and the policies of post-Westphalian countries, which promoted the new concept.

In the current study I showed that, with regard to the concept and practice of the operations in the time period under discussion, ad hoc alliances took shape between states in accordance with their interests in specific issues. Thus, for example, both Western and developing states operated on behalf of changing the composition of the Security Council and its powers and procedures. It seems that China supported a variety of UN goals in Somalia, even though these totally contradicted the principles of the traditional operations, while the United States opposed the operation in Somalia from the beginning of 1994, and tried to block the advancement of these peacekeeping operations in accordance with the second-generation concept. Simultaneously, the United States worked together with Islamic states to promote enforcement and promote human rights in Bosnia. On the other hand, all the UN member states supported the operation in Cambodia (in principle).

Other conclusions of the study relate to the modus operandi of central players in the organisation from 1988 to 1995. The discussion mainly focuses on the functioning of the five permanent members of the Security Council – the United States, the Soviet Union/Russia, the United Kingdom, China and France – but not only them. After the end of the Cold War, the five permanent members lost their ideological compass in which governments often chose whether to join up with liberal–capitalist states or the socialist–communist bloc. This alliance would then guide them in formulating clear policy regarding every conflict taking place in the world, between or within states. After the Cold War, the states dealt with each conflict on its own merits, and were largely able to agree on the execution of operations as a means to deal with conflicts. Usually, the goals of the operations did not reflect clear interests of the powers in the conflict arena, but rather showed lack of interest; thus, the interests of the local players became much more prominent. When a new operation contradicted the interests of the five permanent members of the Security Council, they opposed it. A clear example is the sweeping support given by the five permanent members of the Security Council to the Cambodian operation, as they had no desire or need to promote direct interests in that country. By contrast, their differences of opinion in the former Yugoslavia operation deepened as the intervention became more and more prolonged. The five permanent members were able to agree on one thing: to try to present a united front of their activities to the world, in order to retain their special status in the UN. When most of the organisation's members applied intense pressure on them to change the Security Council's composition, authorities and modus operandi, they chose to limit the use of operations rather than agree to reforms.

The Soviet Union's representatives in the UN at the end of the 1980s, acting under the influence of Gorbachev's 'new thinking', were the engine that drove the process of change in the concept and implementation of peacekeeping operations. In effect, they leveraged the diplomatic process that led to the end of the Cold War and called for development and activation of the peacekeeping operations as part of the new world order. As part of the 'new thinking', they supported the deployment of operations to resolve the conflict in Afghanistan, the conflict between Iran and Iraq, the conflicts in Namibia, Angola and Cambodia. As part of the change, the Soviet Union representatives supported reforms in the goals of the operations. However, they did not want to jeopardise their traditional success principles, and simultaneously they wanted to retain the special status reserved for Russia (the Soviet Union's heir) in the Security Council and in the organisation's institutions.

In the course of 1992, the first year after the dissolution of the Soviet Union, Russian diplomats adopted positions similar to those of the former regime with regard to discussions on the concept. However, when Russia had to address specific conflicts, it abandoned the arenas of Cambodia and Somalia, leaving them to the other UN members for treatment. While Russia did express support for the organisation's activities, it did not allocate any forces. By contrast, Russia viewed the conflict in the former Yugoslavia as more important because it was geographically closer, thus the conflict directly threatened Russia's interests. In this instance, Russia adopted an independent stance that, as the conflict deepened, became more and more oppositional towards the other states. While it allocated several hundreds of soldiers to the peacekeeping forces in the states of the former Yugoslavia, its policy approach would not allow it to use force against the Serb players. Simultaneously, Russia established the CIS, a regional organisation comprising the territories of the Former Soviet Union, and executed regional peacekeeping operations of its own in order to maintain its regional influence.

When the Cold War ended, the United States found itself in the position of being the only superpower left in the world with economic and military superiority. As we see in several chapters of this study, the US representatives in the UN often adopted an independent position, distinct from the positions adopted by most of the other UN members. At least until 1991, the USA retained its dissenting attitude in the UN and refused to relate seriously to calls for developing the UN peacekeeping operation concept as the main model for the maintenance of international peace and security. Instead, the USA felt that each instance should be addressed on a case-by-case basis by evaluating it according to its strategic interests. This position changed somewhat when special international circumstances were created (at the end of 1990) that led to the multinational coalition to liberate Kuwait from Iraq. Furthermore, the diplomatic momentum created with the dissolution of the Soviet Union pushed the United States into the UN discussion at the time regarding the new world order. In principle, the USA supported the concepts raised in Boutros-Ghali's Peace Agenda. However, the US representative emphasised that, once the Security Council decided to execute new multidimensional operations, all the world's nations must supply the appropriate and necessary resources – not just the United States. Simultaneously, the USA torpedoed all attempts to make changes in the modus operandi of the Security Council, limited the resources given to the Secretariat, and did not meet the timetable for the assessment payments it owed to the organisation. This last step threatened to undermine the organisation's financial ability to conduct operations. Finally, the USA allocated only a few forces to most of the operations.

One exception was the case of Somalia between December 1992 and March 1994, when the United States openly supported the advancement of peace enforcement and peacebuilding goals in Somalia and even allocated forces to this purpose (although these were few in number, relative to the extensive needs of the operation). American forces worked alongside UN forces although the Americans operated a separate, independent command system of their own. Later on, the USA even decided to withdraw all its forces from the country, and, from this point on, its representatives in the UN refused to support the continuation of the operation. During that time period, the administration of new US President Bill Clinton discussed the option of increasing the role and powers of the UN regarding conflicts in the world, and the possibility that the United States would even cooperate with such processes. However, discussions of this type were quickly shelved, lest the United States lose its freedom of action in the world. The United States' modus operandi – promoting its own interests in every conflict – was also salient in the former Yugoslavian conflict. In that conflict, the USA refused to allocate significant military ground forces and sabotaged EC (and, later on, EU) initiatives to resolve the conflict. Finally, with regard to the former Yugoslavia, the United States operated unilaterally and contrary to the resolutions of the Security Council (of which the United States is a member!) and imposed peace, in order to end the conflicts in Croatia and Bosnia.

The other two permanent Western states in the Council, the United Kingdom and France, cooperated more consistently with UN institutions than did the Soviet Union and the United States. From the end of 1991, they were the most enthusiastic supporters of enlarging the peacekeeping operations concept and the execution of such operations. Their various representatives supported the development of rapid reaction forces, execution of humanitarian operations, and advancement of human rights. In principle, they were also in favour of the use of force during operations, when necessary. However, when the time came to execute the operations in practice, they did not provide consistent support and generally opposed the use of force.

The United Kingdom focused on arenas in which it had vested interests; in other words, the former Yugoslavia. By contrast, its contribution to operations in Cambodia and Somalia was negligible. Its absence from the Somali arena was salient in light of the fact that Somaliland had been a former British colony. By contrast, Italy demonstrated great involvement in Somalia, largely because it had been Somalia's colonial power. France demonstrated a greater commitment to operations than did the United Kingdom, and was an important contributor to all the large UN peacekeeping operations in that era. Nevertheless, France refused to provide large resources to the Cambodian operation to advance more ambitious goals such as advancement of human rights, and even opposed the use of force. Regarding the Somali front, France allocated forces only in the period of the US intervention, and insisted that its forces be stationed in relatively quiet (non-violent) areas. France's largest contribution was in the former Yugoslavia, in which it had an errant, declared interest in stabilising the conflict. This was so that the conflict would not influence the steps that were being taken at the time to transform the European Community into the European Union (with all that it entailed), which in turn could counterbalance the global power of the United States.

These two permanent member states of the Security Council, the United Kingdom and France, struggled to preserve their special privileges in the Council and refused to increase the resources allocated to the UN Secretariat on a regular basis, except for lending personnel to the peacekeeping operations department. One of the reasons that they contributed forces to the UN was to strengthen their influence in the organisation. They also paid their UN assessments on time for similar reasons, but they turned down the appeal to increase the scope of their participation in the overall costs.

As opposed to the other four permanent Council members, the China representatives argued openly that the ideas raised in the UN regarding a concept change were controversial and incoherent. The basis of their criticism was the argument that the various initiatives ignored the fact that countries act first and foremost to promote their own interests. They expressly emphasised that multidimensional operations do not always support or promote peace (absence of war); and the latter is the main objective of the UN. They refused to change the composition of the Council or to allocate additional resources to the Secretariat that could have helped in smoother running of the operations. However, when China's interests were involved, its involvement also increased. China's representative took an active part in discussions of the Special Committee from 1989 onwards, and in additional discussions conducted in the organisation regarding peacekeeping operations. China allocated many forces, but only to the Cambodia operation, where it even severed relations with its long-standing ally, the Khmer Rouge faction, to promote the mission's success. Since China had no direct interests in Somalia and Yugoslavia, it did not send forces. With regard to all conflicts under discussion, the Chinese representatives argued that the goal of political arrangement should always remain superior to other goals such as humanitarian aid and advancement of human rights. Yet the Chinese representatives did not object to Security Council resolutions in various arenas even when they called for the execution of large multidimensional operations with authority to use force, so long as these resolutions won the sweeping support of most of the countries adjacent to the contested region.

Another conclusion of the study relates to the importance and centrality of the Secretariat in the UN diplomatic discourse. We see, throughout the entire study, that the Secretariat functioned, in effect, as a sixth permanent member of the Security Council. Thus, with regard to the UN, the Secretariat was roughly equivalent to a power. The Secretariat employees, and mainly the Secretary-General, attended the discussions on the concept and practices of the operations. They also administered the operations and produced reports which had a central role in moulding the organisation's views regarding conflicts and ways to resolve them. Thus, the Secretariat continuously strived to enlarge its functions, powers and position. It was more successful in doing so when the powers, regional organisations and UN countries in general were indecisive regarding the preferred method of conflict resolution. In order to consolidate its power, the Secretariat strived to get the UN member states to hand over powers and resources into its hands, thus removing these resources from control of the member states.

Clearly, the real power of the Secretariat depended, to a large extent, on the Secretary-General of the time and his worldview. During the tenure of Javier Pérez de Cuéllar (until December 1991), the Secretariat adopted a wary stance towards the numerous initiatives that arose regarding the execution of large, multidimensional peacekeeping operations in active conflicts. The reservations evinced by the Secretariat, or more accurately by de Cuéllar, stemmed from his scepticism regarding the willingness of the members of the international community to allocate the necessary resources for the new operations. As discussed in Chapter 2, the Secretariat assumed that future operations (after the end of the Cold War) would be smaller in scope, if more complex. De Cuéllar held reservations about international intervention in the conflicts in Cambodia, the former Yugoslavia and

Somalia, mainly because he was highly doubtful regarding the commitment of the international community to large multidimensional operations. Nevertheless, he tried to prepare the Secretariat towards administration of the unprecedented operation in Cambodia.

De Cuéllar's successor Boutros Boutros-Ghali brought with him a different approach regarding the role of the Secretary-General. He believed that with the conclusion of the Cold War, it was up to the Secretary-General to serve as global leader in the new world order. In accordance with his worldview, Boutros-Ghali encouraged UN interventions in intrastate and international conflicts, with special focus on Africa. Boutros-Ghali wanted the UN interventions to include multidimensional operations that would advance political arrangement as well as other objectives such as humanitarian aid, economic development, democratisation and security reform. From the various reports he submitted to the Council, it seems that he tried to combine all the activities under one conceptual roof with unique administrative and organisational ramifications. But in contrast to de Cuéllar's modus operandi and sensitivity to international politics, Boutros-Ghali ignored the interests, abilities and willingness of the members of the international community to maintain such operations. Boutros-Ghali's direct confrontation with the American administration led, finally, to an unprecedented decision among the Americans to block Boutros-Ghali's appointment for another term of office. Instead, he was replaced by Kofi Annan, Deputy Secretary-General in the UN Peacekeeping Department. Boutros-Ghali's activities had positioned the Secretariat in an unprecedented influential position. Between June and October 1993, the UN functioned as a quasi-sovereign in south-central Somalia. However, this experiment in Somalia also exposed the built-in weakness of the UN, which is the product of the agreements and alliances of its members. In the absence of support on the part of the main players in the organisation, the Secretariat lacked all operational ability.

In contrast to the Somali arena, where the Secretariat enjoyed extensive freedom of action, in the former Yugoslavian conflict, numerous countries (mainly European ones), as well as Russia and the United States, clipped the wings of the Secretariat and reduced its influence. As a result, the Secretariat was pushed into a corner with regard to the conflict in the former Yugoslavia and forced to implement the ambitious goals imposed on it by the Security Council, though it had inadequate means to do so. The high expectations and multiple goals on one side, coupled with the limited resources and means allocated to carry out the goals on the other, inflicted great harm on the reputation and credibility of the organisation and especially of the Secretariat. The UN's public image suffered great damage. The situation only changed from 1999 when new operations in East Timor and Kosovo were executed, after the Secretariat received the powers to administer large multidimensional operations with resources to match. Moreover, its prestige was gradually rehabilitated due to lessons-learned reports published under the new able Secretary-General, Kofi Annan.

After the Cold War, UN interventions were greatly affected by regional organisations or at least the countries in close geographical proximity to the areas of conflict. During the Cold War period, the UN strictly enforced its policy that countries close to conflicted areas or countries with direct interests in the conflicts could not take part in the relevant operations. By contrast, after the Cold War, the picture changed. This hypothesis can explain why two operations – both second-generation, multidimensional operations that were deployed simultaneously – led to opposite results. In Yugoslavia, the great influence of the EU contributed to disintegration of the country, while in Somalia, the OAU, the Arab League, and the OIC insisted on preserving the country's integrity. In both instances, the political arrangement was justified on the basis that it would promote peace. In Cambodia, ASEAN also held an important role when it pressured all the sides to cooperate with the UN and hold elections. The ASEAN organisation promised that, at the conclusion of the conflict and upon the election of a new government, Cambodia would then be integrated in ASEAN regional economic arrangements.

One of the findings of this study is that the status and importance of the veteran Western contributor states underwent significant erosion with regard to UN operations. These contributor states included Australia, Denmark, Norway, New Zealand, Finland, Canada and Sweden. These states reached their height in the course of the Cold War when they helped form the concept of the operations and allocated many units to them. Starting from the late 1980s, these countries were among the regular supporters of a change in the goals and success principles of the operations, and they advocated reforms in the operations' administration and management. The decline in their key position as contributors to development of the concept began in 1992 when the large Western powers such as the United States, the United Kingdom and France began to take part in the discussion and bring up their own initiatives. The erosion process in the status of the veteran Western contributor states was even more salient with regard to their actual influence on the operations. Aside from the special case of Cambodia, in which Australia promoted a unique operation, the veteran countries had minor influence on the delineation of the operations' objectives in Somalia and in the former Yugoslavia. With the exception of Australia, none of them allocated forces to Cambodia. In Somalia, these countries were represented by only a few dozens of soldiers each (with the exception of Canada's short-lived contribution). By contrast, most of the contributor states to the former Yugoslavian conflict had a clear interest in protecting European stability, and therefore allocated thousands of soldiers to the operations. In other words, they operated like many other countries, which contributed and allocated forces to those operations that served their interests. Another expression of the erosion in the position of the veteran Western contributor states was the fact that they were pushed from the top of the list of contributor states to the middle, with regard to the sum total of forces taking part in UN peacekeeping operations.

The picture changes completely when we examine the contribution of developing states. During the Cold War period, most developing countries contributed little to the operations and most were unfamiliar with the operations' format. This situation changed after the conclusion of the Cold War, when a larger number of countries began to contribute to the peacekeeping operations. At the time, most of the developing countries lacked experience regarding participation in the operations and their forces did not receive the proper training, organisation and equipment they needed. Therefore, these countries were dependent on the training and support of the Western countries, and this latter group did not always come through with the requisite help. Similarly, only a limited number of developing countries allocated forces to the operations; these were Bangladesh, India and Pakistan. Other countries such as Jordan, Malaysia, Egypt and Nigeria also allocated large numbers of forces.

There is no one clear reason that could account for the large contributions of these countries to peacekeeping operations. However, the present research findings indicate that there is a clear correlation between the interests of those countries in the specific arenas in which they chose to donate forces or other resources and their desire to be involved and have influence over the decision-making process in the UN. Another reason was the financial rewards given by the UN to contributor countries; in the case of developing countries, this remuneration was considerable. From the onset of the 1990s until the date of writing these words, the national affiliation of UN forces in the various operations has remained more or less similar, because the developing countries are the ones who contribute the lion's share of the forces.

Since lack of space in this part prevents me from addressing the modus operandi of all the UN member states, I choose to briefly demonstrate a conclusion of the study by focusing on the activities of the Islamic states, which comprise a political bloc of great influence in the organisation. In 1992, many of these countries advocated the development of new goals for the operations. Yet the various representatives from these countries emphasised the importance of the traditional principles of the operations: operating from a neutral, non-biased approach; support and backup of the international community and local players; and non-use of force. However, when the various operations were actually deployed, these countries would decide whether to support the operations on a case-by-case basis. In other words, there was a great gap between UN rhetoric (theory) and actual practice. Regarding the Cambodia operation: the Islamic states that allocated forces to Cambodia backed the traditional principles. By contrast, some of these countries were in favour of an enforcement action against Aidid's faction in Somalia. In Yugoslavia, the Islamist states functioned as a large, homogeneous bloc and advocated enforcement according to its accepted meaning in the UN Charter, and called for using force against the Serbs (because Muslims were the targets of the Serbs).

Regarding administrational and organisational aspects, the Islamic states tended to support reforms in the composition of the Security Council and the way the Council functioned. Yet they refused to support an increase in the number of

Secretariat staff members, unless this increase was tied to the regional representation principle. Their refusal was based on the rationale that an increase in the number of Secretariat staff members would give them greater representation in the Secretariat, thus ensuring a rise in their influence. Similarly, they argued that the ones to bear the burden of financing the expanding UN budget should be the powers, mainly the five permanent members of the Security Council. Regarding their actual contributions to the operations, many Islamic states were large contributors, including Indonesia, Bangladesh, Jordan, Egypt, Morocco and Pakistan. When we examine the scope of forces they allocated, the timing of these allocations and the time period in which these forces participated in an operation, we understand the calculations that guided the contributor states.

Jordan only allocated forces to the operation in Bosnia. Egypt, a large and influential country, allocated only 100 policemen to the Cambodia operation, a battalion of about 400 soldiers to Bosnia throughout the entire intervention and a similar scope of forces to Somalia only starting from the end of 1992. But in 1994, Egypt increased its forces (to Somalia) to about 1,600 soldiers. Pakistan, the largest contributor among the Islamic states, allocated different amounts to different operations. In Cambodia, Pakistan allocated just over 1,000 soldiers; in Bosnia it allocated almost 3,000 soldiers (though only from the end of 1994). Meanwhile, Pakistan allocated almost 7,000 soldiers to Somalia. Indonesia's contributions were in reverse proportion to those of the other Islamic states. Indonesia was very involved in Cambodia as one of the key players that led the peace process and was the largest contributor of all, having allocated almost 1,800 soldiers. But Indonesia allocated only about 450 soldiers to the Bosnia operation (in the second half of 1995), and did not allocate any soldiers at all to Somalia.

### In summary

Between the late 1980s and the early 1990s, there was a major shift in the position of the UN in the world. After the organisation had been shunted aside for most of the Cold War years, it returned to enjoy international centre stage; the large, multidimensional peacekeeping operations were catalysts in this process. The UN member states mobilised themselves to promote those initiatives that encouraged the achievement of multiple goals such as democratisation, humanitarian aid, resettlement of refugees, demobilisation of armed forces, economic development and advancement of good government to resolve active conflicts. Simultaneously, an intensive discussion was held between the member states and UN institutions regarding the potential of these operations. Nevertheless, even when the goals of the operations and their modes of implementation were interpreted broadly and enlarged, the course of international politics did not undergo a real change. True, the UN tool-box has continued to improve since then – in the guise of the International Criminal Court, the

*Responsibility to Protect* and the myriad peacebuilding and peace-supporting operations. However, the member states continue to exploit new and old UN initiatives alike, in accordance with their international politics, alliances and interests.

These last conclusions sharpen the difference between the work of international political theoreticians and that of practitioners. Statesmen and researcher Henry Kissinger wrote the following in his 2001 book, *Does America Need a Foreign Policy?*

> The ultimate dilemma of the statesman is to strike a balance between values and interests and, occasionally, between peace and justice. The dichotomy between morality and interest, between idealism and realism, is one of the standard clichés of the ongoing debate over international affairs. No such stark choice is, in fact, available. Excessive 'realism' produces stagnation; excessive 'idealism' leads to crusades and eventual disillusionment.[2]

Between 1988 and 1995, tension was constantly and clearly evident between realism and idealism in the work of the UN on peacekeeping. Research of periods that pre-date or antedate this period constitutes fertile ground for historical analysis not only of the influence of peacekeeping on conflict resolution but also on its normative and institutional role in global affairs.

### Notes

1 W. J. Durch and V. K. Holt, *The Brahimi Report and the Future of UN Peace Operations* (Washington, DC: Henry L. Stimson Center, 2003).
2 H. Kissinger, *Does America Need a Foreign Policy? Toward a Diplomacy for the 21st Century* (New York: Simon & Schuster, 2001), p. 286.

# Bibliography

Adebajo, A., 'Ethiopian/Eritrea', in D. M. Malone (ed.), *The UN Security Council: From the Cold War to the 21st Century* (Boulder, CO: Lynne Rienner, 2004), pp. 575–588.
—— *UN Peacekeeping in Africa: From the Suez Crisis to the Sudan Conflict* (Boulder, CO: Lynne Rienner, 2011).
Adelman, H. and A. Suhrke, 'Rwanda', in D. M. Malone (ed.), *The UN Security Council: From the Cold War to the 21st Century* (Boulder, CO: Lynne Rienner, 2004), pp. 483–499.
Adibe, C., *Managing Arms in Peace Process: Somalia* (New York and Geneva: United Nations, 1995).
Ajello, A. and Wittmann, P., 'Mozambieuqe', in D. M. Malone (ed.), *The UN Security Council: From the Cold War to the 21st Century* (Boulder, CO.: Lynne Rienner, 2004), pp. 437–450.
Akashi, Y., 'The Challenges Faced by UNTAC', *Japan Review of International Affairs*, 7:3 (Summer 1993), 185–201.
Albright, M. and B. Woodward, *Madam Secretary* (New York: Miramax Books, 2003).
Albritton, R. B., 'Cambodia in 2003: On the Road to Democratic Consolidation', *Asian Survey*, 44:1 (January 2004), 102–109.
Allard, K., *Somalia Operations: Lessons Learned* (USA: CCRP, 1995).
Antonini, B., 'El Salvador', in D. M. Malone (ed.), *The UN Security Council: From the Cold War to the 21st Century* (Boulder, CO: Lynne Rienner, 2004), pp. 423–436.
Autesserre, S., *The Trouble with the Congo: Local Violence and the Failure of International Peacebuilding* (Cambridge: Cambridge University Press, 2010).
Bailey, S. D., *Voting in the Security Council* (Bloomington, IN: Indiana University Press, 1969).
Bailey, S. D. and S. Daws, *The Procedure of the UN Security Council* (Oxford: Clarendon Press, 3rd edn, 1998).
Baker, J. A., III and T. M. DeFrank, *The Politics of Diplomacy: Revolution, War and Peace* (New York: G.P. Putnam's Sons, 1995).
Barnett, M. and M. Finnemore, *Rules for the World: International Organizations in Global Politics* (Ithaca, NY: Cornell University Press, 2004).
Barnett, M., H. Kim, M. O'Donnell and L. Sitea, 'Peacebuilding: What Is in a Name?', *Global Governance*, 13:1 (2007), 35–58.
Baumann, R. F., G. W. Gawrych and W. E. Kretchnik, *Armed Peacekeepers in Bosnia* (Fort Leavenworth, Kansas: Combat Studies Institute Press, 2004).

Beker, A., *The United Nations and Israel: From Recognition to Reprehension* (Lexington, MA: Lexington Books, 1988).
Bellamy, A., P. Williams and S. Griffin, *Understanding Peacekeeping* (Cambridge, UK: Polity Press; Malden, MA: Blackwell, 2nd edn, 2010).
Benner, T., S. Mergenthaler and P. Rotmann, *The New World of UN Peace Operations* (Oxford: Oxford University Press, 2011).
Bennett, C., *Yugoslavia's Bloody Collapse: Causes, Course and Consequences* (London: Hurst & Company, 1998).
Berdal, M., 'The Security Council and Peacekeeping', in V. Lowe, A. Roberts, J. Welch and D. Zaum (eds), *The United Nations Security Council and War: The Evolution of Thought and Practice since 1945* (Oxford: Oxford University Press, 2010), pp. 175–204.
Berdal, M. and S. Economides (eds), *United Nations Interventionism, 1991–2004* (Cambridge: Cambridge University Press, 2007).
Beresford, M., 'Cambodia in 2004: An Artificial Democratization Process', *Asian Survey*, 45:1 (January 2005), 134–139.
Berman, F., 'the Authorization Model: Resolution 678 and Its Effects', in D. M. Malone (ed.), *The UN Security Council: From the Cold War to the 21st Century* (Boulder, CO: Lynne Rienner, 2004), pp. 153–161.
Bildt, C., 'Holbrooke's History', *Survival*, 40:3 (1998), 187–191.
Le Billon, P., 'The Political Ecology of Transition in Cambodia 1989–1999: War, Peace and Forest Exploitation', *Development and Change*, 31:4 (2000), 785–805.
—— 'Logging in Muddy Waters: The Politics of Forest Exploitation in Cambodia', *Critical Asian Studies*, 34:4 (2002), 563–583.
Boudreau, T. E., *Sheathing the Sword: The UN Secretary-General and the Prevention of International Conflict* (New York, Westport, CT, London: Greenwood Press, 1991).
Boutros-Ghali, B., 'Introduction', in UN, *The United Nations and Cambodia, 1991–1995* (New York: United Nations Department of Public Information, 1995).
—— *An Agenda for Development* (New York: United Nations Department of Public Information, 1995).
—— 'Introduction', in UN, *The Blue Helmets: A Review of United Nations Peace-Keeping*, 3rd edn (New York: United Nations Department of Public Information, 1996), pp. 3–9.
—— *Unvanquished: A U.S.-U.N. Saga* (New York: Random House, 1999).
Bowett, D. W., *United Nations Forces: A Legal Study of United Nations Practice* (London: Stevens & Sons, 1964).
Boyd, A., *Fifteen Men on a Powder Keg: A History of the UN Security Council* (London: Methuen, 1971).
Briggs, H. W., 'Chinese Representation in the United Nations', *International Organization*, 6:2 (1952), 192–209.
Burg, S. L. and P. S. Shoup, *The War in Bosnia-Herzegovina: Ethnic Conflict and International Intervention* (Armonk NY: M.E. Sharp, 1999).
Bush, G. and B. Scowcroft, *A World Transformed* (New York: Alfred A. Knopf, 1998).
Call, C. T. and V. Wyeth (eds), *Building States to Build Peace* (Boulder, CO: Lynne Rienner, 2008).

Caplan, R., *A New Trusteeship? The International Administration of War-Torn Societies* (Oxford: Oxford University Press, 2002).
—— *Exit Strategies and State Building* (Oxford: Oxford University Press, 2012).
Cassanelli, L., *Victims and Vulnerable Groups in Southern Somalia* (Ottawa, Canada, May 1995).
Chandler, D. P., *The Tragedy of Cambodian History: Politics, War, and Revolution since 1945* (New Haven, CT: Yale University Press, 1991).
—— *A History of Cambodia*, 2nd edn (Boulder, CO: Westview Press, 1992).
—— 'Three Visions of Politics in Cambodia', in M. W. Doyle, I. Johnstone and R. C. Orr (eds.), *Keeping the Peace: Multidimensional UN Operations in Cambodia and El Salvador* (Cambridge: Cambridge University Press, 1997), pp. 25–52.
Chesterman, S., *You the People: The United Nations, Transitional Administration and State-Building* (Oxford: Oxford University Press, 2004).
—— 'East Timor', in M. Berdal and S. Economides (eds), *United Nations Interventionism, 1991–2004* (Cambridge: Cambridge University Press, 2007), pp. 192–216.
—— 'Articles 97–99', in B. Simma, D. E. Khan, G. Nolte, A. Paulus and N. Wessendorf (eds), *The Charter of the United Nations: A Commentary* (Oxford: Oxford University Press, 3rd edn, 2012), pp. 1991–2021.
Clarke, W., 'Testing the World's Resolve in Somalia', *Parameters*, 23:4 (1993–1994), 42–58.
Clarke, W. and J. Herbst (eds) *Learning from Somalia: The Lessons of Armed Humanitarian Intervention* (Boulder, CO: Westview Press, 1997).
Claude, I. L. Jr., *Swords into Plowshares: The Problems and Progress of International Organization* (New York: Random House, 2nd edn, 1961).
von Clausewitz, C., *On War*, trans. M. Howard and P. Paret (Princeton, NJ: Princeton University Press, 1976).
Clymer, K. J., *The United States and Cambodia, 1969–2000: A Troubled Relationship* (London; New York: Routledge, 2004).
Cohen, L. J., *Serpent in the Bosom: The Rise and Fall of Slobodan Milošević* (Boulder, CO: Westview Press, 2002).
Compagnon, D., 'Somali Armed Movements: The Interplay of Political Entrepreneurship and Clan-Based Factions', in C. Clapham (ed.), *African Guerrillas* (Oxford: James Currey, 1998), pp. 73–90.
Cordesman, A. H. and A. Wagner, *The Lessons of Modern War: The Iran–Iraq War* (Boulder, CO: Westview Press, 1990).
Cordovez, D. and S. S. Harrison, *Out of Afghanistan: The Inside Story of the Soviet Withdrawal* (New York: Oxford University Press, 1995).
Corwin, P., *Dubious Mandate: A Memoir of the UN in Bosnia, Summer 1995* (Durham, NC and London: Duke University Press, 1999).
van Creveld, M., *The Rise and Decline of the State* (Cambridge: Cambridge University Press, 1999).
de Cuéllar, J. P., *Pilgrimage for Peace: A Secretary General's Memoir* (New York: St. Martin's Press, 1998).
Dallaire, R. with B. Beardsley, *Shake Hands with the Devil: The Failure of Humanity in Rwanda* (Croydon, Surrey: Arrow Books, 2004).

Daws, S., 'The Origin and Development of UN Electoral Groups', in R. Thakur (ed.), *What Is Equitable Geographic Representation in the Twenty-first Century?* (Hong Kong: United Nations University, 1999), pp. 11–29.

Deac, W. P., *Road to the Killing Fields: The Cambodian War of 1970–1975* (College Station, TX: Texas A&M University Press, 1997).

Diehl, P. F., D. Druckman and J. Wall, 'International Peacekeeping and Conflict Resolution: A Taxonomic Analysis with Implications', *The Journal of Conflict Resolution*, 42:1 (1998), 33–55.

Diehl, P. F. and A. Balas, *Peace Operations* (Cambridge: Polity Press, 2nd edn, 2014).

Dinstein, Y., *War, Aggression and Self-Defence* (Cambridge: Cambridge University Press, 4th edn, 2005).

Doyle, M. W., *UN Peacekeeping in Cambodia: UNTAC's Civil Mandate* (Boulder, CO: Lynne Rienner, 1995).

—— 'Authority and Elections in Cambodia', in M. W. Doyle, I. Johnstone and R. C. Orr (eds), *Keeping the Peace: Multidimensional UN Operations in Cambodia and El Salvador* (Cambridge: Cambridge University Press, 1997), pp. 134–164.

Doyle, M. W., I. Johnstone and R. C. Orr (eds), *Keeping the Peace: Multidimensional UN Operations in Cambodia and El Salvador* (Cambridge: Cambridge University Press, 1997).

Doyle, M. W. and N. Sambanis, *Making War and Building Peace: The United Nations since the 1990s* (Princeton, NJ: Princeton University Press, 2006).

Drysdale, J., 'Foreign Military Intervention in Somalia: The Root Cause of the Shift from UN Peacekeeping to Peacemaking and Its Consequence', in W. Clarke and J. Herbst (eds.), *Learning from Somalia, The Lessons of Armed Humanitarian Intervention* (Boulder, CO: Westview Press, 1997), pp. 118–134.

Duignan, P., *NATO Its Past, Present, and Future* (Stanford, CA: Hoover Institution Press, 2000).

Durch, W. J. (ed.), *The Evolution of UN Peacekeeping: Case Studies and Comparative Analysis* (Basingstoke: Macmillan, 1993).

—— 'Introduction to Anarchy: Intervention in Somalia', in W. J. Durch (ed.), *UN Peacekeeping, American Politics, and the Uncivil Wars of the 1990s* (New York: St. Martin's Press, 1996), pp. 311–365.

—— *UN Peacekeeping, American Policy and the Uncivil Wars of the 1990s* (London: Macmillan, 1997).

Durch, W. J. and V. K. Holt, *The Brahimi Report and the Future of UN Peace Operations* (Washington DC: Henry L. Stimson Center, 2003).

Ebner, C., 'Article 100', in B. Simma, D. E. Khan, G. Nolte, A. Paulus and N. Wessendorf (eds), *The Charter of the United Nations: A Commentary* (Oxford: Oxford University Press, 3rd edn, 2012), pp. 2022–2053.

Economides, S., 'Kosovo', in M. Berdal and S. Economides (eds), *United Nations Interventionism, 1991–2004* (Cambridge: Cambridge University Press, 2007), pp. 217–245.

Ehteshami, A., 'The Arab States and the Middle East Balance of Power', in J. Gow (ed.), *Iraq, The Gulf Conflict and the World Community* (London: Brassey's, 1993), pp. 55–73.

von Einsiedel, S. and D. M. Malone, 'Haiti', in M. Berdal and S. Economides (eds), *United Nations Interventionism, 1991-2004* (Cambridge: Cambridge University Press, 2007), pp. 168-191.

Eldon, S., 'East Timor', in D. M. Malone (ed.), *The UN Security Council: From the Cold War to the 21st Century* (Boulder, CO: Lynne Rienner, 2004), pp. 551-566.

Fassbender, B., 'Pressure for Security Council Reform', in D. M. Malone (ed.), *The UN Security Council: From the Cold War to the 21st Century* (Boulder, CO: Lynne Rienner, 2004), pp. 341-355.

—— 'Article 2(1)', in B. Simma et al. (eds), *The Charter of the United Nations: A Commentary* (Oxford: Oxford University Press, 3rd edn, 2012), pp. 133-165.

Filipović, Z., *Zlata's Diary: A Child's Life in Sarajevo* (New York: Viking, 1994).

Findlay, T., *Cambodia: The Legacy and Lessons of UNTAC* (Oxford: Oxford University Press, 1995).

—— 'Introduction', in T. Findlay (ed.), *Challenges for the New Peacekeepers* (Oxford: Oxford University Press, 1996).

—— *Challenges for the New Peacekeepers* (Oxford: Oxford University Press, 1996).

—— *The Use of Force in UN Peace Operations* (Oxford: Oxford University Press, 2002).

Finnemore, M., *The Purpose of Intervention: Changing Beliefs about the Use of Force* (Ithaca, NY: Cornell University Press, 2004).

Forman, S. and A. Grene, 'Collaborating with Regional Organizations', in D. M. Malone (ed.), *The UN Security Council: From the Cold War to the 21st Century* (Boulder, CO: Lynne Rienner, 2004), pp. 295-309.

Fortna, V. P., 'United Nations Transition Assistance Group', in W. J. Durch (ed.), *The Evolution of UN Peacekeeping: Case Studies and Comparative Analysis* (Basingstoke: Macmillan, 1993).

Fox, G. H., 'Democratization', in D. M. Malone (ed.), *The UN Security Council: From the Cold War to the 21st Century* (Boulder, CO: Lynne Rienner, 2004), pp. 69-84.

Franck, T. F., 'The Secretary-General's Role in Conflict Resolution: Past, Present and Pure Conjecture', *European Journal of International Law*, 6:3 (1995), 1-29.

Frantzen, H. A., *NATO and Peace Support Operations, 1991-1999* (London: Frank Cass, 2005).

Freeman, W. D., R. B. Lambert and J. D. Mims, 'Operation Restore Hope: US Centcom Perspective', *Military Review*, 73:9 (1993), 61-72.

Fukuyama, F., *State-Building: Governance and World Order in the 21st Century* (Ithaca, NY: Cornell University Press, 2004).

Ganzglass, M. R., 'The Restoration of the Somali Justice System', in W. Clarke and J. Herbst (eds), *Learning from Somalia: The Lessons of Armed Humanitarian Intervention* (Boulder, CO: Westview Press, 1997), pp. 20-41.

Garthoff, R. L., *The Great Transition: American-Soviet Relations and the End of the Cold War* (Washington, DC: Brookings Institution Press, 1994).

Giddens, A., *The Nation-State and Violence: Volume Two of A Contemporary Critique of Historical Materialism* (Cambridge: Polity Press, 1985).

Gleditsch, N. P., P. Wallensteen, M. Eriksson, M. Sollenberg and H. Strand, 'Armed Conflict 1946-2001: A New Dataset', *Journal of Peace Research*, 39:5 (2002), 615-637.

Glegerich, T., 'Articles 36-38', in B. Simma, D.-E. Khan, G. Nolte and A. Paulus (eds), *The Charter of the United Nations: A Commentary* (Oxford: Oxford University Press, 3rd edn, 2012), pp. 1119-1170.

Glitman, M., 'US Policy in Bosnia: Rethinking a Flawed Approach', *Survival*, 38:4 (1996-1997), 66-83.

Goodrich, L. M., E. Hambro and A. P. Simons, *Charter of the United Nations Commentary and Documents* (Boston, MA: World Peace Foundation, 1969).

Gordenker, L., *The UN Secretary-General and the Maintenance of Peace* (New York & London: Columbia University Press, 1967).

Goulding, M., 'The Evolution of United Nations Peacekeeping', *International Affairs*, 69:3 (July 1993), 451-464.

—— *Peacemonger* (London: John Murray, 2002).

—— 'The UN Secretary-General', in D. M. Malone (ed.), *The UN Security Council: From the Cold War to the 21st Century* (Boulder, CO: Lynne Rienner, 2004), pp. 267-280.

Gow, J., 'The Soviet Involvement', in J. Gow (ed.), *Iraq, The Gulf Conflict and the World Community* (London: Brassey's, 1993), pp. 121-137.

—— *Triumph of the Lack of Will: International Diplomacy and the Yugoslav War* (London: Hurst & Company, 1997).

Greilsammer, I., 'European Reaction to the Gulf Challenge', in G. Barzilai, A. Klieman and G. Shidlo (eds), *The Gulf Crisis and its Global Aftermath* (London: Routledge, 1993), pp. 208-227.

Grove, E., 'UN Armed Forces and the Military Staff Committee: A Look Back', *International Security*, 17:4 (1993), 172-182.

Guleid, A. and J. L. Davies, 'Is It Peace for Somalia?', *New African*, 319 (1994), 7-9.

Halberstam, D., *War in a Time of Peace: Bush, Clinton, and the Generals* (New York: Touchstone, 2002).

Hall, M. and T. Young, *Confronting Leviathan: Mozambique since Independence* (London: Hurst, 1997).

Hassan, A., 'Build a New Somalia', *New African*, 320 (June 1994), 19.

Higgins, R., *United Nations Peacekeeping 1946-1967 Documents and Commentary*, Vol. I: The Middle East (London: Oxford University Press, 1969).

—— *United Nations Peacekeeping 1946-1967 Documents and Commentary*, Vol. II: Asia (London: Oxford University Press, 1970).

—— *United Nations Peacekeeping 1946-1967 Documents and Commentary*, Vol. III: Africa (Oxford: Oxford University Press, 1980).

—— *United Nations Peacekeeping Documents and Commentary*, Vol. IV: Europe 1946-1979 (Oxford: Oxford University Press, 1981).

Holbrooke, R. C., *To End a War* (New York: The Modern Library, 1999).

Howe, J. T., 'Relations Between the United States and the UN in Somalia', in W. Clarke and J. Herbst (eds) *Learning from Somalia, The Lessons of Armed Humanitarian Intervention* (Boulder, CO: Westview Press, 1997), pp. 173-190.

Ifantis, K., *NATO and the New Security Paradigm: Power, Strategy, Order and the Transatlantic Link* (London: Frank Cass, 2003).
International Institute for Strategic Studies – IISS, *The Military Balance 1991-1998* (London: Brassey's, 1991-1998).
Iriye, A., *Cultural Internationalism and World Order* (Baltimore, MD: Johns Hopkins University Press, 1997).
—— *Global Community: The Role of International Organizations in the Making of the Contemporary World* (Berkeley, CA: University of California Press, 2002).
—— *Global Interdependence: The World after 1945* (Cambridge, MA: Belknap Press, 2013).
Ishizuka, K., *Ireland and International Peacekeeping Operations 1960-2000* (London: Routledge, 2004).
Jakobsen, P. V., 'The Transformation of United Nations Peace Operations in the 1990s: Adding Globalization to the Conventional "End of the Cold War Explanation"', *Cooperation and Conflict*, 37:3 (2002), 267–282.
—— *Nordic Approaches to Peace Operations: A New Model in the Making?* (London & New York: Routledge, 2006).
Johansson, P., 'The Humdrum Use of Ultimate Authority: Defining and Analysing Chapter VII Resolution', *Nordic Journal of International Law*, 78:3 (2009), 309–344.
Johnston, H. and T. Dagne, 'Congress and the Somalia Crisis', in W. Clarke and J. Herbst (eds), *Learning from Somalia, The Lessons of Armed Humanitarian Intervention* (Boulder, CO: Westview Press, 1997), pp. 191–206.
Jones, B. D., 'Rwanda', in M. Berdal and S. Economides (eds.), *United Nations Interventionism, 1991-2004* (Cambridge: Cambridge University Press, 2007), pp. 139–167.
Kaldor, M., *New and Old Wars: Organized Violence in a Global Era* (Cambridge: Polity Press, 1999).
Kennedy, P., *The Parliament of Man: The Past, Present and Future of the United Nations* (New York: Vintage Books, 2006).
Kertcher, C., *Peacemaking or Statebuilding* (a Master's thesis submitted to Tel Aviv University, 2002).
—— *The Search for Peace – Or for a State: UN Intervention in Somalia 1992-95* (Jerusalem: The Harry S. Truman Research Institute for the Advancement of Peace, 2003).
—— 'Same Agenda, Different Results: The UN Interventions in Cambodia and Somalia after the Cold War', in: U. Rabi (ed.), *International Intervention in Local Conflicts: Crisis Management and Conflict Resolution Since the Cold War* (London: I.B. Tauris, 2010), pp. 19–33.
—— 'From Cold War to a System of Peacekeeping Operations: The Discussions on Peacekeeping Operations in the UN during the 1980s up to 1992', *Journal of Contemporary History*, 47:3 (2012), 611–637.
Kiernan, B., *The Pol Pot Regime: Race, Power, and Genocide in Cambodia under the Khmer Rouge, 1975-1979* (New Haven, CT: Yale University Press, 1996).
—— 'The Demography of Genocide in Southeast Asia; The Death Tolls in Cambodia, 1975-79, and East Timor, 1975-80', *Critical Asian Studies*, 35:4 (2003), 586–590.

Kissinger, H., *Diplomacy* (New York: Simon & Schuster, 1994).
—— *Does America Need a Foreign Policy? Toward a Diplomacy for the 21st Century* (New York: Simon & Schuster, 2001).
Klein, Y., 'Soviet Policy during the Gulf Crisis', in G. Barzilai, A. Klieman and G. Shidlo (eds), *The Gulf Crisis and Its Global Aftermath* (London: Routledge, 1993), pp. 191–207.
Koops, J., *UN SHIRBRIG and EU Battlegroups* (Oxford: Oxford Council on Good Governance, 2007).
Krisch, N., 'The Security Council and the Great Powers', in V. Lowe, A. Roberts, J. Welch and D. Zaum (eds), *The United Nations Security Council and War: The Evolution of Thought and Practice since 1945* (Oxford: Oxford University Press, 2010), pp. 133–153.
—— 'Articles 39–42', in B. Simma, D.-E. Khan, G. Nolte and A. Paulus (eds), *The Charter of the United Nations: A Commentary* (Oxford: Oxford University Press, 3rd edn, 2012), pp. 1272–1356.
Lamborn, A. C., 'Theoretical and Historical Perspectives on Collective Security: The Intellectual Roots of Contemporary Debates about Collective Conflict Management', in J. Lepgold and T. G. Weiss (eds), *Collective Conflict Management and Changing World Politics* (Albany, NY: SUNY Press, 1998), pp. 31–56.
Lampe, J. R., *Yugoslavia as History: Twice There Was a Country* (Cambridge: Cambridge University Press, 2000).
Langran, I. V., 'Cambodia in 2000: New Hopes are Challenged', *Asian Survey*, 41:1 (January 2001), 156–163.
Ledgewood, J. L. and K. Un, 'Global Concepts and Local Meaning: Human Rights and Buddhism in Cambodia', *Journal of Human Rights*, 2:4 (2003), 531–549.
Lepgold, J. and T. G. Weiss, 'Collective Conflict Management and Changing World Politics: An Overview', in J. Lepgold and T. G. Weiss (eds), *Collective Conflict Management and Changing World Politics* (Albany, NY: SUNY Press, 1998), pp. 3–21.
Lewis, I. M., 'Clan Conflict and Ethnicity in Somalia: Humanitarian Intervention in a Stateless Society', in D. Turton (ed.), *War and Ethnicity Global Connections and Local Violence* (Rochester, NY: University of Rochester Press, 1997), pp. 179–201.
Lewis, I. and J. Mayall, 'Somalia', in M. Berdal and S. Economides (eds), *United Nations Interventionism, 1991–2004* (Cambridge: Cambridge University Press, 2007), pp. 108–139.
Liasi, T., 'Last Days of Saigon?', *New African*, 326 (1995), 35.
Lizee, P. P., 'Cambodia in 1995: From Hope to Despair', *Asian Survey*, 36:1 (1996), 83–88.
—— 'Cambodia in 1996: Of Tigers, Crocodiles and Doves', *Asian Survey*, 37:1 (1997), 65–71.
Lorenz, F. M., 'Confronting Thievery in Somalia', *Military Review*, 74:8 (August 1994), 46–55.
—— 'Weapons Confiscation Policy During the First Phases of Operation "Restore Hope"', *Small Wars and Insurgencies*, 5:3 (Winter 1994), 409–425.
Lowe, V., A. Roberts, J. Welch and D. Zaum, 'Introduction', in V. Lowe, A. Roberts, J. Welch and D. Zaum (eds), *The United Nations Security Council and War: The Evolution of Thought and Practice since 1945* (Oxford: Oxford University Press, 2010), pp. 1–58.

—— *The United Nations Security Council and War: The Evolution of Thought and Practice since 1945* (Oxford: Oxford University Press, 2010).
Luard, E., 'China and the United Nations', *International Affairs*, 47:4 (1971), 729–744.
—— *A History of the United Nations*, Vol. I: The Years of Western Domination, 1945–1955 (Basingstoke: Macmillan, 1982).
—— *A History of the United Nations*, Vol. II: The Age of Decolonization, 1955–1965 (Basingstoke: Macmillan, 1989).
Lyons, T. and A. I. Samatar, *Somalia: State Collapse, Multilateral Intervention, and Strategies for Political Reconstruction* (Washington, DC: Brookings Institution, 1995).
Mackinlay, J. and J. Chopra, 'Second-Generation Multinational Operations', *Washington Quarterly*, 15:3 (1992), 113–34.
Mahbubani, K., 'The Permanent and Elected Members', in D. M. Malone (ed.), *The UN Security Council: From the Cold War to the 21st Century* (Boulder, CO: Lynne Rienner, 2004), pp. 253–266.
Malone, D. M., *Decision-Making in the Security Council: The Case of Haiti, 1990–1997* (Oxford: Clarendon Press, 1998).
—— *The UN Security Council: From the Cold War to the 21st Century* (Boulder, CO: Lynne Rienner, 2004).
—— 'Conclusion', in D. M. Malone (ed.), *The UN Security Council: From the Cold War to the 21st Century* (Boulder, CO: Lynne Rienner, 2004), pp. 617–649.
Manor, Y., *The 1975 'Zionism is Racism' Resolution: The Rise, Fall, and Resurgence of a Libel* (Jerusalem: The Jerusalem Center for Public Affairs, 2010).
Maren, M., *The Road to Hell: The Ravaging Effect of Foreign Aid and International Charity* (New York: Free Press, 1997).
Martin, I., 'International Intervention in East Timor', in J. M. Welsh (ed.), *Humanitarian Intervention and International Relations* (Oxford: Oxford University Press, 2004).
Martin, M. A., *Cambodia: A Shattered Society* (Berkeley, CA: University of California Press, 1994).
Mayall, J. (ed.), *The New Interventionism, 1991–1994: United Nations Experience in Cambodia, Former Yugoslavia, and Somalia* (New York: Cambridge University Press, 1996).
McGregor, C., 'China, Vietnam, and the Cambodian Conflict: Beijing's End Game Strategy', *Asian Survey*, 30:3 (1990), 266–283.
Mendelson, S. E., *Changing Course: Ideas, Politics, and the Soviet Withdrawal from Afghanistan* (Princeton, NJ: Princeton University Press, 1998).
Menkhaus, K., 'International Peacebuilding and the Dynamics of Local and National Reconciliation in Somalia', in W. Clarke and J. Herbst (eds), *Learning from Somalia, The Lessons of Armed Humanitarian Intervention* (Boulder, CO: Westview Press, 1997), pp. 42–63.
Murray, L. G., *Clinton, Peacekeeping and Humanitarian Intervention: Rise and Fall of a Policy* (Abingdon, Oxon: Routledge, 2008).
Nachmani, A., *International Intervention in the Greek Civil War: The United Nations Special Committee on the Balkans, 1947–1952* (New York: Praeger, 1990).

Nahory, C., 'The Hidden Veto', *Global Policy Forum*, May 2004.
Narine, S., 'ASEAN and the ARF: The Limits of the "ASEAN Way"', *Asian Survey*, 37:10 (1997), 961–978.
—— 'ASEAN and the Management of Regional Security', *Pacific Affairs*, 71:2 (1998), 195–214.
Natsios, A. S., 'Humanitarian Relief Intervention in Somalia: The Economics of Chaos', in W. Clarke and J. Herbst (eds), *Learning from Somalia, The Lessons of Armed Humanitarian Intervention* (Boulder, CO: Westview Press, 1997), pp. 77–95.
Neff, S. C., *War and the Law of Nations: A General History* (Cambridge: Cambridge University Press, 2005).
Netherlands Institute for War Documentation (NIOD), *Srebrenica: A 'Safe' Area: Reconstruction, Background, Consequences and Analyses of the Fall of a Safe Area* (Amsterdam: Netherlands Institute for War Documentation, NIOD, 2002).
Oakley, R. B. and J. I. Hirsch, *Somalia and Operation Restore Hope: Reflections on Peacemaking and Peacekeeping* (Washington, DC: United States Institute of Peace, 1995).
O'Neill, J. T. and N. Rees, *United Nations Peacekeeping in the Post-Cold War Era* (Abingdon, Oxon: Routledge, 2005).
Opitz, P. J., 'Collective Security', in H. Volger (ed.), *A Concise Encyclopedia of the United Nations* (Hague: Kluwer Law International, 2002), pp. 25–32.
Owen, D., *Balkan Odyssey* (New York: Harcourt Brace, 1995).
Paris, R., *At War's End: Building Peace After Civil Conflict* (Cambridge: Cambridge University Press, 2004).
Patman, R. G., 'Disarming Somalia: The Contrasting Fortunes of United States and Australian Peacekeepers During United Nations Intervention, 1992–1993', *African Affairs*, 96:385 (1997), 509–533.
Peou, S., 'Cambodia in 1997: Back to Square One?', *Asian Survey*, 38:1 (January 1998), 69–74.
—— 'Cambodia in 1998: From Despair to Hope?', *Asian Survey*, 39:1 (January 1999), 20–26.
Peterson, M. J., *The UN General Assembly* (London and New York: Routledge, 2006).
Powell, C. L. and J. E. Persico, *My American Journey* (New York: Ballantine Books, 1996).
Prunier, G., 'The Experience of European Armies in Operation Restore Hope', in W. Clarke and J. Herbst (eds), *Learning from Somalia: The Lessons of Armed Humanitarian Intervention* (Boulder, CO: Westview Press, 1997), pp. 135–147.
Pugh, M. and N. Cooper (eds), *Whose Peace? Critical Perspectives on the Political Economy of Peacebuilding* (Houndmills, Basingstoke: Palgrave Macmillan, 2011).
Ramet, S. P., *The Three Yugoslavias: State-Building and Legitimation, 1918–2005* (Washington, DC: Woodrow Wilson Center Press, 2006).
Ramses, A., 'Sino-Vietnamese Normalization in the Light of the Crisis of the Late 70s', *Pacific Affairs*, 67:3 (1994), 357–383.
Randelzhofer, A. and O. Dörr, 'Article 2(4)', in B. Simma, D.-E. Khan, G. Nolte and A. Paulus (eds), *The Charter of the United Nations: A Commentary*. (Oxford: Oxford University Press, 3rd edn, 2012), pp. 200–234.

Randelzhofer, A. and G. Nolte, 'Article 51', in B. Simma, D.-E. Khan, G. Nolte and A. Paulus (eds), *The Charter of the United Nations: A Commentary* (Oxford: Oxford University Press, 3rd edn, 2012), pp. 1397–1428.

Ratner, S., *The New UN Peacekeeping: Building Peace in Lands of Conflict after the Cold War* (New York: St. Martin's Press, 1995).

Reichenstein, B., 'Regionalization', in H. Volger (ed.), *A Concise Encyclopedia of the United Nations* (Hague: Kluwer Law International, 2002), pp. 458–464.

Ress, G. and J. Walter, 'Article 53', in B. Simma et al. (eds), *The Charter of the United Nations: A Commentary* (Oxford: Oxford University Press, 3rd edn, 2012), pp. 1478–1524.

Rikhye, I. J., *The Theory and Practice of Peacekeeping* (New York: St. Martin's Press, 1984).

Rikhye, I. J., M. Harbottle and B. Egge, *The Thin Blue Line: International Peacekeeping and Its Future* (New Haven, CT: Yale University Press, 1974).

Roberts, A., 'The Crisis in UN Peacekeeping', in C. A. Crocker, F. O. Hampson and P. Aall (eds), *Managing Global Chaos: Sources of and Responses to International Conflict* (Washington, DC: United States Institute, 1996), pp. 297–319.

—— 'The Use of Force', in D. M. Malone (ed.), *The UN Security Council: From the Cold War to the 21st Century* (Boulder, CO: Lynne Rienner, 2004), pp. 133–152.

Roberts, A. and D. Zaum, *Problems and Opportunities of Selective Security Today* (Oxford: Oxford University Press, 2008).

Rose, M., *Fighting for Peace: Bosnia 1994* (London: Harvill Press, 1998).

Ross, R. S., 'China and the Cambodian Peace Process', *Asian Survey*, 31:12 (1991), 1170–1185.

Russell, R. B., *A History of the United Nations Charter: The Role of the United States 1940–1945* (Washington, DC: The Brookings Institution, 1958).

Sahnoun, M., *Somalia: the Missed Opportunities* (Washington, DC: United States Institute of Peace, 1994).

Sanderson, J., 'The Cambodian Experience: A Success Story Still?', in R. Thakur and A. Schnabel (eds), *United Nations Peacekeeping Operations: Ad Hoc Missions, Permanent Engagement* (Tokyo, New York: United Nations University Press, 2001), pp. 155–166.

Schindlmayer, T., 'Obstructing the Security Council: The Use of the Veto in the Twentieth Century', *Journal of the History of International Law*, 3:2 (2001), 218–234.

Schlesinger, S., *Act of Creation: The Founding of the United Nations: A Story of Superpowers, Secret Agents, Wartime Allies and Enemies, and Their Quest for a Peaceful World* (Boulder, CO: Westview Press, 2003).

Schwebel, S. M., *The Secretary-General of the United Nations: His Political Powers and Practice* (New York: Greenwood Press, 1969, originally published in 1952).

Schweisfurth, T., 'Articles 34–35', in B. Simma, D.-E. Khan, G. Nolte and A. Paulus (eds), *The Charter of the United Nations: A Commentary* (Oxford: Oxford University Press, 3rd edn, 2012), pp. 1086–1118.

Segal, D., 'Five Phases of United Nations Peacekeeping: An Evolutionary Typology', *Journal of Political and Military Sociology*, 23:1 (1995), 65–79.

Seybolt, T., *Humanitarian Military Intervention: The Conditions for Success and Failure* (Oxford: Oxford University Press, 2008).

Shaw, M. N., *International Law* (Cambridge: Cambridge University Press, 2003).
Shawcross, W., *Sideshow: Kissinger, Nixon and the Destruction of Cambodia* (Bungay, Suffolk, UK: Fontana Press, 1980).
—— *Deliver Us From Evil: Peacekeepers, Warlords and a World of Endless Conflict* (New York: Simon & Schuster, 2000).
Sheehan, M., *The Balance of Power: History and Theory* (London: Routledge, 1996).
Short, P., *Pol Pot: Anatomy of a Nightmare* (New York: H. Holt, 2005).
Shrader, C. R., *The Muslim-Croat Civil War in Central Bosnia: A Military History, 1992-1994* (College Station, TX: Texas A & M University Press, 2003).
Simma B., D. E. Khan, G. Nolte, A. Paulus and N. Wessendorf (eds), *The Charter of the United Nations: A Commentary* (Oxford: Oxford University Press, 3rd edn, 2012).
Skogmo, B., *UNIFIL: International Peacekeeping in Lebanon* (Boulder, CO: Lynne Rienner, 1989).
Smith, H., 'Intelligence and UN Peacekeeping', *Survival*, 36:3 (1994), 174-192.
Smith, H. E., G. S. Nieminen and M. Kyi Win, *Historical Dictionary of Thailand* (Lanham, MD: Scarecrow Press, 2nd edn, 2005).
Smith, R., *The Utility of Force* (London: Penguin, 2006).
Smouts, M. C., 'The Political Aspects of Peace-Keeping Operations', in B. Stern (ed.), *United Nations Peace-Keeping Operations: A Guide to French Policies* (Tokyo: United Nations University Press, 1998), pp. 7-39.
Soffer, J., 'All for One or All for All: The UN Military Staff Committee and the Contradictions within American Internationalism', *Diplomatic History*, 21:1 (1997), 45-69.
Solarz, S. J., 'Cambodia and the International Community', *Foreign Affairs*, 69:2 (1990), 99-115.
Song, J., 'The Political Dynamics of the Peacemaking Process in Cambodia', in M. W. Doyle, I. Johnstone and R. C. Orr (eds), *Keeping the Peace: Multidimensional UN Operations in Cambodia and El Salvador* (Cambridge: Cambridge University Press, 1997), pp. 53-81.
Sorenson, D. S. and P. C. Wood (eds), *The Politics of Peacekeeping in the Post-Cold War Era* (London: Frank Cass, 2005).
Stöckl, A., 'Article 101', in B. Simma *et al.* (eds), *The Charter of the United Nations: A Commentary* (Oxford: Oxford University Press, 3rd edn, 2012), pp. 2054-2088.
Synge, R., *Mozambique: UN Peacekeeping in Action 1992-1994* (Washington, DC: United States Institute of Peace, 1994).
Thompson, J., 'The Military Coalition', in J. Gow (ed.), *Iraq, The Gulf Conflict and the World Community* (London: Brassey's, 1993), pp. 138-161.
Thornberry, C., 'Namibia', in D. M. Malone (ed.), *The UN Security Council: From the Cold War to the 21st Century* (Boulder, CO: Lynne Rienner, 2004), pp. 407-422.
Tillema, H. K., *International Armed Conflicts since 1945: A Bibliographic Handbook of Wars and Military Interventions* (Boulder, CO: Westview Press, 1991).
Tomushcat, C., 'Article 33', in B. Simma, D.-E. Khan, G. Nolte and A. Paulus (eds), *The Charter of the United Nations: A Commentary* (Oxford: Oxford University Press, 3rd edn, 2012), pp. 1069-1085.

Touval, S., *Mediation in the Yugoslav Wars* (Houndmills, Basingstoke: Palgrave Macmillan, 2002).

Traub, J., *The Best Intentions: Kofi Annan and the UN in the Era of American World Power* (New York: Farrar, Straus and Giroux, 2006).

Tripodi, P., *The Colonial Legacy in Somalia, Rome and Mogadishu: From Colonial Administration to Operation Restore Hope* (Basingstoke: Macmillan, 1999).

Tripp, C., 'Iraq and the War for Kuwait', in J. Gow (ed.), *Iraq, The Gulf Conflict and the World Community* (London: Brassey's, 1993), pp. 16–33.

Un, K. and J. Ledgerwood, 'Cambodia in 2001: Toward Democratic Consolidation?', *Asian Survey*, 42:1 (January, 2002), 100–106.

—— 'Cambodia in 2002: Decentralization and Its Effects on Party Politics', *Asian Survey*, 43:1, (January 2003), 113–119.

United Nations, *The Blue Helmets: A Review of United Nations Peace-Keeping* (New York: United Nations Department of Public Information, 1985).

—— *The Blue Helmets: A Review of United Nations Peace-Keeping* (New York: United Nations Department of Public Information, 2nd edn, 1990).

—— *The Blue Helmets: A Review of United Nations Peace-Keeping* (New York: United Nations Department of Public Information, 3rd edn, 1996).

—— *A Handbook on the Peaceful Settlement of Disputes Between States* (New York: United Nations Department of Public Information, 1992).

—— *United Nations and Apartheid 1948–1994* (New York, United Nations Department of Public Information, 1994).

—— *The United Nations and Cambodia, 1991–1995* (New York: United Nations Department of Public Information, 1995).

—— *The United Nations and Mozambique: 1991–1995* (New York: United Nations Department of Public Information, 1995).

—— *The United Nations and Somalia, 1992–1996* (New York: United Nations Department of Public Information, 1996).

—— *Yearbook of the United Nations, 1987* (New York: United Nations Department of Public Information, 1992).

—— *Yearbook of the United Nations, 1994* (New York: United Nations Department of Public Information, 1995).

—— *Yearbook of the United Nations, 1995* (New York: United Nations Department of Public Information, 1997).

—— 'Top UN peacekeeping official warns of 'overstretch' as mission staff numbers surge', *UN News Centre*, 4 October 2006.

—— *United Nations Peacekeeping Operations Principles and Guidelines* (New York: Department of Peacekeeping Operations, 2008).

—— *A New Partnership Agenda: Charting a New Horizon for UN Peacekeeping* (New York: Department of Peacekeeping Operations, 2009).

Uphoff Kato, E., 'Quick Impacts, Slow Rehabilitation in Cambodia', in M. W. Doyle, I. Johnstone and R. C. Orr (eds), *Keeping the Peace: Multidimensional UN Operations in Cambodia and El Salvador* (Cambridge: Cambridge University Press, 1997), pp. 186–205.

Urquhart, B., *Hammarskjold* (New York: Harper Colophon Books, 1994).
—— *A Life in Peace and War* (New York: Harper & Row, 1987).
Volger, V. (ed.), *A Concise Encyclopedia of the United Nations* (Hague: Kluwer Law International, 2002).
de Waal, A., *Famine Crimes: Politics & Disaster Relief Industry in Africa* (London: African Rights & International African Institute in association with J. Currey, Oxford & Indiana University Press, Bloomington, 1997).
Walter, C., 'Articles 52, 54', in B. Simma *et al.* (eds), *The Charter of the United Nations: A Commentary* (Oxford: Oxford University Press, 3rd edn, 2012), pp. 1445–1477, 1525–1534.
Weggel, O., 'Cambodia in 2005: Year of Reassurance', *Asian Survey*, 46:1 (January 2006), 155–161.
Weiss, T. G., *The United Nations and Civil Wars* (Boulder, CO: Lynne Rienner, 1995).
—— 'The Humanitarian Impulse', in D. M. Malone (ed.), *The UN Security Council: From the Cold War to the 21st Century* (Boulder, CO: Lynne Rienner, 2004), pp. 37–54.
Weiss T. G. and S. Daws (eds), *The Oxford Handbook on The United Nations* (Oxford: Oxford University Press, 2007).
Weiss, T. G., D. P. Forsythe and R. A. Coate, *The United Nations and Changing World Politics* (Boulder, CO: Lynne Rienner, 3rd edn, 2001).
Welsh, J. M. (ed.), *Humanitarian Intervention and International Relations* (Oxford: Oxford University Press, 2004).
Weschler, J., 'Human Rights', in D. M. Malone (ed.), *The UN Security Council: From the Cold War to the 21st Century* (Boulder, CO: Lynne Rienner, 2004), pp. 55–68.
Westad, O. A., *The Global Cold War: Third World Interventions and the Making of Our Times* (Cambridge: Cambridge University Press, 2005).
Wheeler, N. J., *Saving Strangers: Humanitarian Intervention in International Society* (Oxford: Oxford University Press, 2000).White, N. D., *Keeping the Peace: The United Nations and the Maintenance of International Peace and Security* (Manchester & New York: Manchester University Press, 2nd edn, 1997).
Whitworth, S., *Men, Militarism, and UN Peacekeeping: A Gendered Analysis* (Boulder, CO: Lynne Rienner, 2004).
Williams, B., 'Returning Home: The Repatriation of Cambodian Refugees', in M. W. Doyle, I. Johnstone and R. C. Orr (eds), *Keeping the Peace: Multidimensional UN Operations in Cambodia and El Salvador* (Cambridge: Cambridge University Press, 1997), pp. 165–185.
Williams, M. C., 'New Soviet Policy Towards Southeast Asia: Recognition and Change', *Asian Survey*, 31:4 (1991), 364–377.
Winkelmann, I., 'Groups and Grouping in the United Nations', in H. Volger (ed.), *A Concise Encyclopedia of the United Nations* (Hague: Kluwer Law International, 2002), pp. 158–162.
—— 'Regional Groups in the UN', in H. Volger (ed.), *A Concise Encyclopedia of the United Nations* (Hague: Kluwer Law International, 2002), pp. 455–458.
Wiseman, H., 'United Nations Peacekeeping: An Historical Overview', in H. Wiseman (ed.), *Peacekeeping Appraisals & Proposals* (New York: Pergamon Press, 1983), pp. 19–58.

Wolfrum, R., 'Article 1', in B. Simma, D.-E. Khan, G. Nolte and A. Paulus (eds), *The Charter of the United Nations: A Commentary* (Oxford: Oxford University Press, 3rd edn, 2012), pp. 107–120.
Woodhouse, T. and O. Rambotham (eds), *Peacekeeping and Conflict Resolution* (London: Frank Cass, 2000).
Woods, J. L., 'US Government Decision-Making Process During Humanitarian Operations in Somalia', in W. Clarke and J. Herbst (eds), *Learning from Somalia, The Lessons of Armed Humanitarian Intervention* (Boulder, CO: Westview Press, 1997), pp. 151–172.
Zimmerman, A., 'Article 27', in B. Simma *et al.* (eds), *The Charter of the United Nations: A Commentary* (Oxford: Oxford University Press, 3rd edn, 2012), pp. 871–938.
Zimmerman, W., *Origins of a Catastrophe: Yugoslavia and Its Destroyers* (New York: Times Books, 1997).

*Online secondary sources*

Helander, B. M., H. M. Mukhtar and I. M. Lewis, 'Building Peace from Below? A Critical Review of the District Councils in the Bay and Bakool Regions of Southern Somalia', in http://Arlaadinet.com, April 1995, accessed on 18 April 2015.
United Nations, 'Press Conference by Jean-Marie Guéhenno Under-Secretary-General for Peacekeeping Operations', in www.un.org/en/peacekeeping/articles/pr_JMG.pdf, 4 October 2006, last accessed 30 October 2015.

# Index

Abdić, Fikret 112
Addis Ababa Peace Agreement 128, 163–165, 170, 172
Afghanistan 33, 38, 50, 58–59, 69–70, 72, 77, 199
African Union (AU) 3, 38
   see also Organization of African Unity (OAU)
Ahtisaari, Martti 61
Aidid Mohamed Farrah 125, 129, 164–165, 168–175, 182, 205
Akashi, Yasushi 68, 100, 102, 105–106
Albanian Kosovars
   see also Kosovo
Algeria 94
Angola 33, 51, 55, 59, 63, 67, 77, 199
   Movimento Popular de Libertaçao de Angola (MPLA) 59
   União Nacional para a Independência Total de Angola (UNITA) 59
Annan, Kofi 99, 146, 166, 203
Arab Emirates 66
Arab League 19, 65, 126, 131n4, 171, 204
Argentina 54, 187n, 188n
Asia-Pacific Group 19
Asian Development Bank 194
Association of Southeast Asian Nations (ASEAN) 70, 88, 204
Australia 52, 68, 70–74, 76, 105, 143, 155, 174, 204
Austria 52, 83n, 157

Bahrain 66
Baidoa (Somalia) 167
Bailey, Sidney 18
Baker, James A. III 84
Bakool (Somalia) 165
Bangladesh 54, 94, 161, 168, 187–188n79, 205–206
Banja-Luka (Bosnia) 183
Baranja (Croatia) 179
Barre, Siad 124–125, 163, 167–168
Bay (Somalia) 165
Belgium 79n, 119, 137
Belgrade (Serbia) 178
Bellamy, Alex 3, 32, 86
Bicesse Accords 59
Bihac (Bosnia) 122
Bosnia/Bosnia-Herzegovina 3, 34, 40, 68, 78, 99, 109–112, 114, 116–123, 125–131, 142–143, 150, 173, 176–184, 188n76, 192n154, 194n177, 197–198, 201, 206
   Bosnian-Croats 111–112, 117, 120–121, 182–183
   Bosnian-Muslims 3–4, 111–112, 117–122, 136n102, 139n159, 142, 176, 180–182, 205
   Bosnian-Serbs 3–4, 111–112, 115, 117–121, 139n159, 142, 176, 180–183, 194n177
Botswana 110, 168

Boutros-Ghali, Boutros 37, 68, 76, 86–92, 95, 97, 101, 105, 108, 114, 118–119, 124, 126–127, 130, 138n146–139n173, 145–146, 149–150, 159–162, 174–175, 196, 200, 203
Brahimi Report 36, 197
Brazil 54, 171, 178
Brindisi, Port 157
Brunei 194n183
Bulgaria 83n80, 144
Bunche, Ralph 26
Bush, George (senior) 65

Cairo 145
  Convention 153
  *see also* Non Aligned Movement (NAM)
Cambodia 1, 3, 7, 9, 27, 33–34, 41, 48n77, 50–51, 53–55, 64, 67–73, 75–79, 83n90, 85–86, 92, 99–110, 123–125, 128, 130, 133n86, 142, 151, 155–156, 163, 165–166, 168–171, 175, 177, 179, 190n116, 196–199, 201–202, 204–206
  International Committee on the Reconstruction of Cambodia (ICRC) 103–104
  Supreme National Council (SNC) 103, 105–106, 128
Cambodian People's Party/Phnom Penh government (CPP/SOC) 69, 100–108, 135n85
  *see also* Kampuchean People's Revolutionary Party (KPCP)
Canada 2, 26, 51–52, 74, 77, 143–144, 148, 155–156, 158, 204
Capstone Doctrine (UN) 36
Carrington, Peter 113, 137n117
Central African Republic 38
Chad 33–34
Chile 54, 188n79
China People's Republic of China (PRC) 2, 7, 19, 24, 39, 54, 65, 69–70, 95, 97, 103, 112, 120, 152, 171, 178, 181, 198–199, 201–202
China, Republic of China (ROC) Taiwan 19
Clinton, Bill 200
Coate Roger.A. 16
Committee of 33
  *see also* Special Committee for Peacekeeping Operations (SCPKO)
Commonwealth of Independent States (CIS) 158, 199–200
Congo, The Democratic Republic of 25, 27–28, 36–38, 64, 67, 101
Costa Rica 33, 60
Croatia 34, 109, 111–117, 121, 123, 130–131, 173, 176–179, 182–184, 192n154, 194n183, 201
  Croatian-Serbs 34, 111–116, 177–179, 182
  *see also* Bosnian-Croats, Bosnia
Cuba 59, 63, 81n49, 94
de Cuéllar, Javier Pérez 54–55, 60, 62 –63, 75–76, 113–114, 118, 202–203
Cyprus 25, 27–28, 39, 58, 67
Czech, the Republic of 110, 180

Darod clan (Somalia) 125, 168
Declaration on the Right of Peoples to Peace from 1984 16
Declaration of the International Year of Peace 1985 16
Delalić, Ramiz Ćelo 120
Democratic Kampuchea (DK) 69, 100–104, 107
  *see also* Khmer Rouge
Denmark 51–52, 79, 143–144, 157–158, 184, 204
  *see also* Nordic countries
Djibouti 171
Dominican Republic 25, 60
Dutch 27–28, 46n51, 180

East Timor 3, 36–38, 49n87, 68, 78, 197, 203
Eastern European Group 19, 53, 57, 130, 198–199
Eastern Slavonia (Croatia) 78, 179
Economic and Social Council (ECOSOC) 17, 21, 43n18
Economic Community of West African States (ECOWAS) 35, 48n78
Egypt 25–29, 54, 65, 67, 94, 145, 152, 168, 186n45, 188n79, 205–206
El Salvador 33, 51, 55, 60–61, 67, 79n1, 151, 161
Erdut Agreement 179
Ethiopia 17, 48n83, 169
European Community (EC) 53–54, 65–66, 75, 109, 112–113, 116–117, 119, 123, 126, 130, 137n117, 144, 200–201
European Union (EU) 37–38, 88, 143–144, 158, 181, 183, 188n76, 200–201, 204
  European Council 54
  see also Western European Union
Evans, Gareth 70–71, 105

Fifth Committee 9
Fiji 94, 188n79
Finland 52, 204
  see also Nordic countries
Ford Foundation 160
Forsythe, David P. 16
Fourth Committee 8, 81n61, 145, 185n, 189n
  see also Special Committee for Peacekeeping Operations (SCPKO); Special Political Committee (SPC)
France 2, 17, 23, 26, 51, 53–54, 56, 65, 70, 72, 77, 79n13, 95, 98, 101, 103, 112–113, 118–119, 137n119, 151–152, 168, 171, 194n182, 198, 201, 204
  see also Permanent 5 (P5)

Gambari, Ibrahim 147
Geneva Accords (Afghanistan) 58
Georgia (FSU) 33, 86, 96, 133n42
Germany, Federal Republic of 79n13, 112–113, 118, 137n119, 156
Goražde (Bosnia) 122
Gorbachev, Mikhail 50–51, 58–59, 70, 77, 158, 199
Gospić 177
Goulding, Marrack 63, 76, 107, 113–114, 118, 145
Guéhenno, Jean-Marie 36
Greece 79n13, 109, 118, 181
Griffin, Paul 3, 32, 86
Group of 77 19
  see also Non Aligned Movement (NAM)
Guatemala 33, 60

Haiti 33, 85, 98–99, 133n42, 152
Hammarskjöld, Dag 26–27
Hannay, David 126
Hassan II, king of Morocco 131
Hawiye clan (Somalia) 125, 167–168
Honduras 33, 60
Howe, Jonathan 113
Hun Sen 69, 103, 106–108
Hussein, Saddam 64–66
Hutu 34, 99

Iceland 52
Independent Commission on Disarmament and Security Issues (also known as the Palme Commission) 53
India 23, 25, 39, 54, 67, 83n82, 120, 157, 161, 168, 173, 188n79, 191, 205
Indonesia 23, 28, 71–72, 188n79, 206
International Committee of the Red Cross (ICRC) 72, 97, 122
International Conference on Former Yugoslavia (ICFY) 179, 183
International Court of Justice 17

International Criminal Tribunal for the Former Yugoslavia (ICTY) 110
Iran 50, 58–59, 64, 77, 194, 199
Iraq 33, 38, 50, 57–59, 64–67, 77–78, 79n1, 81n49, 87, 96, 98, 118, 133n42, 161, 183, 199–200
Ireland 52, 79n13, 155, 184
Iriye, Akira 16, 43n20
Israel 19, 23, 25–30, 39, 58, 65, 67
Italy 79n13, 137n119, 168, 171, 201
Ivory Coast 38
Izetbegović, Alija 112

Japan 38, 54, 68, 75, 83, 103, 156
Jordan 29, 188n79, 205–206

Kampuchean People's Revolutionary Party (KPCP) 69–71, 76, 100, 104
  *see also* Cambodian People's Party (CPP)
Kenya 187n46, 188n79
Khmer People's National Liberation Front (KPNLF) 69, 100, 102, 107
Khmer Rouge 68–71, 73, 100–104, 107, 109, 202
  *see also* Democratic Kampuchea (DK)
Kismayu (Somalia) 169
Kissinger, Henry 207
Knin (Croatia) 115
Kosovo 3, 36–38, 40, 68, 78, 110–112, 188n, 197, 203
Kosovo Force (KFOR) 37
Kouyaté, Lansana 173
Kovanda, Karel 180
Krajina (Croatia) 115
Kuwait 25, 33, 50–51, 55, 58, 64–67, 77, 79, 133, 161, 177, 183, 200

Latin American and Caribbean Group (GRULAC) 17, 19
League of Nations 13, 17–18, 62
Lebanon 25, 27, 29–30, 58, 116, 161
Legwaila, Joseph 110

Liberia 33, 37–38, 85, 133n42
Libya 34, 38, 66
Lie, Trygve 24
Loridon, Michel 101
Luard, Evan 28

Macedonia 34–35, 99, 109–112, 121, 123, 131, 176, 192n154
Maglaj 193n
Mahdi, Ali 125, 164, 169
Malaysia 94, 106, 148, 168, 185n27, 187–188n79, 194n183, 205
Mali 153
Manchuria 17
Mao Zedong 24
Markale (Sarajevo, Bosnia) 181
Martin, Marie Alexandrine 105
Maslenica (Croatia) 177
Mello, Sérgio Vieira de 103
Mexico 54
Middle East 23, 29, 65
Military Staff Committee (MSC) 15, 65, 152
Milošević, Slobodan 109, 111, 182
Mogadishu (Somalia) 3, 125–127, 142, 146, 164, 167–173, 175, 185
MOLINAKA (Cambodia) 108
Montenegro 109–111, 116
Mozambique 33, 85, 98–99, 151, 161

Nairobi Declaration 173
Namibia 33, 54, 59, 61–64, 67, 70, 72, 74, 77, 143, 151, 199
National United Front for an Independent, Neutral, Peaceful, and Cooperative Cambodia (FUNCINPEC) 69, 100, 102–103, 107–108
Nepal 168
Netherlands *see* Dutch
New Horizon (UN) 36
New Zealand 52, 74, 143–144, 155, 171, 174, 204

Nicaragua 33, 54, 60–61, 64, 74
  Contras 60
  Sandinista National Liberation Front 60
Nigeria 147, 168, 205
Nojuma, Sam 62
Non Aligned Movement (NAM) 19, 54, 70, 144–145, 152–153, 189n96
Nordic countries 52, 74–75, 77, 143–144, 155–156
  see also Denmark; Finland; Iceland; Norway; Sweden
Norodom, Sihanouk 70, 108
Norodom Ranariddh 103, 108
North Atlantic Treaty Organization (NATO) 3, 35, 37–38, 48n78, 49n89, 110, 122, 124, 150, 158, 178, 181–183, 194n117
North Korea 24–25, 39, 46n47
Norway 52, 158, 204

Olhaye, Roble 171
Oman 66
Organization of African Unity (OAU) 126, 158, 171, 204
  see also African Union (AU)
Organization of the Islamic Conference (OIC) 123, 126, 204
Organization for Security and Cooperation in Europe (OSCE) 37, 48n78
Osman, Mohamed Sheikh 167
Owen, David 121–123

Pakistan 23, 25, 39, 54, 58, 94, 126, 139n159, 157, 161, 168, 170–171, 173–174, 188n79, 192n139, 205–206
Palestinian Authority 19
Papua New Guinea 83n80
Paris Agreements 72–73, 100, 102–105, 108
Paris Conference 69, 72
Pearson, Lester B. 26

Permanent Five (P5) 7, 15, 17–19, 21–22, 23–24, 26, 28, 33, 54, 56–57, 71–72, 74–76, 78, 95, 98, 126, 128, 146–148, 151–155, 157–158, 162, 171, 198–199, 201–202, 206
  see also China; France; Russia; Union of Soviet Socialist Republics (USSR); United Kingdom; United States
Peruća dam (Croatia) 115, 177
Philippines 188
Phnom Penh (Cambodia) 101, 103
Pochentong (Cambodia) 103
Poland 30, 103, 158
Porcell, Gerard 107

Qatar 66

Rafiuddin, Ahmed 69
Rhodesia 30
Roberts, Adam 3, 32
Romania 144
Rose, Michael 120
Rovenský, Dušan 110
Russia 3, 7, 39, 95, 98, 143, 151–152, 158, 171, 178, 181, 198–199, 203
  see also Union of Soviet Socialist Republics (USSR)
Rwanda 3, 33–34, 85, 98, 99, 133n42, 142, 148, 152, 154, 160, 189n83

Sader, Pablo Emilio 80n27
Sanderson, John 68, 102
Sarajevo 34, 118–122, 138–139, 180–182
Saudi Arabia 66, 194n183
Schewebel, Stephen 21
Scowcroft, Brent 78, 141n195
Seam Reap (Cambodia) 106
Senegal 94
Serbia 109–116, 139n159, 181–183, 199, 205
Serbs 111–112, 181–183, 199, 205
  see also Bosnian-Serbs; Croatian-Serbs
Sierra Leone 3, 36

Sinai Peninsula 25-9
Slovenia 109, 111-13
Smith, Rupert 182
Somalia 1, 3, 7, 9, 33-35, 38-41,
    48n77, 85-86, 92, 96, 99, 118,
    123-131, 133n42, 138n148,
    140n178, 141n195, 142-143, 146,
    150, 154-156, 159, 161-177, 179,
    182, 185n20, 185n27, 191n132,
    192n139, 196-206
  *Moryaan* (gangs) 162, 169
  Transitional National Council (TNC)
    128, 165
  United Somali Congress/Somali
    National Alliance USC/SNA 125,
    129, 169-170, 175, 182
Somaliland 164, 174-175, 201
Spain 79n13, 137n119
South Africa 19, 59, 62-63
South Korea 24-25, 39
South Sudan 38
South West Africa People's Organization
    (SWAPO) 62-63
Special Committee for Peacekeeping
    Operations (SCPKO, or Special
    Committee) 7, 51-52, 54, 56, 71,
    75, 81n61, 92-94, 99, 144-145, 153,
    160, 185n15, 202
  *see also* Fourth Committee; Special
    Political Committee (SPC)
Special Political Committee (SPC) 8, 93
  *see also* Fourth Committee; Special
    Committee for Peacekeeping
    Operations (SCPKO)
Srebrenica (Bosnia) 3-4, 121-122,
    136n102, 139n173, 142, 176,
    180, 182
Sri Lanka 30
Srpska Republic (Serbs) 183
Standby High Readiness Brigade
    for United Nations Operations
    (SHIRBRIG) 157-158
Stung Treng (Cambodia) 103

Sudan 38, 194n183
Sweden 51-52, 158, 204
  *see also* Nordic countries
Syria 29, 38, 40, 58, 66

Tajikistan 33, 96
Thailand 54, 69, 76, 102-103, 152, 188n79
Topalović, Mušan 'Caco' 120
Tuđman, Franjo 115, 177
Tuzla (Bosnia) 122, 180

Unified Task Force (UNITAF) 123-124,
    127-128, 168-169
Union of Soviet Socialist Republics
    (USSR) 9, 15, 17, 20, 22-28, 30,
    50-53, 56-60, 63, 65, 69-70, 77-78,
    83n80, 87, 89, 96, 98, 112, 198-201
  *see also* Russia
United Kingdom 2, 7, 17, 20, 23, 26, 28,
    51, 53-54, 65, 70, 77, 79n13, 87,
    95, 98, 112-113, 118-119, 126,
    137n119, 151-152, 171, 194n182,
    198, 201, 204
United Nations Advanced Mission in
    Cambodia (UNAMIC) 34, 68, 79n1,
    99, 133n42
United Nations Angola Verification
    Mission I (UNAVEM I) 59
United Nations Angola Verification
    Mission II (UNAVEM II) 59-60,
    79n1, 133n42
United Nations Children's Fund 167
United Nations Development
    Programme (UNDP) 72
United Nations Disengagement
    Observer Force (UNDOF) 29
United Nations Emergency Force I
    (UNEF I) 25-27
United Nations Emergency Force II
    (UNEF II) 29-30
United Nations Good Offices Mission
    in Afghanistan and Pakistan
    (UNGOMAP) 58

Index                                     229

United Nations High Commissioner for Refugees (UNHCR) 59, 72, 102–103, 115, 119–120, 167
United Nations India–Kuwait Observation Mission (UNIPOM) 25
United Nations Interim Administration Mission in Kosovo (UNMIK) 37
United Nations Interim Force in Lebanon (UNIFIL) 29–30, 58, 116
United Nations Iran–Iraq Military Observer Group (UNIIMOG) 58
United Nations Iraq–Kuwait Observation Mission (UNIKOM) 58
United Nations Military Observer Group in India and Pakistan (UNMOGIP) 23
United Nations Mission in Liberia (UNMIL) 37–38
United Nations Mission for the Referendum in Western Sahara (MINURSO) 79n1, 133n42
United Nations Mission for Verification of Electoral Process in Nicaragua (ONUVEN) 61
United Nations Observation Group in Lebanon (UNOGIL) 25
United Nations Observer Group in Central America (ONUCA) 60–61
United Nations Observer Mission in El Salvador (ONUSAL) 61, 79n1, 133n42
United Nations Operation in the Congo (ONUC) 25, 27–28
United Nations Operation in Côte d'Ivoire (UNOCI) 38
United Nations Operation in Somalia I (UNOSOM I) 35, 123, 125, 133n42
United Nations Operation in Somalia II (UNOSOM II) 35, 123, 128–129, 131, 133n42, 163

United Nations Organization Mission in the Democratic Republic of the Congo (MONUC, MONUSCO) 37
United Nations Peacekeeping Force in Cyprus (UNFICYP) 25, 28
United Nations Protection Force (UNPROFOR) 34, 109–110, 116, 121, 123, 133n42, 163, 176, 179–184
United Nations Secretariat
  Department of Humanitarian Affairs (DHA) 96
  Department of Peacekeeping Operations (DPKO) 27, 36, 48, 96
  Department of Political Affairs (DPA) 96
  Office for Special Political Affairs (OSPA) 26, 30–31, 113
United Nations Special Committee on the Balkans (UNSCOB) 23
United Nations Supervision Mission in Syria (UNSMIS) 38
United Nations Temporary Executive Authority (UNTEA)/United Nations Security Force in West New Guinea (UNSF) 25
United Nations Transition Assistance Group (UNTAG) 61, 63
United Nations Transitional Administration in East Timor (UNTAET) 37
United Nations Transitional Authority in Cambodia (UNTAC) 34, 50, 58, 68–69, 83n90, 99–102, 105–107, 133n42
United Nations Truce Supervision Organization (UNTSO) 23
United Nations Trusteeship Council 17
United Nations Yemen Observation Mission (UNYOM) 25
United Somali Congress/Somali National Alliance (USC/SNA) 125, 170, 175, 182

United States 2, 7, 15, 17, 19–20, 22–28, 38–39, 51, 53–54, 58–60, 63, 65–67, 69–70, 75, 77, 86, 95, 98, 112–113, 117–118, 123, 127–129, 131, 151–152, 168–169, 171–173, 175, 181–184, 194n183, 198–201, 203–204
Uniting for Peace 24, 26
Urquhart, Brian 30–31
Uruguay 56, 80n27, 188n79

Vance, Cyrus 113–114, 121–123
Venezuela 139
Vietnam 68–70, 76, 102, 106
   Vietnamese minority in Cambodia 102

Waldheim, Kurt 29–30
Weiss, Thomas G. 16
Western European and Others Group (WEOG) 17, 130, 198–199
Western European Union 113, 137n119
Western Sirmium (Croatia) 179
West Irian (Western New Guinea) 25, 27–28, 46n51
Western Sahara 33, 51, 55, 67, 77, 79n1, 133n42

Williams, Stewart 3, 32, 86
World Food Programme 167
World Health Organization 167

Yemen 25, 66, 81n49
Yugoslavia 1, 3, 7, 9, 33–35, 41, 48n77, 85–86, 92, 96, 99, 109–24, 126–127, 130, 133n42, 142–143, 146, 154–156, 161–163, 166–168, 171, 175–184, 196–197, 199–205
   Federal Republic of Yugoslavia, FRY (Serbia and Montenegro) 116, 143, 176–177, 182
   Muslim Minority 111
   Socialist Federal Republic of Yugoslavia (SFRY) 109, 180
   Yugoslavia National Army (YNA) 111, 114–115, 117
   *see also* Bosnia; Croatia; Macedonia; Serbia

Zagreb (Croatia) 178
Zaum, Dominik 3, 32
Žepa (Bosnia) 122, 182
Zhaoxing, Li 171
Zimbabwe 120, 168, 187, 188n79

EU authorised representative for GPSR:
Easy Access System Europe, Mustamäe tee 50,
10621 Tallinn, Estonia
gpsr.requests@easproject.com

www.ingramcontent.com/pod-product-compliance
Ingram Content Group UK Ltd.
Pitfield, Milton Keynes, MK11 3LW, UK
UKHW021850210426
5322IPUK00022B/588